Toward the New

Toward the New America

James K. Bell and Adrian A. Cohn
College of San Mateo

D. C. Heath and Company
Lexington, Massachusetts

Printed in the United States of America

Library of Congress Number: 72-111479

For Lisa and for Simon

Contents

The Black Experience

Psychedelos

Eros

Arts

Preface

Toward the New America may be called a new-world reader: a collection of essays, stories, and poems that depict America whirling toward the future. It is designed to catch impressions of a world in transition, to adumbrate the forces and features of a profound and sweeping American revolution. We do not need to remind any reader of the alarming manifestations of that revolution: race riots and armed militants in our cities, near chaos on our college campuses, widespread use of drugs, flagrant and contemptuous disregard for conventional ethics, and the development of arts in which, seemingly, anything goes. Whether or not this revolution is right and healthy, it's happening. And we believe that American students want to talk about it, think about it, and write about it. That is the justification for this book.

Our thesis, briefly stated, is that the will to change — the effective impetus, energy, and creative drive to alter the quality of American life — originates with the young.

It is not our purpose to fit individuals into Procrustean categories, but it seems manifest that the young we speak of here form an extensive American community consisting of three rather amorphous and ill-defined groups.[1] There are, first, the radical young, a small but powerful minority, usually college and ex-college students, who directly challenge the American Establishment. Their orientation is essentially political, but their targets include social systems, educational institutions, giant corporations, and the military. When they must, the radical young use confrontation and violence to achieve their aims. Secondly, there are the black activists, who subscribe to a broad range of political doctrines, but seem to be united around their sense of the injustices done the Negro in America. They extol blackness, and they aim at social and political change. Then there is a third and much larger segment of the young — including millions of students in our high schools and colleges — who may sympathize with the aims of the other groups, and who may be intermittently involved in their causes, but who reject American traditions and values by simply ignoring them. This heterogeneous tribe is creating a culture of its own; the members of the tribe are stereotyped by their devotion to bizarre fashions, permissive sex, drugs, rock music, and movies. Their values, their behavior, and their arts certainly militate against American traditions — and may help bring about their metamorphosis. The collective force of these three groups, it seems clear, *will* shape the future of America.

But let us reiterate the *intention* of this book: to sketch a picture of the country in the process of change, and to do so with contemporary prose and poetry. As teachers and editors, we are advocating only excellence — excellence of thought, of perception, of language. So, although we focus on revolutionary changes in American society, we do so because these things are important; they absorb the

[1] This analysis has been worked out in detail by Edward Kern in an article entitled "Can It Happen Here?" (*Life,* Oct. 17, 1969).

attention of contemporary writers and readers. There is motion, urgency, and excitement here. There is also art.

In selecting and arranging the materials for this book, we have tried first of all to use truly contemporary writing that will stimulate creative thought and discussion. We have kept other purposes before us at the same time: to provide good models for the writing of our students, by a judicious choice of essays; to appeal to the imagination and emotions of our students, as well as to their intellect, by including stories and poems of the highest quality; and to introduce to an academic audience the work of such fine young writers as Gene Fowler and Kristen Hunter.

Finally, we have tried to treat the anthology itself as an intricate and evocative work of art.

Introduction: To the Student

This is a book about your world and its future. The book begins in your genesis — the great wars your fathers fought to save democracy. And it pictures, in the midst of America's general health, prosperity, and freedom, some of the violence in the world your elders saved for you: an American President dies in Dallas while school children in Gallinas, Georgia, "solemn and happy," rise to sing "My Country 'tis of Thee," and cheer; a black man learns his place in a white world.

All this sounds rather cynical. But we do not believe that it is cynical to observe that you grew up in a time of great fear, or that that time is still with us, or that a lot of us have grown indifferent to a surfeit of violent death. To paraphrase Paul Simon, Darkness is our old friend.

In general, however, we believe that this book is optimistic about the future. If it begins with violence, death, and alienation in the first section ("A Natural History of the Dead"), it does so in order to suggest some of the evils against which young and old alike rebel. It evokes the wasteland, the spiritual deserts, the places hostile to men; and it invokes an existential paradox, that men live on the most intense and creative level only after they confront death. In the words of Eugene Rosenstock-Huesay, "We think because we are going to die."

Against the backdrop of this first section, we have placed five scenes from the drama of contemporary *life:* "Revolutions," "The Black Experience," "Psychedelos," "Eros," and "Arts." Their common theme is an implied question: what is *right* for the future America? We believe that some quite specific answers to that question may be inferred from every essay, story, and poem in this book. But the book gives *you* the challenge of interpretation, judgment, and synthesis.

We would only like to observe here that, in general, the book proceeds from the darkness of war and alienation to the joyous affirmation of art. The student rebels dealt with in "revolutions" share a hostile, angry mood, and although their criticism of American society may be constructive, their methods are often destructive. In "The Black Experience" there is, likewise, anger and frustration in the awareness of the black writer that he and his people are cut off from the mainstream of American life. "Psychedelos," on the other hand, represents an ambivalent cultural development. Drugs in themselves may be neither good nor bad, but people may use them well or badly, creatively or destructively. In the same way, "Eros" presents both negative and positive views of the new sexual permissiveness, with the positive views seeming, finally, to outweigh the negative. The section on "Arts," however, is almost entirely affirmative. It opens with a detailed analysis of the ideas of Marshall McLuhan, who believes that the new arts — with their emphasis on the aural and tactile senses — are leading toward a new kind of social unity; and it concludes with a poem of real power and vision — Gene Fowler's

Shaman Songs — which sums up the movement and tone of the entire book. *Shaman Songs* protests many of the human weaknesses and social evils criticized by other selections in this book, but it augurs a rebirth, a renaissance of the human spirit, through the medium of art.

Let us assert then that the American writers we bring together here are not unanimously negative in their appraisal of the future America. Many of them express the conviction that men of good will, guided by a vision of social justice, personal integrity, and freedom for the arts, may yet succeed in creating a new America.

James K. Bell
Adrian A. Cohn

College of San Mateo

Toward the New America

A Natural History of the Dead

A Natural History of the Dead

Night's wing hides the sun.
Gene Fowler, Shaman Songs

The existentialist philosopher defines life as that process which produces corpses. He does so in the belief that we are not really alive until we know *we are going to die. After such knowledge, Albert Camus says, we have two alternatives: we can commit suicide, believing that life is futile, meaningless, and absurd; or we can live with a new commitment to values we choose for ourselves. Without such knowledge, we live pointless, alienated, inauthentic lives.*

We live in a time in which the threat of violent, catacylsmic death is omnipresent. Instantaneous communication allows us to see *what death has done each day: we witness the political assassination, the riot, the airplane crash, the hurricane, the broken bodies on a distant battlefield. In the midst of death, we grow indifferent to it.*

But the great writer, by touching our emotions, can teach us to feel *the ineffable agony of dying. "Let us therefore see," as Ernest Hemingway says, "what inspiration we may derive from the dead."*

We begin with physical death in its most brutal form — war. In "A Natural History of the Dead," a story of World War I, Ernest Hemingway writes with ironic detachment of death on the battlefield. He calmly and objectively depicts, for instance, the appearance of bodies that are left in the sun; he compares the dying of men with the dying of animals; and he shows us what some men did in the presence of death. The story is offensive and horrific, but with a purpose. It strips war of all its glamour, heroics, and patriotic sham to uncover a deeply disturbing truth. In "The Solitary Life of Man," Leo E. Litwak views the inhumanity of war in a different way. He portrays the terrible loneliness of a man at war as he tells the story of Melford Kuhn, a World War II hero who mocks his decorations, curses brass hats, and rejects country, family, and buddies. He believes that only he himself is "relevant"; he has "learned that the dread of dying is a knife that hacks at all sentiments and kills those which have no validity." Kuhn is locked in the tight carapace of this knowledge.

Robert Lowell's poem "For the Union Dead" uses reflections on an incident from the Civil War as a point of departure for his observations on modern men. As he pauses near "The Old South Boston Aquarium," he has a vision of a primitive, reptilian world where "giant finned cars nose forward like fish;/a savage servility slides by on grease."

Other writers in this section deal with other ways of dying. In "That Day," Robie Macauley shows us how the citizens of a small town in Georgia celebrated the assassination of John F. Kennedy. Lawrence Ferlinghetti, in "Sometime During Eternity," gives us a hipster's version of the Crucifixion, while Herbert Gold, in "Death in Miami Beach," explores the thesis that "The state of madness can be defined partly as an extreme of isolation of one human being from everyone else. It provides a model for dying." Another extreme of isolation is depicted by Alan Harrington in "Life in the Crystal Palace," an account of a "happy family," the five hundred employees of a great corporation who are isolated in limbo, overprotected, and, in a sense, dead. In "American Primitive," William Jay Smith portrays his "Daddy," whose "pockets are stuffed with folding money":

He hangs in the hall by his black cravat,
The ladies faint, and the children holler:
Only my Daddy could look like that,
And I love my Daddy like he loves his
Dollar.

And in "The Sound of Silence," Paul Simon addresses the lonely crowd: "Ten thousand people maybe more,/People talking without speaking,/People hearing without listening." His words echo "in the wells of silence." The warning goes unheard.

A Natural History of the Dead

Ernest Hemingway

It has always seemed to me that the war has been omitted as a field for the observations of the naturalist. We have charming and sound accounts of the flora and fauna of Patagonia by the late W. H. Hudson, the Reverend Gilbert White has written most interestingly of the Hoopoe on its occasional and not at all common visits to Selborne, and Bishop Stanley has given us a valuable, although popular, *Familiar History of Birds.* Can we not hope to furnish the reader with a few rational and interesting facts about the dead? I hope so.

When that persevering traveller, Mungo Park, was at one period of his course fainting in the vast wilderness of an African desert, naked and alone, considering his days as numbered and nothing appearing to remain for him to do but to lie down and die, a small moss-flower of extraordinary beauty caught his eye. "Though the whole plant," says he, "was no larger than one of my fingers, I could not contemplate the delicate confirmation of its roots, leaves and capsules without admiration. Can that Being who planted, watered and brought to perfection, in this obscure part of the world, a thing which appears of so small importance, look with unconcern upon the situation and suffering of creatures formed after his own image? Surely not. Reflections like these would not allow me to despair; I started up and, disregarding both hunger and fatigue, travelled forward, assured that relief was at hand; and I was not disappointed."

With a disposition to wonder and adore in like manner, as Bishop Stanley says, can any branch of Natural History be studied without increasing that faith, love and hope which we also, every one of us, need in our journey through the wilderness of life? Let us therefore see what inspiration we may derive from the dead.

In war the dead are usually the male of the human species although this does not hold true with animals, and I have frequently seen dead mares among the horses. An interesting aspect of war, too, is that it is only there that the naturalist has an opportunity to observe the dead of mules. In twenty years of observation in civil life I had never seen a dead mule and had begun to entertain doubts as to whether these animals were really mortal. On rare occasions I had seen what I took to be dead mules, but on close approach these always proved to be living creatures who seemed to be dead through their quality of complete repose. But in war these animals succumb in much the same manner as the more common and less hardy horse.

Most of those mules that I saw dead were along mountain roads or lying at the foot of steep declivities whence they had been pushed to rid the road of their encumbrance. They seemed a fitting enough sight in the mountains where one was accustomed to their presence and looked less incongruous there than they did later, at Smyrna, where the Greeks broke the legs of all their baggage animals and pushed them off the quay into the shallow water to drown. The numbers of broken-legged mules and horses drowning in the shallow water called for a Goya to depict them. Although, speaking literally, one can hardly say that they called for a Goya since there has only been one Goya, long dead, and it is extremely doubtful if these animals, were they able to call, would call for pictorial representation of their plight but, more likely, would, if they were articulate, call for some one to alleviate their condition.

Regarding the sex of the dead it is a fact that one becomes so accustomed to the sight of all the dead being men that the sight of a dead woman is quite shocking. I first saw inversion of the usual sex of the dead after the explosion of a munition factory which had been situated in the countryside near Milan, Italy. We drove to the scene of the disaster in trucks along poplar-shaded roads, bordered with ditches containing much minute animal life, which I could not clearly observe because of the great clouds of dust raised by the trucks. Arriving where the munition plant had been, some of us were put to patrolling about those large stocks of munitions which for some reason had not exploded, while others were put at extinguishing a fire which had gotten into the grass of an adjacent field; which task being concluded, we were ordered to search the immediate vicinity and surrounding fields for bodies. We found and carried to an improvised mortuary a good number of these and, I must admit, frankly, the shock it was to find that these dead were women rather than men. In those days women had not yet commenced to wear their hair cut short, as they did later for several years in Europe and America, and the most disturbing thing, perhaps because it was the most unaccustomed, was the presence and, even more disturbing, the occasional absence of this long hair. I remember that after we had searched quite thoroughly for the complete dead we collected fragments. Many of these were detached from a heavy, barbed-wire fence which had surrounded the position of the factory and from the still existent portions of which we picked many of these detached bits which illustrated only too well the tremendous energy of high explosive. Many fragments we found a considerable distance away in the fields, they being carried farther by their own weight.

On our return to Milan I recall one or two of us discussing the occurrence and agreeing that the quality of unreality and the fact that there were no wounded did much to rob the disaster of a horror which might have been much greater. Also the fact that it had been so immediate and that the dead were in consequence still as little unpleasant as possible to carry and deal with made it quite removed from the usual battlefield experience. The pleasant, though dusty, ride through the beautiful Lombard countryside also was a compensation for the unpleasantness of the duty and on our return, while we exchanged impressions, we all agreed that it was indeed fortunate that the fire which broke out just before we arrived had been brought under control as rapidly as it had and before it had attained any of the seemingly huge stocks of unexploded munitions. We agreed too that the picking up of the fragments had been an extraordinary business; it being amazing that the human body should be blown into pieces which exploded along no anatomical lines, but rather divided as capriciously as the fragmentation in the burst of a high explosive shell.

A naturalist, to obtain accuracy of observation, may confine himself in his observations to one limited period and I will take first that following the Austrian offensive of June, 1918, in Italy as one in which the dead were present in their greatest numbers, a withdrawal having been forced and an advance later made to recover the ground lost so that the positions after the battle were the same as before except for the presence of the dead. Until the dead are buried they change somewhat in appearance each day. The color change in Caucasian races is from white to yellow, to yellow-green, to black. If left long enough in the heat the flesh comes to resemble coal-tar, especially where it has been broken or torn, and it has quite a visible tarlike iridescence. The dead grow larger each day until sometimes they become quite too big for their uniforms, filling these until they seem blown tight enough to burst. The individual members may increase in girth to an unbelievable extent and faces fill as taut and globular as balloons. The surprising thing, next to their progressive corpulence, is the amount of paper that is scattered about the dead. Their ultimate position, before there is any question of burial, depends on the location of the pockets in the uniform. In the Austrian army these pockets were in the back of the breeches and the dead, after a short time, all consequently lay on their faces, the two hip pockets pulled out and, scattered around them in the grass, all those papers their pockets had contained. The heat, the flies, the indicative positions of the bodies in the grass, and the amount of paper scattered are the impressions one retains. The smell of a battlefield in hot weather one cannot recall. You can remember that there was such a smell, but nothing ever happens to you to bring it back. It is unlike the smell of a regiment, which may come to you suddenly while riding in the street car and you will look across and see the man who has brought it to you. But the other thing is gone as completely as when you have been in love; you remember things that happened, but the sensation cannot be recalled.

One wonders what that persevering traveller, Mungo Park, would have seen on a battlefield in hot weather to restore his confidence. There were always poppies in the wheat in the end of June and in July, and the mulberry trees were in full leaf and one could see the heat waves rise from the barrels of the guns where the sun struck them through the screens of leaves; the earth was turned a bright yellow at the edge of holes where mustard gas shells had been and the average broken house is finer to see than one that has been shelled, but few travellers would take a good full breath of that early summer air and have any such thoughts as Mungo Park about those formed in His own image.

The first thing that you found about the dead was that, hit badly enough, they died like animals. Some quickly from a little wound you would not think would kill a rabbit. They died from little wounds as rabbits die sometimes from three or four small grains of shot that hardly seem to break the skin. Others would die like cats; a skull broken in and iron in the brain, they lie alive two days like cats that crawl into the coal bin with a bullet in the brain and will not die until you cut their heads off. Maybe cats do not die then, they say they have nine lives, I do not know, but most men die like animals, not men. I'd never seen a natural death, so called, and so I blamed it on the war and like the persevering traveller, Mungo Park, knew that there was something else, that always absent something else, and then I saw one.

The only natural death I've ever seen, outside of loss of blood, which isn't bad, was death from Spanish influenza. In this you drown in mucus, choking, and how you know the patient's dead is: at the end he turns to be a little child again, though with his manly force, and fills the sheets as full as any diaper with one vast, final, yellow cataract that flows and dribbles on after he's gone. So now I want to see the death of any self-called Humanist[1] because a persevering traveller like Mungo Park or me lives on and maybe yet will live to see the actual death of members of this literary sect and watch the noble exits that they make. In my musings as a naturalist it has occurred to me that while decorum is an excellent thing some must be indecorous if the race is to be carried on since the position prescribed for procreation is indecorous, highly indecorous, and it occurred to me that perhaps that is what these people are, or were: the children of decorous cohabitation. But regardless of how they started I hope to see the finish of a few, and speculate how worms will try that long preserved sterility; with their quaint pamphlets gone to bust and into foot-notes all their lust.

While it is, perhaps, legitimate to deal with these self-designated citizens in a natural history of the dead, even though the designation may mean nothing by the time this work is published, yet it is unfair to the other dead, who were not dead in their youth of choice, who owned no magazines, many of whom had doubtless never even read a review, that one has seen in the hot weather with a half-pint of maggots working where their mouths have been. It was not always hot weather for the dead, much of the time it was the rain that washed them clean when they lay in it and made the earth soft when they were buried in it and sometimes then kept on until the earth was mud and washed them out and you had to bury them again. Or in the winter in the mountains you had

[1] The reader's indulgence is requested for this mention of an extinct phenomenon. The reference, like all references to fashions, dates the story but it is retained because of its mild historical interest and because its omission would spoil the rhythm.

to put them in the snow and when the snow melted in the spring some one else had to bury them. They had beautiful burying grounds in the mountains, war in the mountains is the most beautiful of all war, and in one of them, at a place called Pocol, they buried a general who was shot through the head by a sniper. This is where those writers are mistaken who write books called *Generals Die in Bed,* because this general died in a trench dug in snow, high in the mountains, wearing an Alpini hat with an eagle feather in it and a hole in front you couldn't put your little finger in and a hole in back you could put your fist in, if it were a small fist and you wanted to put it there, and much blood in the snow. He was a damned fine general, and so was General von Behr who commanded the Bavarian Alpenkorps troops at the battle of Caporetto and was killed in his staff car by the Italian rearguard as he drove into Udine ahead of his troops, and the titles of all such books should be *Generals Usually Die in Bed,* if we are to have any sort of accuracy in such things.

In the mountains too, sometimes, the snow fell on the dead outside the dressing station on the side that was protected by the mountain from any shelling. They carried them into a cave that had been dug into the mountainside before the earth froze. It was in this cave that a man whose head was broken as a flower-pot may be broken, although it was all held together by membranes and a skillfully applied bandage now soaked and hardened, with the structure of his brain disturbed by a piece of broken steel in it, lay a day, a night, and a day. The stretcher-bearers asked the doctor to go in and have a look at him. They saw him each time they made a trip and even when they did not look at him they heard him breathing. The doctor's eyes were red and the lids swollen, almost shut from tear gas. He looked at the man twice; once in daylight, once with a flashlight. That too would have made a good etching for Goya, the visit with the flashlight, I mean. After looking at him the second time the doctor believed the stretcher-bearers when they said the soldier was still alive.

"What do you want me to do about it?" he asked.

There was nothing they wanted done. But after a while they asked permission to carry him out and lay him with the badly wounded.

"No. No. No!" said the doctor, who was busy. "What's the matter? Are you afraid of him?"

"We don't like to hear him in there with the dead."

"Don't listen to him. If you take him out of there you will have to carry him right back in."

"We wouldn't mind that, Captain Doctor."

"No," said the doctor. "No. Didn't you hear me say no?"

"Why don't you give him an overdose of morphine?" asked an artillery officer who was waiting to have a wound in his arm dressed.

"Do you think that is the only use I have for morphine? Would you like me to have to operate without morphine? You have a pistol, go out and shoot him yourself."

"He's been shot already," said the officer. "If some of you doctors were shot you'd be different."

"Thank you very much," said the doctor waving a forceps in the air. "Thank you a thousand times. What about these eyes?" He pointed the forceps at them. "How would you like these?"

"Tear gas. We call it lucky if it's tear gas."

"Because you leave the line," said the doctor. "Because you come running here with your tear gas to be evacuated. You rub onions in your eyes."

"You are beside yourself. I do not notice your insults. You are crazy."

The stretcher-bearers came in.

"Captain Doctor," one of them said.

"Get out of here!" said the doctor.

They went out.

"I will shoot the poor fellow," the artillery officer said. "I am a humane man. I will not let him suffer."

"Shoot him then," said the doctor. "Shoot him. Assume the responsibility. I will make a report. Wounded shot by lieutenant of artillery in first curing post. Shoot him. Go ahead shoot him."

"You are not a human being."

"My business is to care for the wounded, not to kill them. That is for gentlemen of the artillery."

"Why don't you care for him then?"

"I have done so. I have done all that can be done."

"Why don't you send him down on the cable railway?"

"Who are you to ask me questions? Are you my superior officer? Are you in command of this dressing post? Do me the courtesy to answer."

The lieutenant of artillery said nothing. The others in the room were all soldiers and there were no other officers present.

"Answer me," said the doctor holding a needle up in his forceps. "Give me a response."

"F— yourself," said the artillery officer.

"So," said the doctor. "So, you said that. All right. All right. We shall see."

The lieutenant of artillery stood up and walked toward him.

"F— yourself," he said. "F— yourself. F— your mother. F— your sister. . . ."

The doctor tossed the saucer full of iodine in his face. As he came toward him, blinded, the lieutenant fumbled for his pistol. The doctor skipped quickly behind him, tripped him and, as he fell to the floor, kicked him several times and picked up the pistol in his rubber gloves. The lieutenant sat on the floor holding his good hand to his eyes.

"I'll kill you!" he said. "I'll kill you as soon as I can see."

"I am the boss," said the doctor. "All is forgiven since you know I am the boss. You cannot kill me because I have your pistol. Sergeant! Adjutant! Adjutant!"

"The adjutant is at the cable railway," said the sergeant.

"Wipe out this officer's eyes with alcohol and water. He has got iodine in them. Bring me the basin to wash my hands. I will take this officer next."

"You won't touch me."

"Hold him tight. He is a little delirious."

One of the stretcher-bearers came in.

"Captain Doctor."

"What do you want?"

"The man in the dead-house —— "

"Get out of here."

"Is dead, Captain Doctor. I thought you would be glad to know."

The Solitary Life of Man

Leo E. Litwak

"See, my poor lieutenant? We dispute about nothing. In time of war we dispute about nothing."

"F— you," said the lieutenant of artillery. He still could not see. "You've blinded me."

"It is nothing," said the doctor. "Your eyes will be all right. It is nothing. A dispute about nothing."

"Ayee! Ayee! Ayee!" suddenly screamed the lieutenant. "You have blinded me! You have blinded me!"

"Hold him tight," said the doctor. "He is in much pain. Hold him very tight."

Melford Kuhn had done his duty and with courage. He had received a Silver Star for carrying a wounded buddy a thousand yards while under fire from a pillbox. He mocked the decoration. He cursed brass hats. He disdained all that was rear echelon. He was judged to be the most effective platoon sergeant in the company. This judgment was the buttress of his pride.

There were a few truths that had so affected him that all else seemed irrelevant. A shell fragment has a trajectory defined by its initial velocity and direction and the successive forces impressed upon it. Flesh and bone were not impressive forces. The fragment could act as bullet, knife, cleaver, bludgeon. It could punch, shear, slice, crush, tear. It could be surgical in its precision or make sadistic excess seem unimaginative.

And what happened to brass-hat zeal when the brain was exposed, when guts unfolded, when a flayed stump drooled blood? Didn't the lieutenant turn away from Morgan's shredded stump, mumbling, "I can't. Oh, no!"? Kuhn fixed the tourniquet. Yet they became zealots again when the dying was a few days past and they were in the company of their brother officers and they could begin the falsification of history which proposed heroes and cowards and right action and blunders.

He had learned that the dread of dying is a knife that hacks at all sentiments and kills those which have no validity. He scorned those who approached combat from the perspective of honor, ambition, and the other sentiments of gallantry which flourish when there is no risk of dying.

He felt that ignorance had been pared away from him until only the core of truth was left. The more imminent death became, the narrower was his focus, until now, after two years of combat, he had reached hard fact. Not country, not family, not buddies, but only he himself was relevant. And as his focus narrowed, he became more taciturn, less concerned with the vanities which depended on a wider community.

He loathed Solomon. Solomon was a supply sergeant, assigned to battalion headquarters, who had no reason for being at the front. He should have been two miles back, in a village already secured, nicely housed, nicely fed, profiting from the German obsequiousness which made everything available to acquisitive hands. Solomon was forty-five, a swarthy, big-nosed man, his face creased, tall, gaunt, with a gentle manner. He was dressed like a soldier, yet Kuhn regarded him as a caricature of a soldier. His clothes were glistening new issue, and he used all the tricks of dressing which the combat soldier learns through necessity. He wore a field jacket over his wool sweater, OD trousers tucked into combat boots, a knit wool cap under his helmet liner and steel helmet. Solomon, with his pious talk, his admiration for heroes, his fear of cowardice, his flagrant sympathizing, had become intolerable to Kuhn. Solomon used the sanctimonious language which charmed officers back in battalion headquarters, but he had no flair for the bitter invective which the GI recognized as the language of a friend.

The platoon was assembled, ready to mount the truck. The company jeep arrived with a galvanized can filled with hot coffee. The men lined up and dipped into the coffee with their canteen cups. It was a chill morning, and Solomon stood at the rear of the line, his arms wrapped around his chest, his hands tucked into his armpits.

"Solomon — " Kuhn waved him over to his side and walked him out of earshot of the others. "What are you doing here, Solomon?"

Solomon smiled, misunderstanding Kuhn's intention. "I think I should take my chances with the rest of the boys, Mel. Let them have their coffee first."

"That's damn nice of you. You could be sitting down to breakfast back in battalion."

"It weighs on my conscience, Mel, that I should be safe while the boys up here take all the risks."

"This isn't a club for healthy consciences. I'm not interested in your conscience. There isn't one of us who wouldn't be back in battalion if he had the chance. All you're doing up here, Solomon, is taking someone's coffee."

Solomon shivered. He pulled one arm free and shrugged with it. "You're right. I'll go without coffee."

"Solomon! We're going to take a village this morning. Suppose we have trouble? What do you do, Solomon?"

"What I can do I don't know. But whatever you want I should do, I'll try."

"I've got no job for you." He wanted to snarl, "Stop cringing, Stupid!" Instead he glared his dislike. "Rodansky tells me you bother him with your kraut pitying. How come you're giving Rodansky trouble?"

Solomon rubbed his eyes. He wore OD wool gloves with leather palms. He was more than twenty years older than Kuhn.

"Rodansky is bothered by the German boy. I know he's bothered. So he didn't offend me."

"I don't care if you're offended. You're no problem of mine. I care about my platoon. And you're just trouble for me. I don't want you around, Solomon."

Solomon nodded. "I'll ride back with the jeep. I apologize, Mel."

Kuhn walked away from him.

Rodansky had been on guard duty the day before. He had heard a noise in the bushes at the edge of the platoon area. He had challenged, then had fired, and Kuhn had found him standing beside the dying man. The German lay behind a bush, his arms extending through it. He wore a great-coat. His wool cap had fallen off. His hair was in the midst of the bush, an abundant, dirty yellow. He wasn't armed, and Kuhn rolled him over. The German wheezed through his chest.

"I told him to put up his hands. *'Hands auf,'* I said."

"What a mess. He's a kid."

The boy was already soggy gray. The slug had hit at an angle, swerved within the compass of the chest, and his heart was bared. *"Warum hast du — "* Neither Kuhn nor Rodansky understood German and they did not respond to the boy's muttering.

Kuhn straightened up as others in the platoon joined them. "He won't last till the aid station. Leave him here. Is the medic around? It doesn't make any difference."

Then Solomon came up, gasping with fear, blanching when he heard the moans. He fell to his knees beside the boy and touched his face. He listened to the muttering. "He wants to know why did we shoot." Solomon looked up, asking the question in his own right. "He says he wanted to surrender. *'Wir haben nicht gewissen,'* " he explained to the boy, his voice trembling with compassion. "He wants to know if he's dying."

"He's dead, Solomon! Tell him he's dead. *Tot,*" Rodansky shouted at the boy. "Kraut *tot!*"

"Nein," Solomon said in turn. He told the boy they would soon have him in a hospital. *"Wir haben nicht gewissen,"* he concluded in hopeless apology.

A few weeks before, twelve men from the platoon had been killed in front of a pillbox. There had been considerable variety in their deaths. They'd been zeroed in by eighty-eights. The GIs had swallowed these deaths as part of the nourishment of combat whose grotesqueries provisioned their daily fare.

Rodansky caught Solomon's arm as they left the boy to the medic.

"What the hell you doing in the army, Solomon — an old man like you? Why aren't you back with the girls, getting the dough, saluting the flag? What are you here for, Solomon?"

Solomon was still shocked by the sight of the naked heart beating in a sheath of slime. His face mirrored the open-mouthed pallor of the dying German.

He raised his arms waist high and let them flop. He repeated this gesture several times before answering Rodansky. "He asked is he dying. He came to surrender. Why did we shoot, he wants to know. He's maybe only sixteen. The poor boy!"

"Poor boy!"

"It doesn't matter to me all of a sudden that he's German. His chest was breathing, Harry. Did you hear it? Ah! I wish we didn't shoot. It's a pity, a pity, Rodansky."

Though they had recently come from a

reserve area where shower facilities were available, Rodansky hadn't washed or shaved. His helmet was set low on his forehead, and he peered from under it like a man taking a cautious look in the midst of a barrage. He released his grip on Solomon's arm to squeeze his rifle with both hands. He shook the rifle at Solomon, his lips twisting for an adequate expression of his outrage. "I shot, you old bastard, not you! You bastard! We fight your wars and then you come around and preach!"

It was clear that he meant the "you" generically. Solomon revealed his identity with every shrug, with every anecdote, with his intonation, with his liberal use of such notions as Pity and Justice, with his faithful attendance at Saturday services.

Kuhn shared Rodansky's loathing for this old man who presumed to give them lessons in sentiment when he was so little experienced in the passion that proved integrity, the fear of death. The following morning he ordered Solomon back to the rear.

They had come so fast into Germany that they passed through villages still entrucked, leaving the security of the area to the reserve companies that followed. The widely spaced convoy rattled down poor country roads, claiming a new segment of Germany with each turn of the wheels. The Germans who lined the streets cheered the convoy with the enthusiasm of the liberated. When the soldiers dismounted and formed squads to scour a village, they found the Germans more tractable than any ally. *"Nach kirche!"* the GIs shouted. The Germans took up the cry and without further urging streamed to church where they were instructed by the military government. The town was left in the hands of the GIs. These were irreverent hands, not limited by any law. They stripped watches from the grinning Germans. They ransacked the German houses for guns and cameras and silver and food. The Germans yielded their homes to GI boots which trampled their linens and muddied their beds. The women were cheerful offerings to appease the conqueror. Good food, good servants, good plumbing, good women, they were a magnificent fee to conquer. Kuhn despised them. Good cameras, good watches, good pistols, they were as good to Kuhn as any European. Kuhn had a Luger, a Leica, a fine Swiss watch.

Ahead of them, beyond the reach of GI boots, there was law supported by a seemingly death-defying ardor. There was German law and German pride ahead of them. Ahead of them were boasts that the German spirit would endure death rather than humiliation. Behind them they left a disordered mob prepared to sacrifice everything German and human to preserve themselves. Without urging, the Germans denied all that they had been and betrayed any compatriot whose betrayal benefited them.

Kuhn had so far not failed himself. He had not lost himself in the solvent of dread. He had made trembling legs advance. He had made his panicked hands obey him. He had refused to be overwhelmed by fatigue. Whatever beliefs he possessed he was sure of, since they had endured. Yet his victories had not relieved him from oppression. He was more and more oppressed. Instead of being restored by the intervals between hazards, he spent the time anticipating future catastrophes. He didn't know the extent of his endurance. He feared that moment when his courage would fail him and he would act badly.

As the truck bore them across a German valley, he scanned the sky for aircraft. He studied the roadside for cover. He planned his escape from the truck. The sky was too clear, the land too hilly, the opportunities for ambuscade unsettling. He didn't rely on the scouting jeeps to discover snipers. He only trusted his own vision. He tried imagining the city of Helo where they were to dismount and assemble for an assault. He wondered whether the Germans would be supported by tanks and artillery, whether they would be yielding or would resist.

The banter of the GIs irritated him. He considered their ability to forget hazards a kind of amnesia, fortunate if one could settle for something other than truth. The men were crammed on benches that ran the length of the truck on both sides. They squatted on the floor. They pressed together, shoulders and hips joined, knees against backs, rifles held between legs, loosened helmet straps clanging against steel with each toss of the truck.

" — outside of Trier, remember?" Reilly summoned his buddies to hear the anecdote. "That pillbox with the railroad tunnel?" He and Rodansky had left their squad to check a farmhouse. It was a place with an inner court and a ripe compost pile and pigs and chickens and Russian laborers. Rodansky found a book filled with sketches. These showed a man and woman going all out for love. Various attitudes were sketched in provocative detail. The farm wife entered. Rodansky looked at her, then at the sketchbook. "This is you?" He held up the book and tapped his finger on the woman depicted. The farm wife nodded. "This is me!" Rodansky shouted, pointing to the man. He threw off his harness, dropped his rifle on the table, and pursued her into the bedroom.

Rodansky admitted his conquest and in response to their urging detailed it. He was filled with a charge that raised him mile high. "She didn't run no further than that bed. All feathers it was, so she sunk out of sight with her legs poking up. We didn't get past page one. It's lucky for me there was a war on."

What perhaps the men most admired was Rodansky's ability to forget the pillbox where a few hours previously they had lost an entire squad. Rodansky was able to lust when only terror seemed appropriate. He made places and people who were strange to the GIs less intimidating by humbling them. He'd had limey women in England, Frog and Belgian girls, fräuleins — and in circumstances which seemed to rule out any passion but fear. Once he'd disappeared into a cellar with a fräulein while they struggled for a village. Machine guns directed tracers at the GIs from the high ground beyond. They could see Tiger tanks maneuvering on the hillside for a counterattack. And afterwards what they remembered of that village was, not the GI and German dead, not their panic when it seemed that the enemy tanks would assault them, but Rodansky taking a recess from war in order to satisfy an appetite they were delighted had survived.

Kuhn saw in this eagerness to return to manageable passions a betrayal of experience which he attributed not only to GIs, but to allies and enemies everywhere, and above all to those who remained in the rear echelons, never risking death. Instead of being readied for disaster by his relaxing intermissions, Rodansky was becoming untrustworthy. He bitched too much, he talked too much. He failed to tend himself when they were in reserve.

And Kuhn believed that if fear hadn't predominated, Rodansky could have taken the German boy prisoner.

The convoy ascended a steep hill. From the crest they looked down upon a valley. The day was clear, and they were able to view a dozen villages, each centered around a church, ringed first with plowed fields and then with forest. The wind came from the east and brought a piney smell and a vague sound which seemed composed of church bells, the lowing of cattle, the barking of dogs, but nothing of war. Across the valley, straggling beneath the distant hills was the city of Helo. No tanks were visible, no Germans, there was no sound of artillery, no machine-gun staccato to presage resistance ahead. On the left, some two miles distant, they observed another column, preceding them toward Helo. The information was passed back that B and C Companies of their battalion would take the city, with small resistance expected, and that their company would follow in reserve.

The men were jubilant. This was a fine big city that had been spared air raids, and they were getting it peacefully. What novelties in bedding, what steals in cameras, what city fräuleins were available? They relished the chickens they would gut; hams, sausages, preserves they would loot; wine from cellars; and finally sleep.

They dismounted six miles from Helo with orders to sweep the area before the city. Kuhn's platoon controlled a sector three hundred yards wide, consisting mainly of open field and farmhouses. He broke the platoon into squads, instructing the squad leaders to keep track of their men. "There's a crossroads about three miles from here. We'll assemble there in two hours. Keep moving. Call me if there's any trouble."

The mission was uneventful. Kuhn reached the assembly point with time to spare. The day had warmed sufficiently to make the march uncomfortable. Chester Grove, the platoon messenger, accompanied Kuhn. Grove was a farmer from Oklahoma, a lumpish man who admired Kuhn. He nervously broached topics which he hoped would interest Kuhn.

"If we get it now, Sarge, when it's almost over, what a joke."

"It's a long way from over."

"It's been a couple weeks since we run into artillery. Everyone's relaxed. I tell you, Sarge, you can be trained for a lot of things. Experience makes you better if you want to be an athlete or a farmer or for screwing. You get smarter reading books. There's a lot of things where practice makes perfect. But, Sarge, when I hear a shell I don't have the nerve I first had. I figure that every time I wasn't killed I was in luck and there's only so much luck a man has before the cards change."

The squads arrived, Reilly's squad reporting last. The men sprawled along the roadside, munching at K-rations and food looted in the course of the march.

"Everybody here?"

"Rodansky ain't showed up," Reilly reported. "Give him a few minutes, Sarge. He'll be along."

"Where is he?"

"You know old Rodansky, Sarge. He could find himself a woman and a bed Sunday morning in church."

"Where is he?"

"Back in that farmhouse." Reilly pointed to a farmhouse in a grove of trees, half a mile from the assembly point.

"He's got five more minutes." When the five minutes passed, Kuhn nodded. "Okay,

Reilly. Let's get him."

Plodding and sour-faced, there were a few buddy indiscretions Reilly wouldn't forgive. He might regret excess in killing, cowardice, gold-bricking, but so long as it was family that was in error he was tolerant. The broadness of his view did not extend beyond the family of buddies.

"Old Rodansky, when he's on tail, it takes a direct hit from a eighty-eight to get him off."

"I'll get him off."

"Take it easy, Sarge. Harry's okay."

"You think this war is a joke, Reilly?"

They walked directly into the kitchen. Rodansky's rifle was on a counter near a tile oven. His field jacket, hung with grenades, lay on a chair.

Kuhn shouted for Rodansky. He walked to the door beside the oven and kicked it. "Rodansky! Come out of there!"

Reilly caught his arm. "Hold on, Sarge. He'll come."

Kuhn shoved the door open. The room was dark. There was a burst of motion from the high bed. Rodansky scrambled from the bed, gripping his pants. He came toward the light, fumbling with his belt, his shirt undone, blinking, stunned, a sweaty smell accompanying him. The woman crouched on the other side of the bed.

"That's a lousy trick, Kuhn. It's no skin off your nose. What are you getting so goddam GI for?"

Kuhn struggled with a murderous impulse he didn't understand. "I catch you again leaving your rifle around like that and I'll bust the hell out of you."

"Bust me. I'm a PFC."

"I can bust you good, Rodansky. You know what I mean? You want to push harder and find out?"

Kuhn hurried back to the platoon without waiting for Reilly and Rodansky.

C Company had the outskirts of Helo. A tank man pissed from a doorway, his free hand gripping a bottle of wine. Chemical mortars had fired the bordering houses, and no efforts were made to stop the burning. B Company had sequestered an entire block, and the men of B Company had already cashed in on the available bounty.

Instead of approaching the heart of town, the reserve company was directed along its periphery. For a moment, peering down a winding street, they glimpsed a sizable plaza that promised the amenities of city life they had long missed. They were marched through a residential area, then to a dirt road, and soon the city was on their left, open field on their right, and it was evident they were not intended to share the fortunes of the other companies in the battalion.

In an open field, two miles beyond the city, they came to barracks enclosed with barbed wire. There were three buildings that formed a *U*-shape. The buildings were mere boxes, with small windows covered with steel mesh. The ground surrounding the buildings was hard clay.

The prospect was barren, and Kuhn shared the general dismay. The battalion jeep was at the entrance to the compound. A group of officers huddled around the jeep while the company halted. The captain and platoon leaders conferred with the major. Solomon was with them. He waved to Kuhn.

Kuhn's platoon was detached from the company and entered the grounds where they assembled around their officer. The rest of the company returned to the city.

"We're only going to be here a few hours. We have to make Brumberg by morning. We go by truck. There'll be hot chow. Get some rest, boys." Lieutenant Gordon was a ruddy-cheeked man of twenty-five, his natural stoutness trimmed down by rigorous living. "Now, about this place — I'm not going to give you the usual crap about looting and fraternizing. I know what goes on. This is a *Lager.* The middle barracks there has thirty women in it — Hungarians. These girls have had a very rough time. Stay away from them. They think the GI is something different, and I want them thinking that way when we leave. Sergeant!" He summoned Kuhn. "Sergeant, I want you to put out a guard detail for the women's barracks. Any man caught fraternizing I'll court-martial."

There were wooden bunks in the long room. A potbellied stove was in the center of the room, firewood heaped behind it. The men flung down their rifles, helmets, and harness. They sprawled in their bunks on bare springs.

Kuhn waited for them to settle down before assigning details. He felt dizzy and knew the dizziness to precede a blackout. These periods of amnesia had become frequent. Dread settled on him like a fog and, sometimes for several moments, he couldn't distinguish his place, his role, his purpose. He nerved himself to endure these moments. He took off his helmet and swabbed his forehead with his wool cap. Their names tumbled across his tongue, and he scanned the barracks but couldn't find the faces to fit the names. Then slowly their faces merged with the fog. He felt as distant from them as if they had been background to a dream. He couldn't pluck out the sense of their words. He fumbled for his detail book and turned the pages. The headings were senseless, there was no clue in the words recorded. He felt nauseated but was determined not to reveal his panic and continued turning the pages. Rebel, Reilly, Rodansky. Grove, Nelson, Schultz. The words became a rhythm which was compulsively reiterated.

"Mel, Mel." The blackout lasted a few seconds. He was not detected. Solomon gripped his sleeve. "Can I talk to you, Mel? In private? A few seconds? Are you busy?"

The smiling, seamed face was in focus.

"Rebel, your squad takes the first tour of guard duty. Let's make it till eleven. Nelson, from eleven to three. Schultz, from three if we need your squad. One post in front, one in back."

He followed Solomon into the yard. The jeep had left. The yard was empty. The sun was already low over the plowed fields. They could hear the distant motors in the city, the heavy rumble of tanks, a faraway shout.

"They're Jewish girls, Melford. Yesterday, before the Germans left, they cut off their hair and marched them naked through the streets. They're lucky they are alive. They come from a village, Mel, where all the Jews are dead except these girls. The Germans made them whores."

"What do you want from me, Solomon?"

"In two days it's Pesach — Passover — Mel. Tonight, while we're still here, I want that you and I should help these girls to celebrate their luck. I want we should have a meal which we can pretend is a seder."

The sun was covered by the clouds rolling in from the horizon. Long shadows spread from the forest across the furrows of the encompassing fields. The forest hadn't been cleared of enemies. Germans, by-passed by their column, might now be waiting at the edge of the forest. The road to Helo went through the forest, and Kuhn was to be briefed at company headquarters in Helo. There were rumors that Brumberg, their next objective, was a focus of resistance. He had to get to town before dark to secure the password.

"I want you to meet the girls, Kuhn. It will give them a real pleasure."

"What time is it?"

"It's four o'clock. I have permission from the major to hold a seder, Mel. These poor kids. There are some of them babies yet — fifteen, sixteen."

"I got troubles without you around, Solomon. What do you want? A seder?"

Rebel came out to begin the first tour of duty. "Where shall I dig in, Sarge?"

"In back. Near the wire."

Solomon caught his arm, and Kuhn shoved him away. "Don't touch me, you jerk."

But his single-mindedness brooked no offense. "It's not a question do I annoy you or do you like me or are you worried. The question has to do with these girls. I don't ask any big sacrifice from you, like to give up your life. I only ask you to be a little decent to some girls who, because you are a Jew — even if it annoys you — they would feel some pleasure to meet you."

"You're what annoys me, Solomon."

"Do you so much value yourself, Kuhn, that you can't take a little time for these poor girls?"

"Get off my back." He left Solomon abruptly and returned to the barracks. He told Reilly to take over the platoon while he and Grove went to headquarters for the briefing.

Rodansky lay on his bunk, still harnessed, his knees raised, his arms folded across his chest, his eyes closed.

Reilly accompanied Kuhn to the barbed-wire gate. "How about these gals, Sarge?"

"You heard the lieutenant. They're off-limits."

"What he don't know won't hurt him."

"It'll hurt you, Reilly. It's my orders you listen to. Stay away from them. I hold you responsible, Reilly. You're in charge. Don't get smart."

"What the hell. We're moving out in a few hours."

"I'm telling you straight. I'll break you, Reilly. Don't give me any of that buddy business. No screwing around. Get it?"

Reilly winked. "Got it."

Lately, Kuhn had sensed resistance among the men. He felt eyes following him, averted when he turned. They were handling him as they did officers, accepting orders with sardonic geniality, grins becoming smirks.

"I'll make it a point to check, Reilly."

There was no part of army life which was natural to Kuhn. He had no flair for communal living. He had early discovered that his efforts to establish himself as a buddy made him foolish. He could only pretend sympathy and when the pretense wearied him his antipathy showed.

Forests were strange to him. Initially he had not been able to orient himself in forests. He was not familiar with forest sounds, had poor vision in the mirkiness of the forest gloom. There were men who could walk confidently in the dark. They could discriminate sounds and know when to be easy and when to be tense. They could relax vigilance. A snapped twig, a sensed motion, danger felt, and without doing violence to their nerves, they were again prepared. But to Kuhn, all sounds were ominous. He had no sense for danger and was always on guard. He feared the infiltration of enemies and he couldn't take advantage of lulls. Yet Kuhn had mastered his natural disadvantages and by never yielding to terror he had established himself as the equal of any soldier in the company.

The pines leaned together across the road. Kuhn and Grove advanced into pockets of gloom, the only sound being the gravel scattered by their boots. Kuhn held his carbine ready, bracing against panic whenever they approached an area of darkness. He felt himself vulnerable to any violence. If a German should leap from the forest, he would turn and run. He would abandon Grove. If captured, he would beg. He clicked off the safety of his carbine and hunched his shoulders.

He was trembling when finally they were past the forest and had entered the town.

"Maybe we'll get a ride back," Grove suggested.

"They don't run a taxi service."

Cobbled streets twisted up the hill toward the church. Half-timbered houses fronted solidly on the narrow streets, their upper stories cantilevered. The gutters were strewn with wires laid by the Signal Corps. The intersections were placarded with directions indicating the various units in the area. MPs supervised traffic at intersections. Convoys of trucks rolled through. The front which had been at Helo a few hours previously was already several miles beyond.

Company headquarters were located in the main square which centered about the church. Market stalls, shuttered and locked, fringed the square. The area was being used as a motor-pool and was crowded with trucks and jeeps. There were no civilians in sight, and the soldiers who were not attending to their vehicles were rummaging for loot.

The captain briefed them on the coming objective. Brumberg was defended by twelve batteries of German artillery. This was, perhaps, a sizable element of the remaining enemy resistance. Their company was to participate in a task force that included tanks, TDs, and air support. They had earned this privilege by virtue of their great record. The captain was proud. The lieutenants were proud.

Kuhn loathed himself after a session with the officers. A gentlemanly jargon was in common use. The noncoms, as well as the officers, lent themselves to a collegiate view of war. Even Kuhn while in the company of officers was impressed by their vision of combat. They had seen what shell fragments could do. They had smelled blood and knew that it was a fecal smell. They had seen how the perspective of a dying man narrows until it is confined to himself. And yet they could still approach combat with collegiate sentiments. They ate well. They drank the best of Scotch, served from German tumblers. They were established in the mayor's residence and handsomely bedded. Kuhn withdrew from the party spirit that prevailed. He saw them as a spic-and-span hazing crew with a boy-scout ardor for protocol and a sophomoric concern for reputation.

The major, who had joined the briefing, approached Kuhn. "How's my boy Solomon doing, Sergeant? You keep an eye on that old man, hear?" The charge was confided with the easy bonhommie that a master — a decent paternalistic master — has for his underlings. He was a ruddy, bulky, senatorial type, his uniform tailored to fit his bulk, his polished, stiff bearing a mark of his caste. "I love that big-hearted sonofagun. He found himself some Jewish girls who were treated very badly. And Solomon — well he couldn't have been more concerned if it was him the krauts tortured. We could do with more like Solomon." He held Kuhn's elbow and spoke confidentially: "By the way, Sergeant, I've fixed a little surprise for Solomon. Some of the mail has arrived from Division, and the chaplain has sent up some Jewish flat bread — matzos — and I sent it on to your outfit together with the hot chow. The old man will get a kick out of it. See that he's taken care of, Sergeant. Right?" He squeezed Kuhn's elbow.

The password was Easter Bunny.

The twilight was well advanced when they started back toward the platoon. It was chill again, and Kuhn shivered in his woolens which were still damp from sweating. They left the town. The moment they were on the country road the clamor of motors and rummaging GIs diminished. They entered the forest. Grove walked down the center of the road, his rifle clanking against his canteen, the sling of his rifle slapping against the buckles of his harness. Kuhn listened to him chew the chicken leg he had taken from the officers' mess. He used both hands to hold the leg, his head jerking back as he tugged at the meat. He flung the bone away and wiped his hands on his trousers. He belched, then reached into the pocket of his field jacket for a chocolate bar. He stripped the paper, crumpled it into a ball, flung it into the underbrush beside the road. Kuhn was dizzy with expectation of a bullet. He felt like a target.

"You pig!"

"What?"

"Quiet!"

"I was just eating, Sarge."

"They can hear you eating in Berlin. Where did you learn to eat, on your pig farm? You'll bring every kraut in ten miles."

"There're no krauts around."

"You're not getting me killed, Grove. This is enemy territory. How do you know this forest is secure? There are twelve batteries of kraut artillery at Brumberg. Brumberg is only ten miles from here."

"I won't eat then. If my eating is going to lose the war, okay, I won't eat."

"Whisper, Stupid! This isn't an officers' club."

"You're making more noise than me, Sarge."

"Shut up and let's move."

They trudged on opposite sides of the road, less concerned now with possible ambushes than with their hatred of each other. Kuhn listened to Grove's muttering, realized his own childishness, and yet couldn't restrain his loathing for this and all other buddies. He felt himself dying in a stupid war among stupid men whose understanding was confined to what sex and stomach could sense.

"Twelve batteries — they're honored."

Grove steamed with the insult. "You'd think you was General Patton. Who the hell are you to tell me how to eat? I can eat any damn way I please. I was the only friend you had in this platoon. With the friends you got, it ain't kraut shrapnel you have to worry about. Sonofabitch. They better section-eight you before you crack wide open."

They were still far from the barracks when they heard the party. It was night, and the windows hadn't been completely blacked out, and cracks of light sprayed over the plain.

"We move out in three hours and they're screwing up! I warned Reilly!"

The guard was near the door. It was Rebel. He was so intent upon the sounds from the barracks that he didn't observe their approach.

"*Hands auf,* you jerk! Put down that rifle.

If I was a kraut you'd be a dead man and so would everyone else in this platoon. This isn't your post, Rebel. I could court-martial you, Stupid. What the hell's going on?"

"Solomon brought them in, Sarge. He said it was okay. He said he'd take responsibility. The major gave him permission."

"Who's running this outfit, me or Solomon!"

"It ain't my fault, Sarge."

"The password is Easter Bunny. Got it? We're moving out in three hours. We're joining Task Force Onaway. We've been volunteered. There's twelve batteries of kraut artillery at Brumberg. You feel like kicking your heels, Rebel?"

"How come us, Sarge? Why don't they give some other company the chance?"

"We're honored, Stupid. What's the password?"

"Easter Bunny."

A long table had been constructed from planks fitted over sawhorses. There were candles on the table. Mess kits had been placed in front of the seated women. Hot chow was presented in huge GI pots. The women were shawled. They wore knee-length smocks, half-sleeved, open-throated. They were pallid and puffy-faced, an unhealthy taint that was as much the color of apathy as the consequence of poor food and imprisonment. Dead men had this color. Bodies moldering in trenches had this smell.

Yet now they could laugh. Now they felt no pain. Now they were ready to forget the several hundred krauts who had mounted them. So newly rescued from terror, could their equilibrium be so quickly restored? Kuhn shrank from the sight of them. How could they laugh? How could they respond to the buddy teasing? How could they live after their complete humiliation? They had given everything away.

The men stood behind them, helping with the preparations for the feast. They beckoned Kuhn to share the fun. "Climb in, Sarge. There's room for everybody."

"Grab a matzo, Sarge. Good old Solomon — "

Solomon beamed. Solomon, with his brood of chicks, thought he was among gentlemen.

"Reilly! What did I tell you!"

"Solomon's got orders from the major. I figured you was outranked, Sarge."

"I saw the lights a mile away. Is this what you call a blackout?"

"It ain't hardly dark."

"Clear out these women. I don't want any more screwing around. We move out in three hours."

"That's three hours. That's not now."

"I said, clear them out, Reilly," he slowly advised.

"What's the pitch? We're nice boys. These are friendly gals. What's eating you, Kuhn?"

"Twelve batteries of kraut artillery. That's what's eating me. Come morning we'll be at Brumberg."

"I'll be there, Kuhn, and so will the boys. Meantime, I don't see any artillery. Maybe I'll get kilt in the morning. Right now I'm not getting kilt."

"Melford!" Solomon shouted. "My friend! I want you to meet someone." He beckoned Kuhn with both hands, speaking excitedly to the woman beside him.

"Melford, I want you to meet Leona." In German he told Leona that Kuhn was the Jewish sergeant he had told her about. All the women turned to watch the introduction.

She was the only one not shawled. Her straight black hair was cropped at the neck. Leaning on her elbows, puffing a cigarette, she had seemed a beauty across the room — a dark, slim woman, great-eyed, fine-featured. But up close the ravage was apparent. The skin was jaundiced, and the face was dry and brittle. The swollen cords of her throat traced her gauntness. Her sprawled legs exhibited the welts of lice bites. There was a sore on her lower lip.

"It is a year now since I see a Jewish man," she told him in a rasping voice. She arose to greet him. She didn't bother to find out whether he would accept the identity she imposed on him. She came to him with the stiff gait of a pregnant woman, her arms half raised, and walked up in reach of the embrace she expected.

He was so strongly repelled by her that it required a physical effort to remain in her presence. She seemed to him fouled by all the abuse she had suffered. Her walk was infirm. The broadness of her hips, the puffy ankles were an unnatural contrast to the bony shoulders and skinny arms. The musty smell which repelled him seemed to have its source in her scabs and her welts. That she was still a young woman made her seem even more repellent. What hadn't she allowed to happen to her? What hadn't she endured in order to avoid death? Dared she claim him as kin? Face him as her equal?

"Everyone's had it tough." He stood his distance.

"Solomon has much praised you to us."

"Solomon is sometimes foolish. Solomon is a big talker. Pardon me, Leona, but now I have to talk to Solomon. I have to speak privately."

He took Solomon outside and when the door was closed, seized him and slammed him against the barrack wall. Solomon's helmet fell across his forehead. He lost his balance and grabbed Kuhn's arm.

"Mel!"

"I hate the way you smile, Solomon! I hate the way you wiggle on your belly to get laughs. I hate you for all the asses you've kissed. I hate you for being so stupid!"

"Because I'm a Jew maybe?" Solomon hissed, gasping under the hand that pinned him to the wall. "You hate me because I'm a Jew, Kuhn?"

"In three hours we go for a ride. At the end of the ride we get out and walk. And while we walk we get killed. The man ahead, the man behind, they get killed. Their bellies open. Their legs tear off. Their heads explode. That's what I concentrate on, Solomon. That's the important thing. And you, Smiley, you Fat-lips, you Big-heart — you drag your ass up here where it doesn't belong and you clap your head and say, 'Poor little kraut who doesn't have a chest — ' You come up here and hunt out Jews and you say, 'Okay! Let's stop everything, boys, let's be nice to the Jew girls. They've had it so bad, take pity. Pity the poor Jews who are whores.' And you know what the boys think of you, Solomon? Who is this old jerk with the clean uniform and good food in his belly who comes up here and says, 'Time out, let's take pity.' Pity? What's that word? They use it back in headquarters? Those gentlemen back there, the ones who tell us we have the honor to get killed? They use words like honor, too, don't they, Solomon?"

He shook Solomon while he spoke. He clutched the lapels of Solomon's field jacket, and the old man gasped and choked, his head wobbling as he submitted to what appeared to him a murderous assault. His lips slackened, white showed in his eyes, his face was gray with shock, he embraced Kuhn's hands with his own.

"You want to kill me?" he hissed.

Kuhn felt the trembling hands on his own and tightened his grip.

"I'm old enough to be your father," Solomon said as if amazed. "Is this the way you treat me?"

"What have you ever learned, you bastard!" But suddenly he couldn't endure the terror in Solomon's eyes. He pushed Solomon against the wall once more and dropped his hands.

"Are you a Hitler or a God you can treat me like this? What gives you the power?"

Kuhn felt drugged in the aftermath of violence. He looked at Solomon as if he could see there the reflection of himself, see his brutishness mirrored there, see reflected in the older man's disillusionment his own deterioration.

"I learned how it is about dying," Kuhn muttered. "I learned what is bullshit. What I learned you have no idea of. Why are you so surprised, Stupid? Don't you know what the world is like?"

Solomon breathed deeply, his seamed face now resolute. "Don't be too proud, Kuhn," he answered hoarsely. "Don't think you only have felt what no one else has felt. There is always someone has had it worse."

"Have your seder, Solomon. But stay away from me. Stay away from me and stay away from this platoon."

He did not respond to the bitter dignity of Solomon's defiance. "It's not only your war, Kuhn."

Toward the east, in the direction of Brumberg, the sky pulsed from dark to lightening white. This was the artillery prepartion of Brumberg. The damp chill pinched his toes and shivered his thighs. He raised the collar of his field jacket. It required intense listening to discern the pervasive bass rumble of the distant shelling. The furrows in the field seemed to writhe and twist after steady scanning. Clots of gloom separated from the forest wall and merged with the field. There was laughter in the barracks behind him. They were snug in their lighted room, warmed by the stove, guarded front and rear by entrenched GIs. But what was this one drop of light contrasted with the great puddle of darkness in which they were immersed?

When Solomon left, Kuhn felt the darkness swarm over him. It pressed a bubble of loneliness that rose from his guts to his throat. He despairingly summoned his exhausted pride to suppress this gas of pity.

He was close to tears when Rodansky came around the corner, followed by the girl. She was no more than seventeen. Shawled, her form distorted by the poor-fitting smock, there was still no mistaking her beauty. There was an idiot innocence in her eyes, as though she had preserved herself from further defeat by withdrawing her awareness from all that her body had suffered. She clutched Rodansky's arm when she saw Kuhn. She cowered at the sight of him.

Rodansky was in a fever, tensed from head to toe, his eyes darting in quest of escape. He jerked to a halt and spread out his arms to stop the girl when he saw Kuhn. His fear showed. He stood his ground, nerving himself for punishment. "Okay . . . so what are you going to do about it?"

He was strangely saddened by Rodansky's terror. Was his effort to find release of such pathetic consequence that he could now turn pale at the sight of Kuhn?

"There's kraut artillery waiting for us, Rodansky."

"You can wait for it, Kuhn. I don't ask any favors. At least I got my kicks in."

"Take the girl in, Rodansky. Get some chow. We move out in two hours."

Rodansky guided the girl into the barracks. She followed him docilely, averting her face as she passed Kuhn.

A flare ignited with a hiss, turning the sky greenish-white. It was the first of a series of flares aimed toward Brumberg. Planes flew overhead toward Brumberg. In front of him, the forest appeared in silhouette, the trees as sharply defined as paper cutouts. He remained frozen after the darkness again settled.

He had to clean his carbine, get the ammo distributed, receive the final brefing from the lieutenant. But until his loneliness was relieved, no action was possible.

Solomon was seated at the head of the table. He addressed both the seated girls and the standing GIs. Kuhn went to the opposite end of the table and sat by Leona. He did not reject her hand which gripped his under the table.

Somehow Solomon had made a congregation of his audience. There was pious intensity in their listening.

" — so that is why tonight we talk about the meaning of this day. And to make this meaning clear is why I ask why this night is different from all other nights. It has to do when our people were in Egypt. They were slaves."

For The Union Dead

Robert Lowell

Relinquunt omnia servare rem publicam.

The old South Boston Aquarium stands
in a Sahara of snow now. Its broken
windows are boarded.
The bronze weathervane cod has lost
half its scales.
The airy tanks are dry.

Once my nose crawled like a snail on
the glass;
my hand tingled
to burst the bubbles,
drifting from the noses of the cowed,
compliant fish.

My hand draws back. I often sigh still
for the dark downward and vegetating
kingdom
of the fish and reptile. One morning
last March,
I pressed against the new barbed and
galvanized

fence on the Boston Common. Behind
their cage,
yellow dinosaur steam shovels were
grunting
as they cropped up tons of mush and
grass
to gouge their underworld garage.

Parking lots luxuriate like civic
sand piles in the heart of Boston.
A girdle of orange, Puritan-pumpkin-
colored girders
braces the tingling Statehouse, shaking

over the excavations, as it faces Colonel
Shaw
and his bell-cheeked Negro infantry
on St. Gaudens' shaking Civil War relief,
propped by a plank splint against the
garage's earthquake.

Two months after marching through
Boston,
half the regiment was dead;
at the dedication,
William James could almost hear the
bronze Negroes breathe.

The monument sticks like a fishbone
in the city's throat.
Its colonel is as lean
as a compass needle.

He has an angry wrenlike vigilance,
a greyhound's gentle tautness;
he seems to wince at pleasure
and suffocate for privacy.

He is out of bounds. He rejoices in man's
lovely,
peculiar power to choose life and die—
when he leads his black soldiers to death,
he cannot bend his back.

On a thousand small-town New England
greens,
the old white churches hold their air
of sparse, sincere rebellion; frayed flags
quilt the graveyards of the Grand Army
of the Republic.

That Day

Robie Macauley

It was a day of fantastic good luck. Such marvelous fortune as I could hardly remember in all my 38 years. I almost got a kind of religious feeling about it, as if you could see the Hand of God. I remember when I heard the news I just sat there in my desk chair like I was in a trance, just as if I could see the clouds roll by, the black waters recede, the sun break through and the trees and meadows turn green with hope. That was the way it struck me, sort of like a vision.

The day hadn't begun in any special way that I recall — at least there weren't any special omens around. I remember that I got out of bed and touched my toes 20 times, the way I always do. Then I wandered around the house not in such a good humor. I knocked at Sissy's door and yelled at her to get up. Kid would stay there until she got bedsores if somebody didn't yell at her. Then I went out on the sun porch and saw Bud bouncing a tennis ball against the garage door instead of finishing up the homework he hadn't done last night. At that rate, they'll have to give him an old-age pension to get him out of the seventh grade. I opened the window and told him what I thought about people who bounced a damn tennis ball around instead of doing their work.

It sure was a pretty November day, I had to admit. And maybe, after all, it did you more good to fool around with a tennis ball than study some of those half-baked things they give them in school nowadays. He had to write a report on the UN last

The stone statues of the abstract Union
Soldier
grow slimmer and younger each year—
wasp-waisted, they doze over muskets,
and muse through their sideburns.

Shaw's father wanted no monument
except the ditch,
where his son's body was thrown
and lost with his "niggers."

The ditch is nearer.
There are no statues for the last war here;
on Boylston Street, a commercial
photograph
showed Hiroshima boiling

over a Mosler Safe, "the Rock of Ages,"
that survived the blast. Space is nearer.
When I crouch to my television set,
the drained faces of Negro school
children rise like balloons.

Colonel Shaw
is riding on his bubble,
he waits
for the blessed break.

The Aquarium is gone. Everywhere,
giant finned cars nose forward like fish;
a savage servility
slides by on grease.

month; I wouldn't be surprised if there were Communists in the schools even down here.

The sun made me feel a little better, though. And there was a good, rich smell in the kitchen — Georgina with the coffee perking and the eggs and bacon on. "Miz Huber just get up. She say you go ahead and eat," Georgina told me. No news — it happens that way every morning, but Georgina knows it makes me nervous the way everybody in our family goofs off in the morning, and this is her way of telling me the world is in working order. I like Georgina. She hasn't got mean and pushy the way a lot of them have lately.

And all the rest of it went along in the everyday way, insofar as I can remember. I went into the dining room and pulled the front news section off the paper. Gives me a rotten stomach half the morning if I look at it — I know by experience. The kind of thing that goes on unchecked these days. It's a nice room. From where I sit by the French windows, I can look out and see the big oak, all our stretch of green lawn down to the tennis court, and it's mighty pretty. Don't bother me; don't let me see the news; give me some good bacon and eggs and corn bread and coffee, and I'll start the day just as cheerful as any man.

Just as usual, Sissy and Bud came to the table a little later than they should, but still before their mother showed up. Louise was just in time to give me a goodbye peck on the cheek as I was going out the door. I got the Cadillac out of the garage, got onto the highway, made the three miles into town in less than ten minutes, parked behind the office and went in. Until around noon, as I said, it was just an ordinary morning, no different from any other if you happened to be a pretty well-off lawyer with a nice practice, an apartment-house owner, club member, ex-councilman, member of the First Methodist, and what they call in the papers "solid citizen" of Gallinas, Georgia. At noon, the whole world changed.

Three years ago, Simms and Huber bought an old brick house in the center of town and fixed it up into a mighty smart office. We had the old floors sanded down and refinished, the old woodwork repaired, put in lots of rich-looking rugs and drapes, filled the place with authentic antiques, and even got a fairy up from Atlanta to do "the decor." There's a Yankee musket ball, souvenir of Sherman, buried in the wainscot in the hall. We had a glass plate put over it and a silver wreath hung to mark the spot.

(Actually, old Major Beard, who used to own the house, was a real bad drunk in his later years. He used to keep a loaded pistol on the table by his chair, and when he was drinking, he'd take it into his head to get rid of one of the servants, or maybe one of his family. I've never been so sure that Sherman was to blame.)

Some people thought we ought to have an office in the new all-glass-and-steel Commercial Building. Not me. I like this old-fashioned setting. Or did until the marches started.

Then things got rough. They came down Forrest Street onto Jackson and right past our office on the way to the courthouse. We had a flower border out front — Miss Munson's idea — and they trampled that down. They pushed against the fence so it began to sag in some places. They sang and screamed and waved their signs like monkeys let loose from the zoo. We stood it the first time; had to — the town wasn't really prepared. That night somebody, one of the drunk ones I guess, threw a brick into our big front window. You can bet Len and I were in Clemson Todd's office first thing next morning. He looked green. He never bargained for this kind of trouble when he put up his name for mayor. I'll always remember him as a big-ass kid in high school, scared of the teacher. And we scared him some that morning ourselves.

But even with twice the number of police in riot helmets and squad cars around, tear gas and dogs when things got ugly, they still raised hell the whole month long. I don't know why the worst of it had to happen right outside our windows. One day a tear-gas bomb in our front yard and the next day blood all over our front steps where the police got one of them. That's when I bought a shotgun for the office, hired Nash Pettigrew for night watchman and gave Clemson holy hell about getting them off our street.

After he brought in the fire trucks with the hoses and the town got a real riot squad organized, things got a sight better and the demonstrations tapered off. Better, but not permanent-better. On the outside things were quiet, but I began to have the feeling that sleep at night would never quite be the same thing again. Lots of folks at the club said that it was just the outside agitators — and if we got shed of them, things would go back to normal. But I knew different. It appeared to me like we were living in the middle of a huge dry forest, dry as tinder. You could stop some people who started fires, but then there would be lots of fires that sprang up here and there just of themselves. What was needed was a big thing, like a real seven-day torrent, to give us some peace again.

Well, that particular morning Len and I spent in my office going over some cases due to come up on the next docket. I don't recall a thing else. Len left a little before noon because he had to see a man about buying a piece of land out on the Gainesville Road. A little later, I sent Peggy Munson out for some roast-beef sandwiches and a bottle of beer. Sometimes I just like to have a quiet lunch alone in my office and play the radio some, restaurants in this town being what they are. I got settled down. The girls went away to lunch and the place was quiet. There was some kind of show-tune music on the radio. And right up to that point it had been a common kind of morning without anybody, least of all me, suspecting any different. Suddenly the music broke off and, great God, it began to happen.

I don't remember anything except sitting there listening, awe-struck, for maybe the better part of an hour. Then I snapped the radio off and just sat there in that new kind of silence, not thinking any particular thoughts but carried off in that kind of wonderful trance.

What brought me out of it finally was a kind of tapping at my door. I said, "Come in," and it was Peggy Munson, not saying a thing, just standing there. She looked like somebody had hit her on the skull with a baseball bat. I could tell there was something awful wrong with her.

"Good Lord, Peggy," I said. "What's the matter?" Her hands hung down and her eyes kept staring at me with a kind of concussed look. I got up and started over toward her.

She started to speak in a queer voice. It was something like, "Did you . . . no . . . what. . . ." Then she said, "I feel sick, Mr. Huber. I'm going home."

I said, "Lie down, Peggy. Let me call Doc Thurman. Or maybe I'd better run you over to the hospital right away."

"No, no!" she said. "I'll be all right. Just let me go home. Mary's taking me in her car." And she almost ran out to the sidewalk, where Mary was waiting with the motor running.

So that's it, I thought — could it be? Nice girl like Peggy, from a good family. After the other, it was almost too much to take in. The phone was ringing and I went back into my office.

It was Louise, and she sounded almost hysterical, even more than she usually does on the telephone. "Have you heard the news?" she said. "Praise God, isn't it just the most exciting thing?" I managed to get in the fact that I had heard it.

"I was having lunch at Lois Graves' — five of us girls — and you should've seen the faces around the table. Kind of scary to begin with, but when it began to percolate through what this meant, you never saw five happier souls in your life. Babbling and hugging each other like crazy. And listen, Charlie Ray."

"I'm still listening."

"I came right home and I've been on the phone ever since. I got a report from June Sugden, who happened to be over at the school. She said it was just *impressive* how they all reacted. They understood right away. They *know.* The whole seventh grade stood up, just as solemn and happy as can be, and you know what they did? They sang, *My Country 'Tis of Thee* first and they cheered afterward. Buddy right there in the front row. Seventh graders and they realized right off what a lot of older folks are still too dumb to realize. You know what, Charlie Ray, it gives me hope. Just after everything was looking so bad. It's God's way of telling us. Oh, don't be so tongue-tied. Don't you think it's a marvel? You come home right away and we'll go over to the club for drinks. I just *have* to hear what people are saying."

Len came in as I was hanging up. He didn't say anything, but, with the big smile on his face, he didn't have to. We shook hands silently. Then he said, "I'll see you at the club. All of us are going over — a kind of victory celebration, you might say."

The streets were pretty well deserted, and I wheeled the big Cadillac right through town at a good clip and out to the highway. No cop would be mean enough to give me a ticket at a time like this.

When I got to our lane, I slowed down — you never can tell about dogs or kids there. I came up past the Weiners' place going about 20 and I saw Doc Weiner out digging in his garden — it crossed my mind to stop and ask him if he'd heard the news.

They are our nearest neighbors, but we've made it a point not to have much to do with them, of course. As neighbors, we've never had anything to complain about — they keep to their side of the grove and we keep to ours. As Louise points out, they *are* rich Yankee Jews and, you know, give them an inch. . . . But I had a sudden curiosity to speak to Weiner and so I slowed up and stopped.

Then I noticed something mighty funny about what he was doing. He was digging furiously in one spot, spading out big chunks of dirt like he had to have a foxhole in the next five minutes. He wasn't very used to digging, but he sure was putting his heart into this one.

I opened the car door, started to get out, and called to him, "Hey, Doc, did you hear the news?"

At that he looked up, and I think he noticed me for the first time. I couldn't believe my eyes. The man was crying. He turned away quickly without so much as a word, and walked stiff-legged back toward his house.

Well, Frau Weiner, whatever her name is, doesn't look like an easy one to get along with. That was my first thought. Then I remembered that they had a boy in the Army, and I wondered if something had happened to him. Unlikely — they don't see much action in the Quartermaster Corps, where this kid undoubtedly was. Anyway, why worry, it could be anything. They are an emotional race. I climbed back in the car and went home.

The scene at the club was like New Year's Eve. I don't think the bar had done so much business since the day Repeal came in. Everybody was sitting around talking a mile a minute, laughing, slapping each other on the back. I grabbed a waiter first thing, literally grabbed him by the arms and hauled him over to a table where the Simms, Pete and Martha McIntyre and the Whitlaws were sitting. They had just come and hadn't been served yet.

"Listen, you bring us four of the biggest, coldest bottles of champagne you can find," I said to the waiter. We sat down and everybody began to babble at once. It was like they all couldn't quite believe it. They knew it was good, but they didn't know quite how good or quite what to make of it. It was like one of those things you have to get drunk over before you can begin to make sense of it. And it seemed to me that we'd all got a little drunk right when we were first hit.

The champagne came. I picked up a bottle and when I popped the cork, there were loud mock screams and wild laughs from all over the room — then hand clapping.

We all had a glass, but the men soon turned to bourbon and branch. We were all old friends, lived alike and thought alike, but now we seemed to have an even closer bond than ever before. It was turning into one of the warmest, most heartfelt thanksgiving parties I've ever had the good fortune to witness.

I think we were all on the way to being stoned before they began to serve dinner. Louise sang *Happy Days Are Here Again* and her hair came down over her face. Pete did an imitation that everybody hugely enjoyed.

Just as we were getting up, I mean staggering up, to leave the bar and go in to the dining room, Len came back from the lounge where he'd been checking the TV program.

He pulled me aside and said, "Listen, Charlie. The news isn't so good."

I said something like, "Whaddya mean, no good? Don't poop the party."

"I'm serious," he said. "They caught the guy."

"In a barn near Bowling Green," I said.

"No, I'm not kidding. They caught the guy and *he wasn't one of ours."*

"What was he, then?"

"The guy who fired the shots was a Commie. It was on TV. Don't you see how that changes everything, Charlie? Don't you see, goddamn it?"

It kind of spoiled that day for me.

Sometime During Eternity

Lawrence Ferlinghetti

Sometime during eternity
some guys show up
and one of them
who shows up real late
is a kind of carpenter
from some square-type place
like Galilee
and he starts wailing
and claiming he is hep
to who made heaven
and earth
and that the cat
who really laid it on us
is his Dad

And moreover
he adds
It's all writ down
on some scroll-type parchments
which some henchmen
leave lying around the Dead Sea somewheres
a long time ago
and which you won't even find
for a coupla thousand years or so
or at least for
nineteen hundred and fortyseven
of them
to be exact
and even then
nobody really believes them
or me
for that matter

You're hot
they tell him

And they cool him

They stretch him on the Tree to cool

And everybody after that
is always making models
of this Tree
with Him hung up
and always crooning His name
and calling Him to come down
and sit in
on their combo
as if he is <u>the</u> king cat
who's got to blow
or they can't quite make it

Only he don't come down
from His Tree

Him just hang there
on His Tree
looking real Petered out
and real cool
and also
according to a roundup
of late world news
from the usual unreliable sources
real dead

Death in Miami Beach

Herbert Gold

The state of madness can be defined partly as an extreme of isolation of one human being from everyone else. It provides a model for dying. Only an intermittent and fragmentary awareness of others interrupts the black folding of the layers of self upon each other — this also defines the state of that dilemma known as "mental health."

There is a false madness induced by the accidents of isolation which prisoners, travelers, and the very ill may sometimes experience without giving up their return ticket. Surely you out there all know what I mean from your own troubles and painful decisions. To say that it is false madness does not soften its extremity. The mask of existence fits harshly on your skin, but it is in fact your only skin; and when harshly your skin is peeled off — beneath it you are naked and your naked isolation is no joy to you.

During a period of work on a long job of writing in the winter of 1958, I deliberately withdrew myself from all those who knew my name and traveled by automobile in slow stages through the deep South to Miami Beach, Key West, Havana, and finally back up toward Detroit. No one asked me to write a novel, no one asked me to go away; but I did anyway. I was tempted by the prospect of dreaming through my story amid a pleasant chaos of sun and sea, all other responsibilities suspended, and so I arranged it for myself.

Work is very fine, but after the day's work, isolation, silence, and death seemed to follow me through the zazzy carnival of Miami, the casual resort indolence of Key West, and the smoky, blistered elegance of a tourist's Havana. In Havana, from the rooftop of the Ambos Mundos Hotel, I could see Batista's police loafing with their weapons in front of public buildings; occasionally there were bombs; once a body happened to be left in the street and people hurried by as if they knew nothing, nothing, nothing at all but the next step before them.

At Key West, a few days before Christmas, I visited the turtle slaughterhouse. It is one of the few tourists attractions on this spot of island, "North Havana," raised far out into the sea off the coast of Florida. Visitors take their kiddies by the hand and lead them to see the nice turtles.

Before being killed and canned, the turtles swim in dense kraals, bumping each other in the murky water, armor clashing, dully lurching against the high pens. Later, trussed on a plank dock, they lie unblinking in the sun, their flippers pierced and tied. The tough leather of their skin does not disguise their present helplessness and pain. They wear thick, sun-hardened accumulations of blood at their wounds. Barbados turtles, as large as children, they belong to a species which has been eliminated locally by ardent harvesting of the waters near Key West, but the commercial tradition still brings them here to be slaughtered. Crucified like thieves, they breathe in little sighs, they gulp, they wait.

At a further stage, in the room where the

actual slaughtering occurs, the butchers stride through gore in heavy boots. The visitor must proceed on a catwalk; a misstep will plunge him into a slow river of entrails and blood. Because it was near Christmastime, the owners of the plant had installed a speaker system for musical divertissement of the butchers, and while the turtles dried under the sun or lay exposed to the butchers' knives, Christmas bells tolled out, electronically amplified, "God Rest Ye Merry, Gentlemen," or the Bing Crosby recording of *"Adeste Fideles."*

These commercial details are not intended to support a special plea on behalf of the humane harvesting of Barbados turtles. In fact, let me grant that I sought out this scene and visited the abattoir without having any proper business there at all: merely curiosity and the need to confirm my imagination about it. I should be judged for vulgarity by the man who chooses out of purity not to follow me, not by the man I saw lurking outside, with a face ravaged by the horrified fascination which makes it impossible for him to visit his dreams. What had I done which he could not permit himself? Was I filthied, was I weakened by pleasure but obscurely nourished, was I fed on coveted turtle joys after trampling in turtle blood? Had I asked permission from the butcher and plied a knife with my own hands on the belly of one of the slow, unblinking, dragon-headed, ancient sea-beasts? And did it arch its graceful dragon neck in reproach as I stabbed? He stared at me like a jealous lover, imagining my wickedness, rabid and hopeless, wanting to bury his head in the reek on my hands.

Most of us turn from the vision of death only out of weakness, and this is no turning from death. Serve up your turtle steak, gourmet friend, with no protest from me; I'll eat at your table. ("A nice rendition," one gentleman said of Bing Crosby to his wife. Turtle is tasty, somewhat gamy meat. Protein nourishes the brain — brings oxygen and freedom.)

A few days later, in Miami Beach, I participated in two trivial accidents. My hotel was in one of the oldest, therefore least expensive, parts of the town, only a short block from the sea and a short block from restaurants and therefore very convenient to my casual schedule: breakfast at Whelan's, a stretch of writing, a long swim, lunch, a pleasant bit of loafing on the beach, then perhaps some sunbaked work at my typewriter on the tar roof ("solarium"), and another swim before dinner. I had the habit in the morning of disregarding the elevator, hurrying down a back stairway of the Webster Hotel, through an alley, and so shortcutting to the drugstore. One day, wearing tennis shoes, I felt an evil slide and crunch underfoot, and knew first by the shrinking in my heart and then by simple inspection that I had stepped on a small animal.

It seemed to be a variety of cockroach. It had been perhaps an inch and a half long, longer with its wings spread, and it had strayed from the raised platform nearby where the hotel stored its rubbish. Now it lay twitching, legs scrambling in the air without moving, and a yellow ooze seeped from its body within the crushed carapace. I suppose it was already dead despite all this nervous movement. I went for a walk, told myself that this was a silly matter to be fretful about (I was merely isolated), and finally took my habitual breakfast: orange juice, scrambled eggs, toast, coffee.

An hour later the dead beast was glued by its own innards to the paving of the alley; the Florida sun was moving through the sky above it. But now there was also a row of ants leading to it, another leading away, like twin caterpillars dissembling their unity of purpose. They were not merely eating, of course, they were carrying off the meat to their hill someplace. But the dead roach still twitched, and when the tickling jaws struck, it fluttered, squeezed, blindly pushed in its place. The ants went scrambling away, each carrying its minuscule steak.

All afternoon the shell of the roach lay there. Its row of legs no longer waved of their own power, but there were still tremors as the eating ants tugged at it. Unfatigued and busy, they were determined to wipe this slate clean.

Shortly before dark I again came down the back stairway. Now the familiar arena had changed. Another foot had struck, more strange and haphazard than my own. The shell of the roach was destroyed; there were also dead ants freckling the stone; stillness and death. The ants were suddenly individual in death; the undulating columns were erased. And the work of eating was permanently interrupted for both eaters and eaten.

The next morning when I walked through the alley no sign remained. A sweeper had done her work; there were straight, mechanical striations — a friendly broom. Good. But I bent to look for some sign or memorial to the departed beast on this stretch of alley which I now knew very well. There was none. Marks of broom; new arrangements of pebbles and dust; history here had entered upon an epoch which was strange to me.

Then finally a homely death entered what might pass for society in my isolated Miami Beach — the world of the soda fountain at Whelan's, where strollers came into an air-conditioned place to shake off the sand of the beach, sip a Coke, buy lotions and plastic sunglasses, and sometimes order a quick meal.

I was taking my breakfast, according to my habit, on a stool at the counter. By this time I was acquainted with Frank, the short-order cook, who had emigrated from Second Avenue in New York twenty years ago for his health and, for sweet health's sake, still managed to cover the leathery pouched skin of age with a fierce Miami tan, despite his long hours in Whelan's service. It relieved the silence to exchange a few morning words with a man who by now knew my face: "Two scrambled light."

"Same as yesterday, Mister."

"Yes, like yesterday." (Triumph in my voice: He remembers me!) "Whole-wheat toast. You got marmalade today?"

"Marmalade." Frank knew my face and my eggs.

Other eaters, like me, were forking up eggs and grits and sipping their Cokes or coffee when the woman entered. She was blotched with sunburn, had a swollen nose, and a mouth open so wide for noise that all her features were distorted. Emitting emergency alarm signals, turning her head and staring, demanding passage, demanding attention, a shouting vehicle, she pushed a stumbling old man along with her. "Ohh," she screamed, "a Bromo! For God's sake a Bromo! My husband is dying, a Bromo, for God's sake!"

The man's face was blue and he seemed barely conscious. He swayed stiffly as she steered him toward a stool near me.

"Oh, a Bromo right now, please!" she wailed.

Frank, behind the counter, looked sideways at her, pretended the impossible — that he did not hear her — and went on making a bacon-lettuce-and-tomato sandwich on whole-wheat toast, light on the mayonnaise.

Two or three of us jumped up to support the old man. His skin had a thick purple glow that said death to all our eyes.

"Oh, have mercy, a Bromo for my poor husband!" the woman screamed. "He didn't do nothing to you! For God's sake why don't you give it to him?"

Floundering, I watched Frank finish the bee-ell-tee, slide it onto a plate, and hand it to his customer. The hotrodder bent his head to the spilling sandwich and ate as if his life depended on it, thrustingly. In the meantime, the pharmacist, a short man in a white coat, sweating profusely despite the air conditioning, came bustling from his cubicle and said, "Heart attack? You want I should call a doctor, Missus?"

"Ohh, please, dear God, a Bromo!" she shouted.

"I'll call a doctor, he'll be right over."

"Bromo for a dying man! Why don't you give it to him? Mercy, mercy!"

The pharmacist was on the telephone and the howling woman subsided in shrill spasms. Her husband swayed on the stool, his eyes shut, while his wife leaned sobbing against his back to keep him from toppling onto the ground. She refused to let anyone touch him in order to lay him out on the floor — someone's idea — as if this ministry would commit him once and for all to the hands of death. Naturally, my innards shrank from this; the layers of the self closed tight; the flower of feeling was shut, sealed. I wanted to rush in some place, rush away; strike, destroy, *run;* kill Frank, kill the hotrodder, because a man was dying and nobody could do anything. Thus righteousness substitutes for being straight with the world. I was sly and scared. Thus I occupied myself with rage at my friend Frank, who pretended to hear nothing and stubbornly refused to make the glass of Bromo Seltzer.

During the five minutes before the doctor arrived, the scene altered rapidly and tensely. Of course, all the breakfasters but the determined hotrodder stopped their eating. The kid in the leather jacket asked for pretzels with his Coke for sustained strength behind the wheel. The rest of us drifted, lurking behind the sick man on his stool. His wife wept and cursed and heaved out her sobs because no one would supply a Bromo.

Then abruptly the man shook himself and opened his eyes and tried to stand up. He stumbled; his wife pushed him back onto the stool. He shook his head and mumbled. Then rapidly the purple color diminished; his eyes stopped their blind rolling; he began to talk with his wife. He was returning to the living. He and his wife had a whispered consultation. She nodded rapidly at him, like a bird.

Suddenly she alighted and flew out the door. The man, left behind on the stool, said hoarsely, "Lemme have a glass of water, will you, pal?"

Frank gave him the water.

Now the doctor entered, rolling his sleeves down and carrying his black bag open. He had apparently run a block in the tropical morning heat.

"Haha!" said the formerly dying man. Just like that: "Hahaha! Hi, Doc!"

"You're the sick man?" said the doctor. "Let's see now —"

"Hahaha! Don't touch me, Doc," said the old man, leaning away. "Listen, Doc, it's a funny thing. My wife gets herself all excited — aggravated."

"You mean you're all right?" the doctor said.

"Just like a little attack was all I had, hahaha," said the old man.

"You're okay?"

"Look, Doc, I ain't been eating right, you know, enjoying myself, hahaha. A little attack. I get them sometimes. Like a little attack is all."

"Okay," said the doctor firmly, "you don't want me to look at you? Okay." He nodded briskly to the pharmacist, said, "I've got a patient in my office," and trotted off again into the heat.

The old man smiled and gazed without malice at Frank, who had refused him the Bromo. Instead of leaving a tip he left him one word of explanation before he headed off after his wife. The word was deposited on the counter behind him with an apologetic smile: "Constipation."

Eggs in the plates of all the late breakfasters were left cold and shiny. The hotrodder alone had finished his sandwich, Coke, and pretzels, and left whistling. Angry at last, I discharged an unformulated hostility on Frank: "Why the devil didn't you give the man his Bromo?"

His reply seems an obvious bit of logical disquisition at this remove, but there in the shadow of panic and crisis it struck me with the force of revelation. Rubbing a dirty cloth on the counter — formulating and reformulating a smear of grease before me — he said, "If he was dying of a heart attack, what good would a Bromo do him? And if he was not dying, what good is a Bromo?"

"Yes, but."

"So I have to do my job, but I don't have to listen to nuts."

"But you didn't say anything! That woman was hysterical."

He looked at me with undisguised pity for my ignorance. "That's why I didn't say anything. I been in trouble for saying things before, I learned."

He went back to work; the pharmacist was back in his cubicle, counting pills into a bottle; the doctor had returned to his office. It was eleven o'clock and Frank took down the sign about the breakfast special. A man came in frightened to ask for the special, and Frank pointed to the sign, which was upside down on the counter, and said, "It's five minutes after eleven already. But I'll give it to you." The look of despair faded from the man's face.

In a few days I finished my own job and began the long drive out of the false Florida summer into the northern winter, my wheels passing over all sorts of unfelt beasties, my gullet accepting steaks and chops, my heart leaping with no better welcome to death than before. In Detroit my daughter asked me, "What's God's last name? How big is the whole world? Where do you go when you die?"

The foregoing inconclusive words were written two years ago. Now I have seen fit to return to my cafeteria-and-old-folks slum on lower Collins Avenue, and ostensibly for the same lure of cheap sun, sky, water, beach, boredom. I write, I swim. I stroll on Lincoln Road, I eat steaks and pizza, I sniff the sea with my sunburnt beak, I suck in my belly and run barefoot on the sand, I sleep, I write. In front of one of the new hotels I found a nude in plaster, beckoning, with her hand lifted as if hitching a ride. All aboard, you masturbators. Some of the fruit juice and hamburger stands have disappeared; new ones have opened. The Ellis Department Store, Here Since 1919, is closed, looks ransacked, has a box of Fruit of the Loom T-shirts spilled in the window and a U.S. Federal Court bankruptcy notice affixed to its sealed door.

I met a waitress in a restaurant which advertises nine-course dollar dinners. She has a pretty, lively, thirty-five-year-old girl's face, with all the black brightness of eye a man could want; she turns out to be Corsican and we speak French; an artillery sergeant brought her to Florida and apparently tired of her brightness of eye. She has a rattling Corsican accent, likes Edith Piaf records, and gives me extra shrimp bits in my shrimp bits salad. So some things change. Last time I heard no Edith Piaf and earned no extra forkfuls of shrimp. The sirloin steak she brings me spreads its wings and seems ready to flop off the plate. My gut talks French and I take ease in the flattery of food. I wait and at last she slips into my booth with me and sighs. It is eleven o'clock, time to begin real life. Her history is sad. I feel obliged to offer some recompense for the evil done her by men and luck, and so I listen, wondering how her eyes can remain so bright as the disasters and disillusionments unroll.

When I said good night, she replied with a funny, rapidly fiddling, diddling, twenty-one-fingered gesture at her mouth. I asked what it meant. "Fun and glee," she said, "fun and glee! *Maintenant je suis une vraie Américaine.*" Her eyes burn like stars, but like the stars, she has darkness between them.

A day and a night and another day. The first week passes.

I eat salty bagels in the sun, I listen to the teenage girls after school with their curious mixture of Florida cracker and Bronx accents. I go back into the damp of my room — the peculiar dank assault of cheap tropical bedrooms — and think my novel through once again, examining the pile of manuscript with my intentions in motion like a column of ants working over the struggling body of an insect. And when the life seems to weaken, I leave it and go out onto the beach or into the street.

Madness consists partly in an extreme of isolation? Partly. But the demented tumble down from their associations and memories into other associations and memories; they are sent away into the future with a map of the past which conforms to no agreed past and to no other map — and yet it is their only chart, their history and route, their needs which are unfailingly present. The lonely traveler also brutally inflicts absolute possession of his movements upon the endless day, and the novelty of what he sees joins him in yet another way to his deepest desires and dreads. He returns, he never lets go. There is no escape even in isolation; there is no isolation, merely interrupted and distorted association, until death claims us. Then every man is an island entire of itself.

In love, we seek freedom and purity even more than the comfort of diminished isolation. Those few fortunate ones who have the talent can bear the paradox of love. The rest of us are harassed by our contradictory demands — *join me, make me free.* With age and aging, the model of all voyages (lean and grow, diminish and weary), comes final approach to the ultimate simplicity which love seeks to confound — death. A paradox forever out of balance to answer a grave black simplicity: *we are ill used.* The facts we make for ourselves disappoint the intentions with which we make them. The opposable thumb, which is said to be responsible for civilization and history, gives us no answers here, though with it we can grasp our pens and break insects in our hands. Finally we die, opposable thumbs and all.

In the meantime, I visit my story. We exchange visits. I laugh over it, frown and worry over it, and urge it forward. Then I leave it for the Miami streets. The book follows me; it does not let me visit unaccompanied; it enters me instead and I try to shake it off as an adept at voodoo fights against possession by the importunate god. The opposable thumb is of no use in this contest; both the prize and the weapons have reached beyond tools, even tools of thinking; I am the quadruple god's horse — dream of love, hope of meaning, joy of power, relish in being. Too much burden on one soul. Who asked me to feel sorry or glad for others? They were merely pious who asked me. Why follow their orders? I decide: I *won't.* But I cannot escape my self, which also gives orders. The flower of feeling opens; the flower shuts; it obeys the freshness of weather. All emotion flowing from health or illness partakes of the pathetic fallacy, identifying moral value with the gifts of nature. My feet want to run; I am wearing Keds, and feel light on the foam rubber soles; but the heat of the sun holds me to earth.

There is a hotel on Washington Boulevard which specializes in "economical, comfortable living for the retired." It is a huge dark building like the Women's House of Detention in Greenwich Village, but without the bars on the rooms, and there are purple lights playing on the palm trees outside, soft music piped throughout the grounds, and the frequent blare of a loudspeaker: "Missus Goldberg to the telephone! Missus Goldberg! *Sadie, answer the phone!*" when the children call from New York. The streets of the neighborhood are filled with chattering of mournful elder statesmen, mostly losers after sixty years of continual negotiation, men with chagrined pouches slipping sideways beneath their eyes, women with hair bursting onto their cheeks and upper lips, as if all at once, near the end, they have decided to make a final try at being better men than their husbands.

To walk through the crowd during the hour following their afternoon naps is to wade in senility. There is a deep-sea lack of light despite all the sun and brisk resort clatter; you gasp for life and run to look in a dusty window. Narcissus wants to be just thirty-five, *"nel mezzo del cammin di nostra vita,"* and not seventy, not seventy! The crowd flutters by. "She thought she could be my daughter-in-law! A girl like that! To be my daughter-in-law! And you know what? Now she is." "I used to be in business. I had a good business. It was a nice store, good location. Furniture. I should have kept my location." "What does the weather report say? Does the weather report ever say anything but the weather?" "Moishe died. He had an attack. Well, we all got to go."

Is it the same voice, the same rhythm? It is the same crowd — grief, isolation, death. There almost always seems to be an ambulance pulling up or pulling away.

It is fine to tell a story, which feels like

affirmation, but afterwards, after the morning's writing, then what? Writing is an expression of affirmation, power, longing, but not a proper cause of these emotions in the writer. He is a guide into delight and dread because he can escape victimization (he thinks); he has left a little trail of paper behind him as he threads his way into the maze, and can find his way back (he believes — though the roar of the maze sets up a disarray in anything as fragmentary as his intentions about return). He tracks the minotaur with an open mind. "Maybe I'll like it," he says, "and maybe I won't. At least I'll see." He initiates passion only because he has it — otherwise self-delusion and covetous self-therapy. And so it is not good to be alone for long, entirely alone.

But at least for a time, until they dim out, loneliness sharpens the eyes. I feel like a safecracker; loneliness has also sharpened my fingertips, and my entire body throughout feels the clicking tumblers as I yearn toward the combination. I come to focus, I work. But afterwards, then what? I have retreated from the distractions of Manhattan. There are no telephone calls. No friendship, no duties, no hazards of pique or pleasure. I shall work till the battery runs down, frozen and stilled by this busy emptiness under the sun. I ask myself: Can the silent column of ants reconstruct the living roach at its leisure underground? No, only a tree can make a tree, only a winged roach can make a winged roach. A column of ants works by an invisible will which resides in no one of its jointed parts, but only a swollen green ant can breed an urgent ant.

As I walk on Lincoln Road, the smart shopping area of "the Beach," I ogle the oglers, the sunburned sun-worshipers basted with oil, cream, tonic, and lotion — the touts, boxers, fairies, grandmothers, exiled Cubans, local hotrodders and their gumchewing molls, sportsmen, natty invalids in gabardine, drunks, stockbrokers, antique collectors, Semites and anti-Semites all taking the air together on Lincoln Road. Hill people, swamp people, and ex-pugs sell newspapers flown in from all over — New York, Chicago, Los Angeles ("Smogsville!" cackles a refugee). And New York is harried by flu and Chicago is black with coal and damp. And here we all are on Lincoln Road, with a delicious breeze, courtesy of the steakhouse pumping cool air into the street. So let's buy the hometown paper to see how miserable we might have been, for others are.

On Lincoln Road, fair Lincoln Road in Miami Beach, the Negroes have been freed; freed of existence, that is; only a few black ghosts slip discreetly by. Even if they were not so discreet, they would be invisible, though for a new reason: they are going someplace, namely, to work, or at another hour, home. For them, Lincoln Road is a mere artery for transit, while for the others, Lincoln Road is parlor, sunroom, promontory into health and beauty. For the visitors, Lincoln Road is a slow matter, a recipe for yearned-for slowness, sloth, strolling ease, delicacy of control. The cocky Broadway chapparoonies are wearing their new pleatless "Miami-Tailored Daks." Their bellies do the work of belts, hiding the place where belts would be. Now I'm so slow I don't need a belt, the pants proudly announce; I'm just walkin' along, just struttin' down the avenue, just here and pleasant with myself, and when I take a breath, the expandable elastic waistband expands with me. In the men's room of a bar off Lincoln Road, hung with photographs of wrestlers, there is a curious vending machine which is decorated with a crown and raised scepter and submits a product called DE-LA: "Say Delay, a light lubricating ointment designed to aid in the prevention of premature climax. Odorless. Safe. Stainless. Easy to apply. Directions on package. 50¢ coins only. Machine does not give change."

Machine makes comment, however. Machine is trying to tell us something.

The Negro girl who cleans my room gets yelled at, screamed at, all morning. "Stupid, stupid, stupid! A single room only gets two towels, one face, one bath!" She smiles slyly to herself as if she knows where the manager's DE-LA is hidden. This is the southland, I am reminded, where we have grits for breakfast. But it is not quite dat ole Dixie, boss, which changeth not, nor can age alter it. It is Miami Beach. The Sholem Aleichem Literary Society ("Managed by Tourists — Managed for Tourists") has a For Rent sign on it. "Owner Will Remodel for Any Business."

I decide as I walk: I'll write my book till the battery runs down, though distraction seems necessary; other duties, friends, "real life."

The sirens of the police ambulances work up and down the Beach all day and night, announcing the news as they carry away the attacked, the fallen, the stroked, the perished. A population of the aged sheds its members at the merest trifle of an excuse — a bottle of cold pop in the sun, a skipped nap, somebody raising his voice suddenly — or no excuse at all. It touches life and someone dies. It treads carelessly and someone dies. The sirens whir and howl and Negroes courteously open the back door for the corpse. For some reason people smile at the ambulance as they stroll, sucking ice cream. Perhaps they dream of an accident, a distraction: *Siren meets white Thunderbird, boy of forty cut off in his prime, had a girl in there with him, not his wife.* Perhaps thinking: *Not me this time.*

One of those impossible coincidences. Today I met Dr. Meyer leading his blind wife. He was our family doctor in Cleveland, addicted to practical jokes, who always said he wanted to do research, and in fact he had some sort of connection with one of the important drug laboratories. When he retired from practice, he announced to my parents over a bottle of wine that now he would begin his true life's work. I had decided that his practical jokes, bought in Jean's Fun House on East 9th Street — buzzers, false flies, stomach noises, leaky cups — were a symptom of childish anger at adult responsibility. But now that he could retire from practice and try his hand at research. . . . It turned out that his wife had inoperable cataracts; she went blind fast, and he went sour, quiet, mean; and they left Cleveland for Miami Beach, where I saw him leading her, walking with the stiff, frightened step of the unaccustomed blind. He is shrunken; only today do I notice that he is a small man — when I was a boy, he was immense. At present, and forever until the very end, his life's work is to steer his wife to the beach in the morning and sit with her to describe what he sees. He has replaced both practical jokes and dreams of a laboratory with loyalty to his wife, but virtue has made him a furious runt.

Fantasies of thighs, breasts, bellies as I nap on the beach. I awaken, sticky with salt. My nose is peeling. Shall I visit the Corsican waitress again tonight? Shall I ask the Meyers to dinner? But I have made this disappearance into Miami Beach in order to avoid the troubles of others and of myself. I swim again. I doze again. I dream of sex with a woman I overheard describing the proper way to kill a chicken "so it don't suffer. You ask anyone, they'll tell you. And there's nothing like fresh-killed chicken. You can't trust the butchers."

A man in the coffee shop later said to the cashier: "I been sick, that's why you ain't seen me. Doctor said coronary thrombosis. You ever heard of that?"

"Naw. Lots of people got coronaries, but that thrombosis, that's a new thing. The docs keep finding new things so they can charge us."

"Well, I'll tell you, it left me feeling pretty weak."

I went one night to see a road company version of *My Fair Lady* at the Miami Beach Auditorium, which more frequently provides hospitality for wrestling or boxing matches. A maggoty, bored imitation of Rex Harrison, a thick Eliza without any bounce. The audience is quietly taking in the famous sight. They write on their postcards home: Tonight we saw a Broadway show, but the girl was fat.

Crazy Louie on the beach — a frantic grandfather with Latin records, maracas, castanets, silk Cuban shirts, feathers, straw skirt, rubber Halloween masks, a huge earring loosely hooked to his ear by a bent hairpin, thick glasses sliding down his nose, leathery withered legs, dancing and dancing, all sinews and grins and shakes to some inner song while the portable phonograph goes rattle-and-scrape, screech, rattle, and scrape. Amazingly, the crowd which regularly gathers on the sand nearby seems to enjoy his music; some of them shake, too, dreaming of the days when they had lust to squander on their legs. Dr. Meyer's wife smiles as he describes the scene. "Are you smiling, Meyer?" she asks. He says yes, but is lying. Crazy Louie bangs his castanet under her nose and screams *"Ole!"* and she jumps. At last Dr. Meyer smiles.

Then he tells her that sometimes the beginnings of arteriosclerosis can be detected at age twenty-five. "Cuts off the blood supply to the brain. The psychiatrists think they're smart, but they can't do anything about the histological system. The brain dries up like a scab."

"Meyer, you shouldn't use such language."

"You mean histology?"

"I mean scab, Meyer."

Crazy Louie is dancing and cackling, kicking sand. The old ladies in their bathing skirts fan themselves contentedly as he enters his Afro-Cuban apocalypse. On the beach there is a rural, village tolerance of madness. Louie doesn't do any harm. His children sent him down. He is new since my last visit.

And where are my old friends?

The cockroach in the alley is long gone, of course, and its grandchildren unto many generations. But I have found cheap sun again for my sinus, and white ocean breaking against the distractions of Manhattan in winter, spring, summer, fall. I think of a friend, a Jewish chauvinist, arguing with his girl: "When your people were still living in trees and hitting each other with sticks, my people already had sinus trouble."

The Spinoza Forum is gone, replaced by a motel. Dr. Wolfson still goes to the beach every afternoon. But the neighborhood is changed. He has nothing to say to me except that raw beets, honey, and tangerines keep a man virtuous and healthy, no matter what his age.

The woman who knew Thomas Wolfe

— did I forget to mention that last time? — and swam as if she wanted to die, and worked as a B-girl . . . gone. She wanted to reconstruct some cabin-in-the-woods dream of perfection, but she could never find the missing pieces. Life is not a jigsaw puzzle; once it has been scrambled, the old picture is gone.

The racing-car driver with whom I chatted a couple of times at breakfast — gone.

The column of ants at the cockroach — gone.

The drummed-up acquaintances — even their names forgotten.

The hotel clerk who wanted to explore in Guatemala — perhaps he is exploring in Guatemala. The new manager of the hotel has never even heard of him.

And the man who died — dead.

I know this for certain, for I have finally discovered an old friend. Frank, the gray bozo behind the counter at Whelan's, is still there. I had taken up new eating habits and did not return to Whelan's during my first week in Miami Beach, but then I did and found him, still building hamburger platters and scrambling eggs. At first he did not remember me. He never knew my name. When I reminded him of the incident about the man who died, and of our long breakfast friendship, a look of irritation captured his face — demands were being made on him — but then his cross mug creased into a smile. He did remember me! He only needed to be reminded!

"You know that old fool," he said. "Later really did die. He's dead. Later died."

There was a new cat in the store. A new special on toothbrushes. A new pharmacist.

I had a hamburger on our old friendship, and Frank put an extra slice of tomato on the side to *prove* that he remembered me. But why should he? He had been an experience for me — the same now, with balder eyebrows — but what was I to him? For me he existed as an example of something, a moment of frightening history, a troubled memory which I had set down in words. I had needed a friend then, but he did not. I was frightened by death then, and worse, by a way of receiving death, but he was not and perhaps never admits that he might be.

Why does he stay in Miami Beach?

Yes, for a job. Yes, for the sun. But why there?

All right, then why not there?

Why do I go back?

Why did I go back? What happened to those dead and dying ones? They died and were dead; they were swept away. I thought, the first time I went to Miami Beach, that I had made a free choice to be isolated, but I discovered that everyone comes to the state of isolation in time — though not freely. What I did out of apparent health and youth, in the pleasure of work, those others did in sickness and age, in the anxiety of boredom. But eventually work is done, health turns to decay, youth turns to ripeness turns to age; feebleness and dying must precede death except for fighter pilots, who are anachronisms. Miami Beach is an extension, adult education course in how to die, pursued with great seriousness by the enrollees. The old folks work at it with deliberate and modest intensity, in group sessions, complimenting each other on their tans, their sport shirts, their postgraduate skill at finding a proper weather. The young vacationers flush in on packaged tours, immerse themselves in the ceremonial indulgences of resort hotels, eat, swim, and enjoy their honeymoon wrestling, take in Eartha Kitt or Leo de Lion, sigh with boredom and excess, buy bottles of Man Tan at the air terminal ("Arrive With Fresh Sun On Your Cheeks!"), and flee back to real life with a secret conviction that this is leisure? Strictly for the birds, brother.

That first time in Miami Beach, I was a curious observer, obscurely moved, with the face of a man who fearfully unwinds a rope as he visits his dream of the turtle slaughterhouse. The second time (the last time!), two years' change had begun to discover my implication to me; I broke the rope; the model of death is real; the dream of dying is real. The tanned, reduced, heliotropic Doctor Meyer recognized me despite his wife's blindness ("Hannah! Look who's here!"), and when I spoke to her, she gropingly embraced me. This was why I went back — to feel Mrs. Meyer's arms hotly convulsed about my neck, as if I were still a boy in Cleveland, and to know that I was not a young man from Cleveland visiting Miami Beach as he had toured carnivals, the war, the Caribbean, Europe, and taken the boat ride around Manhattan. I was a winter visitor, tired of town, come for the sun, who had been there before.

Am I now satisfied with what I found? Which is: "Later really did die. Later died." Just as in the alley two years ago, in that swept space where there was no longer any roach and no column of ants, history enters upon new epochs which begin to grow familiar to me.

Life in the Crystal Palace

Alan Harrington

Happy families are all alike, said Tolstoy. Whether this is true of great corporations I don't know, because I have belonged to only one. The company I have been with for more than three years is one of the world's largest, having some thirty-four thousand employees in the United States and overseas. There are more than five hundred of us here at headquarters — and we are a happy family. I say this without irony, not for the reason that I am in the public-relations department, but because it is the truth. We give every appearance of happiness. We are also in many respects pretty much alike, at least on the surface.

It is not that our company makes us behave in a certain way. That kind of thing is out of date. Most of our people tend to live and talk alike, and think along the same general lines, for the simple reason that the company treats us so well. Life is good, life is gentle. Barring a deep depression or war, we need never worry about money again. We will never have to go job-hunting again. We may get ahead at different speeds, and some will climb a bit higher than others, but whatever happens the future is as secure as it can be. And the test is not arduous. Unless for some obscure reason we choose to escape back into your anxious world (where the competition is so hard and pitiless and your ego is constantly under attack) we will each enjoy a comfortable journey to what our house organ calls "green pastures," which is, of course, retirement.

"Is this sort of existence worth living?" you ask. I think that depends on who you are and also on the person you could become. There are two ways of looking at it: (1) If you are not going to set the world on fire anyway, it is better to spend your life in nice surroundings; (2) looking back, you *might* have had a more adventuresome time and struggled harder to make your mark in the world if the big company hadn't made things soft for you.

But it is all too easy to be glib in disapproving of the kindly corporation. We are then in the position of scorning the earthly paradise, and that cannot be done lightly. To be honest, we should put aside the convenient clichés — that big business firms, for example, are by their very nature heartless, exploitive, enforcers of conformity, etc. It is commonly assumed that a big, apparently impersonal authority is made up of bad fellows. How much more bewildering and exasperating to discover that they are good fellows!

I went into my job at the corporation with a poor spirit. I was suspicious of large companies, and swore that nobody was going to turn me into a robot. My situation was untenable anyway. I had just sold my first novel, a satire about a man who, under the pressure of business, had turned himself into a Nothing. In a year the grenade would go off, and of course the writer would be fired.

Particularly disconcerting in the early days was the gentleness of my new associates. Most public-relations offices are filled with edgy, hustling people. Here there was such courtesy and regard for your comfort . . . it was unfair. When I arrived, everyone turned and smiled, and they all came over to say how glad they were that I was with them. The boss took my arm and had me in for a long talk. "We want you to be happy here," he said earnestly. "Is there anything we can do? Please let us know." When you discover that the members of the company team really care about you it is a shock to the nervous system. The skeptical newcomer stands there, shifting his feet, not knowing what to do with his preconceived resentment.

I went through the orientation course, and completed all the forms and saw that I was protected against everything. I had a momentary fearful sensation of being enfolded in the wings of the corporation and borne aloft. "How's everything going?" inquired one of the orientation men, and I grunted at his civil question.

Now I was one of the group, hunched gloomily over a typewriter amid smiling faces. With the exception of the department head and assistant manager, our public-relations staff worked in one large room. We did our jobs in leisurely fashion with a carpet of non-glare fluorescent lighting above and a thick wall-to-wall carpet below. The usual office noises were hushed. Typewriters made a faint clack. Our mild jokes were lost in the air. It seemed to be a strange pressure chamber in which there was no pressure. This was a temporary arrangement. Next year the company was moving to a new office building in the suburbs, and it would be a fabulous place — a great office-palace on a hilltop surrounded by fields and woodlands. Everybody talked about the palace and what a marvelous headquarters it would be. The enthusiasm bored me, and I thought: "Well, I'll never see it."

That was a long time ago. Today I continue to live in the city but commute in reverse to the suburbs, and every weekday I sit down to work in the country palace. Here, after three years, are some general impressions of our corporate life:

The corporation is decent. Most of our men have deep, comfortable voices. You have stood beside them in slow elevators, and heard these vibrant tones of people whose throats are utterly relaxed. And why shouldn't they be relaxed? Once you join our company, so far as the job is concerned, you will have to create your own anxieties. The company won't provide any for you.

There is no getting around it — our working conditions are sensational. The lower and middle echelons arrive at nine and, except in very rare instances, go home at quarter-to-five. Many of the higher executives work longer and harder, according to their inclinations, but seldom in response to an emergency. Rather it is a pleasure for them.

This is a company whose products move easily in great packages across the continent. Demand is constant and growing, since our products are good for people and contribute to the nation's health and well-being. The supply is adjusted from time to time in order to keep prices at a reasonable level. There is no reason for anyone to kill himself through overwork.

The savage, messianic executive of the type described in Rod Serling's *Patterns* would find himself out of place here. In fact, he would be embarrassing. In the unlikely event of his coming with us, the moment he started shouting at anybody he would be taken aside and admonished in a nice way. (We do have one high-ranking officer a bit like that, but he is old and close to retirement. He is very much the exception.)

A full recital of our employee benefits would — and does, in the indoctrination period — take all day, but here are just a few of them. We have a fine pension fund, a fantastically inexpensive medical program for you and your family, and a low-premium life-insurance policy for double your salary. The company will invest five per cent of your pay in blue-chip stocks and contribute on your behalf another three per cent. The company picks up half of your luncheon check. When we moved to the suburbs, the company paid its employees' moving expenses and helped them settle in their new homes. For those who didn't wish to move . . . a bus waits at the railroad station for commuters from the city and drives them to the hilltop office building.

The only unsatisfactory working condition, I think, is that you must be content with a two-week vacation until you have been with the company for ten years. In other words, the experience you may have gained elsewhere, precisely the experience the company has *bought,* counts for nothing in terms of vacation time. But this policy is fairly standard practice. It certainly inhibits a man's desire (say, after nine years) to change companies for a better job. Thus, it is at least a minor pressure against free-spirited enterprise. All the benefits exert pressure, too. There is nothing sinister about them, since admittedly they are for your own material comfort — and isn't that supposed to be one of the goals of mankind? What happens is that, as the years go by, the temptation to strike out on your own or take another job becomes less and less. Gradually you become accustomed to the Utopian drift. Soon another inhibition may make you even more amenable. If you have been in easy circumstances for a number of years, you feel that you are out of shape. Even in younger men the hard muscle of ambition tends to go slack, and you hesitate to take a chance in the jungle again.

On top of all this, it is practically impossible to be fired. Unless you drink to alcoholism or someone finds your hand in the cash box, the company can afford to keep you around indefinitely. Occasionally under great provocation — such as a scandal that reaches the tabloids — there may be a transfer. Once in a while a prematurely crusty old-timer is retired. Otherwise the ax will not fall.

Every so often I hear my seniors at the corporation inveigh against socialism, and it seems strange. I think that our company resembles nothing so much as a private socialist system. We are taken care of from our children's cradles to our own graves. We move with carefully graduated rank, station, and salary through the decades. By what marvelous process of self-deception do we consider our individual enterprise to be private? The truth is that we work communally. In our daily work most of us have not made an important decision in years, except in consultation with others.

Good people work here. Since joining the

company I have not heard one person raise his voice to another in anger, and rarely even in irritation. Apparently when you remove fear from a man's life you also remove his stinger. Since there is no severe competition within our shop, we are serene. We do compete mildly perhaps, by trying to achieve good marks in the hope that our department head will recommend a promotion or an increase to the Salary Committee. Cutting out the other fellow and using tricks to make him look bad is hardly ever done. At higher levels, now and then, executive empires will bump into each other and there will be skirmishes along the border. But these are for the most part carried on without bullying and tablepounding, and the worst that can happen to the loser is that he will be moved sideways into a smaller empire.

It would be wrong to say that our employees are not lively. They smoke and drink and love, and go on camping trips, go skiing, and operate power boats, and read things and go to the movies, and ride motorcycles like anybody else. In the office they know what to do (usually after consultation) in almost any circumstance. What a great many of them have lost, it seems to me, is temperament, in the sense of mettle. We speak of a mettlesome horse. Well, these are not mettlesome people. They lack, perhaps, the capacity to be mean and ornery when the ego is threatened — because at our company we do not threaten people's egos. Rather the ego tends to atrophy through disuse.

Another curious thing is our talent for being extremely friendly without saying anything to each other. I remember a conversation that went something like this:

"Jim! Where did you come from? I haven't seen you in — I guess it's been about a year and a half."

"Just about that, Bill. A year and a half at least."

"What are you up to, for goodness' sake?"

"I've been in Washington, and now I'm going back overseas."

"Always on the move!"

"Well, I guess I am. I just thought I'd come down and have a chat with you before leaving."

"It's great that you did. How's your family?"

"Fine, Bill, how is yours?"

"They're fine, too."

"The years go by, don't they?"

"They sure do."

"Well. . . ."

"Well. . . ."

"Well, I guess I'd better be moving along."

"It's been wonderful talking to you, Jim. Look, before you get on the plane, why don't you come down for another talk?"

"I will, boy. You can count on it."

Also common among our employees is a genuine and lively interest in the careers of upper-level executives whom they may never have laid eyes on. As the gentlemen move from one station to another, their progress is followed with exclamations and inside comments. "Hmm, Jackson has moved to Purchasing! I thought so." "Look at Welsh — he's taken over the top spot in Patagonia. Anybody can tell that they're setting him up for a vice-presidency." Who *cared* about Jackson and Welsh? At one point, I did. I had to prepare a press release about them, and update — add two more lines to — their official biographies.

The role of the corporation's top directors in our cosmos is an interesting one. In our company, members of the board are not remote figures from outside who drop in to attend meetings now and then. They are on the job every day. They recognize us, nod, and often say hello. I have found these august gentlemen to be amiable and even shy in the presence of their inferiors, but their appearance on the scene is the occasion of total respect, body and soul, such as I have never witnessed outside the army. They are not feared either. They conduct themselves in a friendly, most democratic manner. It is not awe they inspire but, so far as I can see, pure admiration. I was once talking to a young man in the employee-relations department when his eyes, gazing over my shoulder, suddenly lit up with joy. I turned, expecting to see our pretty receptionist, but it was a director passing by and giving us a wave of his hand.

Team play is the thing. Team play means that you alone can't get too far out ahead of the troops. You can't, because in our company it is necessary to consult and check over everything. Someone will ask whether this doesn't lead to a certain amount of mediocrity. It does. We have a substantial number of mediocre people in the company — that is, men and women of ordinary ability who would probably never originate anything under any circumstances.

But where organizing an effort is concerned it is sometimes better to have mediocre talent than a bunch of creative individuals who disturb the situation by questioning everything. In terms of performance, if you have a slow but sure operation, mediocre personnel, including your nephews, can carry it out beautifully. In *planning,* mediocrity has and still does hurt the company.

Our method is to get together and talk it out, each one of us contributing his mite. Why have one man make a decision when thirty-three can do it better? The consequence of this policy is that our executives commit few errors — although sometimes they arrive at the right decision three years too late. But the sure markets for the company's products bring in so much money that the mistake is buried under mountains of dollar bills. Our interminable round of conferences may also be counted on to produce by default serious errors of omission. These don't hurt noticeably either, for the reason cited above.

I got over my impatience at the slow pace of things, but I felt it once at a lecture given to senior and junior executives on the new central filing system that would go into effect when we reached the palace. A fierce little girl, a vestal of the files, told us how it was going to be. We sat, without anyone suggesting it, according to rank, and I could work out the possible course of my company career, if I stayed with it, just by looking at the assemblage of heads in front of me — bald and white in the front rows, then pepper-and-salt, and gradually back where I was, the black, brown, and blond heads of hair. I thought of my own head, slowly changing through the years as I moved up a row or two, with never a chance by a brilliant coup of jumping while still brown-headed . . . or even pepper-and-salt — over several rows and landing among the white thatches. How could I make such a leap when anything I accomplish I do as a member of a group?

A little more tension would be welcome. This may be based on fragmentary evidence, but I suspect that when people are not placed under at least a minimum of tension they seek it out in their dreams. One day I overheard our press-relations man conferring with our public-relations manager, Mac Tyler, who said: "Maybe next time, Walt, you had better try it the other way." The press man came out of the office and saw me. "Boy!" he said, "I sure got a bawling out on that!"

Another man of some rank joined his local Democratic Party, and worked hard at it during the presidential campaign. But he felt guilty about what he had done. Finally he rushed upstairs and confessed to the president of the corporation. "Gosh," he told me afterward in a disappointed tone, "he didn't mind at all. He just put his hand on my shoulder and said: 'Don't worry, Fred, I'm a Jeffersonian Republican myself!' "

We conform by choice. Critics of big business are constantly on the watch for the kind of over-cooperation that a company explicitly demands of its members. Our company doesn't demand anything. Oh, there is tactful pressure on us to join the annuity and insurance program, and a rather strong insistence on Red Cross and Community Chest contributions, but nothing serious.

What you have to watch out for is the amount of compliance you fall into by yourself, without realizing it. Something like this almost happened to me when my book was published. Far from resenting the satire, most of our employees who read it enjoyed the book. I was asked to autograph dozens of copies, and several were bought and prominently displayed in the company lending library. I had thought of myself as a writer in temporary captivity. Now that was no longer possible. A captive of what? Good Will?

I began to feel what I now recognize was a gradually deepening contentment. If you are on the watch for the symptoms, here are a few: (1) You find that you are planning your life defensively, in terms of savings plans and pensions, rather than thinking speculatively of moving up fast — faster than the others. (2) You become much less impatient over inefficiency, shrug your shoulders and accept it as the way things are. (3) Your critical faculties become dull; you accept second-best; it seems unsporting to complain. (4) Nothing makes you nervous. (5) You find that you are content to talk to people without saying anything. (6) You mention something like (improvising now) "our Human Development Department" to outsiders and learn with surprise that they think you have made a joke.

During this period of contentment, which lasted quite a few months, I did not concern myself with anything beyond the requirements of my job. I became easy-going and promiscuously nice, and had a harmless word for everybody. Finally, I was reminded that this sort of thing was the mark of a fat soul. A succession of incidents helped indicate what was wrong.

We are remote from the lives of others. Shortly before we moved to the country the press-relations man and I were looking out of our eleventh-floor window in the direction of the waterfront. We saw a half-circle of men gathered on a far-off pier. "Isn't that what they call a shape-up?" he asked with faint curiosity. It was easy to tell that he barely imagined that these men existed and that their quaint customs were real.

Some weeks before, I had looked down on a gentleman in a homburg and cutaway, running among the crowds in the financial district. He carried a bouquet of red roses wrapped in green paper. You don't associate this street with flowers, and it was exciting to see him running, holding his green wrapping like a torch of something beautiful in this place. And then he died on his feet, twisting over and slumping to the pavement. His head rested against the wall of a building. He rested with the flowers flung across his knees and his fine hat askew, and the absurd and living gallantry that produced this death *could* only be nothing to us or to anyone in the crowds that simply swerved around him and kept going, because of the way we are concentrated and oriented away from things like that.

How remote we were too from the crazy musicians who arrived on a blustery fall day with the idea that, since this was a financial center, there would be a rain of coins from the tall buildings in response to their trumpet, guitar, and bass fiddle. The wind swirled their jazz among the canyons. I saw that no one was paying them the slightest attention. Feeling guilty, I threw them a quarter, but they didn't see it. They danced and made jazz in the cold, while upstairs we went on with our work, and they didn't exist, and it was nobody's fault.

It isn't that we should have been expected to know about longshoremen, or care particularly about the man in the homburg, or throw coins to the brave musicians, but we have simply, systematically, avoided letting these aspects of life into our field of vision. We came in from the suburbs and plundered the city, and left each night without having the least idea of what was going on there. Even our daily experience in the rapid transit was spent behind a newspaper; taxis shielded us from the bad sections of town. We never heard guitars strumming on the dirty doorsteps, nor comprehended the possible excitement of disorderly feelings that make other people so much more alive than we are.

And when the corporation moved to the country our isolation from all that became completely splendid. Now most of us could anticipate fifteen- and thirty-minute rides in car pools from our suburban homes to a suburban office. You could almost hear an official sigh of contentment on the day that we moved.

This way to the palace. Point your car along a winding drive-way up the green hillside shaded with great elm trees. Enter the wide and friendly doorway and look at the murals in our lobby. They will tell you the story of our industry. As you go through the offices, you will probably marvel as we did at all the comforts and services we have. Imagine a sea of blond desks with tan chairs, outdoor lighting pouring in everywhere, roomy offices with individually-controlled air-conditioning and area-controlled Music by Muzak coming out of the walls. We need few private secretaries. All we have to do is pick up a phoning device and dictate our message to a disc that whirls in a sunny room in another part of the building. Here a pool of stenographers type all day long with buttons in their ears. We don't see them and they don't see us, but they know our voices.

A high-speed pneumatic tube system winds through the entire building. We send material from one office to another not by messenger but by torpedo containers traveling twenty-five feet a second. Simply have the attendant put your paper, magazine, or memo in the plastic carrier. He inserts the container in the tube, dials the appropriate number, and, whoosh, it is shot across the building. There is a complete sound system throughout headquarters. If, for example, a bad storm is forecast, there will be an "Attention Please," and you may go home early. At noon, enjoy movies in an auditorium the size of a small theater, visit the library, watch the World Series on color TV, or play darts and table tennis in the game room. The finest catering service and a staff of friendly waitresses bring you luncheon. Then go to the company store, pitch horseshoes, or take a brief stroll under the elms.

What happens to an office force when it is offered facilities like these? At first there were a few small complaints. The main difficulty is that we find it all but impossible to get off the campus. You can speed several miles to town for a quick lunch. Otherwise you stay on the grounds until closing. City employees everywhere have the chance to renew, at least slightly, their connection with the world during lunch hour. When we first came many of us rambled in the woods and picked flowers, but we seldom do that anymore.

As for our work-efficiency, I think it has diminished a bit as a result of what one of my friends calls "our incestuous situation." When you are isolated in the country it is not easy to feel that sense of urgency that distinguishes most businessmen.

I sometimes have a feeling of being in limbo. More than ever one feels — ungratefully — over-protected. While on the job, I actually can't feel hot or cold. I can't even get sick. This will sound ridiculous, but when the company obtained a supply of influenza shots, I found myself in the absurd position of refusing one. For some reason I wanted a chance to resist the flu in my own way.

What is the moral of all this? I am not quite sure but some time ago Dostoyevsky put it in *Notes from Underground:*

> Does not man, perhaps, love something besides well-being? Perhaps he is just as fond of suffering? Perhaps suffering is just as great a benefit to him as well-being?

. . . In the 'Crystal Palace' (suffering) is unthinkable. . . . You believe, do you not, in a crystal palace which shall be forever unbreakable — in an edifice, that is to say, at which no one shall be able to put out his tongue, or in any other way to mock? Now, for the very reason that it must be made of crystal, and forever unbreakable, and one whereat no one shall put out his tongue, I should fight shy of such a building.

American Primitive

William Jay Smith

Look at him there in his stovepipe hat,
His high-top shoes, and his handsome collar;
Only my Daddy could look like that,
And I love my Daddy like he loves his Dollar.

The screen door bangs, and it sounds so funny—
There he is in a shower of gold;
His pockets are stuffed with folding money,
His lips are blue, and his hands feel cold.

He hangs in the hall by his black cravat,
The ladies faint, and the children holler:
Only my Daddy could look like that,
And I love my Daddy like he loves his Dollar.

The Sound of Silence

Paul Simon

Hello darkness my old friend,
I've come to talk with you again,
Because a vision softly creeping,
Left its seeds while I was sleeping
And the vision that was planted in my brain
Still remains within the sound of silence.

In restless dreams I walked alone,
Narrow streets of cobble stone
'Neath the halo of a street lamp,
I turned my collar to the cold and damp
When my eyes were stabbed by the flash of a neon light
That split the night, and touched the sound of silence.

And in the naked light I saw
Ten thousand people maybe more,
People talking without speaking,
People hearing without listening,
People writing songs that voices never share
And no one dares disturb the sound of silence.

"Fools!" said I, "You do not know
Silence like a cancer grows.
Hear my words that I might teach you
Take my arms that I might reach you."
But my words like silent raindrops fell
And echoed, in the wells of silence.

And the people bowed and prayed
To the neon God they made.
And the sign flashed out its warning
In the words that it was forming.
And the sign said:
"The words of the prophets are
written
on the subway walls and tenement
halls"
And whispered in the sounds of silence.

(Simon and Garfunkel)

Revolutions

I will reach into your
fiery heart, pull out
the sky.

Gene Fowler, Shaman Songs

For more than two decades after World War II, U.S. college and university campuses were relatively quiet places. The faculty largely concerned itself with research, publishing, teaching, and attending committee meetings. Students seemed largely preoccupied with attending class, putting together term papers, or preparing for exams — in short, acquiring the degree that would qualify them for a better job in an affluent society. Indeed, many a professor frankly expressed dismay that students were so apathetic to what was going on around them.

Demonstrations on most campuses were either rare or non-existent. Revolts might brew, but where they did they did so rather quietly. For example, a well-known football coach at a mid-western university was dismissed as the result of a campaign originated by a student editor, in the editorial columns of the university daily, because the coach refused to play his black players. In the early 1950's, a group of students and faculty at the University of Wisconsin calmly and quietly pooled their efforts to begin what was to be the political downfall of Senator Joseph McCarthy, and the revival of the Democratic party as a dynamic political force in that state.

But by the mid '60's, many of the nation's campuses were no longer quiet. As the 1970's drew near, increasing numbers of students were in revolt. At Columbia, and other universities and colleges, students seized administrative offices and classroom buildings. Nor were confrontations confined to the campus. In California, students marched on induction centers and stood in front of troop trains. And history will record the impact that demonstrators at the 1969 Democratic National Convention in Chicago — many of them students — had on the outcome of the national election that year.

What caused the shift in the student mood? Dr. George Wald, a Nobel laureate, speaking extemporaneously at M.I.T., March 4, 1969, remarked that unless one assumes that students are totally irresponsible, student unrest must have some meaning. It does have a meaning; in the face of such problems as almost unimpeded militarism and unchecked population growth, Dr. Wald declared that today's youth is by no means certain that it has a future. Of course, some critics will question, even doubt, student responsibility and their depth of understanding. In reply to such skeptics, Dr. Martin Duberman, in "On Misunderstanding Student Rebels," argues that today's students are more mature, both physically and mentally, than were the youth of generations not too far past. They are responsible political activists, who are mature enough to possess a distinctiveness of their own which will not allow them to be indifferent to an environment filled with social injustice and in dire need of change.

However, in "The Politics of Violence," Arthur M. Schlesinger Jr. takes exception with Dr. Duberman. While recognizing the need for change, Schlesinger ponders the method. He criticizes the proclaimed self-righteous morality of the intemperate New Left as "an assault on rationality in politics . . . a reversion to and rationalization of the strain of hatred and violence in our own national tradition." In "Anti-Americanism in America," Midge

A Generation in Search of the Future

George Wald

Decter also voices criticism of some who urge change — the radical intellectuals. In their revolt against the 1960's, a disquieting and disillusioning decade that made the need for change so urgent, radical intellectuals, Mrs. Decter says, have wrought an incredible shift. In 20 years they have succeeded in swinging from an anti-Soviet to an anti-American position in which "the refusal to countenance political complexity remains the same." All the contributors to this section agree that a major catalyst to student unrest in the 1960's was the Vietnam War. In "Open Letter to an American Liberal," the final essay in this section, Kenneth Tynan urges the American young to "defeat the military-industrial machine by noncooperation and passive resistance," in the belief that "they could change the face of America within a decade."

Thus college campuses are no longer the tranquil places they once were. A myriad of youthful voices cry out for change. But what needs to be changed? How shall the changes be made? What kinds of institutions should be developed to replace existing institutions?

All of you know that in the last couple of years there has been student unrest, breaking at times into violence, in many parts of the world: in England, Germany, Italy, Spain, Mexico, Japan, and, needless to say, many parts of this country. There has been a great deal of discussion as to what it all means. Perfectly clearly, it means something different in Mexico from what it does in France, and something different in France from what it does in Tokyo, and something different in Tokyo from what it does in this country. Yet, unless we are to assume that students have gone crazy all over the world, or that they have just decided that it's the thing to do, it must have some common meaning.

I don't need to go so far afield to look for that meaning. I am a teacher, and at Harvard I have a class of about three hundred and fifty students — men and women — most of them freshmen and sophomores. Over these past few years, I have felt increasingly that something is terribly wrong — and this year ever so much more than last. Something has gone sour, in teaching and in learning. It's almost as though there were a widespread feeling that education has become irrelevant.

A lecture is much more of a dialogue than many of you probably realize. As you lecture, you keep watching the faces, and information keeps coming back to you all the time. I began to feel, particularly this year, that I was missing much of what was coming back. I tried asking the students, but they didn't or couldn't help me very much.

But I think I know what's the matter. I think that this whole generation of students is beset with a profound uneasiness, and I don't think that they have yet quite defined its source. I think I understand the reasons for their uneasiness even better than they do. What is more, I share their uneasiness.

What's bothering those students? Some of them tell you it's the Vietnam war. I think the Vietnam war is the most shameful episode in the whole of American history. The concept of war crimes is an American invention. We've committed many war crimes in Vietnam — but I'll tell you something interesting about that. We were committing war crimes in World War II, before the Nuremberg trials were held and the principle of war crimes was stated. The saturation bombing of German cities was a war crime. Dropping those atomic bombs on Hiroshima and Nagasaki was a war crime. If we had lost the war, it might have been *our* leaders who had to answer for such actions. I've gone through all that history lately, and I find that there's a gimmick in it. It isn't written out, but I think we established it by precedent. That gimmick is that if one can allege that one is repelling or retaliating for an aggression, after that everything goes.

And, you see, we are living in a world in which all wars are wars of defense. All War Departments are now Defense Departments. This is all part of the doubletalk of our time. The aggressor is always on the other side. I suppose this is why our ex-Secretary of State Dean Rusk went to such pains to insist, as he still insists, that in Vietnam we are repelling an aggression. And if that's what we are doing — so runs the doctrine — everything goes. If the concept of war crimes is ever to mean anything, they will have to be defined as categories of *acts,* regardless of alleged provocation. But that isn't so now.

I think we've lost that war, as a lot of other people think, too. The Vietnamese have a secret weapon. It's their willingness to die beyond our willingness to kill. In effect, they've been saying, You can kill us, but you'll have to kill a lot of us; you may have to kill all of us. And, thank heaven, we are not yet ready to do that.

Yet we have come a long way toward it — far enough to sicken many Americans, far enough to sicken even our fighting men. Far enough so that our national symbols have gone sour. How many of you can sing about "the rockets' red glare, the bombs bursting in air" without thinking, Those are *our* bombs and *our* rockets, bursting over South Vietnamese villages? When those words were written, we were a people struggling for freedom against oppression. Now we are supporting open or thinly disguised military dictatorships all over the world, helping them to control and repress peoples struggling for their freedom.

But that Vietnam war, shameful and terrible as it is, seems to me only an immediate incident in a much larger and more stubborn situation.

Part of my trouble with students is that almost all the students I teach were born after World War II. Just after World War II, a series of new and abnormal procedures came into American life. We regarded them at the time as temporary aberrations. We thought we would get back to normal American life someday.

But those procedures have stayed with us now for more than twenty years, and those students of mine have never known anything else. They think those things are normal. They think that we've always had a Pentagon, that we have always had a big Army, and that we have always had a draft. But those are all new things in American life, and I think that they are incompatible with what America meant before.

How many of you realize that just before World War II the entire American Army, including the Air Corps, numbered a hundred and thirty-nine thousand men? Then World War II started, but we weren't yet in it, and, seeing that there was great trouble in the world, we doubled this Army to two hundred and sixty-eight thousand men. Then, in World War II, it got to be eight million. And then World War II came to an end and we prepared to go back to a peacetime Army, somewhat as the American Army had always been before. And, indeed, in 1950 — you think about 1950, our international commitments, the Cold War, the Truman Doctrine, and all the rest of it — in 1950, we got down to six hundred thousand men.

Now we have three and a half million men under arms: about six hundred thousand in Vietnam, about three hundred thousand more in "support areas" elsewhere in the Pacific, about two hundred and fifty thousand in Germany. And there are a lot at home. Some months ago, we were told that three hundred thousand National Guardsmen and two hundred thousand reservists — so half a million men — had been specially trained for riot duty in the cities.

I say the Vietnam war is just an immediate incident because as long as we keep that big an Army, it will always find things to do. If the Vietnam war stopped tomorrow, the chances are that with that big a military establishment we would be in another such adventure, abroad or at home, before you knew it.

The thing to do about the draft is not to reform it but to get rid of it.

A peacetime draft is the most un-American thing I know. All the time I was growing up, I was told about oppressive Central European countries and Russia, where young men were forced into the Army, and I was told what they did about it. They chopped off a finger, or shot off a couple of toes, or, better still, if they could manage it, they came to this country. And we understood that, and sympathized, and were glad to welcome them.

Now, by present estimates, from four to six thousand Americans of draft age have left this country for Canada, two or three thousand more have gone to Europe, and it looks as though many more were preparing to emigrate.

A bill to stop the draft was recently introduced in the Senate (S. 503), sponsored by a group of senators that runs the gamut from McGovern and Hatfield to Barry Goldwater. I hope it goes through. But I think that when we get rid of the draft we must also drastically cut back the size of the armed forces.

Yet there is something ever so much bigger and more important than the draft. That bigger thing, of course, is the militarization of our country. Ex-President Eisenhower, in his farewell address, warned us of what he called the military-industrial complex. I am sad to say that we must begin to think of it now as the military-industrial-labor-union complex. What happened under the plea of the Cold War was not alone that we built up the first big peacetime Army in our history but that we institutionalized it.

We built, I suppose, the biggest government building in our history to run it, and we institutionalized it.

I don't think we can live with the present military establishment, and its eighty-billion-dollar-a-year budget, and keep America anything like the America we have known in the past. It is corrupting the life of the whole country. It is buying up everything in sight: industries, banks, investors, scientists — and lately it seems also to have bought up the labor unions.

The Defense Department is always broke, but some of the things it does with that eighty billion dollars a year would make Buck Rogers envious. For example, the Rocky Mountain Arsenal, on the outskirts of Denver, was manufacturing a deadly nerve poison on such a scale that there was a problem of waste disposal. Nothing daunted, the people there dug a tunnel two miles deep under Denver, into which they have injected so much poisoned water that, beginning a couple of years ago, Denver has experienced a series of earth tremors of increasing severity. Now there is grave fear of a major earthquake. An interesting debate is in progress as to whether Denver will be safer if that lake of poisoned water is removed or is left in place.

Perhaps you have read also of those six thousand sheep that suddenly died in Skull Valley, Utah, killed by another nerve poison — a strange and, I believe, still unexplained accident, since the nearest testing seems to have been thirty miles away.

As for Vietnam, the expenditure of firepower there has been frightening. Some of you may still remember Khe Sanh, a hamlet just south of the De-militarized Zone, where a force of United States Marines was beleaguered for a time. During that period, we dropped on the perimeter of Khe Sanh more explosives than fell on Japan throughout World War II, and more than fell on the whole of Europe during the years 1942 and 1943.

One of the officers there was quoted as having said afterward, "It looks like the world caught smallpox and died."

The only point of government is to safeguard and foster life. Our government has become preoccupied with death, with the business of killing and being killed. So-called defense now absorbs sixty per cent of the national budget, and about twelve per cent of the Gross National Product.

A lively debate is beginning again on whether or not we should deploy antiballistic missiles, the ABM. I don't have to talk about them — everyone else here is doing that. But I should like to mention a curious circumstance. In September, 1967, or about a year and a half ago, we had a meeting of M.I.T. and Harvard people, including experts on these matters, to talk about whether anything could be done to block the Sentinel system — the deployment of ABMs. Everyone present thought them undesirable, but a few of the most knowledgeable persons took what seemed to be the practical view: "Why fight about a dead issue? It has been decided, the funds have been appropriated. Let's go on from there."

Well, fortunately, it's not a dead issue.

An ABM is a nuclear weapon. It takes a nuclear weapon to stop a nuclear weapon. And our concern must be with the whole issue of nuclear weapons.

There is an entire semantics ready to deal with the sort of thing I am about to say. It involves such phrases as "Those are the facts of life." No — these are the facts of death. I don't accept them, and I advise you not to accept them. We are under repeated pressure to accept things that are presented to us as settled — decisions that have been made. Always there is the thought: Let's go on from there. But this time we don't see how to go on. We will have to stick with these issues.

We are told that the United States and Russia, between them, by now have stockpiled nuclear weapons of approximately the explosive power of fifteen tons of TNT for every man, woman, and child on earth. And now it is suggested that we must make more. All very regrettable, of course, but "those are the facts of life." We really would like to disarm, but our new Secretary of Defense has made the ingenious proposal that now is the time to greatly increase our nuclear armaments, so that we can disarm from a position of strength.

I think all of you know there is no adequate defense against massive nuclear attack. It is both easier and cheaper to circumvent any known nuclear-defense system than to provide it. It's all pretty crazy. At the very moment we talk of deploying ABMs, we are also building the MIRV, the weapon to circumvent ABMs.

As far as I know, the most conservative estimates of the number of Americans who would be killed in a major nuclear attack, with everything working as well as can be hoped and all foreseeable precautions taken, run to about fifty million. We have become callous to gruesome statistics, and this seems at first to be only another gruesome statistic. You think, Bang! — and next morning, if you're still there, you read in the newspapers that fifty million people were killed.

But that isn't the way it happens. When we killed close to two hundred thousand people with those first, little, old-fashioned uranium bombs that we dropped on Hiroshima and Nagasaki, about the same number of persons were maimed, blinded, burned, poisoned, and otherwise doomed. A lot of them took a long time to die.

That's the way it would be. Not a bang and a certain number of corpses to bury but a nation filled with millions of helpless, maimed, tortured, and doomed persons, and the survivors huddled with their families in shelters, with guns ready to fight off their neighbors trying to get some uncontaminated food and water.

A few months ago, Senator Richard Russell, of Georgia, ended a speech in the Senate with the words "If we have to start over again with another Adam and Eve, I want them to be Americans; and I want them on this continent and not in Europe." That was a United States senator making a patriotic speech. Well, here is a Nobel laureate who thinks that those words are criminally insane.

How real is the threat of full-scale nuclear war? I have my own very inexpert idea, but, realizing how little I know, and fearful that I may be a little paranoid on this subject, I take every opportunity to ask reputed experts. I asked that question of a distinguished professor of government at Harvard about a month ago. I asked him what sort of odds he would lay on the possibility of full-scale nuclear war within the foreseeable future. "Oh," he said comfortably, "I think I can give you a pretty good answer to that question. I estimate the probability of full-scale nuclear war, provided that the situation remains about as it is now, at two per cent per year." Anybody can do the simple calculation that shows that two per cent per year means that the chance of having that full-scale nuclear war by 1990 is about one in three, and by 2000 it is about fifty-fifty.

I think I know what is bothering the students. I think that what we are up against is a generation that is by no means sure that it has a future.

I am growing old, and my future, so to speak, is already behind me. But there are those students of mine, who are in my mind always; and there are my children, the youngest of them now seven and nine, whose future is infinitely more precious to me than my own. So it isn't just their generation; it's mine, too. We're all in it together.

Are we to have a chance to live? We don't ask for prosperity, or security. Only for a reasonable chance to live, to work out our destiny in peace and decency. Not to go down in history as the apocalyptic generation.

And it isn't only nuclear war. Another overwhelming threat is in the population explosion. That has not yet even begun to come under control. There is every indication that the world population will double before the year 2000, and there is a widespread expectation of famine on an unprecedented scale in many parts of the world. The experts tend to differ only in their estimates of when those famines will begin. Some think by 1980; others think they can be staved off until 1990; very few expect that they will not occur by the year 2000.

That is the problem. Unless we can be surer than we now are that this generation has a future, nothing else matters. It's not good enough to give it tender, loving care, to supply it with breakfast foods, to buy it expensive educations. Those things don't mean anything unless this generation has a future. And we're not sure that it does.

I don't think that there are problems of youth, or student problems. All the real problems I know about are grown-up problems.

Perhaps you will think me altogether absurd, or "academic," or hopelessly innocent — that is, until you think of the alternatives — if I say, as I do to you now: We have to get rid of those nuclear weapons. There is nothing worth having that can be obtained by nuclear war — nothing material or ideological — no tradition that it can defend. It is utterly self-defeating. Those atomic bombs represent an unusable weapon. The only use for an atomic bomb is to keep somebody else from using one. It can give us no protection — only the doubtful satisfaction of retaliation. Nuclear weapons offer us nothing but a balance of terror, and a balance of terror is still terror.

We have to get rid of those atomic weapons, here and everywhere. We cannot live with them.

I think we've reached a point of great decision, not just for our nation, not only for all humanity, but for life upon the earth. I tell my students, with a feeling of pride that I hope they will share, that the carbon, nitrogen, and oxygen that make up ninety-nine per cent of our living substance were cooked in the deep interiors of earlier generations of dying stars. Gathered up from the ends of the universe, over billions of years, eventually they came to form, in part, the substance of our sun, its planets, and ourselves. Three billion years ago, life arose upon the earth. It is the only life in the solar system.

About two million years ago, man appeared. He has become the dominant species on the earth. All other living things, animal and plant, live by his sufferance. He is the custodian of life on earth, and in the solar system. It's a big responsibility.

The thought that we're in competition with Russians or with Chinese is all a mistake, and trivial. We are one species, with a world to win. There's life all over this universe, but the only life in the solar system is on earth, and in the whole universe we are the only men.

Our business is with life, not death. Our challenge is to give what account we can of what becomes of life in the solar system, this corner of the universe that is our home; and, most of all, what becomes of men — all men, of all nations, colors, and creeds. This has become one world, a world for all men. It is only such a world that can now offer us life, and the chance to go on.

On Misunderstanding Student Rebels

Martin Duberman

The young, it is becoming clear, are regarded with considerable hatred in our country. Resentment against them cannot be explained simply as a reaction to the style of a particular generation, for in recent years the young have been attacked on such divergent grounds that the grounds themselves take on the appearance of pretext. In the 1950s we denounced students for their inertia, their indifference to public questions, their absorption in the rituals of fraternities and football, their dutiful pursuit of "achievement." In the 1960s we condemn them for the opposite qualities: for their passion, their absorption in public questions, their disgust with the trivia of college parties and athletics, their refusal to settle for mechanical processes of education.

Since the past two college generations have been denounced with equal vehemence for opposite inclinations, it seems plausible to conclude that it is not those inclinations but the very fact of their youth that makes them the target for so much murderous abuse. This conclusion may seem to contradict the fact that American society, above all others, is known for its adoration of youth. But that itself, paradoxically, is one cause of adult hostility: our youth-obsessed elders resent the eighteen-year-old's easy possession of the good looks and high spirits they so desperately simulate.

Adult anger at the physical superiority of the young has usually been contained by the comforting assumption that eighteen-year-olds are at least the moral, intellectual, and emotional inferiors of their elders. College students have traditionally been viewed as apprentices, almost as supplicants. And until recently they accepted their role as dutiful petitioners for entry into the world of adult insight and skill.

As no one needs reminding, they no longer accept that role, though most of their elders continue the struggle to confine them to it. Today's eighteen-to-twenty-year-old considers himself an adult, by which he does not mean (as so many forty-year-olds unconsciously do) that he has ceased growing, but that he has grown up enough to make his own decisions. In every sense, even statistically, his case is a strong one.

The weight of recent physiological and psychological evidence establishes the student claim that today's eighteen-year-olds mature more rapidly than those of earlier generations. Physically, they are taller and heavier than their counterparts at the turn of the century. Boys reach puberty around age fourteen, and girls begin to menstruate at the average age of twelve years, nine months (in both cases almost two years earlier than in 1900).

Moreover, there is much evidence that this earlier physical maturity is matched by emotional and intellectual precocity. According to Dr. C. Keith Conners, director of the Child Development Laboratory at Massachusetts General

Hospital, both emotional and intellectual growth are today largely completed by age eighteen. By this Dr. Conners means that the difficult trials of adolescence are over, the basic patterns of personality have become stabilized, and the ability to reason abstractly — to form hypotheses and make deductions — has been established. This does not mean, of course, that no further maturity is possible after age eighteen. Additional information and experience do (or at least should) provide material for continuing reassessments. But that, of course, is (or should be) true of all of us.

In terms of knowledge already possessed, moreover, the graduating high school senior of today, thanks both to the media and to the stepped-up pace of academic work, is well informed on any number of topics — the new math, say, or the physical properties of the atom — of which his elders are ignorant. And as for experience, I am not at all sure that the eighteen-year-old who has had his senses activated by early sexual relations, strobe lights, pot, soul, and rock, and his political instincts honed by Vietnam, the draft, and the civil rights movement, should not be considered more vitally alive, more instinctually sound, than the typical forty-year-old who has spent his additional twenty years glued to the tube, the routinized job, the baseball and stock statistics.

The Academic Mandarins

It is bad enough that we have refused to extend to students the rights and responsibilities which their maturity warrants. What is perhaps worse is that many of those who hold positions of power or prestige in our universities have learned so little from the upheavals which that refusal has produced. A recent spate of books and articles by such men demonstrates anew their uneducability; they make it clear, by their continuing patronization and belittlement, that students still have an uphill fight in their struggle to be taken seriously.

One case in point, though not the most egregious, is that of George F. Kennan. When Kennan's article "Rebels Without a Program" (aptly characterized by Richard Poirier as "a new containment policy for youth") appeared in the New York *Times* Sunday Magazine for January 21, 1968, it drew such an unprecedented reply from students and teachers (including a letter from me) that the Atlantic Monthly Press decided to issue the article, the replies, and a lengthy rebuttal by Kennan as a separate volume, *Democracy and the Student Left.* In that rebuttal, Kennan does acknowledge that the public questions agitating the country are indeed "so harrowing" and "harbor such apocalyptic implications that it is silly to suggest," as he originally had, that college students should go about their studies as usual.

But having acknowledged that "harrowing" problems face the country, Kennan proceeds, by a curious indirection, to minimize them. He lectures student activists on their "inability to see and enjoy the element of absurdity in human behavior" (adding, gratuitously, that he suspects their love lives, no less than their politics, are "tense, anxious, defiant and joyless"), on their "social science" rhetoric, and on their indifference to "nature as a possible compensating or sustaining factor in the face of social or political frustration." Kennan fails, however, to make clear how the merit of the issues the students raise in any way depends on the "inadequate" manner in which they raise them. I, for one, cannot see how the Vietnam War or the plight of our ghetto-dwellers might become more attractive or tolerable if viewed with an awareness of "the element of absurdity in human behavior" or described in a rhetoric free of social science jargon or escaped from by periodic trips to the wilderness.

Kennan insists that the students' obliviousness to nature, *et al,* is symptomatic of their "lack of interest in the creation of any real style and distinction of personal life generally." By which he means, as he goes on to specify, their lack of "manners," their untidiness, their disinterest in "personal hygiene," their refusal to cultivate the "amenities." It is debatable that this description is either accurate or significant, as applied to the nonpolitical, drug-oriented "hippies," but it is certainly not a valid description of campus activists, the ostensible subjects of Kennan's critique.

The main point, of course, is not that the new generation lacks "any real style," but that Kennan is unable to perceive much of its distinctiveness. Kennan is a good eighteenth-century *philosophe,* distrustful of "enthusiasm," and preoccupied with the rationalist credo of restraint and temperance in all things. Since "passion" is suspect, it follows (albeit unconsciously) that no injustice warrants fervent disapproval. What the new generation believes and Kennan apparently does not is that "moderation" can itself become a form of paralysis, even of immorality — like the moderate protest of Pope Pius XII against the extermination of Jews.

If Kennan's condescension toward the different life-style of the young were peculiar to him, it could be more readily ignored. But in fact his attitude is the characteristic response of the older generation to the younger. Any number of other examples are possible, but I will mention only two of the more prominent: Sidney Hook and Jacques Barzun.

Hook has published two statements (that I know of) on the recent ferment at Columbia, a long article, "The Prospects of Academe," in *Encounter* for August, 1968, and a brief note in the *Psychiatry and Social Science Review.* It is difficult to choose between them in deciding the high point to date for gray-bearded arrogance. In the shorter piece Hook flatly states that the Columbia rebels "had no grievances," and that they were interested solely in "violence, obscenity and hysterical insult." In the longer article Hook characterizes the protesters as "callow and immature adolescents" whose dominant mood, like that of all adolescents, is "irrationalism." While denouncing students for their passion, this self-appointed defender of "reason" and of the university as the "citadel of reason" himself indulges in a rhetoric so inflamed ("Fanatics don't lack sincerity. . . . They drip with sincerity — and when they have power, with blood — other people's blood") that by comparison the most apocalyptic students seem models of sobriety. Hook even declares that "there are some things one should not be moderate about" — which is exactly what the student activists (and Barry Goldwater) have said. The students, of course, mean it is acceptable to be passionately against war and racism. Hook (and Goldwater) mean it is acceptable to be passionately against those who passionately protest war and racism.

The Case of Jacques Barzun

Hook's themes — that college students are adolescents, that the best proof of their childishness is that they are "emotional" and that emotion (in others) is bad — are to be found in their most explicit form in Jacques Barzun's new book, *The American University.* In a note in the book's preface Barzun, who was dean of faculties and provost at Columbia from 1958 to 1967, explains that the manuscript was in the hands of the publisher six weeks before the student outbreak on April 23, 1968. But lest we be tempted on that account to excuse some of the positions he adopts in his book, Barzun further adds that despite the outbreak he has "found no reason to change or add to the substance of what I had written months earlier." Among the views he has found no need to modify is his statement that Grayson Kirk has always shown himself "ready and eager for progressive changes." Barzun does not pause to define "progressive," but one can't help thinking he uses the word in its original sense to describe the reforms that preceded World War I. Certainly nothing in his attitude toward students would place him beyond the year 1915.

Barzun begins his discussion of the college population by adopting the Olympian view: they are, after all, young men, and that means "turbulence is to be expected, heightened nowadays by the presence of girls. . . ." In other words, a certain amount of inherent anger adheres to the condition of being young (it *is* a "condition," in Barzun's view), and anger must find its outlet. The nature of the outlet is almost a matter of indifference: if "the people of the town" do not provide a convenient target, well then, it might just as well be politics.

Still in the Olympian vein, Barzun further suggests — it is as close as he ever comes to implicating society — that "perhaps our lack of proper ceremonies for initiation into the tribe leaves the young to devise their own proof of manhood." Barzun loves dismissing the young with this kind of casual irony. Its elegant offhandedness is a useful device for keeping a proper distance between the generations. It is also useful — though of this Barzun seems unaware — for expressing the savagery which he likes to think is confined to the student population. Barzun claims the undergraduates would themselves welcome rites of initiation, for what they really want, he insists, is more, not less, discipline. When they speak of the impersonality of the university, they mean, it seems, "the looseness of its grip upon them." Kennan makes the same point in almost the same words: students are currently objecting to parietal rules, he asserts, because "the rules have relaxed too much rather than that they have been relaxed too little." According to both men, students are starved for structure, are desperate to be introduced to the rigors of logic. In Barzun's phrasing, they are looking for "order," for "intellectual habits"; they sense that this is the balance they need, for like all youngsters they are in a "fever and frenzy," "their mind is monopolized by their inner life."

To meet this "rage for order," Barzun and Kennan posit a properly antiseptic university, a place of "respite and meditation" whose "proper work," in Barzun's phrase, is "in the catacombs under the strife-torn crossroads." He fills this subterranean cemetery with properly lifeless figures; they are "somewhat hushed,"they give pause, as at Chartres, to the "spiritual grandeur of their surroundings." Yet just as one begins to feel, in the rush of Christian imagery, that Barzun has spent so many years surrounded by campus Gothic as to have lost all sense of distinction between the university and the church, he stoutly declares that *his* catacombs will not be peopled by early Christians. He dislikes that breed; it was marked by the same distasteful qualities he associates with today's young radicals: "indifference to clothes and cleanliness, a distrust and neglect of reasoning . . . a freedom in sexuality, which is really a lowering of its intensity and value . . . and — most symptomatic — a free field given to the growth of hair."

Barzun also shares with Kennan and Hook the proposition that "emotion" has no place on campus, and that since student rebels tend to be emotional, it can be safely assumed they are also unreliable. All three men equate (and thereby confuse) "emotion" with "irrationality," and all employ a vocabulary of neat opposites — "reason" versus "emotion" — that separates what our experience combines. They see education as "the cultivation and tempering of the mind" but fail to see that "enthusiasm" is one path by which that tempering proceeds. (For an understanding of the role emotion might and should play in learning, they would do well to read a remarkable new book by George B. Leonard, *Education and Ecstasy.* Though Leonard's discussion is chiefly centered on the lower grades, almost everything he says has applicability to higher education as well, especially his remark that schools as presently structured tame the "unnamed powers" of their students — their chief effect is to "limit possibilities, narrow perceptions and bring the individual's career as a learner (changer) to an end." Leonard foresees schools where the children will not emerge as mere knowledge machines but as beings who have also learned about their bodies, emotions, and senses. His is as authentically the voice of the future as Barzun's is that of the past.)

Barzun is also huffy at other "nonsense" currently being peddled about teaching, especially the idea that teacher and student should explore together, each learning from the other. This view, he asserts, has done "immense harm to both parties. The teacher has relaxed his efforts while the student has unleashed his conceit." And of what does that "conceit" consist? Barzun is quick to tell us: the conviction that they (the students) have something to contribute. "Only rarely," he declares, with a hauteur appropriate to the century from which most of his ideas spring, does a teacher "hear from a student a fact he does not know or a thought that is original and true . . . to make believe that their knowledge and his are equal is an abdication and a lie."

And so we are back, as always in Barzun's schema, to the confinement of his starting assumption: students are children and, usually, fools. His contempt for undergraduates is pervasive. They are, very simply, not to be trusted; "student reliability is at a low ebb," he warns, and especially in that of radical students, who have but one purpose: to destroy. The evidence Barzun marshals to justify his contempt is so exasperatingly trivial (as well as suspect in its accuracy) that it demeans its compiler far more than the students. The undergraduates, he asserts, cheat a lot on exams and papers; they obtain pocket money by stealing books from the college bookstore; they keep library books out as long as they like and let fines go unpaid; they deny their roommates "the slightest considerateness"; students of both sexes live "pig-style" in their dormitories; their conversations "usually cannot follow a logical pattern," and so on.

The first thing to be said about these accusations is that Barzun has seized upon the occasional practices of a few undergraduates in order to damn a whole generation. The second is that even if these qualities did characterize a whole generation, they hardly seem heinous when compared with the sins of the fathers — when compared, that is, with racism at home and imperialism abroad.

The distressing consequence of this obsession with the peccadillos of the young is an avoidance of those genuinely important problems to which the young are calling attention. Mandarins like Barzun, Kennan, and Hook are so preoccupied with manners that they forget matter. They are so certain of the rightness of their own patterns of thought and action and so eager to denounce all deviations by the young from those patterns that they blind themselves (and others) to the serious questions this new generation has raised — questions about the nature of education, the proper functions of a university, the very quality of American life.

What Activists Are Really Like

A dozen or so studies have been made of student activists at a variety of universities, and the findings have been conveniently summarized in a recent essay by Stanford's Nevitt Sanford. The group portrait that emerges (confirmed by Kenneth Keniston's new book, *Young Radicals*) is strikingly different from the slanderous one being peddled by Messrs. Barzun and Hook.

The activists, first of all, constitute only a small minority, though a growing one, of all college students; at Berkeley, for example, their number is put at about 15 percent. Second, there are important differences, in almost all measurable categories, between activists on the campus and other students. The activists score consistently higher on a wide variety of personality tests, including theoretical skills, aesthetic sensitivity, degree of pyschological autonomy, and social maturity. They are also the better students, with significantly higher grade-point averages than the nonactivists. In trying to account for the recent emergence of student activism, Sanford points to various changes since the 1930s in family life and child training. But he feels that student activism is primarily a response to social conditions both within the university and in the world at large. Since the latter are the more widely known determinants of student rebelliousness, I will confine my remarks to conditions in the university.

One set of grievances on the campus centers on what does — or does not — go on in the classroom. As David Riesman has written, "Colleges on the whole have been very backward as compared with industry or the Army in their curiosity about their own inner processes." Until recently they have accepted lectures, grading, and examinations as part of the Natural Order of Things and have seen no reason to question the long-standing assumptions that Teacher is the possessor and arbiter of Truth, that his function is to transmit knowledge (narrowly defined as accumulated information) to students, and that their function is to memorize it.

Any challenge to this conventional wisdom is still viewed with scorn by the vast majority of faculty and administrators — and of the student population as well. Barzun, for example, gives short shrift to any protest against grades and tests; "no person by way of being educated," he announces, "resents examinations; they are so instructive." Should a student activist or one of his allies among the younger faculty reply that exams and grades chiefly instruct students in how to please their professors, in how to compete with one another, in how to settle for orthodox questions and answers, and in how to suppress their own originality, Barzun's answer would be — hogwash. He sees the activists' demand for autonomy and for the freedom to pursue their own lines of inquiry as cant, as another example of their "mental confusion." By way of proof, Barzun triumphantly recounts a recent episode in a large Midwestern university: when students in a philosophy of education class of 300 complained that they had little say in their own education, the professor asked how many did in fact want to take responsibility for their work, and only ten hands went up. The moral, as Barzun draws it, is that students calling for self-regulation merely "ape the advertiser's soapy mind." But that is not the moral at all. Our educational system has been so successful in turning out automatons that the vast majority of its products are terrified at the thought of taking over responsibility for their own lives. The fact that only ten hands went up is itself a severe indictment of our educational practices. Instead of proving that "all is well," it proves that we are in desperate trouble — that maybe only 3.3 percent of our *citizens* are willing to make their own decisions.

Barzun similarly misses the point the undergraduate dissenters are making about the lecture system. That point has been well put in a recent issue of the *Yale Alumni Magazine* by Alan Weiner, a graduating senior. The present system, he wrote, encourages "debilitating dependence"; each student, taking dutiful notes at lecture, produces by the end of the semester (and for exams) a "paraphrased copy" of the lecturer's text, "one copy differing from the other less in content than in penmanship." Weiner recognizes that lectures, at their best, can be useful — a good lecture can provide a lucid introduction to some particularly difficult area of study so that the student "is spared the initial paralysis of venturing alone into *terra incognita*"; it can offer a fundamental reinterpretation not yet published or widely accepted; and it can "show a brilliant man in the process of putting ideas together." But such moments in the lecture room are rare, so rare that they do not justify the maintenance of a system which far more typically inculcates sloppiness, omniscience, plagiarism, and theatricality in the lecturer, and passivity, boredom, resentment, and cynicism in the student.

And what is the answer of men like

Barzun to the growing resentment of the lecture system? That the protesters do not understand the true nature of their dissatisfaction. The real trouble, Barzun declares, is that the university has "let lapse the *formality* of lecturing — its form — which was its principal merit." What is wanted by way of change, in other words, is not to dismantle the lecture system but to return it to its pristine shape, to reintroduce "formal presentation" and even "staginess and rhetorical effects," since these impart something Barzun labels "didactic energy." Given this gross misreading of student discontent, it might be well to remember in speaking hereafter of the "generation gap" that incomprehension is not confined to one side.

Where the System Fails

Discontent with teaching practices in our universities embraces more than the lecture system. Even where small seminars or discussion groups prevail (an expensive device few universities can afford), the needs of the students are not given anything like equal consideration with the needs of teachers. As two students in the *Yale Daily News* recently put it, the present system fails to help undergraduates appropriate facts and skills "in the interest of making lives, not just living." In assuming that the university's main, almost exclusive, function is to produce and transmit information, we have given top priority to promoting those faculty members most likely to assist in the manufacture of knowledge. This means, of course, that the university has come to be staffed chiefly by those concerned with research and writing rather than those concerned with educating the young — that is, with helping them to discover what their interests and talents are, in helping them to change. As Alfred North Whitehead said long ago, "So far as the mere imparting of information is concerned, no university has had any justification for existence since the popularisation of printing in the fifteenth century." Yet most professors do look on the imparting of information as the sum and substance of their responsibility. They make little or no effort to show, either in their subject or in their person, how knowledge can influence conduct and inform action (which, as William Arrowsmith has pointed out, is not really surprising, since they are themselves products of the same noneducation).

Most professors are interested only in students who are themselves potential scholars; they are concerned with training future colleagues, not with helping the individual young person grow in his own directions. The lack of interest taken by most professors in most students, their refusal to reveal or engage more than a small share of their own selves, have made many of the best students cynical about knowledge and about those who purvey it. They hoped to find in their professors models on whom they might pattern their lives; instead they find narrow specialists busy with careers, with government contracts, with the augmentation of status and income. They hoped to find a curriculum which would help them to uncover and pursue their interests; instead they find one primarily tailored to the needs of the faculty specialists. They hoped to discover a mode of living which would help them to integrate their intellectual curiosity with the demands of their senses and emotions; instead they find, in Erich Fromm's words, an education "more and more cerebral . . . [where] people are taught concepts, but are not taught or confronted with the experience which corresponds to these concepts." They hoped to find some acknowledgment of their worth and some encouragement toward its further development; instead they find disinterest, patronization, overt dislike. They find, in short, what Nietzsche called "the advancement of learning at the expense of man."

With considerable justice, therefore, the students, particularly the more talented and sensitive ones, reject the university and its faculty as self-serving, self-justifying, self-enclosed. They learn to seek their education — the expanding of insight and option — outside the formal academic curriculum, to seek it in talk and games with friends, in films, clothes, and cars, in Sergeant Pepper's Lonely Hearts Club Band, in the lyrics of Bob Dylan, in the Doors, in pot and acid. And if some of these sources prove as phony or as dangerous as the mechanical exercises of the campus, surely much of the responsibility lies with an academic community that has encouraged, almost forced, its students to look for life-enhancement where it can.

Is the University a Democracy?

Most of the powers within the academic community will not even acknowledge the right of students to complain, let alone the cogency of those complaints. To the request that they be allowed a voice in planning the curriculum, a Jacques Barzun replies that they have done nothing to "earn" a voice. To the lament that their studies seem outmoded or irrelevant, Barzun retorts that "relevance is a relationship in the mind and not a property of things" — which apparently means that although students might want to study urban affairs, if they will instead study cockle shells *in the right way,* they will discover all there is to know about life in the ghettos. And to the students' suggestion that they have some formal power in such matters as choosing faculty, passing on applications for admission, or helping to decide on the expansion of the physical plant, Barzun responds with hoots of derision and George Kennan with cold anger.

Both gentlemen remind the undergraduates that the university is not, and was never meant to be, a democracy. Barzun does believe that students should have the right of self-government in their own dormitories, for he acknowledges that they are "socially mature enough not to need domestic proctoring" (a curious and seemingly arbitrary departure from his usual premise that undergraduates are children). But Kennan will not go even this far in extending power to undergraduates. The university, by virtue of its position as owner of the dormitories, has no choice in Kennan's view but "to lay down certain minimal norms for the manner in which that use can proceed. This would be true," he insists, "even if the inhabitants were older people." But it is not true, for Kennan's (and my own) university, Princeton, owns a great deal of faculty housing, and in none of it are the tenants subjected to the demeaning regulations in regard to visitors, and so on, which are imposed upon the students.

With the exception of this disagreement over parietal rules, Barzun and Kennan are firmly united in their contention that the university cannot and should not be a democracy. Kennan, in this instance, is the more peremptory of the two. "Even if university trustees and administrators had a right to shift a portion of their responsibilities for university affairs to the student, which they do not," he writes, the student would in any case "be unqualified to receive it." The very suggestion, he warns, is part of the current tendency of American society "to press upon the child a premature external adulthood."

Barzun rests most of his case on the grounds of impracticality. The university cannot function as a democracy, he argues, because it is "extremely difficult to get from student bodies either a significant vote, or a council or committee that is representative. . . . Add that student newspapers have long ceased to purvey anything approaching a public opinion, and it is clear that democracy is that last name a political scientist would apply to the government by outcry which has lately gained favor as an extracurricular activity." The absurdity of this argument (and its loaded terminology) is best seen when placed in another context. Is it *easy* to get a "significant" or "representative" vote from the United States Congress? Do our commercial newspapers "purvey anything approaching a public opinion"? Shall we, on those accounts, abandon both the Congress and the public press as unworkable institutions? In trying to make a case against democracy in the university, in other words, Barzun has forced himself — I assume, inadvertently — into making a case against democracy in general. The "insurmountable obstacles" which he finds to democratic institutions on the campus are likewise in the path of democracy within the larger society. Indeed, they loom less large on campus; given the limited size of a university, the opinions of its constituency could be canvassed and tabulated far more easily than in the society as a whole — that is, if the will to do so existed.

The other argument most often heard for denying students any say in university affairs is that they are "mere transients." True, but so are many professors, and so (to change the context) are members of the House of Representatives, who are elected for only two years. Besides, the *interests* of the student population do not shift as often as the population itself; Clark Kerr, in fact, detects signs that students are beginning to look upon themselves as a "class." But even if the interests of the undergraduates did continually change (and they probably should), life does, after all, belong to the living, or, in the case of the universities, a campus to its *present* constituents.

The University as Landlord

In addition to student grievances over what happens in the classroom and on the campus, there is another major source of disaffection: the university's relationship to the world around it — its role as landlord of neighboring property, and, on the broader canvas, its role as the recipient of government largesse and provider of government expertise.

The upheavals of last spring at Columbia brought to focus the problem of the university's relationship to the society at large. One of two key issues during that upheaval was Columbia's pending construction of a gym in a public park used by Harlem residents. This issue by itself might be thought of minor importance (if, that is, one is not a resident of Harlem), but in fact it was the latest of a long series of encroachments by Columbia into the surrounding ghetto, an encroachment which usually involved evicting tenants with little concern for their wishes and welfare. (Even now Columbia continues its encroachment; as James Ridgeway reports in his new book, *The Closed Corporation: American Universities in Crisis,* Columbia is still secretly extending its real estate holdings in Harlem, and its "relocation office" is still forcing families out of buildings it wants to tear down.)

Various groups, including students, faculty, Harlem residents, and the city, had appealed to the Columbia administration to review its policies on the gym construction — all to no avail. It is simply false to say, as Sidney Hook has, that "instead of seeking peacefully to resolve them [grievances] through existing channels of consultation and deliberation, the SDS seeks to inflame them." Not only did student groups, including SDS, attempt to get a peaceful hearing, but they had to make those attempts against formidable obstacles, for as Amitai Etzioni, professor of sociology at Columbia, has written, "due process, even in the loose sense of established channels for expression and participation, is not institutionalized at Columbia or at most other universities." Even after the upheavals of last spring, the suggestion that precise channels be established for student participation continues to infuriate men like Barzun. One would think that anyone who so deplores student "immaturity" would at least recognize the standard argument of psychologists that immaturity is prolonged, even heightened, by an exclusion from responsibility. But apparently, despite his rhetoric in defense of "orderly process," Barzun prefers occasional barricades to regularized communication.

He even goes so far as to deny the reality of issues like the gym construction. Universities must expand, he argues, and expansion inevitably brings conflict with the university's immediate neighbors. But shall the needs of several hundred citizens, he rhetorically asks, "prevail over the needs of . . . a national university?" Besides, the area around a university is usually a "deteriorating" one (as regards Columbia, Barzun has elsewhere referred to its surrounding neighborhood as "uninviting, abnormal, sinister, dangerous"), so it is a matter of simple "self-protection" for the university to take "steps." The "steps," as Barzun defines them, include "bringing in the police against crime and vice, hiring special patrols, and buying real estate as fast as funds and the market permit." This might look, Barzun concedes, like "waging war on the inhabitants," but what they forget is that with the university's expansion goes "increased employment and trade." The residents of Harlem apparently do not see it that way, and they and their student allies have decided that all else failing, it becomes necessary to invoke the doctrine of "self-protection" for themselves as well. (In his long book, Barzun has almost no discussion of Columbia's relations with Harlem; when I came to a chapter entitled "Poverty in the Midst of Plenty," I thought I had finally come to a detailed review of those relations, but the chapter turned out instead to be about the financial problems of the university.)

Why Innovation Is Crucial

The second major issue in the Columbia dispute last spring concerned the university's affiliation with the Institute for Defense Analyses (IDA), an affiliation which in turn symbolized the university's dependence on government grants and involvement with government research. Barzun and others like to defend the university as a "center of research," and they contrast that "proper" function with the "misguided" one of the university becoming a center of "experience." But it is one thing to defend the university theoretically as a research center, and quite another to ask specifically "research in what and for what?"

The multiple and tangled relationships that have developed between our leading universities and the large corporations and the federal government raise doubts about the proper boundaries of "research." This is especially true of what James Ridgeway calls the university's "war machinery" — its complicity in everything from antisubmarine-warfare research at Columbia to counterinsurgency planning at the University of Michigan. Today more than two thirds of university research funds come from agencies of the federal government closely connected with defense matters, and about one quarter of the 200 largest industrial corporations in the country have university officials on their board of directors. It is certainly an open question these days whether the university is engaged in research in order to pursue "truth" or to acquire status, power, and profit. Columbia's own farcical involvement with the Strickman cigarette filter is but one of many examples of the university's placing greed ahead of integrity.

There are, I should stress, no simple formulas for establishing the "right" relationship universities should form with public corporations and governments. It is *because* there are no easy answers that the matter should be subjected to open debate, with all interested parties bringing to bear their insights and perspectives. And by "all," I include students. They are rightly disturbed over the university's entanglement with war and private profit, and they ask that their concern be registered and their views considered. They are entitled to nothing less, for until students began to protest such matters as IDA affiliation, the universities were doing business as usual, blind to the implications of their own actions. The same is true of the university's record regarding innovation in education and the procedures of campus government — I mean real innovation, not the substitution of blue tape for red. Before student activists began forcing a variety of campus and classroom issues into the open, the university's concern was minimal.

What we are witnessing, then, is not a sporadic and superficial, but a sustained and far-reaching, attack on the university's smug and antique bearing. The student activists are not rebelling against their parents' values, but applying those values to the institutions with which they find themselves involved. They are not confused children, uncertain of their motives or aims, but determined adults who have found their education and their society seriously wanting.

I doubt if we have ever had a generation — or at least a minority of one — that has engaged itself so earnestly on the side of principled action, that valued people so dearly and possessions so little, that cared enough about our country to jeopardize their own careers within it, that wanted so desperately to lead open, honest lives and to have institutions and a society which would make such lives possible. It is a generation for which we should be immensely grateful and of which we should be immensely proud. Instead, we tell them that they are frenzied children; that we will try to be patient with them but that they should not push us too far; that they too in time will grow to understand the *real* ways of the world. To say that this condescension or blindness on the part of the older generation is a "pity" does not fit the dimensions of the case. It is a crime.

The Politics of Violence

Arthur M. Schlesinger, Jr.

The world today is asking a terrible question — a question which every citizen of this Republic should be putting to himself: what sort of people are we, we Americans?

And the answer which much of the world is bound to return is that we are today the most frighening people on this planet.

We are a frightening people because for three years we have been devastating a small country on the other side of the world in a war which bears no rational relationship to our national security or our national interest.

We are a frightening people because we have already in this decade murdered the two of our citizens who stood preeminently before the world as the embodiments of American idealism — and because last night we tried to murder a third.

We are a frightening people because the atrocities we commit hardly touch our official self-righteousness, our invincible conviction of our moral infallibility.

The ghastly things we do to our own people, the ghastly things we do to other people — these must at last compel us to look searchingly at ourselves and our society before hatred and violence rush us on to more evil and finally tear our nation apart.

We cannot take the easy course and blame everyone but ourselves for the things we do. We cannot blame the epidemic of murder at home on deranged and solitary individuals separate from the

From *Harper's Magazine,* August, 1968. Reprinted by permission of Arthur M. Schlesinger, Jr.

rest of us. For these individuals are plainly weak and suggestible men, stamped by our society with a birthright of hatred and a compulsion toward violence.

We cannot blame our epidemic of murder abroad on the wickedness of those who will not conform to our views of how they should behave and how they should live. For the zeal with which we have pursued an irrational war suggests the internal impulses of hatred and violence demanding outlet and shaping our foreign policy to their ends.

We must recognize that the evil is in us, that it springs from some dark, intolerable tension in our history and our institutions. It is almost as if a primal curse had been fixed on our nation, perhaps when we first began the practice of killing and enslaving those whom we deemed our inferiors because their skin was another color. We are a violent people with a violent history, and the instinct for violence has seeped into the bloodstream of our national life.

We are also, at our best, a generous and idealistic people. Our great leaders — Lincoln most of all — have perceived both the destructive instinct and the moral necessity of transcending destruction if we are going to have any sort of rational and decent society. They have realized how fragile the membranes of our civilization are, stretched so thin over a nation so disparate in its composition, so tense in its interior relationships, so cunningly enmeshed in underground fears and antagonisms, so entrapped by history in the ethos of violence.

Now, as our nation grows more centralized, our energy more concentrated, our inner tensions more desperate, our frustrations in our own land and in the world more embittered, we can no longer regard hatred and violence as accidents and aberrations, as nightmares which will pass away when we awake. We must see them as organic in our national past; we must confront them; we must uncover the roots of hatred and violence and, through self-knowledge, move toward self-control. And we must exert every effort in the meantime to protect and strengthen the membranes of civility against the impulses of destruction.

In this effort, a special responsibility lies on our intellectual community. For one can expect primitive emotions on the part of those who occupy the right wing of our national politics. But the intellectual community should be the particular custodian of the life of reason. It should be the particular champion of discipline and restraint. It should be the particular enemy of hatred and violence.

Little is more dismaying than the way in which some, a few, in the intellectual community have rejected the life of reason, have succumbed to the national susceptibility for hatred and violence, have, indeed, begun themselves to exalt hatred and violence as if primitivism in emotion constituted a higher morality. I do not suggest that such intellectuals are responsible for the atrocities committed at home and abroad. I do suggest that they have contributed to the atmosphere which has begun to legitimize hatred and violence. I do suggest that they are reinforcing the assault on civility and hastening the decomposition of the American social process.

Some wonder, no doubt, whether that social process is worth saving. But the alternative to process is anarchy, where those who use the means of violence win out; and the intellectual community will always lose in this competition. Our process, with all its defects, is a process of change — peaceful change — on which all decency and rationality depend.

Let me make it clear that I am not talking about the student uprisings of recent weeks. I have no question that on balance the world stands to gain from student protest. No doubt such protest has on occasion led to excess. But it is already a shameful state of affairs when excess proves the only way of attracting the attention of complacent university administrations and indifferent faculties to the problems and perplexities of the coming generation.

The causes of student insurgency vary from college to college, and from country to country. It would seem likely that the primary incitement in our own nation has been the war in Vietnam — a war which has tempted our government into its course of appalling and insensate destruction, a war which, through the draft, has demanded that young Americans kill and die where they can see no rational relationship between personal sacrifice and national interest. But the cause is also more than the Vietnam war. For that war has come for many to prefigure a larger incomprehensibility, a larger absurdity, even a larger wickedness, in our official society. For some it has come to seem, not an aberration, but the inevitable result of the irremediable corruption of the American system.

I cannot share the belief that there was something foreordained and ineluctable about the war in Vietnam — that the nature of American society would have compelled any set of men in Washington to pursue the same course of folly. This really seems determinist nonsense. One can still understand, though, why the contradictions of our society weigh so heavily on the young — the contradictions between the righteousness of a Secretary of State and the ruthlessness of a B-52; between the notion that violence is fine against simple folk 10,000 miles away and shocking against injustice in our own land; between the equality demanded by our constitutional structure and the equality denied by our social structure; even between the accepted habits of one generation and the emerging habits of the next, as when a parent tipsy on his fourth martini begins a tirade against marijuana.

The very weight of these contradictions has produced a rush of despair about libertarian democracy itself. By libertarian democracy I mean simply the system in which the rule of the majority at any given time rests on the guarantee of the right of minorities to convert themselves into new majorities. Such a system assumes political action to be in its essence a rational process — that is, a deliberate choice of means to achieve desired ends. As a rational process, libertarian democracy requires the widest possible freedom of discussion and debate; and this implies, of course, a considerable indulgence of wrongheadedness and imbecility along the way.

This has been the American theory, as

laid down, for example, in the Constitution and the Bill of Rights. And, in the course of our national history, libertarian democracy has led to many useful results. It has also led to many frustrations. It has left problems unsolved, wrongs unredressed, and sinners unpunished. It cannot be relied upon to produce rapid and conclusive change. The very insistence on reasonableness and due process has seemed at times a pretext for inaction and therefore a mask for injustice. This has been particularly the case in recent years. From the moment we started bombing North Vietnam in February 1965, our government appeared rigidly and sanctimoniously unresponsive to reasoned criticism of its course. Increasingly persuaded that change was impossible within the constitutional order, people started to turn to civil disobedience, emotional agitation, and even violent protest. A sense began to arise that libertarian democracy itself was impotent in the new world of economic, military, and intellectual corporatism. One saw a growing conviction, especially among the young, that party politics were a façade and a fake. One saw a growing cynicism about democratic institutions, a growing defection from the democratic process. In due course, the spreading sense of the impotence of libertarian democracy generated a creed systematically and candidly opposed to libertarian democracy.

The new creed has two parts. The first part is an attempt to clear away what its theorists regard as the noxious rubbish of the Bill of Rights. The new creed thus perceives the First Amendment as the keystone, not of liberty, but of a wicked apparatus of tolerance employed by an oppressive social order to thwart basic change. I do not wish to do this new doctrine an injustice, so I will state in the words of its leading advocate — that is, Herbert Marcuse — its belief that it is *necessary* and *right,* as a matter of principle, to suppress views with which one disagrees and to howl down those who utter such views.

Mr. Marcuse begins with the proposition that contemporary society has absorbed and abolished the historic means of social revolution. It has done this through an ingenious and despicable combination of welfarism, tolerance, and manipulation. Capitalism, in short, subverts potential opponents by offering a measure of apparent economic security and personal freedom.

Mr. Marcuse is determined to expose this state of affairs. As he sees it, any improvement in the condition of the powerless and the oppressed only plays into the hands of the rulers — and is therefore to be regretted. And the device of tolerance is particularly evil because it renders "the traditional ways and means of protest ineffective — perhaps even dangerous because they preserve the illusion of popular sovereignty."

The way to revive the hope of social change, Mr. Marcuse suggests, is therefore to do away with tolerance: "Certain things cannot be said, certain ideas cannot be expressed, certain policies cannot be proposed, certain behavior cannot be permitted without making tolerance an instrument for the continuation of servitude." He is commendably specific about what he would forbid. His program, as he states it,

> would include the withdrawal of toleration of speech and assembly from groups and movements which promote aggressive policies, armament,

chauvinism, discrimination on the grounds of race and religions, or which oppose the extension of public services, medical care, etc. Moreover, the restoration of freedom of thought may necessitate new and rigid restrictions on teachings and practices in the educational institutions.

Mr. Marcuse's call for the forcible suppression of false ideas is, I have suggested, only the first part of the new creed. Nor is such an assault on the Bill of Rights new, even for radicals. The Stalinists of the 'thirties, for example, had no compunction in arguing in much the same way that civil freedom should be denied those who resist the Stalinist truth. What particularly distinguishes the New Left of the 'sixties from previous American radicalisms is the second part of its creed — and here not the summons to revolution, which again is familiar, but the refusal to state revolutionary goals except in the most abstract and empty language. To put it more precisely, what distinguishes the New Left is not only its unwillingness to define what it aims for after the revolution but its belief that such reticence is a virtue.

On its positive side, the new creed becomes, so to speak, a kind of existentialism in politics — a primitive kind, no doubt, but still rooted in some manner in the existential perception that man dwells in an absurd universe and defines himself through his choices. In extreme cases, this perception may lead to *voyages au bout de la nuit:* as Nietzsche said, "Nihilism represents the ultimate logical conclusion of our great values and ideals — because we must experience nihilism before we can find out what value these 'values' really had." In its serious form, existentialism can lead to an immense and intense sense of individual responsibility as every man realizes that only he can provide his own escape from the enveloping nothingness around him. In its vulgar form, however, with which we are dealing here, existential politics becomes the notion that we must feel and act before we think; it is the illusion that the experience of feeling and action will produce the insight and the policy.

Existential politics in this form springs much more from Sorel than from Kierkegaard. Georges Sorel, you will recall, drew a distinction between myths, which, he said, were "not descriptions of things, but expressions of a determination to act," and utopias, which were intellectual products, the work of theorists who "seek to establish a model to which they can compare existing society." Sorel regarded utopias — that is, rational programs — as contemptible. The myth must be the basis of action; the myth would produce the revolution, which would thereafter produce its own program; and "the myth," Sorel emphasized "must be judged as a means of acting on the present; any attempt to discuss how far it can be taken literally as future history is devoid of sense." So, in the footsteps of Sorel, the New Leftists believe in the omnipotence of the deed and the irrelevance of the goal. The political process is no longer seen as the deliberate choice of means to move toward a desired end. Where libertarian democracy had ideally demanded means consistent with the end, and where the Stalinist left of the 'thirties contended that the end justified the means, the New Left propounds a different doctrine: that the means create the end.

Let us not ignore the attractions of the existential approach. After all, there are many absurdities in our world. Our country has never undertaken anything more absurd in its history than the Vietnam war. After all, a man does make himself by his decisions. After all, our conventional liberalism is to a discouraging degree a liberalism of promises and excuses. After all, social renewal can only come from personal commitment.

All these things help explain, I think, the appeal of the new creed. Yet this creed contains so much in the way of fakery and fallacy — to put it bluntly, it is so preposterous and so depraved — that I do not see how it can be long entertained by any serious democrat.

Let us look first at the negative part; the demand for the forcible suppression of false ideas. This immediately raises a self-evident question: how is one to tell which ideas are admissible and which are to be suppressed? "In the interplay of theory and practice," Mr. Marcuse replies, "true and false solutions become distinguishable. . . . Freedom is liberation, a specific historical process in theory and practice, and as such it has its right and wrong, its truth and falsehood." But who is to make this determination? What agency is the repository of final judgment on truth and falsehood? Here, alas, Mr. Marcuse lets us down. His standards are hopelessly vague, and in the end he places his confidence in what he mystically calls "the democratic educational dictatorship of free men."

This is not very satisfactory; so let us pursue the question a step further. I suppose that the new creed does not expect to make such judgments through a man. But, if not through a man, these judgments must be made through a mechanism, which means through men. Such a mechanism would plainly have to have an extraordinary degree of power. What assurance can there ever be that this power would be used disinterestedly — that is, for the good and the true, should there ever be a means of defining the good and the true — rather than in the interests of the men operating the mechanism? What will this mechanism become — what have such mechanisms ever become — but a means for the suppression of all criticism of the manipulators of the mechanism? So the mechanism, in the end, rests on an assumption of human infallibility.

But the assumption of human infallibility has never been justified in the long and varied history of mankind. It implies the rule of those whom Mr. Dooley long ago defined as men who do what they think "th' Lord wud do if He only knew the facts in th' case" — and Mr. Dooley was defining a fanatic.

Not only do men who claim infallibility in politics do far more evil than good; but the systematic suppression of supposedly false ideas would deeply constrict and impoverish human knowledge and understanding. "There is no error so crooked," Tupper said, "but it hath in it some lines of truth." Or, as Norman Mailer recently put it, "Sometimes a profound idea is buried in a particularly ugly notion." Human creativity takes a marvelous and sinister diversity of forms. How dare anyone assume the right to censor and deny the unlimited freedom of human expression? "I tolerate with the utmost latitude the right of others to differ from me in opinion without imputing to them criminality," wrote Jefferson. "I know too well the weakness and uncertainty of human reason to wonder at its different result."

The demand for the forcible suppression of "false" ideas would be an enormously effective way of calling a halt to human progress. Nor does the other half of the new creed make any more sense: that is, the conviction that one should feel and act first and think later, that the means create the end. The kind of action supremely required to strike through the mask of official society, we are told, is violence. Without violence, official society, in its present sophisticated condition, will calmly co-opt and emasculate the opposition. Only violence will force official society to drop the smiling mask of tolerance and reveal its inner viciousness. More than this, violence becomes a means of social and individual redemption. As Frantz Fanon has written, "Violence is a cleaning force. It frees the native from his inferiority complex and from his despair and inaction; it makes him fearless and restores his self-respect. . . . Violence alone, violence committed by the people, violence organized and educated by its leaders, makes it possible for the masses to understand social truths."

This is hardly, of course, a new doctrine. Others in this century have propagated the cult of the deed. Mussolini and Hitler celebrated violence, because violence, by abolishing the procedures and civilities of society, opens the way for those who are most successful in the use of force. I do not know about the situation in developing countries; there violence in certain contexts may have the benign effects claimed by Fanon. But surely little is more pathetic than the view that violence in American society will benefit the left. A limited amount of violence may stimulate the process of democratic change; but, if the left, through the cult of the deed, helps create an atmosphere which destroys the process of democracy itself, the winners will be those who use violence best, and they will be on the right.

The new creed, with its dismissal of free discussion and its conviction that violence will mystically generate policy and program, represents an assault on rationality in politics — an assault based on the ultimate proposition that rights and wrongs in public affairs are so absolute and so easily ascertainable that opposition can be legitimately destroyed. This assault on the Bill of Rights and on libertarian democracy is in my judgment wrong, because no one is infallible. It is stupid, because the beneficiaries of this view will not be the idealists of the left but the brutalists of the right. It is dangerous because it represents a reversion to and rationalization of the strain of hatred and violence in our own national tradition: the politics of lynch law against the politics of Lincoln. It is a vote for the worst against the best in our political ethos.

The new creed above all overlooks the fact of human frailty. "Men are not flattered," wrote Lincoln, "by being shown that there has been a difference of purpose between the Almighty and them." Yet men are not gods. That is why absolutism always fails in human society. Democracy requires consent — it insists, that is, that a majority of the electorate be persuaded that one course is preferable to another. If men or mechanisms were infallible, there would be no need for persuasion. But, because they are not, the discipline of consent is indispensable to civilized society. The discipline of consent means the policies must triumph not through divine right or through a "democratic educational dictatorship" but through making sense to a majority of the people; and the condition of bringing a majority along is the best guarantee that policies relate, not to personal fantasy or personal power, but to the greatest good of the greatest number.

This discussion of the new creed may seem irrelevant to the pragmatic insurgencies of our society. And, indeed, so long as these insurgencies remain pragmatic — that is, related to specific issues and specific injustices — they represent a desperately needed pressure against the established complacencies of a self-righteous nation. Yet the new creed exists; it has received serious, if not convincing, formulation; it has won support because of the spreading sense in recent years of the impotence of libertarian democracy; and it has created among some of the young a mystical passion for revolutionary upheaval.

I have said that the new creed will only weaken democracy against its enemies. I would say further that it underestimates the power of rational democracy — that is, the power of the people, in one way or another, to modify the system and alter its course. We have had, I noted earlier, a season of despair about our democracy. But those whom despair led on to desperation underestimated the capacity of public opinion eventually to catch on to what is happening, even in fairly controlled and manipulated societies, and to demand a change in things. This has happened even in authoritarian states, like France. It has happened even in communist states, like Czechoslovakia. And it has happened in our own country.

Here the democratic process has turned out to be more effective than its critics had supposed. The rebellion against libertarian democracy gathered momentum, we have noted, because of the obstinate and righteous determination of our government to pursue a policy of military escalation in Vietnam. Yet in the last six months the democratic process, working in its own inscrutable way, has forced the President to abandon — for a moment, at least — the escalation policy; it has forced him to begin serious peace talks; it has forced him to withdraw from the Presidential contest. These are not inconsiderable accomplishments.

I do not contend that the process works swiftly. Obviously if President Johnson had given his March 31 speech a year earlier, many Americans and Vietnamese, now dead, might be alive; and the evidence against the escalation policy was just as strong on March 31, 1967, as it was on March 31, 1968. Nor do I contend that the process works surely. There is no guarantee against the reescalation of the war. Nor is there any guarantee, given the irresponsibility of the romantic left, against the election of a President committed to continue the persons and policies against which the rebellion began. Nor, alas, is there any guarantee against the resurgence of violence, bloodshed, and murder. Yet, with all its tardiness and inconclusiveness, democracy in America continues to show a certain vitality and efficacy. "The sober, second thought of the people," as Martin Van Buren said years ago, "is never wrong, and always efficient." At any rate, it is wiser in the long run than the certitudes of the absolutists.

Nietzsche once wrote, "Gaze not too deeply into the abyss, lest the abyss gaze into you." Those who claim to be bearers of absolute truth are men who have gazed too deeply into the abyss. They have committed what Hawthorne called the Unpardonable Sin — the sin of self-pride, which destroys discrimination, enslaves people, breeds fanaticism and violence, and concludes in madness and catastrophe. It is sad when the derelicts of our society surrender to the Unpardonable Sin; it is contemptible when our intellectuals exemplify it. Let us strike out against the concrete and particular evils of our time. But let us not yield to that awful despair which dissolves all distinctions in thought and action and hurtles us on to the politics of apocalypse. In the long run, any sane society must rest on freedom and reason. If we abandon this, we abandon everything.

If we are to survive as a nation, we must resist our inbred impulse to violence, not capitulate to it, not celebrate it. We must resist our inbred impulse to intolerance. We must resist our inbred impulse to absolutism. As we identify these impulses, as we strive against them wherever they appear — whether in the gutter press or in the abstractions of intellectuals — we create a chance of defying the winds of unreason. But we cannot suppose that this problem will solve itself. We must, indeed, define ourselves by our choices, but do so by making the choices which respect human reason and human dignity; the choices which acknowledge and nourish the human capacity for mutual respect and affection.

When Martin Luther King was murdered, Robert Kennedy broke the news of his death to a black audience on a street corner in Indianapolis. He said:

> . . . we can make an effort, as Martin Luther King did, to understand and to comprehend, and to replace that violence, that stain of bloodshed that has spread across our land, with an effort to understand with compassion and love. . . . I had a member of my family killed, but he was killed by a white man. But we have to make an effort in the United States, we have to make an effort to understand. . . . What we need . . . is not division; what we need . . . is not hatred; what we need . . . is not violence or lawlessness, but love and wisdom, and compassion toward one another, and a feeling of justice toward those who still suffer within our country, whether they be white or they be black.

Robert Kennedy concluded with a quotation from Aeschylus: "In our sleep, pain which cannot forget falls drop by drop upon the heart until, in our own despair, against our will, comes wisdom through the awful grace of God."

Anti-Americanism in America

Midge Decter

I have a gloomy premonition . . . that we will soon look back on this troubled moment as a golden time of freedom and license to act and speculate. One feels the steely sinews of the tiger, an ascetic, "moral," and authoritarian reign of piety and iron. Robert Lowell in a Partisan Review *symposium*

It is no insignificant trait of contemporary history that in its rhythm of assigning epochs the decade seems to have replaced the century. Who among Americans, and particularly among American intellectuals, cannot pithily characterize the 'twenties, the 'thirties, the 'fifties? Each of them is now from our vantage point seen to have had its own unmistakable social flavor: its own politics, its own sense of life, its own dictates of public and private comportment, its own literature. (Only the 'forties have been scanted in these characterizations, given over as they were to the war and its immediate aftermath and thus to the strains of what was past and what was coming.)

History, to be sure, cannot be so tidy as to mete itself out in ten-year measures. The decade to which we have affixed his name, for instance, did not find Dwight D. Eisenhower in the White House until two years after its inception. Similarly with the 'thirties, which in some important sense can be said to have been over in 1937 or '38. Still, there is more than mere convenience in describing certain patterns of American life and thought in these terms. They do, after all, reflect the rhythm, if not the exact chronology, of our spiritual development. In any case, everyone knows what one means by them: The 'twenties were the time — the 18th Amendment to the Constitution notwithstanding — of the explosive, exuberant, and sure-minded throwing off of American provincialism and small-town puritanism. The 'thirties were the time of a new, grown-up membership in the society of the Old World — a participation in the crises of what looked then to be its detumescence, a tuning-in to its intellectual currents, and finally a bloody and costly sharing in its salvation. And the 'fifties were the years when America self-consciously assumed the role of the world's major conservative power, with everything that such a position implies — including an internal atmosphere ridden with, on the one hand, high and righteous self-definition and, on the other, with a spirit of the most dulling prudence and caution.

An American adult of today, then, has in his ordinary lifetime virtually spanned ages. His mind and imagination have been confronted with the demand that they make room for, accommodate themselves to, five traditional lifetimes' worth of issues, movements, countermovements, revolutions, consolidations, and counterreactions. His life-style — the expression of his sense of social relations, his values, his aspirations — has been assaulted not only by a technology that continually renders itself and the issues it creates obsolete but by shifts in basic fashion that are, to say the least, unnerving in their rapidity. He sees himself separated by experience and attitude not only, as his modernity has prepared him to be, from his children, but even from those five years younger than he. He struggles to incorporate a new system of thought which, somewhere, a new vanguard has already set itself up to discredit.

An exemplary serious and educated American has without yet becoming an old man had something like the following spiritual odyssey. He has, with the writers of the 'twenties, thrown off the repressions and hypocrisies of the traditional bourgeoisie. He has accepted the liberations and burdens of Freudianism. He has, with or without any of the party affiliations that might follow therefrom, taken over the Marxian critique of capitalism and the class society, and, again regardless of party affiliation, on the other side been profoundly influenced by conservative warnings about the depredations against culture of the newly empowered masses. He has discovered the possibilities for totalitarianism — implicit in Marxism, explicit in Leninism — in the attempt at a radical reordering of society. Following on this, he has come to acknowledge the evolution of American capitalism into a variant system no longer comprehended in the categories of its traditional critics and, moreover, to grant its superiority to other economic systems as a means at least for the release of wealth. He has, largely through the agency of the Nazi episode in Europe, discovered in the heart of man an evil no mere social programming can hope to bring totally under control, much less eradicate. And he has discovered in turn that the preoccupation with such evil can be dangerously allied to complacency about those ills and inequities in the life of society that can in fact be remedied. Most recently . . . but of now later.

Taken all together, these ideas may sound like the very recipe for human "wisdom" — each view set off by another which softens, modifies, modulates it, and the whole, a balanced and "stable" amalgam. They have not, however, *been* taken all together, but rather come into intellectual power in a series over four decades, each of them for a time supplying the central impulse to a new movement of thought. Nor in the end would the wisdom resulting from the judicious combination of ideas and the critiques of ideas probably be worth very much. If the description of his odyssey makes the exemplary intellectual[1] sound, with desperate injustice, a little foolish, it must be remembered that such views as he has incorporated are not purchasable by choice but are the hard-won coin of experience and the effort to make sense out of that experience.

Ideas are powerful things, requiring not a studied contemplation but an action, even if it is only an inner action. Their acquisition obligates a man in some way to change his life, even if it is only his inner life. They demand to be stood for. They dictate where a man must concentrate his vision. They determine his moral and intellectual priorities. They provide him with allies and make him enemies. In short, ideas impose an interest in their ultimate fate which goes far beyond the realm of the merely reasonable.

This is what accounts for the rabbit-like rate at which new cultural "generations" are produced in America. For a "generation" under these conditions represents not a new batch of the young who have come of age but a new preoccupation which has found its style and its rhetoric. (It is also what accounts for the fact that many Europeans, and particularly for some reason Englishmen, find American intellectual life to be so full of brute vitality by comparison with their own: the arguments they witness among us are often battles in which men are fighting for their lives.)

[1] Terms such as these are as necessary as they are questionable, and require their user to stop and state his case: by "intellectual" I mean quite simply a man whose life is committed to the direction of his

In any case, to have taken part in what Lionel Trilling once called "the life of the mind" has been a peculiarly double experience: energizing and enervating, offering promise and promising despair. Each succeeding decade has come to an end with its own record of disillusion and bewilderment. Each new decade has begun with its own hinted promise of a revised and corrected, perhaps this time eternal, vision.

Of course, simple stylishness has also played its part in these dizzying shifts of attitude and preoccupation: vogues in thought serve momentarily to brighten the life much as vogues in dress. The point was once brilliantly illuminated by the historian R. A. Nisbet when he observed that one of the most underrated social forces in history is plain boredom. And how could even the most dedicated intellectual community resist the hunger for the new that stalks American society in general and the insatiable media of mass communication in particular? But whatever the motive behind one's submission to them, ideas about the world, as we have noted, are consequential. Even slogans, whose original purpose — take two leading slogans of the 'sixties, "Black Power" and "The War on Poverty" — is only to call people out of some impasse (or solace them while they remain there), can often turn the course of events.

II

And what of the 'sixties — which will soon be drawing to a close? What was their promise, and what will prove to have been their disillusion? Naturally, in one way it is too soon to talk of the 'sixties; something of their drama remains yet to be played out. Nevertheless, certain things are already clear. The first of these is that the 'sixties will — like the 'thirties, though in a rather different sense from them — be seen as a turbulent, a "radical," decade. And the second is that it will be known as the decade of the Vietnam war — despite the fact that consciousness of the war did not become keen or central until the decade was nearly halfway over and despite the possibility, remote as it seems at the moment, that it may end in peace.

Both of these characterizations would have seemed astonishing in 1960; for the decade, to begin at the beginning, opened not with the threat of ugly tension and war but on the contrary, with the promise of a new series of triumphs for American liberal democracy. This promise was one which had lain dormant through the years of war and Cold War, years in which the system was seen to be hanging on by its fingernails and was accounted well merely to have remained intact. A new sense of possibility was, now, not so much to be released as to explode — with all the energy of one of those historic revelations about what might be attainable if people only willed it to be.

The revelation was communicated in the main from two very different sources and in two very different ways. First, intelligibly, from the political reordering implied in the strategy of massive nonviolent protest which had recently been adopted by the civil-rights movement. And second, mystically, through the personality of John F. Kennedy. The meaning of the grand surge of protest that began with the Montgomery bus boycott — and that was obviously, despite whatever horrors along the way, going to make its effect — lay in the assurance that there was after all a

thought. In his *The Steps of the Pentagon* Norman Mailer describes such a man as one deeply limited by the inexorable "logic-of-the-next-step." So be it.

simple, noble, and *aesthetically pleasing* way to bring to an end the age-old scandal of American society. (Criminally callow as this response seems today, what it most reflected was a longing to throw off that sense of social complexity which had since the onset of the Cold War hung like a dead weight over all our imaginings of the future.)

The effect of Kennedy himself is considerably more difficult to define. It had to do with his youth, his beauty, his — odious word — style, his being unlike our — even more odious word — image of a politician. Norman Mailer, for instance, in a long essay describing the Democratic convention that nominated Kennedy, spoke of the quality of cold liberation that came off the man and predicted what did in some way happen, that Kennedy's candidacy and election would help to release a host of energies and impulses long storing up in the psychic underground. Just how this release came about must be a question for future historians of American culture to decide. The point is that Kennedy's presence in the White House did in fact have such an effect — almost without regard to his policies or record. (Just as his assassination three years later set off a widespread feeling of personal desolation that went much deeper than simply shock at the murder of the President.)

Meanwhile, that process in U.S.-Soviet relations which had been converting Containment to Coexistence and Coexistence into something called "the thaw" — however chancy or reversible it might prove to be — had begun to still some of the anxiety that seemed earlier to condition all of life. And perhaps even more important than the abatement of anxiety it afforded, the coming to an end of the Cold War left space in the political thought that it had been so totally occupying for other and fresher problems. Americans suddenly "discovered" that some forty million of their number were still living in great poverty. It was rumored that in a number of universities students were no longer apathetically figuring the angles — as they had done in the decade preceding — but were returning to the passionate study of modern history, social justice, and Marx. The demand for nuclear disarmament was receiving a growing, and growingly respectful, hearing, at least in the major cities and possibly even in Washington. Popular entertainment, on stage, in films, and on the printed page, was being touched by a healing and invigorating new impiety. Books were being written, and widely read, which helped to explain why the 'fifties, after all on the whole a comparatively peaceful and comfortable time, had left so many people feeling so bad, their lives so confined and narrow, their young so cynical or delinquent.

The triumphs for liberal democracy that seemed forthcoming in the early 'sixties were not, to be sure, millennial ones — and perhaps not even material ones. They consisted largely in things of the spirit: public tones and postures, the terms and modes of public debate, the nature of the issues debated, the simple willingness to acknowledge the existence of serious national problems, the eagerness to pursue new thoughts and the hospitality bestowed upon those who thought them, a banishing of priggishness from high places, a new tolerance and even sympathy for the liberties needfully taken by the arts and by artists — in short, those things of the spirit which enlightened Americans, no matter how hard-nosed the times teach them to be, never really lose their abiding faith in. Combined with the proper legislation — not then, as it was usually not, given much searching attention — and the necessary adjustment of our posture toward the rest of the world — to some extent being undertaken by the Kennedy Administration — the new spirit would be moving us a step or two anyway in the direction where the millennium might one day be discovered. Or if not the millennium, then at least the possibility for a reasonably stable world, a reasonably just society in the United States, and a reasonably attractive quality of life.

A great sigh of relief went up among the intellectuals (though that it did so would no doubt now be hotly denied by the majority of them) at the fact that they were, and once more in good conscience could be, liberals. The term "liberal" was not one that many people were to use. In the 'fifties it had come to be something of a dirty word: one generally used it with reference to oneself only in irony and reserved it in its uninverted sense for others who displayed either an unwonted simplemindedness or an unthinking loyalty to old cant. Insofar as it had been known truly to apply to one, liberalism represented a compromise with one's anxious quiescence parading under the banner of the Tragic: it meant a highly articulate, sophisticated, and well-documented accommodation to things as they were. Thus the word was to have little currency in the new prevailing atmosphere; people much preferred "radical." Nevertheless, the early 'sixties were in fact a moment when intellectuals could and did dream of influencing the taste for change being expressed by their government and by the society around them. This moment had arrived, moreover — it is a crucial point — within a system still operating by the most ordinary give-and-take of American politics. It had arrived without apocalypse, without even the help of most intellectuals in bringing it, and without appearing to threaten those comforts the society had already provided. The Negro, it then seemed, might at last be integrated without any fundamental overhauling of that system; the poor might at last be led out of poverty, the peace of the world at least minimally guaranteed, the educational system revamped, etc., etc. — all through the workings of a new spirit of willingness and the application of new and as yet untried ideas ("new ideas" was a favorite commodity of the Kennedy Administration and it sought experts to provide them in every field). Even the notion that an advanced technological society like ours might simply do away with money as the medium for the distribution of life's necessities was advanced by a social thinker or two without any reference to the inevitability of political upheaval. It was the imagination that was to be radical; the system would be plastic enough to incorporate it. The new active liberals had the comfort once more of knowing what there was to care about and, somewhat more vaguely, what it was they wished to advocate. People were beginning to have fun, and congratulated themselves.

III

Some seven or eight years have now gone by since the days described above. Their joyousness has been intentionally exaggerated (without a mention of the Berlin Wall or Bay of Pigs or a survey of the New Frontier's actual record on the issues of civil rights and poverty) because people who are committed to the shaping force of their ideas tend more than others to gloss over the texture of past experience — difficult in any case to keep hold of in the torrential rush of decades. *Of course* not everyone who expressed himself in that period was expressing enthusiasm unbounded. Of course such new political vitality as there was was braced by a hard-won and not so foolishly to be surrendered skepticism.

Nevertheless, something of all this there was — I speak here not of the words alone but of the music, and the music said things are better for earnest men, better than they have been in a long long time.

During seven years, then — five, really — the atmosphere in the universities and centers of culture has sharply turned from a new wave of liberal enthusiasm to a storm of reckless, nihilistic, and profoundly despairing radicalism. All the things that had seemed most hopeful at the beginning of the decade have become precisely the sorest spots in this new radical sensibility.

The desire for a relaxation of American moral fervor against some abstraction called "Communism" has been completely reversed into a powerful moral fervor against some abstraction called "imperialism" or "capitalism" (read, America); and many of the people who most vociferously gave voice to the first now burn their ritual candles at the shrine of the second. The demand that the Negro be given his rightful place in the centers of white society has been muffled under a raucous cry of doom to that society; and many of the same people who applauded that demand and seconded it now applaud and second the longing for destruction that supplanted it. The poor whose release from the ugliness of poverty was to be the first order of social business are now exhorted by those who lead their cause to make a subversive value of their poverty; and many of the people who once sought to offer them some greater share of the nation's wealth now seek to support their subversion of the values needed to create that wealth. The cities that were to provide the centers for America's new forays into a more graceful and vivacious life now teeter at the edge of destruction as viable political and administrative entities — and at the edge, some of them, of destruction period; and many of the people who had been the most eager to take part in the social experimentation they promised to yield are now the most eager to pronounce them hopeless. Hallucinogenic drugs have powered and ratified a new youth culture that dictates disengagement from all forms of social and intellectual discipline, a settlement into creature existence, and a total, exclusive submission to the realm of self; and many of the people who once cheered the emergence of a serious, active, and disciplined youth — particularly after the disengaged and self-full 'fifties — now sympathize with the claims of that culture and, with a reckless disloyalty to the standards once imposed on their own intellectual formation, support its products.

Nothing serves better to illustrate the tone and feel of this shift than the career of Stokely Carmichael. That the man who had once been a leader in a serious, determined, and day-by-day attack on the unequal status of the Southern Negro — an attack whose nonviolence was the mark not of weakness but precisely of its determination to succeed once and for all — should now be spending his days making futile desperado announcements of a coming retaliatory terror against white society seems to sum up a great deal about the current decade. Future generations may one day blandly find in this career merely a symptom of the inevitable dynamics of the Negro Revolution caught at midpoint. For after winning what there was to be won, or very nearly so, in the way of Constitutional redress, the Negro's condition as a powerless minority was logically to require the transfer of his demands from integration to "black power." In the lofty and distant view which the future, looking back, so properly arrogates to itself, there will not necessarily be much attention paid to the violent language and behavior through which the Negro first set out to add his weight to the balance of American urban politics. Nor may the rioting in Northern urban ghettos be recorded as anything more than "incidents" in a certain process of political and social reorganization. Nor, certainly, may the use of the Vietnam war as the justification for the declaration of absolute, worldwide racial enmity — as Carmichael and his colleagues and sympathizers now use it — appear as anything other than the taking advantage of a certain historical coincidence to sharpen the pride and group consciousness of American Negroes. For many of his contemporaries, however, most particularly for those who share with him a coming of age in the 'sixties, Stokely Carmichael embodies something very large and real in their own current sense of life. He has become the very personification of their sudden total and implacable hatred for American society.

As a public spokesman, of course, Carmichael has to some extent been the victim of his listeners; and in this, too, he is peculiarly representative of the time. For they have not resisted him, have not even demanded that he make sense. They ask only that he speak to their mood, like people in search of entertainment. If and when he fails to thrill them, he will simply be abandoned, like so many before him, to the escalations of his own spirit. The role of "box office," like that of boredom, is one that modern social critics would do well to ponder.

But if the fate of civil-rights militancy illustrates the change in temper most dramatically, that is only because it is the most definable and containable of the present welter of public issues. The course from hope to despair has been run at exactly the same pace, and by exactly the same plotting of curve, in the realms of foreign policy, domestic politics, and the arts. The new position of "despair"[2] proceeds from one axiom: the American system has come to evil, it must in one way or another be undermined at its foundations.

The corollaries of this axiom are several, and stand in a complicated relation to one another. The first corollary is that any and all of America's difficulties abroad are of her own making and are thus amenable to her own unilateral unmaking. Supplying documentation for this view is a whole new enterprise in historiography — undertaken by such historians as William Appleman Williams, Staughton Lynd, Gar Alperovitz — which seeks to revise our theories about the onset of the Cold War and the assignment of responsibility for it. The engine driving this enterprise and supplying its tone is the notion that by the

[2] I use quotation marks not because the despair is not real but because it is a despair of adopted posture rather than individual feeling; unlike personal despair, which counsels resignation and silence, it has brought with it a veritable whirlwind of energy, action, sociability, and noisemaking.

end of World War II the United States had become the world's leading imperial power, in the face of whose possibly blind but inevitable will to aggrandizement the Soviet Union had to move to protect itself. Such a notion is, of course, not new, only the application to a more recent history of the theory of "capitalist encirclement" advanced in defense of the Soviet Union in the 'thirties. Many of these historians' most ardent students had not even been born in the 'thirties, however, and by one of those quirks of the American educational system — which appears to teach its students to maintain a proper skepticism only toward the experience and earned wisdom of their elders — they seem not to recognize behind all this merely the reversion to an older formula of Good and Evil than the one their mentors would have them discredit. In practice, the application of this attitude means that while, for instance, in demonstrating one's opposition to the Vietnam war one does not necessarily wish to march under the flag of the Vietcong, neither does one wish to be intolerant of, or make open quarrel with, those who do. One might not necessarily wish to give aid and comfort to one's country's enemies, but it is after all only by virtue of her own lust for power and profit that she *has* enemies.

Another corollary is that any and all of America's domestic difficulties are the result of the ill will of white society. In practice, then, while one might not necessarily wish for the *Schadenfreude* of the anarchic destruction of our cities, neither does one have the heart to make open quarrel with those who do. One need not necessarily favor the terrorization of one's innocent fellow citizens — white *and* black — but after all, no one of white skin, and no one of black skin willing to remain at peace in this society, is by one's own theoretical lights quite innocent.

Nor need one — in the realm of culture — take complete satisfaction from the evidence in one's own party of a growing illiteracy and a complacent disregard for all the hard work, hard thought, and hard spiritual discipline contained within the Western cultural tradition. But neither would one wish to oppose the spiritual freedom claimed by those who do make a principle of such disregard; to do so would not only be "square" but in some sense to affirm and perpetuate a curse on all mankind. For after all, that tradition has been placed in the keeping of heavy-handed and pusillanimous academic bureaucrats and has been made to serve the purposes of an evil status quo.

IV

What has happened to create so nearly seismic a reversal of spirit? Much of the answer can be covered in three words: the Vietnam war. To put the matter very flatly, the government of the United States has become involved in a military venture which to the vast majority of the educated, enlightened, liberal community of Americans seems at the very least senseless and at the worst evil. Implied by these three words, however, is a problem far greater and more thoroughgoing than a merely bitterly unpopular government policy. Any military venture of the United States, to be sure, would in these days be fearfully opposed by that community; the existence of a vast nuclear weaponry throughout the world has, as Hans J. Morgenthau many years ago predicted it would, virtually ruled out the waging of war as a means for settling foreign disputes or securing new arrangements of international power.

The Vietnam war bespeaks a much greater failure than the failure to — or even a foolhardy unconcern to — keep the peace. Coming as it did hard on the heels of a new belief that our foreign policy would at last replace the mechanical reflex ideology of the Cold War with a flexible system of response to individual local problems, Johnson's escalation in Vietnam exposed the fact that the governing establishment of this country placed no credit whatsoever in that belief. Our "commitment" to the Republic of Vietnam could still be thought of as one of a complicated leftover tangle of holding actions and alliances; our direct and relatively large-scale intervention in a civil war — even in countering an intervention made on behalf of the other side — spelled out America's continuing determination to let no further inch of ground fall to the Communists. The same determination was evinced in our intervention in the Dominican Republic, but left by itself the Dominican adventure might still have seemed only an ugly blunder.

There was, then, to be no new American foreign policy, only a new enemy — and an increasingly desperate application of all the old justifications for dealing with him. What had appeared to be a genuine new adjustment of attitude could now be seen to have depended entirely on the fact that for three years our foreign dealings had been in the hands of a man with a penchant for traditional civilized diplomacy and a talent for operating without a full-blown policy. The "new look" under Kennedy had been Kennedy's alone, personal to him and, as it turned out, to only a few of his advisers; it had not been established in government beyond his person. Now, under Johnson, America was once more to return to being (or if you will, remain), in the accent of the late John Foster Dulles, "anti-Commonist." In a sense, it was to be more purely anti-Communist than in the 'fifties, since the demise of a centrally controlled worldwide Communist conspiracy now made it less easy for government spokesmen to maintain their former confusion between the containment of a single hostile power, Russia, and the defeat of a hateful political order, Communism. Not that the attempt has not been made to identify this new holding back of the tide of Asian Communism with the containment of an aggressively expanding China. But in a world which has learned to discount the myth of the Communist monolith — and which is anyway apt, in the face of all the evidence, to remain somewhat skeptical of the picture of China ready and able to swallow all of Southeast Asia country by country — the analogy will not wash.

Thus though Johnson has personally borne the brunt of the blame for the mess in Vietnam, some opponents of the war, with considerable justice, find Johnson himself to be only the perfect representative of a larger, and as they would have it, reactionary ruling class. Enough talk of "aggressive Communism" — particularly in a period of hot, and unpopular, warfare — must sooner or later, it seems, breed its own corresponding talk of "aggressive capitalism." In any case, while a continuing sterility in foreign policy, as under Eisenhower, creates a feeling of acute frustration, the dashing of a promise for better things such as Johnson was responsible for creates a far deeper response of demoralization.

Beyond the war itself and what it means

for the state of American foreign policy, this mood of demoralization has been even further deepened by the almost diabolical lack of public candor with which the citizenry has been treated on this subject. We have very nearly attained to that Orwellian nightmare in which "peace" means "war," "victory" means "defeat," and "consensus" means "individual will." If Johnson has at least an arguable case — and even some of his opponents might still be willing to believe he does — he behaves as if he does not. Senators who dissent from his policy, we are told, no longer have access to his person. Persuasion of the opposition consists almost exclusively of references to public-opinion polls which show them to be in a minority, or pronouncements, such as that given in a newspaper interview by John Roche, a member of the White House staff, to the effect that the President's opponents are isolated and unimportant people. Reports on the progress of the war consist almost exclusively of daily tallies of the enemy dead. And behind all of this there is an atmosphere emanating from Washington of ever-increasing petulance and bad temper — frequently, in this psychologically oriented age, taken to be the mark of an uneasy conscience.

Americans have of course — and with little benefit to the commonwealth — had long training in taking for granted the disparity between government statement and government intention. Had not the Eisenhower Administration assured us that it would not rest content with the mere containment of Soviet power but would seek to do everything within its means to assist in bringing to Eastern Europe full democratic liberation? The majority of Americans were obviously quite content not to have to believe it. Did not both Nixon and Kennedy make stirring martial gestures in the direction of Cuba during their respective Presidential campaigns? Again, people instinctively understood the game and did not take them at face value. Any keeping of separate public and private accounts by the government is bound to leave its citizenry with some measure of anxiety followed by, or intermixed with, a certain creeping cynicism. Yet it makes a considerable difference whether official dishonesty is one which speaks belligerently for the sake of remaining pacific — as was the case under Eisenhower — or whether it is — as with Johnson — one which speaks the love of peace for the purpose of intensifying war. Dullesian hypocrisy about the aims of American policy in Eastern Europe buried us beneath a load of distorting language that often made it next to impossible to discuss, or think about, the problem at hand. Johnsonian hypocrisy about the aims of American policy in Vietnam, tied as it is to the destruction of a country and the killing of its civilian population on the most questionable of military and political grounds, has served to call into question — particularly among the young — the very legitimacy of government authority.

V

"It is enough," Franz Kafka once wrote in his diary, "that the arrow fits the wound it makes." In a very large measure the opposition to the war has come to reflect, and be reflected by, Johnson's conduct of it. In this sense, perhaps, the disaffection that goes so far as to wish a defeat upon one's own country is well deserved by the arrogance that dares pursue its own privately defined terms of victory. In any case, the radical, despairing nihilism that has ballooned among us in the past few years shares a number of spiritual and intellectual characteristics with the present atmosphere in the White House. Notable among these are an unthinking dependence on political formulas expressed in moral terms, a refusal to make certain necessary distinctions, a lack of candor, a shutting off of genuine debate, and an almost personal demand for loyalty, for the closing of ranks.

It would be silly, of course, to lay the entire current disaffection among the community of the enlightened at the door of Lyndon Johnson — or even of the war itself. Some of what accounts for that community's disgust with the state and nature of American society has to do with frustrations that were inevitable, particularly given the high, innocent expectation with which it greeted the early 'sixties. The single most important of these expectations, in fact, was not thwarted but on the contrary raised to fever pitch precisely by Lyndon Johnson: the expectation that there would be full-scale, orderly redress to the American Negro for his unthinkable treatment at the hands of his fellow Americans. Only the most insanely doctrinaire of his opponents would even at this heated point underrate Johnson's role as the foremost civil-rights President in history. The frustration arose from the fact that the Negro wanted and needed two contradictory things (contradictory, at least, within the particular legal and social tradition of the United States): individual rights and dignity on the one hand and group power on the other; and he could no longer wait patiently for the attainment of either. White society was prepared to give him, as an individual, the former. But the latter, because it would cost people something in the way of the diminution of their own power, was not to be given. Power was something that would have to be wrested. The problem very quickly became a grave one for the Negroes — and in a sense even graver for their white sympathizers — because the moral justice and urgency of their case blinded most of their leaders to the fact that they were pursuing two separate and contradictory ends which would require two separate and distinguishable programs of action. Thus long before he was ready for it — which is to say, long before he had forged for himself the necessary community structure to serve him as a base — the Negro had to confront the resistance of the already structured communities into whose network of power he would have to make some incursion. The experience of the resistance, and of his unpreparedness for it, understandably left him in a rage. His white sympathizers, who had dealt only, and guiltily, in terms of morality and so had refused themselves the right to make any cool judgment of his political behavior, were then split into groups willing to share his rage or frightened by it. Having failed on both sides to understand the mechanism of power in which they had involved themselves, angry Negroes and angry white liberals and radicals fell back for an explanation of the new difficulty on a theory of American society as hopelessly and irremediably racist. This theory was perhaps as inevitable as the frustration that gave rise to it. Other things being equal, it would have surrendered some of its simplicity to the exigencies of a day-to-day struggle in which not all would be defeat and not all victory.

But other things did not remain equal

— the country was engaged in a war which these same activists deemed to be an unjust one. And not only engaged in this war, but engaged in it beneath the clouds of an official temper which left very little open to the spirit of public consultation or influence. So the war, while it did not create the frustration of the civil-rights movement, helped to harden that frustration into the atmosphere of a beleaguered camp, and provided real fuel for the idea that "orderly political process" was a snare and a delusion for the complacent.

The same can be said for the sense of futility that now surrounds the war on poverty. The poor, too, were caught in a contradiction — very nearly the same one — and in this case without even the élan or drive which supports people who are making a fight for themselves. But the realization that even so little money as had been spent on the poor could not now be spared from the requirements of that other, realer, war once again hardened ordinary frustration into unheeding bitterness.

And so partly fairly, partly not, all the issues that had roused a spirit of opposition — mainly war and poverty and equality for Negroes, but not only these — were fused into one; and in that fusion much of the opposition — enough of it to leave an ineradicable imprint on the entire culture of this decade — was funneled into a single piously articulated attitude of anti-Americanism.

It is this attitude, and not adherence to any particular school or schools of radical political ideology, that earns one admittance to that precinct of the intellectual community called the New Left. It is this attitude, and not the chronological accident of one's birth date, that entitles one to claim membership in that exclusive and intimidating generation Under Thirty. It is this attitude, and not a commitment to the free adventure of the mind, that now accredits one as a truly free spirit beyond the taint of having sold one's soul for pleasure or profit.

Thus we have, within twenty short years, come full circle. The word "evil" hangs heavy in the language of intellectual discussion just as it came to do in the years after World War II. Then it was applied to the Soviet Union, now to the United States, but the refusal to countenance political complexity that it bespeaks remains the same. Now, as then, dissent from the prevailing currents of fashionable opinion is adjudged to constitute moral failure and places the dissenter beyond the pale of argument. It is astonishing — and more than astonishing — appalling — to realize that the developments of two decades, in a rapidly changing world, have not deterred many of America's most intelligent, most serious, most talented people from their appointed round.

VI

With all due respect, then, to the trials and frustrations of the 'sixties, the response of the intellectual community to those trials and frustrations has been both disastrous in itself and a depressing omen for the future.

At precisely a time when the values for which this community believes itself to stand — the enlargement of intellectual possibility and the devotion to standards of excellence — are being most threatened from the outside, it has responded only in kind, by threatening them further from the inside.

When a historian like Staughton Lynd proclaims Hanoi to be the model for the achievement of freedom by small nations, he is perverting both the use of his intellectual discipline and his mandate as a thinking man.

When the organizers of a movement to withhold federal income tax in protest against the war draw up a statement which identifies the United States with Nazi Germany, they are, while pretending to appeal to the moral sense, perverting that sense.

When Susan Sontag, wishing to express her horror at the fruits of modern technology, launches an attack upon the Faustian spirit of the whole of Western Civilization ending with the observation that "the white race . . . [is] the cancer of humanity," she undermines the very ground on which she herself is entitled to speak or write.

When Andrew Kopkind, a highly talented young journalist, finds in the fascist tactics wielded by a group of Negroes at a conference of radicals a necessary — finally even a hopeful — experience, he reveals a carelessness toward the virtues of freedom that a writer may indulge in only at his peril.

When Robert Brustein, dean of the Yale drama school, indiscriminately and in a tone of deepest self-gratulation lends his sponsorship to any and all works of art whose intention is subversive, he is in fact subverting nothing so much as that artistic integrity to which he professes devotion.

The examples could multiply. They abound in the liberal weeklies, in the highly influential *New York Review of Books,* in some of the quarterlies, and are to be heard from the platform of every forum, symposium, teach-in, and round table on peace.

What is sorriest about this present climate is that it witnesses another betrayal for which yet another high price is sure to be exacted — in disillusionment and bitterness and violent reaction. An intellectual temper which has not the patience to sort out the illegitimate from the legitimate cannot long sustain itself. We learned this from the 'fifties; it will be this decade's lesson, too. The 'seventies will very likely bring a turning back — a turning back from the value of all social passion as well as from the futility of violence. And may we not expect that the disillusion of tomorrow will become the hard, cold, oppressive philosophy of day after tomorrow?

Open Letter to an American Liberal

Kenneth Tynan

Dear Friend:

In the last six months of 1967, 25 children under the age of 14 were executed by the American Army in South Vietnam for giving aid and comfort to the Viet Cong. During the same period, the number of child prostitutes in Saigon increased by 7000, and the bombs dropped by U.S. planes on North Vietnam had a combined explosive power twice as great as that of all the aerial bombardments in World War Two.

Every one of the statements in that paragraph is false. But were you quite sure, as you read them, that they weren't true? Didn't you, in fact, assume that they were accurate? And, if so, did you feel anything more than the customary twinge of weary nausea with which one reacts to the daily barrage of evil news out of Vietnam? The human capacity to be shocked is not unlimited, and the lies I have cooked up differ only in degree from the truths you already know about the strange and ferocious war in which your Government is presently engaged. But suppose you believed my inventions and were genuinely outraged: How would you have protested, and what could your protest hope to achieve? Above all, *what is it like to live in a country where such statements might conceivably be true?*

I ask you because I honestly don't know. I've just returned from my first trip to America in three years. Shortly before I left England, I learned from a Gallup Poll that one out of every four American adults favored the use of atomic weapons to win the war in Vietnam. An appalling statistic, but it didn't greatly surprise me: We Europeans are nowadays as grimly accustomed to bad news about America as you are to bad news about Vietnam. I wonder if you realize exactly what European liberals feel about this war of yours. Do you remember a hypervirile Manhattan intellectual we knew who used to go down to Stillman's gym every so often and climb into the ring for a few rounds with some junior aspirant, generally a Negro, a Cuban or a Filipino? Big deal, you said; he's working off his aggressions on "inferior races." That's how we regard your war. To us, Vietnam is Washington's grisly equivalent of Stillman's gym.

Before 1967 I'd paid about 20 visits to the States, all of them as a friend — critical on occasion, alarmed by McCarthy's rise and relieved by his fall, but always affectionate and ultimately trusting. Last year, for the first time, I came warily, as a suspicious stranger. Just after I arrived, I bought a handful of comics at the airport for the six-year-old son of a liberal buddy of mine. Riffling through them, I came across a copy of *Tod Holton — Super Green Beret* and decided to violate my anticensorship principles by withholding it from the boy. In case you don't know about Tod, he's a schoolboy in Valleyville, U.S.A., to whom "an ancient Far Eastern monk" has entrusted a supernatural Green Beret. Whenever American interests are threatened overseas, "the magic headgear glows." Tod puts the thing on, salutes the flag and instantly vanishes, only to reappear — transformed into an ironfisted superman — wherever the natives are restless. His job is to succor the needy while merrily zapping the Cong. Typical sample of dialog:

SOUTH VIETNAMESE CHILD: Please, sir, some food! Our rice bowls have been empty these three days now!
TOD: Sorry, I didn't have time to stop off at the supermarket! But you can have these chocolate bars!
SOUTH VIETNAMESE CHILD: Many humble thanks, sir!

Having solved the starvation problem, Tod goes on to beat hell out of the Cong — a parcel of bald-pated fiends with Fu Manchu beards — and departs as miraculously as he came. Crowds of pro-American peasants (the assembled Uncle Toms of Vietnam) speed him on his way with wholeheartedly servile cries of gratitude, worthy of Stepin Fetchit on Lincoln's birthday. The strip concludes: "So spreads the fame of the mighty Super Green Beret as he battles on the side of the oppressed and downtrodden all over the world!" The same magazine also features a daredevil trio called the Flying Musketeers, who zoom out to China in their supersonic jet-copter and triumphantly bomb an atomic-missile factory. ("Your country's yours again!" they tell the local chieftain. "You are free once more!") After carrying out this classic pre-emptive strike, they jet back to Washington, where they are hailed by the Pentagon with cheers and congratulations.

So I didn't give that black-and-white, might-is-right, end-justifies-the-means-type propaganda sheet to six-year-old Pete; but I talked about ends and means to his father, and to several other good writers whom I used to count as political sympathizers. I found them drinking on a fairly monumental scale. Every night before dinner they would get somberly sloshed, and the provocation would always be the same: Vietnam, and what to do about it. Should they go on marches, or burn their draft cards in Independence Square, or emigrate to a Mediterranean island, or make one last, desperate attempt to get an unequivocal statement out of Bobby Kennedy? By the time the sun rose over Vineyard Haven, they would usually have decided that they were politically impotent. (But at least they have something to be impotent *about* — a dominant climate of opinion against which to revolt. We in Britain are far more abjectly powerless; we rebel in a vacuum. Even if we persuaded Harold Wilson to protest against the bombing of North Vietnam, it would mean nothing, since he would undoubtedly let L.B.J. know in advance that he was only doing it to placate the left wing of the Labour party.)

Although I saw quite a few of our friends during my three-week stay, I didn't call you; for reasons that I'll try to explain, I felt hesitant and slightly embarrassed. Do you recall the last time we met? It was in London, late in the summer of 1964. Johnson was running for the Presidency on a platform that explicitly pledged him to cool the war; he promised he wouldn't let American boys "do the job that Asian boys should do." To my lasting amazement, you believed him, and you became quite ruffled when I cynically predicted that his first act, after election, would be to escalate. We both agreed, however, that American involvement in Vietnam was militarily a mess and morally a catastrophe. It wasn't until 1965 that your position began to change. You still deplored the war, but I saw that it was taking on, in your mind, a curiously autonomous identity, almost as if it were an inoperable disease, following its predestined course in accordance with its own nature — horribly but blamelessly, like an earthquake or hurricane.

Fate, and not human agency, seemed to be in charge of events; and once you accept this view of history, the next logical step is to absolve human beings from all moral responsibility. Which brings us very close to those interesting theories about war guilt that certain West German pundits have lately been peddling. As one of them has said: "Behind the technical machinery of war, the individual can no longer be cornered. The causal nexus of action and responsibility has been broken. . . . The concepts of guilt and innocence sound like rules of behavior from the nursery — authors should be ashamed to go on churning them out." The same apologist sums up his case in a wonderfully bland sentence. By the end of World War Two, he says, "the means of extermination available *had finally outgrown the power of human decision.*" (My italics.) In other words, the buck ends nowhere. Auschwitz and Hiroshima were nobody's fault — just regrettable by-products of an omnipotent abstraction called "the historical process."

"A plague on both their houses," you said in one of your letters, referring to the American Army and the Viet Cong. And a plague — in the sense of a disaster caused by no human volition and raging beyond human control — was precisely what, in your eyes, the war had become.

You were naturally dismayed when the black news came through on February 7, 1965, that U.S. planes had started to bomb North Vietnam, and you wrote me a sturdy letter of dissent. But it contained a worrying passage in which you suggested that L.B.J. and his advisors were somehow "prisoners of events." There it was again, the old historical process, whereby executioners are mysteriously transmuted into prisoners, and criminals into victims. And although you thought the bombing unjustified, you seemed to regard it as just another downhill step, instead of a seven-league stride toward the point of no return. When noncombatants began to die under your bombs, the people of North Vietnam saw the face of the West as their government had always depicted it. A truth we often forget became self-evident to them: that the aerial bombardment of civilians is a practice in which the Communist countries have never indulged.

It was during 1965 that your attitude finally became clear. Somewhere, in everything you wrote or said about the war, there would be an escape clause, acquitting you of the charge of taking sides. Of course America was wrong to devastate the South and blast the North; but at the same time (you would point out), the Viet Cong had killed a lot of civilians, and were thus equally guilty. As I read these hedging letters of yours, a few lines by Thomas Hardy flitted across my mind:

There seemed a strangeness in the air,
Vermilion light on the land's lean face;
I heard a voice from I knew not where: —

"The Great Adjustment is taking place."

And a safe, respectable adjustment it was. You had taken your stand at last, resolutely facing both ways with the same Olympian frown. You didn't love Big Brother, but nobody was going to accuse you of loving Big Brother's enemies.

Now, it would obviously be lunatic to say that either side in Vietnam had a monopoly of right or wrong. But isn't it just as irresponsible to throw up your hands and declare that there's nothing to choose between them? In my primitive, pragmatic way, I begin by counting the victims. General Westmoreland stated in April 1967 that during the past nine years, 53,000 South Vietnamese civilians had been killed "or kidnaped" by the Viet Cong — i.e., slightly less than 6000 a year. (He neglected to specify how many of these were kidnaped.) But according to an exhaustive Associated Press report issued in October 1966, American artillery and aircraft are killing almost as many Southern noncombatants as that *every month* — quite apart from civilian casualties in raids on the North.

The murder of innocent people is always atrocious; even so, Jean-Paul Sartre was not being entirely cold-blooded when he said:

> I refuse to place in the same category the actions of an organization of poor peasants, hunted, obliged to maintain an iron discipline in their ranks, and those of an immense army backed up by a highly industrialized country of 200,000,000 inhabitants. And then, it is not the Vietnamese who have invaded America or rained down a deluge of fire upon a foreign people. In the Algerian war, I always refused to place on an equal footing the terrorism . . . which was the only weapon available to the Algerians, and the actions and exactions of a rich army of half a million men, occupying the whole country. The same is true in Vietnam.

I'm quoting from an interview given by Sartre shortly before the first session of the Bertrand Russell International War Crimes Tribunal, of which he was the executive president. No doubt you've heard of this extraordinary body, set up by Russell to determine whether the activities of the U.S. in Vietnam could be classified as criminal under the laws by which the Nazis were tried at Nuremberg in 1945. No government or party sponsored the Tribunal; it was paid for by private subscriptions. (Ironically, a great deal of the money came out of the $200,000 that an American publisher gave Russell for the rights to his autobiography.) Its prototype was Nuremberg, where several precedents in international law were firmly established. To initiate or wage aggressive war, to violate the customs of war as laid down in The Hague and Geneva conventions, to commit inhuman acts on civilians — all these were defined as crimes, and the guilty Nazis were duly punished. Inherent in the trials was the doctrine that nobody — not even a head of state — could escape accountability for his deeds. To plead that you were acting under orders was no longer a valid defense. Nuremberg was no mere kangaroo court: In 1946, its legality and its judgments were affirmed by the General Assembly of the United Nations. Justice Robert H. Jackson, chief American counsel at the trials, spoke for his country when he said: "We are not prepared to lay down a rule of criminal conduct against others which we would not be willing to have invoked against us." All that Sartre and Russell did was to take him at his word.

Their Tribunal stated the case for the prosecution. Although they invited evidence from the other side, I think they felt that the defense had already had a pretty thorough airing in the mass media of the West. Naïvely, they hoped that the Western press would report the Tribunal's hearings. Apart from the odd, dismissive paragraph, I saw almost nothing. (The eastern-European papers were just as curt, though for different reasons. The Tribunal's image of gallant little North Vietnam, not only surviving but even winning against all the odds, was not wildly endearing to the Russians; they want Hanoi to come to the conference table, since they are well aware that Chinese communism grows stronger whenever an Asian is killed by a Western bullet.) None of the 15 men and women on the Tribunal needed much convincing that U.S. intervention in Vietnam was *immoral*: Their purpose was to find out whether it could be shown to be *illegal.* Sartre made this distinction quite clearly in the interview I've mentioned above: "There is no question of judging whether American policy in Vietnam is evil — of which most of us on the Tribunal have not the slightest doubt — but of seeing whether it falls within the compass of international law on war crimes."

If an anti-Fascist organization is both shunned by the Soviet bloc and knocked by the West, it can't be all bad. In spite of its admitted bias, I couldn't help respecting the Tribunal's aims. Without international law we perish, and no other body seemed to be concerning itself with applying the rule of law to the bloody carnival of Vietnam. And even if the jury is packed, it's still possible for an outsider to weigh the value of factual evidence. Hence I decided to watch the Tribunal in action; and I'd like to lay on you my impressions, to date, of its brief, beleaguered and fugitive existence.

November 1966: first press conference, held in London. Apart from European and American journalists, I notice a high proportion of Africans, Asians and Latin Americans in the audience, which also includes Dick Gregory. The Tribunal obviously has a powerful appeal to the Third World — i.e., to those nations and individuals who decline to be leaned on by Moscow or Washington. Sartre is unable to attend, but Bertrand Russell puts in an appearance to read a prepared statement. He moves with a terrible fragility, like an ancient wading bird, and the piping, rasping precision of his voice turns the conference into a Cambridge University tutorial, circa 1900. "I have lived through the Dreyfus case" — in seven words, he whisks us back through as many decades. He accuses the U.S. of mounting "a war of annihilation," expresses "admiration and passion" for the people of Vietnam, and departs. (Age and ill health prevented the sage from traveling to Stockholm for the Tribunal's first session. Dean Rusk, who had been invited to nominate a spokesman for the American Government, told a group of journalists that he had no intention of "playing games with a 94-year-old Briton." Sartre promptly issued a crisp rebuff. "Mr. Rusk," he said, "might have replied: 'I do not recognize the legitimacy of the Tribunal, and I will not send anyone to represent the American Government's point of view.' Or else: 'I recognize it as legitimate, and we are so certain that we are right that I will at once send a spokesman to Stockholm.' Or he might have answered: 'I do not recognize the legitimacy of these judges, but we possess such strong arguments and overwhelming evidence that I am not afraid to set before them the reasons for our policies.' But he said none of these things. Instead, he chose an ignominious way out. He sought to ridicule a great old man.")

Months pass. Postponement follows postponement. Harold Wilson won't have the Tribunal in London; with freezing courtesy, De Gaulle slams the door on it in Paris. For a while it looks as if Algeria may be the place, but this plan is unaccountably frustrated, and it's in Stockholm, for a chilly week in May 1967, that the tribunes, witnesses, newsmen and private observers finally forgather. The venue is the *Folkets Hus* (People's House), a Swedish-modern conference hall with a theater in the basement, where the neatly timed current attraction is the off-Broadway protest play *Viet Rock.*

The Tribunal members — grave faces clustered around green-baize tables — comprise a German dramatist (Peter Weiss, author of *Marat/Sade*), a British historian (Isaac Deutscher, biographer of Stalin and Trotsky), a French novelist (Simone de Beauvoir, disciple and companion of Sartre) and, of course, Sartre himself, a busy, bespectacled gnome, exuding intellectual energy. There are also eminent jurists from France, Italy, Japan, Pakistan and Turkey, and two Americans — a pacifist and a minor playwright. The scowling chairman, who looks like a heavyweight bouncer, is the Yugoslav historian Vladimir Dedijer — a highly sympathetic figure, I later discover, who championed the cause of Milovan Djilas when the latter was imprisoned for criticizing Tito. In Stockholm (Dedijer announces) the Tribunal will confine itself to two questions: Is the U.S. guilty of aggression in Vietnam, and to what extent have civilian targets been attacked? Other charges — concerning chemical weapons, inhuman treatment of prisoners, and genocide — will be held over until subsequent sessions.

So the quiet recital of evidence begins, a litany of pain inflicted with nobly paternal motives (after all, the Vietnamese must be protected from themselves), a story — growing monotonous with iteration — of homes and schools, churches and hospitals destroyed for the greater good of those who lived, learned, worshiped and were healed in them. Only thus, it seems, can the people of Vietnam be taught the wisdom of the American way of life. Better this than the heresy, of neutralism or the living death of communism. There's no room for a middle course now. The bombs fall on the just and the unjust — first a wave of high explosive, then a wave of napalm, then a wave of fragmentation bombs (the procedure never varies) — until the survivors come to their senses, realizing at last that they must either welcome the sincere white bombardiers or be branded enemies of freedom. Those who are not for the U.S. are against liberty, and must not marvel if they are hunted and destroyed.

A French lady journalist tells how she accompanied a North Vietnamese peasant to his home after a raid. Tea had been prepared and was hot on the table, but his wife and four children were dead. What end did these deaths serve? The Frenchwoman, who was tortured by the Germans in World War Two, claims to recognize the tactics. To make a member of the Resistance confess, the Gestapo would torture his next of kin; similarly, to make the Viet Cong capitulate, the Americans bomb their compatriots in the North. A Pakistani witness quotes from a conversation he had with a military official in Hanoi.

Question: If the U.S. stops bombing North Vietnam, will you take reciprocal steps of de-escalation? *Answer:* Certainly — we'll stop shooting down American bombers.

The catalog of homicide goes relentlessly on. Of people ravaged by napalm ("His ears just melted," says a witness who was present during a raid); of Northern villages carefully obliterated, despite being far removed from military targets. Film clips and photographs amply support the charges, together with tape recordings made by local citizens. As slide after slide of civilian corpses is projected onto the screen, we acquire a sort of immunity to horror. "*Autres corps des victimes. . . . Autres corps des victimes,*" repeats a Cambodian delegate, showing us pictures of Cambodian peasants who died when American bombers violated their territory. (Ostensibly by accident, but actually, he insists, to chastise Cambodia for its policy of neutralism.) In time it becomes difficult to distinguish a dead body from its background. It looks like something crumpled, spilled, rolled up, discarded — an unwieldy piece of garbage, melting into surroundings of domestic debris. This is the human form as Francis Bacon sees it in his paintings, caught writhing in some private turmoil, as if anticipating its own ultimate putrescence.

A special ghastliness ought to attach to dead lepers. In 1957 the North Vietnamese built a model leper colony to accommodate 4000 patients. They chose a secluded spot for it. Even in our enlightened age, tradition insists that lepers should be kept in isolated areas. American planes demolished the colony in 39 raids, and fired on the inmates as they were being evacuated to caves in the nearby hills. One hundred thirty-nine people were killed. Films and photos establish the loneliness of the site and the extent of the havoc; but I can't pretend that a slaughtered leper looks more moving than any other corpse. This is what French weapons expert Professor Jean-Pierre Vigier is later to define as "psychosocial bombing" — its essential target being civilian morale. The dead act as object lessons to the living. Why, indeed, should Rusk bother to play games with an aged Briton? Here, on the big board, is a far more fascinating game, and one for which he can invent his own rules.

By no means all the evidence goes unchallenged by the members of the Tribunal: These are combative intellectuals, in whom the impulse to argue is almost a reflex. Thus, when a witness describes the bombardment of dikes in the North, a massive Pakistani lawyer sternly demands how much of his account is based on personal experience and how much on official sources. Mostly the latter, the witness admits; and his testimony is brusquely disallowed. Again, a Japanese investigator produces a map taken from a captured American pilot on which (he maintains) hospitals chosen for attack are marked in red. Sartre will have none of this. Perhaps, he suggests, they were marked in red as targets to be *avoided?* The Japanese equivocates; Sartre persists in his skepticism; and the evidence is quashed.

Is this technically a war of American aggression? Three dapper professors — Chesneaux of the Sorbonne, Douglas of Cornell and Kolko of the University of Pennsylvania — present their findings, which differ only in length and relative felicity of phrasing. All reject the conventional thesis, advanced by establishment liberals like Arthur Schlesinger, that this is a war into which America just happened to blunder.

Summary of Chesneaux: American intervention in Vietnam started long before the Geneva Conference of 1954 — Truman said in the previous year that the U.S. was paying half the cost of what was then a French colonial war. Those who believe that this was ever a civil war are kidding themselves: It was (and remains) a struggle between Vietnamese nationalism and foreign-backed puppet governments. "It is the U.S. that has committed subversion in Vietnam, not the N.L.F. [National Liberation Front]."
Summary of Douglas: For at least 17 years, the U.S. has been financially and militarily committed to preventing the country from going neutral. American policy, according to this *nostra culpa* recital, combines "a glib rhetoric with a barbarous reality." (But Douglas could hardly have guessed how far the barbarity would go, or how glib the rhetoric would get. Since he addressed the Tribunal, it's become common form for U.S. commanders to advocate punitive invasions of North Vietnam, Laos and Cambodia. The closed world in which they think and plan is now a complete moral madhouse. They are moving the air war to the frontiers of China — perhaps in the hope of provoking Chinese retaliation. If this takes place, on however small a scale, they will be able, like Tod Holton's cronies, to bomb China's nuclear stations with a clear conscience.)

Gabriel Kolko, Associate Professor of History at the University of Pennsylvania, comes up with the fullest and most clinching indictment of the Great American Aberration. From the beginning, he says, Vietnam has been a testing ground of America's ability to suppress wars of revolutionary nationalism. And the beginning was in 1950, when the success of communism in China first convinced the U.S. that self-determination in southeast Asia was something to be discouraged. Hence America's refusal to endorse the 1954 Geneva agreements, which guaranteed free elections in Vietnam. Between 1955 and 1959, the Diem regime executed more than 16,000 of its political opponents and received more than 70 percent of its budget from the U.S. A new resistance movement erupted among the peasants in 1959, and the N.L.F. was formed at the end of the following year. Soon afterward, the U.S. military build-up began. Excerpt from Kolko's peroration:

> First as a passive senior partner, and then as the primary party, the United States made Vietnam an international arena for the Cold War; and the war should never be considered as a civil conflict, or even secondarily as a by-product of one — for in that form it would hardly have lasted very long against a national and radical movement that the vast majority of the Vietnamese people always sustained.

Should the U.S. therefore pull out? On this question I fancy you'd go along with Schlesinger, who opposes the war but says (in his book on Vietnam) that America has "moral obligations to those South Vietnamese who, under our encouragement and with the expectation of our support, have said and done things which will assure their imprisonment or death if the Viet Cong should take over South Vietnam by force." This is the American liberal's stock case against American withdrawal. But it wouldn't be insuperably difficult, given U.S. good will and careful surveillance by the International Control Commission set up at Geneva, to make sure that free elections, not force, determined the composition of the government; and the I.C.C. could also supervise a general amnesty. Even if the worst happened, and reprisals occurred, could they really be more abominable than what the U.S. is already doing to Vietnam?

As the days pass, and the witnesses come and go, I detect a certain duality in the Tribunal's aims. It is trying to prove that America's military effort is at once effective (i.e., commits atrocities) and ineffective (i.e., cannot win the war). "The accused, your Honor, is not only a multiple ax slayer but harmless." But this is a forensic quibble. What dominates one's mind is wonder at the versatile violence of American war making. Napalm, for example — what a triumph of scientifically administered pain! One of the witnesses offers in evidence a fragment of a napalm bomb that has already exploded. He chips a tiny splinter into an ashtray and applies a match. It burns fiercely for ten minutes. The brain recoils, and the flesh cringes, from the thought of contact with this exquisitely researched product of Western know-how. (Not to mention such other marvels of expertise as the seven "chemical agents" — three of them potentially lethal gases — that the U.S. has now authorized for use in Vietnam. These, together with data relating to bacteriological weapons, will be discussed at the Tribunal's next series of sessions.)

On the fourth morning, the human evidence is shown. Cameramen converge, arc lamps flood the stage and we avidly peer, feeling like ghouls, at a pretty girl in blue, a serene small boy and two impassive men in dark, ill-fitting business suits. These are the first Vietnamese victims of American bombing ever to be seen outside their native country. (From this point onward, I wish you had been there: Hearsay is a great cushion against guilt.)

The men come from the South. Thai Binh Dan, aged 18, is a peasant who was napalmed on May 21, 1966, suffering permanent injuries to his face, arms, hands and legs. Hoang Tan Hun is a 45-year-old rice grower, maimed by a phosphorus bomb earlier in the same month. His left ear has gone, he can't move his head and his left arm is glued to his body.

The girl and the boy are North Vietnamese. Ngo Thi Nga, who is 23, teaches school in a village of 500 homes. On the night of October 22, 1966, she and 15 of her pupils were asleep in the classroom when the American bombs fell. She felt a stabbing pain in the back of her neck, but took as many children to the shelters as she could before fainting. When she came to, she was in hospital. "My head hurt, I couldn't sleep, I vomited everything. Two of the children were dead. The diagnosis said I had a steel pellet lodged in my skull." It is still there. Her sight is getting weaker, and she has crippling headaches. A French doctor testifies that the damage to her brain is incurable. There was no military target — no factory, no power plant, no railroad, no highway, not even a bridge — within 20 kilometers of her village, and no troops had ever been stationed there.

Do Van Ngoc is a moonfaced lad with a voice as shrill and sunny as Shirley Temple's in her prepolitical days. He is nine years old. In the mornings he goes to school and in the afternoons looks after his father's cattle. The afternoon of June 5, 1966, is the one we are concerned with. "I saw three planes coming in from the sea. One of them dropped two bombs. There were big flames, the cattle were on fire, and I jumped into the water of the rice fields because my body was burning. Later I called out to some people passing by and they took me to hospital. I stayed there three months. Then my parents brought me home and I got fat again and went back to school." He is politely asked if he is willing to show his wounds. The cameras move in closer, the audience rises. He strips off his jacket, shirt and pants, and is suddenly naked, in a blaze of light. Above the waist he's unmarked; but his belly, thighs and groin are burned to a deep-brown crisp, corrugated like the crackling on a roast of pork. (A Stockholm physician confirms that the scars could have been caused only by napalm.) Shock inscribes the image on my retina. Mention Vietnam today, and that is what I see. If you dismiss it as a mere propaganda display, I can only agree with you, and pity you. It *was* propaganda; but it was propagating a symbolic and demonstrable truth. Tabloid simplifications are not always lies. I know we are taught to mistrust them; but the moment our skepticism becomes total, we play into the hands of authority, which rejoices whenever a potential rebel is seduced into apathy.

I suppose I am urging you to lose your cool. Can you face the prospect of living without it? About 30 years ago, another great military power intervened to impose a puppet government on another embattled country. You would surely have lined up against the Germans in Spain: Isn't there reason enough to take sides against the Americans in Vietnam? You'll probably argue that to do so would be an empty gesture, but I say the hell with such self-abasement. I know it pleases you to think yourself powerless, but numbers are extremely potent, and your allies are more numerous than you imagine.

So what to do? For one thing, how about setting up a War Crimes Tribunal in the U.S., with a panel of American jurists sitting in judgment on their own political leaders? Arraign your own country in accordance with the international laws it helped to formulate. If the Tribunal produced concrete evidence that the U.S. had acted in breach of these laws, it would not only attract enormous publicity but also open the way for a test case that might be taken before a Federal court — e.g., that of a man who refused the draft because he did not wish to aid and abet his country in committing war crimes. You may remind me of the case of Captain Howard Levy, the Brooklyn dermatologist who got a prison sentence for declining, on conscientious grounds, to give instruction to Green Beret medicos bound for Vietnam; but that sentence was passed by a military court, not a civil one, and Dr. Levy lacked the corroborating weight of witnesses and evidence that a Tribunal could provide.

My idea is to put the basic structure of American democracy to the test: Take the Executive branch to court and challenge the Judiciary to condemn it. And if you think I am being fanciful, let me boost your morale with a quote from Professor Louis Sohn of the Harvard Law School. "Certainly," the professor says, "a U.S. court could find its own Government in violation of international law — and do something about it." If the Judiciary evades its duty, one thing at least will have been made bitterly clear: that the separation of law from politics, on which your Constitution prides itself, is a discredited myth. Your legal system will have confessed its subservience to the political arm.

If, like me, you belong to the 39-plus generation, you and your coevals could be indispensably helpful in the organizing (which must be speedy and well financed) of a juridically sound and politically respectable Tribunal. But what about the young? I'm convinced that most of them would be either radical enough to support the Tribunal or unprejudiced enough not to ignore it. If its findings cut no ice in the official courts, they might decide to opt out of the system, having been shown that it self-evidently did not work. As far as the political establishment is concerned, they would surely be right. But opting out need not mean giving up. Two courses of definite action would still be left to them. They could line up with the Third World I've mentioned and defined above by helping to form — inside America but outside the major parties — a political Third Force of tough-mindedly leftish character. (A solid and obdurate Popular Front would spell nightmares for L.B.J.) Alternatively, they could join the hippies. It's an easier choice, of course, but not to be underrated. Ten years ago I used to attack the Beats for being nonpolitical; I told them to stay in the boat and rock it. Since then, the boat has grown steadily more unrockable. Nowadays, it's a hell-bent war canoe that neither of the major parties can steer away from the rapids. Dropping out of the present setup can be an act of affirmation, more positive than staying in. "You and I, dear brothers, all of us who smoke a little pot and dig a little peace, we are high among the radicals and subversives L.B.J. would like to get rid of." (I'm quoting from a "love release" put out by a Digger community.) "Anything that criticizes the establishment and its asinine war-and-power game is political, subversive. . . . All the heads and hippies, all the black-power people, all the wild and futile Reds with their outmoded economic fantasies and incredibly lovely and naïve idealism, you and I, dear brothers — they're out to get us!"

And did you hear about the Digger who went to Michigan last summer and made a speech so challenging that it stunned the New Left into silence and self-reappraisal? The occasion was a conference held by the Students for a Democratic Society. The Digger said, in part:

> Marxism's a groove, but Russia's a drag, right? Look at us, we're out of it, drop out of it with us. We're going to make this country be what we want. It can be beautiful. We can all be beautiful. . . . Johnson doesn't want you to be beautiful. Resist! You can't *reform* this country. If the New Left took over, it would all be the same, man, because you're not free. You got to drop out, baby. *Free yourselves, and then free the country.* We're doing it. You can do it. We're your brothers. Are you with us?

In other words, defeat the military-industrial machine by noncooperation and passive resistance. Regard the Government as an occupying power, just as Gandhi regarded the British in India. Make bridges, all the time, between the Diggers and the New Left. If American youth would only learn from the patience of the Vietnamese, it could change the face of America within a decade.

No matter what choice it makes, you will be able to help — with advice, with prestige, with propaganda. And that will help all of us, including your friends in Europe. Don't think we like disliking America.

Yours at the barricades,

Kenneth Tynan

The Black Experience

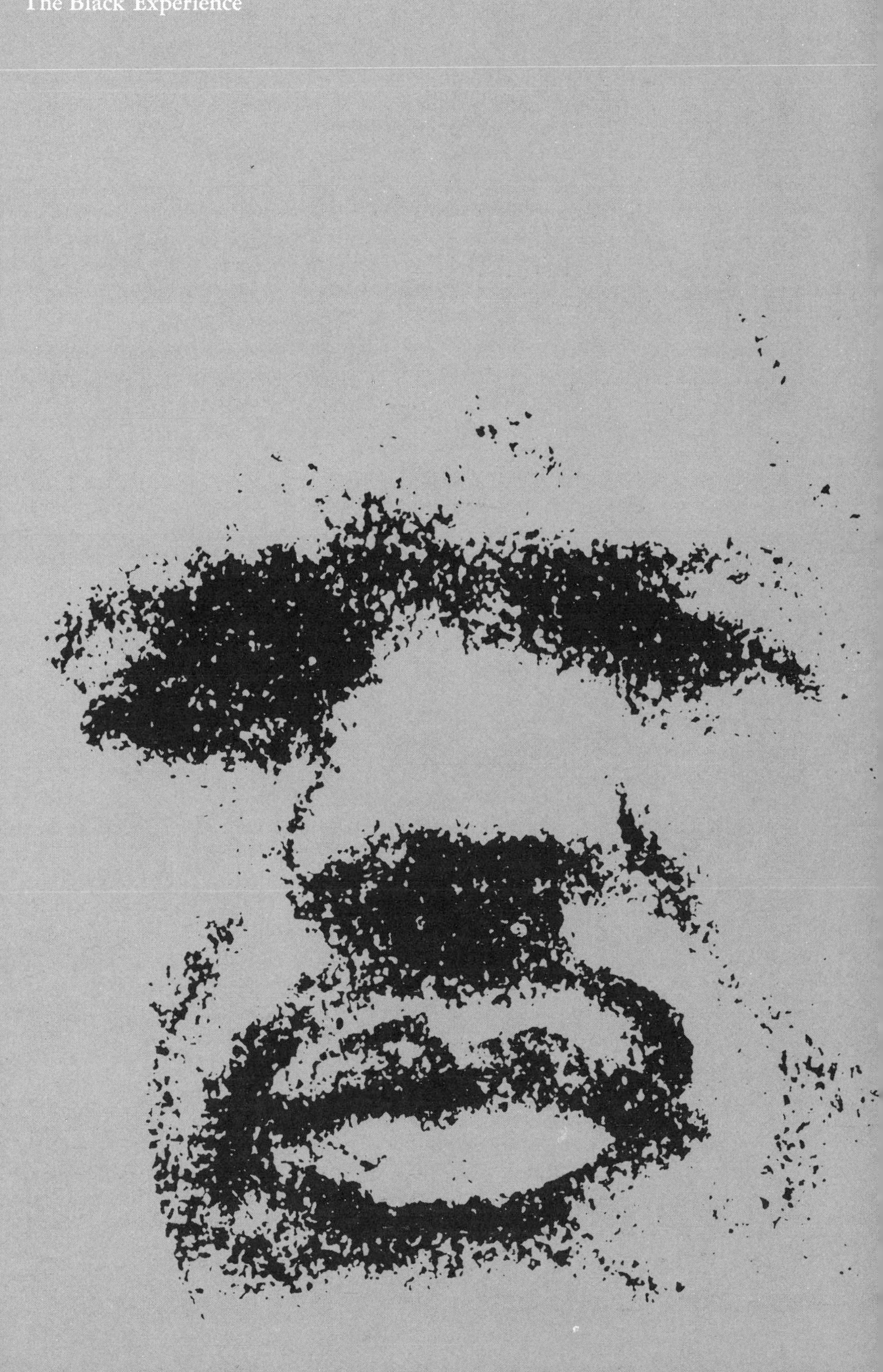

A tribe with fear of the Other.
Foreign man.
Black man.
Sexed man.
High man.
Other.
A tribe with fear of the Other.
Gene Fowler, Shaman Songs

"The price of hating other human beings is loving oneself less," writes Eldridge Cleaver in his essay "On Becoming." For Cleaver, "Rape was an insurrectionary act," a way of expressing the "bloody, hateful, bitter, and malignant nature" of his feelings toward white women. But the knife cuts with both edges. James A. Emanuel writes with profound beauty of Emmett Till, murdered in Mississippi ("allegedly for flirting with a white woman," says Cleaver) and dumped into a river.

In "The Ethics of Living Jim Crow," Richard Wright tells us how he learned, painfully, to "stay in his place," as a black man in a white man's world. Ralph Ellison's "Battle Royal," the first chapter of his autobiographical novel Invisible Man, *presents the story of a sensitive and intelligent youth who is taunted and tormented for the delectation of his town's leading white citizens. Both boys learn the rules of survival, which do not allow for insurrection.*

Warren Miller is a white author who writes convincingly of the Negro's world. In two chapters from his novel Cool World, *he evokes the empty, violent lives of young black men in the ghetto. "Debut," by Kristen Hunter, is the story of a middle-class black girl clawing her way up the social ladder, accepting the values of white society, and rejecting those of her neighborhood as her mother looks on saying, "I do believe she's learned what I've been trying to teach her after all."*

In his poem "Mulatto," Langston Hughes shows us "A little yellow/Bastard boy" rejected by his white father. In "The Negro Mother" Hughes presents a Negro mother thinking of her race's enslavement and dreaming that her dark children will one day be free: "For I will be with you until no white brother/Dares keep down the children of a Negro mother." Then, in a much less solemn tone, Hughes offers a solution to racial hatred in his story "Jazz, Jive, and Jam." As his main character, Jess Simple, says, "With a jazz band, they could work out integration in ten minutes. Everybody would have been dancing together like they all did at the Savoy — colored and white — or down on the East Side at them Casinos on a Friday night where jam holds forth — and we would have been integrated."

Finally, in "The Mystery of Black," another examination of the black experience from a white writer's point of view, Nat Hentoff tries to correct some of the remaining romantic misconceptions about the life the black man leads in America.

On Becoming

Eldridge Cleaver

Folsom Prison
June 25, 1965

Nineteen fifty-four, when I was eighteen years old, is held to be a crucial turning point in the history of the Afro-American — for the U.S.A. as a whole — the year segregation was outlawed by the U.S. Supreme Court. It was also a crucial year for me because on June 18, 1954, I began serving a sentence in state prison for possession of marijuana.

The Supreme Court decision was only one month old when I entered prison, and I do not believe that I had even the vaguest idea of its importance or historical significance. But later, the acrimonious controversy ignited by the end of the separate-but-equal doctrine was to have a profound effect on me. This controversy awakened me to my position in America and I began to form a concept of what it meant to be black in white America.

Of course I'd always known that I was black, but I'd never really stopped to take stock of what I was involved in. I met life as an individual and took my chances. Prior to 1954, we lived in an atmosphere of novocain. Negroes found it necessary, in order to maintain whatever sanity they could, to remain somewhat aloof and detached from "the problem." We accepted indignities and the mechanics of the apparatus of oppression without reacting by sitting-in or holding mass demonstrations. Nurtured by the fires of the controversy over segregation, I was soon aflame with indignation over my newly discovered social status, and inwardly I turned away from America with horror, disgust and outrage.

In Soledad state prison, I fell in with a group of young blacks who, like myself, were in vociferous rebellion against what we perceived as a continuation of slavery on a higher plane. We cursed everything American — including baseball and hot dogs. All respect we may have had for politicians, preachers, lawyers, governors, Presidents, senators, congressmen was utterly destroyed as we watched them temporizing and compromising over right and wrong, over legality and illegality, over constitutionality and unconstitutionality. We knew that in the end what they were clashing over was us, what to do with the blacks, and whether or not to start treating us as human beings. I despised all of them.

The segregationists were condemned out of hand, without even listening to their lofty, finely woven arguments. The others I despised for wasting time in debates with the segregationists: why not just crush them, put them in prison — they were defying the law, weren't they? I defied the law and they put me in prison. So why not put those dirty mothers in prison too? I had gotten caught with a shopping bag full of marijuana, a shopping bag full of love — I was in love with the weed and I did not for one minute think that anything was wrong with getting high. I had been getting high for four or five years and was convinced, with the zeal of a crusader, that marijuana was superior to lush — yet the rulers of the land seemed all to be lushes. I could not see how they were more justified in drinking than I was in blowing the gage. I was a grasshopper, and it was natural that I felt myself to be unjustly imprisoned.

While all this was going on, our group was espousing atheism. Unsophisticated and not based on any philosophical rationale, our atheism was pragmatic. I had come to believe that there is no God; if there is, men do not know anything about him. Therefore, all religions were phony — which made all preachers and priests, in our eyes, fakers, including the ones scurrying around the prison who, curiously, could put in a good word for you with the Almighty Creator of the universe but could not get anything down with the warden or parole board — they could usher you through the Pearly Gates *after you were dead,* but not through the prison gate *while you were still alive and kicking.* Besides, men of the cloth who work in prison have an ineradicable stigma attached to them in the eyes of convicts because they escort condemned men into the gas chamber. Such men of God are powerful arguments in favor of atheism. Our atheism was a source of enormous pride to me. Later on, I bolstered our arguments by reading Thomas Paine and his devastating critique of Christianity in particular and organized religion in general.

Through reading I was amazed to discover how confused people were. I had thought that, out there beyond the horizon of my own ignorance, unanimity existed, that even though I myself didn't know what was happening in the universe, other people certainly did. Yet here I was discovering that the whole U.S.A. was in a chaos of disagreement over segregation/integration. In these circumstances I decided that the only safe thing for me to do was go for myself. It became clear that it was possible for me to take the initiative: instead of simply *reacting* I could *act.* I could unilaterally — whether anyone agreed with me or not — repudiate all allegiances, morals, values — even while continuing to exist within this society. My mind would be free and no power in the universe could force me to accept something if I didn't want to. But I would take my own sweet time. That, too, was a part of my new freedom. I would accept nothing until it was proved that it was good — for me. I became an extreme iconoclast. Any affirmative assertion made by anyone around me became a target for tirades of criticism and denunciation.

This little game got good to me and I got good at it. I attacked all forms of piety, loyalty, and sentiment: marriage, love, God, patriotism, the Constitution, the founding fathers, law, concepts of right-wrong-good-evil, all forms of ritualized and conventional behavior. As I pranced about, club in hand, seeking new idols to smash, I encountered really for the first time in my life, with any seriousness, The Ogre, rising up before me in a mist. I discovered, with alarm, that The Ogre possessed a tremendous and dreadful power over me, and I didn't understand this power or why I was at its mercy. I tried to repudiate The Ogre, root it out of my heart as I had done God, Constitution, principles, morals, and values — but The Ogre had its claws buried in the core of my being and refused to let go. I fought frantically to be free, but The Ogre only mocked me and sank its claws deeper into my soul. I knew then that I had found an important key, that if I conquered The Ogre and broke its power over me I would be free. But I also knew that it was a race against time and that if I did not win I would certainly be broken and destroyed. I, a black man, confronted The Ogre — the white woman.

In prison, those things withheld from and denied to the prisoner become precisely what he wants most of all, of course. Because we were locked up in our cells before darkness fell, I used to lie awake at night racked by painful craving to take a leisurely stroll under the stars, or to go to the beach, to drive a car on a freeway, to grow a beard, or to make love to a woman.

Since I was not married conjugal visits would not have solved my problem. I therefore denounced the idea of conjugal visits as inherently unfair; single prisoners needed and deserved *action* just as married prisoners did. I advocated establishing a system under Civil Service whereby salaried women would minister to the needs of those prisoners who maintained a record of good behavior. If a married prisoner preferred his own wife, that would be his right. Since California was not about to inaugurate either conjugal visits or the Civil Service, one could advocate either with equal enthusiasm and with the same result: nothing.

This may appear ridiculous to some people. But it was very real to me and as urgent as the need to breathe, because I was in my bull stage and lack of access to females was absolutely a form of torture. I suffered. My mistress at the time of my arrest, the beautiful and lonely wife of a serviceman stationed overseas, died unexpectedly three weeks after I entered prison; and the rigid, dehumanized rules governing correspondence between prisoners and free people prevented me from corresponding with other young ladies I knew. It left me without any contact with females except those in my family.

In the process of enduring my confinement, I decided to get myself a pin-up girl to paste on the wall of my cell. I would fall in love with her and lavish my affections upon her. She, a symbolic representative of the forbidden tribe of women, would sustain me until I was free. Out of the center of *Esquire,* I married a voluptuous bride. Our marriage went along swell for a time: no quarrels, no complaints. And then, one evening when I came in from school, I was shocked and enraged to find that the guard had entered my cell, ripped my sugar from the wall, torn her into little pieces, and left the pieces floating in the commode: it was like seeing a dead body floating in a lake. Giving her a proper burial, I flushed the commode. As the saying goes, I sent her to Long Beach. But I was genuinely beside myself with anger: almost every cell, excepting those of the homosexuals, had a pin-up girl on the wall and the guards didn't bother them. Why, I asked the guard the next day, had he singled me out for special treatment?

"Don't you know we have a rule against pasting up pictures on the walls?" he asked me.

"Later for the rules," I said. "You know as well as I do that that rule is not enforced."

"Tell you what," he said, smiling at me (the smile put me on my guard), "I'll compromise with you: get yourself a colored girl for a pinup — no white women — and I'll let it stay up. Is that a deal?"

I was more embarrassed than shocked. He was laughing in my face. I called him two or three dirty names and walked away.

I can still recall his big moon-face, grinning at me over yellow teeth. The disturbing part about the whole incident was that a terrible feeling of guilt came over me as I realized that I had chosen the picture of the white girl over the available pictures of black girls. I tried to rationalize it away, but I was fascinated by the truth involved. Why hadn't I thought about it in this light before? So I took hold of the question and began to inquire into my feelings. Was it true, did I really prefer white girls over black? The conclusion was clear and inescapable: I did. I decided to check out my friends on this point and it was easy to determine, from listening to their general conversation, that the white woman occupied a peculiarly prominent place in all of our frames of reference. With what I have learned since then, this all seems terribly elementary now. But at the time, it was a tremendously intriguing adventure of discovery.

One afternoon, when a large group of Negroes was on the prison yard shooting the breeze, I grabbed the floor and posed the question: which did they prefer, white women or black? Some said Japanese women were their favorite, others said Chinese, some said European women, others said Mexican women — they all stated a preference, and they generally freely admitted their dislike for black women.

"I don't want nothing black but a Cadillac," said one.

"If money was black I wouldn't want none of it," put in another.

A short little stud, who was a very good lightweight boxer with a little man's complex that made him love to box heavyweights, jumped to his feet. He had a yellowish complexion and we called him Butterfly.

"All you niggers are sick!" Butterfly spat out. "I don't like no stinking white woman. My grandma is a white woman and I don't even like her!"

But it just so happened that Butterfly's crime partner was in the crowd, and after Butterfly had his say, his crime partner said, "Aw, sit on down and quit that lying, lil o' chump. What about that gray girl in San Jose who had your nose wide open? Did you like her, or were you just running after her with your tongue hanging out of your head because you hated her?"

Partly because he was embarrassed and partly because his crime partner was a heavyweight, Butterfly flew into him. And before we could separate them and disperse, so the guard would not know who had been fighting, Butterfly bloodied his crime partner's nose. Butterfly got away but, because of the blood, his crime partner got caught. I ate dinner with Butterfly that evening and questioned him sharply about his attitude toward white women. And after an initial evasiveness he admitted that the white woman bugged him too. "It's a sickness," he said. "All our lives we've had the white woman dangled before our eyes like a carrot on a stick before a donkey: look but don't touch." (In 1958, after I had gone out on parole and was returned to San Quentin as a parole violater with a new charge, Butterfly was still there. He had become a Black Muslim and was chiefly responsible for teaching me the Black Muslim philosophy. Upon his release from San Quentin, Butterfly joined the Los Angeles Mosque, advanced rapidly through the ranks, and is now a full-fledged minister of one of Elijah Muhammad's mosques in another city. He successfully completed his parole, got married — to a very black girl — and is doing fine.)

From our discussion, which began that evening and has never yet ended, we went on to notice how thoroughly, as a matter of course, a black growing up in America is indoctrinated with the white race's standard of beauty. Not that the whites made a conscious, calculated effort to do this, we thought, but since they constituted the majority the whites brainwashed the blacks by the very processes the whites employed to indoctrinate themselves with their own group standards. It intensified my frustrations to know that I was indoctrinated to see the white woman as more beautiful and desirable than my own black woman. It drove me into books seeking light on the subject. In Richard Wright's *Native Son,* I found Bigger Thomas and a keen insight into the problem.

My interest in this area persisted undiminished and then, in 1955, an event took place in Mississippi which turned me inside out: Emmett Till, a young Negro down from Chicago on a visit, was murdered, allegedly for flirting with a white woman. He had been shot, his head crushed from repeated blows with a blunt instrument, and his badly decomposed body was recovered from the river with a heavy weight on it. I was, of course, angry over the whole bit, but one day I saw in a magazine a picture of the white woman with whom Emmett Till was said to have flirted. While looking at the picture, I felt that little tension in the center of my chest I experience when a woman appeals to me. I was disgusted and angry with myself. Here was a woman who had caused the death of a black, possibly because, when he looked at her, he also felt the same tensions of lust and desire in his chest — and probably for the same general reasons that I felt them. It was all unacceptable to me. I looked at the picture again and again, and in spite of everything and against my will and the hate I felt for the woman and all that she represented, she appealed to me. I flew into a rage at myself, at America, at white women, at the history that had placed those tensions of lust and desire in my chest.

Two days later, I had a "nervous breakdown." For several days I ranted and raved against the white race, against white women in particular, against white America in general. When I came to myself, I was locked in a padded cell with not even the vaguest memory of how I got there. All I could recall was an eternity of pacing back and forth in the cell, preaching to the unhearing walls.

I had several sessions with a psychiatrist. His conclusion was that I hated my mother. How he arrived at this conclusion I'll never know, because he knew nothing about my mother; and when he'd ask me questions I would answer him with absurd lies. What revolted me about him was that he had heard me denouncing the whites, yet each time he interviewed me he deliberately guided the conversation back to my family life, to my childhood. That in itself was all right, but he deliberately blocked all my attempts to bring out the racial question, and he made it clear that he was not interested in my attitude toward whites. This was a Pandora's box he did not care to open. After I ceased my diatribes against the whites, I was let out of the hospital, back into the general inmate population just as if nothing had happened. I continued to brood over these events and over the dynamics of race relations in America.

During this period I was concentrating my reading in the field of economics.

Having previously dabbled in the theories and writings of Rousseau, Thomas Paine, and Voltaire, I had added a little polish to my iconoclastic stance, without, however, bothering too much to understand their affirmative positions. In economics, because everybody seemed to find it necessary to attack and condemn Karl Marx in their writings, I sought out his books, and although he kept me with a headache, I took him for my authority. I was not prepared to understand him, but I was able to see in him a thoroughgoing critique and condemnation of capitalism. It was like taking medicine for me to find that, indeed, American capitalism deserved all the hatred and contempt that I felt for it in my heart. This had a positive, stabilizing effect upon me — to an extent because I was not about to become stable — and it diverted me from my previous preoccupation: morbid broodings on the black man and the white woman. Pursuing my readings into the history of socialism, I read, with very little understanding, some of the passionate, exhortatory writings of Lenin; and I fell in love with Bakunin and Nechayev's *Catechism of the Revolutionist* — the principles of which, along with some of Machiavelli's advice, I sought to incorporate into my own behavior. I took the *Catechism* for my bible and, standing on a one-man platform that had nothing to do with the reconstruction of society, I began consciously incorporating these principles into my daily life, to employ tactics of ruthlessness in my dealings with everyone with whom I came into contact. And I began to look at white America through these new eyes.

Somehow I arrived at the conclusion that, as a matter of principle, it was of paramount importance for me to have an antagonistic, ruthless attitude toward white women. The term *outlaw* appealed to me and at the time my parole date was drawing hear, I considered myself to be mentally free — I was an "outlaw." I had stepped outside of the white man's law, which I repudiated with scorn and self-satisfaction. I became a law unto myself — my own legislature, my own supreme court, my own executive. At the moment I walked out of the prison gate, my feelings toward white women in general could be summed up in the following lines:

To a White Girl

I love you
Because you're white,
Not because you're charming
Or bright.
Your whiteness
Is a silky thread
Snaking through my thoughts
In redhot patterns
Of lust and desire.

I hate you
Because you're white.
Your white meat
Is nightmare food.
White is
The skin of Evil.
You're my Moby Dick,
White Witch,
Symbol of the rope and hanging tree,
Of the burning cross.

Loving you thus
And hating you so,
My heart is torn in two.
Crucified.

I became a rapist. To refine my technique and *modus operandi,* I started out by practicing on black girls in the ghetto — in the black ghetto where dark and vicious deeds appear not as aberrations or deviations from the norm, but as part of the sufficiency of the Evil of a day — and when I considered myself smooth enough, I crossed the tracks and sought out white prey. I did this consciously, deliberately, willfully, methodically — though looking back I see that I was in a frantic, wild, and completely abandoned frame of mind.

Rape was an insurrectionary act. It delighted me that I was defying and trampling upon the white man's law, upon his system of values, and that I was defiling his women — and this point, I believe, was the most satisfying to me because I was very resentful over the historical fact of how the white man has used the black woman. I felt I was getting revenge. From the site of the act of rape, consternation spreads outwardly in concentric circles. I wanted to send waves of consternation throughout the white race. Recently, I came upon a quotation from one of LeRoi Jones' poems, taken from his book *The Dead Lecturer:*

> A cult of death need of the simple striking arm under the street lamp. The cutters from under their rented earth. Come up, black dada nihilismus. Rape the white girls. Rape their fathers. Cut the mothers' throats.

I have lived those lines and I know that if I had not been apprehended I would have slit some white throats. There are, of course, many young blacks out there right now who are slitting white throats and raping the white girl. They are not doing this because they read LeRoi Jones' poetry, as some of his critics seem to believe. Rather, Le Roi is expressing the funky facts of life.

After I returned to prison, I took a long look at myself and, for the first time in my life, admitted that I was wrong, that I had gone astray — astray not so much from the white man's law as from being human, civilized — for I could not approve the act of rape. Even though I had some insight into my own motivations, I did not feel justified. I lost my self-respect. My pride as a man dissolved and my whole fragile moral structure seemed to collapse, completely shattered.

That is why I started to write. To save myself.

I realized that no one could save me but myself. The prison authorities were both uninterested and unable to help me. I had to seek out the truth and unravel the snarled web of my motivations. I had to find out who I am and what I want to be, what type of man I should be, and what I could do to become the best of which I was capable. I understood that what had happened to me had also happened to countless other blacks and it would happen to many, many more.

I learned that I had been taking the easy way out, running away from problems. I also learned that it is easier to do evil than it is to do good. And I have been terribly impressed by the youth of America, black and white. I am proud of them because they have reaffirmed my faith in humanity. I have come to feel what must be love for the young people of America and I want to be part of the good and greatness that they want for all people. From my prison cell, I have watched America slowly coming wake. It is not fully awake yet, but there is soul in the air and everywhere I see beauty. I have watched the sit-ins, the freedom raids, the Mississippi Blood Summers, demonstrations all over the country, the FSM movement, the teach-ins, and the mounting protest over Lyndon Strangelove's foreign policy — all of this, the thousands of little details, show me it is time to straighten up and fly right. That is why I decided to concentrate on my writings and efforts in this area. We are a very sick country — I, perhaps, am sicker than most. But I accept that. I told you in the beginning that I am extremist by nature — so it is only right that I should be extremely sick.

I was very familiar with the Eldridge who came to prison, but that Eldridge no longer exists. And the one I am now is in some ways a stranger to me. You may find this difficult to understand but it is very easy for one in prison to lose his sense of self. And if he has been undergoing all kinds of extreme, involved, and unregulated changes, then he ends up not knowing who he is. Take the point of being attractive to women. You can easily see how a man can lose his arrogance or certainty on that point while in prison! When he's in the free world, he gets constant feedback on how he looks from the number of female heads he turns when he walks down the street. In prison he gets only hate-stares and sour frowns. Years and years of bitter looks. Individuality is not nourished in prison, neither by the officials nor by the convicts. It is a deep hole out of which to climb.

What must be done, I believe, is that all these problems — particularly the sickness between the white woman and the black man — must be brought out into the open, dealt with and resolved. I know that the black man's sick attitude toward the white woman is a revolutionary sickness: it keeps him perpetually out of harmony with the system that is oppressing him. Many whites flatter themselves with the idea that the Negro male's lust and desire for the white dream girl is purely an esthetic attraction, but nothing could be farther from the truth. His motivation is often of such a bloody, hateful, bitter, and malignant nature that whites would really be hard pressed to find it flattering. I have discussed these points with prisoners who were convicted of rape, and their motivations are very plain. But they are very reluctant to discuss these things with white men who, by and large, make up the prison staffs. I believe that in the experience of these men lies the knowledge and wisdom that must be utilized to help other youngsters who are heading in the same direction. I think all of us, the entire nation, will be better off if we bring it all out front. A lot of people's feelings will be hurt, but that is the price that must be paid.

It may be that I can harm myself by speaking frankly and directly, but I do not care about that at all. Of course I want to get out of prison, badly, but I shall get out some day. I am more concerned with what I am going to be after I get out. I know that by following the course which I have charted I will find my salvation. If I had followed the path laid down for me by the officials, I'd undoubtedly have long since been out of prison — but I'd be less of a man. I'd be weaker and less certain of where I want to go, what I want to do, and how to go about it.

The price of hating other human beings is loving oneself less.

Emmett Till

James A. Emanuel

I hear a whistling
Through the water.
Little Emmett
Won't be still.
He keeps floating
Round the darkness,
Edging through
The silent chill.

Tell me, please,
That bedtime story
Of the fairy
River Boy
Who swims forever,
Deep in treasures,
Necklaced in
A coral toy.

The Ethics of Living Jim Crow
An Autobiographical Sketch
Richard Wright

My first lesson in how to live as a Negro came when I was quite small. We were living in Arkansas. Our house stood behind the railroad tracks. Its skimpy yard was paved with black cinders. Nothing green ever grew in that yard. The only touch of green we could see was far away, beyond the tracks, over where the white folks lived. But cinders were good enough for me and I never missed the green growing things. And anyhow cinders were fine weapons. You could always have a nice hot war with huge black cinders. All you had to do was crouch behind the brick pillars of a house with your hands full of gritty ammunition. And the first woolly black head you saw pop out from behind another row of pillars was your target. You tried your very best to knock it off. It was great fun.

I never fully realized the appalling disadvantages of a cinder environment till one day the gang to which I belonged found itself engaged in a war with the white boys who lived beyond the tracks. As usual we laid down our cinder barrage, thinking that this would wipe the white boys out. But they replied with a steady bombardment of broken bottles. We doubled our cinder barrage, but they hid behind trees, hedges, and the sloping embankments of their lawns. Having no such fortifications, we retreated to the brick pillars of our homes. During the retreat a broken milk bottle caught me behind the ear, opening a deep gash which bled profusely. The sight of blood pouring over my face completely demoralized our ranks. My fellow-combatants left me standing paralyzed in the center of the yard, and scurried for their homes. A kind neighbor saw me, and rushed me to a doctor, who took three stitches in my neck.

I sat brooding on my front steps, nursing my wound and waiting for my mother to come from work. I felt that a grave injustice had been done me. It was all right to throw cinders. The greatest harm a cinder could do was leave a bruise. But broken bottles were dangerous; they left you cut, bleeding, and helpless.

When night fell, my mother came from the white folks' kitchen. I raced down the street to meet her. I could just feel in my bones that she would understand. I knew she would tell me exactly what to do next time. I grabbed her hand and babbled out the whole story. She examined my wound, then slapped me.

"How come yuh didn't hide?" she asked me. "How come yuh awways fightin'?"

I was outraged, and bawled. Between sobs I told her that I didn't have any trees or hedges to hide behind. There wasn't a thing I could have used as a trench. And you couldn't throw very far when you were hiding behind the brick pillars of a house. She grabbed a barrel stave, dragged me home, stripped me naked, and beat me till I had a fever of one hundred and two. She would smack my rump with the stave, and, while the skin was still smarting impart to me gems of Jim Crow wisdom. I was never to throw cinders any more. I was never to fight any more wars. I was never, never, under any conditions, to fight *white* folks again. And they were absolutely right in clouting me with the broken milk bottle. Didn't I know she was working hard every day in the hot kitchens of the white folks to make money to take care of me? When was I ever going to learn to be a good boy? She couldn't be bothered with my fights. She finished by telling me that I ought to be thankful to God as long as I lived that they didn't kill me.

All that night I was delirious and could not sleep. Each time I closed my eyes I saw monstrous white faces suspended from the ceiling, leering at me.

From that time on, the charm of my cinder yard was gone. The green trees, the trimmed hedges, the cropped lawns grew very meaningful, became a symbol. Even today when I think of white folks, the hard, sharp outlines of white houses surrounded by trees, lawns, and hedges are present somewhere in the background of my mind. Through the years they grew into an overreaching symbol of fear.

It was a long time before I came in close contact with white folks again. We moved from Arkansas to Mississippi. Here we had the good fortune not to live behind the railroad tracks, or close to white neighborhoods. We lived in the very heart of the local Black Belt. There were black churches and black preachers; there were black schools and black teachers; black groceries and black clerks. In fact, everything was so solidly black that for a long time I did not even think of white folks, save in remote and vague terms. But this could not last forever. As one grows older one eats more. One's clothing costs more. When I finished grammar school I had to go to work. My mother could no longer feed and clothe me on her cooking job.

There is but one place where a black boy who knows no trade can get a job, and that's where the houses and faces are white, where the trees, lawns, and hedges are green. My first job was with an optical company in Jackson, Mississippi. The morning I applied I stood straight and neat before the boss, answering all his questions with sharp yessirs and nosirs. I was very careful to pronounce my *sirs* distinctly, in order that he might know that I was polite, that I knew where I was, and that I knew he was a *white* man. I wanted that job badly.

He looked me over as though he were examining a prize poodle. He questioned me closely about my schooling, being particularly insistent about how much mathematics I had had. He seemed very pleased when I told him I had had two years of algebra.

"Boy, how would you like to try to learn something around here?" he asked me.

"I'd like it fine, sir," I said, happy. I had visions of "working my way up." Even Negroes have those visions.

"All right," he said. "Come on."

I followed him to the small factory.

"Pease," he said to a white man of about thirty-five, "this is Richard. He's going to work for us."

Pease looked at me and nodded.

I was then taken to a white boy of about seventeen.

"Morrie, this is Richard, who's going to work for us."

"Whut yuh sayin' there, boy!" Morrie boomed at me.

"Fine!" I answered.

The boss instructed these two to help me, teach me, give me jobs to do, and let me learn what I could in my spare time.

My wages were five dollars a week.

I worked hard, trying to please. For the first month I got along O.K. Both Pease and Morrie seemed to like me. But one thing was missing. And I kept thinking about it. I was not learning anything and nobody was volunteering to help me. Thinking they had forgotten that I was to learn something about the mechanics of grinding lenses, I asked Morrie one day to tell me about the work. He grew red.

"Whut yuh tryin' t' do, nigger, get smart?" he asked.

"Naw; I ain' tryin' t' git smart," I said.

"Well, don't, if yuh know whut's good for yuh!"

I was puzzled. Maybe he just doesn't want to help me, I thought. I went to Pease.

"Say, are yuh crazy, you black bastard?" Pease asked me, his gray eyes growing hard.

I spoke out, reminding him that the boss had said I was to be given a chance to learn something.

"Nigger, you think you're *white,* don't you?"

"Naw, sir!"

"Well, you're acting mighty like it!"

"But, Mr. Pease, the boss said . . ."

Pease shook his fist in my face.

"This is a *white* man's work around here, and you better watch yourself!"

From then on they changed toward me. They said good-morning no more. When I was just a bit slow in performing some duty, I was called a lazy black son-of-a-bitch.

Once I thought of reporting all this to the boss. But the mere idea of what would happen to me if Pease and Morrie should learn that I had "snitched" stopped me. And after all the boss was a white man, too. What was the use?

The climax came at noon one summer day. Pease called me to his work-bench. To get to him I had to go between two narrow benches and stand with my back against a wall.

"Yes, sir," I said.

"Richard, I want to ask you something," Pease began pleasantly, not looking up from his work.

"Yes, sir," I said again.

Morrie came over, blocking the narrow passage between the benches. He folded his arms, staring at me solemnly.

I looked from one to the other, sensing that something was coming.

"Yes, sir," I said for the third time.

Pease looked up and spoke very slowly.

"Richard, *Mr.* Morrie here tells me you called me *Pease.*"

I stiffened. A void seemed to open up in me. I knew this was the show-down.

He meant that I had failed to call him Mr. Pease. I looked at Morrie. He was gripping a steel bar in his hands. I opened my mouth to speak, to protest, to assure Pease that I had never called him simply *Pease,* and that I had never had any intentions of doing so, when Morrie grabbed me by the collar, ramming my head against the wall.

"Now, be careful, nigger!" snarled Morrie, baring his teeth. "*I* heard yuh call 'im *Pease!* 'N' if yuh say yuh didn't, yuh're callin' me a *lie,* see?" He waved the steel bar threateningly.

If I had said: No, sir, Mr. Pease, I never called you *Pease,* I would have been automatically calling Morrie a liar. And if I had said: Yes, sir, Mr. Pease, I called you *Pease,* I would have been pleading guilty to having uttered the worst insult that a Negro can utter to a southern white man. I stood hesitating, trying to frame a neutral reply.

"Richard, I asked you a question!" said Pease. Anger was creeping into his voice.

"I don't remember calling you *Pease,* Mr. Pease," I said cautiously. "And if I did, I sure didn't mean . . ."

"You black son-of-a-bitch! You called me *Pease,* then!" he spat, slapping me till I bent sideways over a bench. Morrie was on top of me, demanding:

"Didn't yuh call 'im *Pease?* If yuh say yuh didn't, I'll rip yo' gut string loose with this bar, yuh black granny dodger! Yuh can't call a white man a lie 'n' git erway with it, you black son-of-a-bitch!"

I wilted. I begged them not to bother me. I knew what they wanted. They wanted me to leave.

"I'll leave," I promised. "I'll leave right *now.*"

They gave me a minute to get out of the factory. I was warned not to show up again, or tell the boss.

I went.

When I told the folks at home what had happened, they called me a fool. They told me that I must never again attempt to exceed my boundaries. When you are working for white folks, they said, you got to "stay in your place" if you want to keep working.

II

My Jim Crow education continued on my next job, which was portering in a clothing store. One morning, while polishing brass out front, the boss and his twenty-year-old son got out of their car and half dragged and half kicked a Negro woman into the store. A policeman standing at the corner looked on, twirling his nightstick. I watched out of the corner of my eye, never slackening the strokes of my chamois upon the brass. After a few minutes, I heard shrill screams coming from the rear of the store. Later the woman stumbled out, bleeding, crying, and holding her stomach. When she reached the end of the block, the policeman grabbed her and accused her of being drunk. Silently, I watched him throw her into a patrol wagon.

When I went to the rear of the store, the boss and his son were washing their hands at the sink. They were chuckling. The floor was bloody and strewn with wisps of hair and clothing. No doubt I must have appeared pretty shocked, for the boss slapped me reassuringly on the back.

"Boy, that's what we do to niggers when they don't want to pay their bills," he said, laughing.

His son looked at me and grinned.

"Here, hava cigarette," he said.

Not knowing what to do, I took it. He lit his and held the match for me. This was a gesture of kindness, indicating that even if they had beaten the poor old woman, they would not beat me if I knew enough to keep my mouth shut.

"Yes, sir," I said, and asked no questions.

After they had gone, I sat on the edge of a packing box and stared at the bloody floor till the cigarette went out.

That day at noon, while eating in a hamburger joint, I told my fellow Negro porters what had happened. No one seemed surprised. One fellow, after swallowing a huge bite, turned to me and asked:

"Huh! Is tha' all they did t' her?"

"Yeah. Wasn't tha' enough?" I asked.

"Shucks! Man, she's a lucky bitch!" he said, burying his lips deep into a juicy hamburger. "Hell, it's a wonder they didn't lay her when they got through."

III

I was learning fast, but not quite fast enough. One day, while I was delivering packages in the suburbs, my bicycle tire was punctured. I walked along the hot, dusty road, sweating and leading my bicycle by the handle-bars.

A car slowed at my side.

"What's the matter, boy?" a white man called.

I told him my bicycle was broken and I was walking back to town.

"That's too bad," he said. "Hop on the running board."

He stopped the car. I clutched hard at my bicycle with one hand and clung to the side of the car with the other.

"All set?"

"Yes, sir," I answered. The car started.

It was full of young white men. They were drinking. I watched the flask pass from mouth to mouth.

"Wanna drink, boy?" one asked.

I laughed as the wind whipped my face. Instinctively obeying the freshly planted precepts of my mother, I said:

"Oh, no!"

The words were hardly out of my mouth before I felt something hard and cold smash me between the eyes. It was an empty whisky bottle. I saw stars, and fell backwards from the speeding car into the dust of the road, my feet becoming entangled in the steel spokes of my bicycle. The white men piled out and stood over me.

"Nigger, ain' yuh learned no better sense'n tha' yet?" asked the man who hit me. "Ain' yuh learned t' say *sir* t' a white man yet?"

Dazed, I pulled to my feet. My elbows and legs were bleeding. Fists doubled, the white man advanced, kicking my bicycle out of the way.

"Aw, leave the bastard alone. He's got enough," said one.

They stood looking at me. I rubbed my shins, trying to stop the flow of blood. No doubt they felt a sort of contemptuous pity, for one asked:

"Yuh wanna ride t' town now, nigger? Yuh reckon yuh know enough t' ride now?"

"I wanna walk," I said, simply.

Maybe it sounded funny. They laughed.

"Well, walk, yuh black son-of-a-bitch!"

When they left they comforted me with:

"Nigger, yuh sho better be damn glad it wuz us yuh talked t' tha' way. Yuh're a lucky bastard, 'cause if yuh'd said tha' t' somebody else, yuh might've been a dead nigger now."

IV

Negroes who have lived South know the dread of being caught alone upon the streets in white neighborhoods after the sun has set. In such a simple situation as this the plight of the Negro in America is graphically symbolized. While white strangers may be in these neighborhoods trying to get home, they can pass unmolested. But the color of a Negro's skin makes him easily recognizable, makes him suspect, converts him into a defenseless target.

Late one Saturday night I made some

deliveries in a white neighborhood. I was pedaling my bicycle back to the store as fast as I could, when a police car, swerving toward me, jammed me into the curbing.

"Get down and put up your hands!" the policemen ordered.

I did. They climbed out of the car, guns drawn, faces set, and advanced slowly.

"Keep still!" they ordered.

I reached my hands higher. They searched my pockets and packages. They seemed dissatisfied when they could find nothing incriminating. Finally, one of them said:

"Boy, tell your boss not to send you out in white neighborhoods after sundown."

As usual, I said:

"Yes, sir."

V

My next job was as hall-boy in a hotel. Here my Jim Crow education broadened and deepened. When the bell-boys were busy, I was often called to assist them. As many of the rooms in the hotel were occupied by prostitutes, I was constantly called to carry them liquor and cigarettes. These women were nude most of the time. They did not bother about clothing, even for bell-boys. When you went into their rooms, you were supposed to take their nakedness for granted, as though it startled you no more than a blue vase or a red rug. Your presence awoke in them no sense of shame, for you were not regarded as human. If they were alone, you could steal sidelong glimpses at them. But if they were receiving men, not a flicker of your eyelids could show. I remember one incident vividly. A new woman, a huge, snowy-skinned blonde, took a room on my floor. I was sent to wait upon her. She was in bed with a thick-set man; both were nude and uncovered. She said she wanted some liquor and slid out of bed and waddled across the floor to get her money from a dresser drawer. I watched her.

"Nigger, what in hell you looking at?" the white man asked me, raising himself upon his elbows.

"Nothing," I answered, looking miles deep into the blank wall of the room.

"Keep your eyes where they belong, if you want to be healthy!" he said.

"Yes, sir."

VI

One of the bell-boys I knew in this hotel was keeping steady company with one of the Negro maids. Out of a clear sky the police descended upon his home and arrested him, accusing him of bastardy. The poor boy swore he had had no intimate relations with the girl. Nevertheless, they forced him to marry her. When the child arrived, it was found to be much lighter in complexion than either of the two supposedly legal parents. The white men around the hotel made a great joke of it. They spread the rumor that some white cow must have scared the poor girl while she was carrying the baby. If you were in their presence when this explanation was offered, you were supposed to laugh.

VII

One of the bell-boys was caught in bed with a white prostitute. He was castrated and run out of town. Immediately after this all the bell-boys and hall-boys were called together and warned. We were given to understand that the boy who had been castrated was a "mighty, mighty lucky bastard." We were impressed with the fact that next time the management of the hotel would not be responsible for the lives of "trouble-makin' niggers." We were silent.

VIII

One night, just as I was about to go home, I met one of the Negro maids. She lived in my direction, and we fell in to walk part of the way home together. As we passed the white night-watchman, he slapped the maid on her buttock. I turned around, amazed. The watchman looked at me with a long, hard, fixed-under stare. Suddenly he pulled his gun and asked:

"Nigger, don't yuh like it?"

I hesitated.

"I asked yuh don't yuh like it?" he asked again, stepping forward.

"Yes, sir," I mumbled.

"Talk like it, then!"

"Oh, yes, sir!" I said with as much heartiness as I could muster.

Outside, I walked ahead of the girl, ashamed to face her. She caught up with me and said:

"Don't be a fool! Yuh couldn't help it!"

This watchman boasted of having killed two Negroes in self-defense.

Yet, in spite of all this, the life of the hotel ran with an amazing smoothness. It would have been impossible for a stranger to detect anything. The maids, the hall-boys, and the bell-boys were all smiles. They had to be.

IX

I had learned my Jim Crow lessons so thoroughly that I kept the hotel job till I left Jackson for Memphis. It so happened that while in Memphis I applied for a job at a branch of the optical company. I was hired. And for some reason, as long as I worked there, they never brought my past against me.

Here my Jim Crow education assumed quite a different form. It was no longer brutally cruel, but subtly cruel. Here I learned to lie, to steal, to dissemble. I learned to play that dual role which every Negro must play if he wants to eat and live.

For example, it was almost impossible to get a book to read. It was assumed that after a Negro had imbibed what scanty schooling the state furnished he had no further need for books. I was always borrowing books from men on the job. One day I mustered enough courage to ask one of the men to let me get books from the library in his name. Surprisingly, he consented. I cannot help but think that he consented because he was a Roman Catholic and felt a vague sympathy for Negroes, being himself an object of hatred. Armed with a library card, I obtained books in the following manner: I would write a note to the librarian, saying: "Please let this nigger boy have the following books." I would then sign it with the white man's name.

When I went to the library, I would stand at the desk, hat in hand, looking as unbookish as possible. When I received the books desired I would take them home. If the books listed in the note happened to be out, I would sneak into the lobby and forge a new one. I never took any chances guessing with the white librarian about what the fictitious white man would want to read. No doubt if any of the white patrons had suspected that some of the volumes they enjoyed had been in the home of a Negro, they would not have tolerated it for an instant.

The factory force of the optical company

in Memphis was much larger than that in Jackson, and more urbanized. At least they liked to talk, and would engage the Negro help in conversation whenever possible. By this means I found that many subjects were taboo from the white man's point of view. Among the topics they did not like to discuss with Negroes were the following: American white women; the Ku Klux Klan; France, and how Negro soldiers fared while there; French women; Jack Johnson; the entire northern part of the United States; the Civil War; Abraham Lincoln; U. S. Grant; General Sherman; Catholics; the Pope; Jews; the Republican Party; slavery; social equality; Communism; Socialism; the 13th and 14th Amendments to the Constitution; or any topic calling for positive knowledge or manly self-assertion on the part of the Negro. The most accepted topics were sex and religion.

There were many times when I had to exercise a great deal of ingenuity to keep out of trouble. It is a southern custom that all men must take off their hats when they enter an elevator. And especially did this apply to us blacks with rigid force. One day I stepped into an elevator with my arms full of packages. I was forced to ride with my hat on. Two white men stared at me coldly. Then one of them very kindly lifted my hat and placed it upon my armful of packages. Now the most accepted response for a Negro to make under such circumstances is to look at the white man out of the corner of his eye and grin. To have said: "Thank you!" would have made the white man *think* that you *thought* you were receiving from him a personal service. For such an act I have seen Negroes take a blow in the mouth. Finding the first alternative distasteful, and the second dangerous, I hit upon an acceptable course of action which fell safely between these two poles. I immediately — no sooner than my hat was lifted — pretended that my packages were about to spill, and appeared deeply distressed with keeping them in my arms. In this fashion I evaded having to acknowledge his service, and, in spite of adverse circumstances, salvaged a slender shred of personal pride.

How do Negroes feel about the way they have to live? How do they discuss it when alone among themselves? I think this question can be answered in a single sentence. A friend of mine who ran an elevator once told me:

"Lawd, man! Ef it wuzn't fer them polices 'n' them ol' lynch-mobs, there wouldn't be nothin' but uproar down here!"

Battle Royal

Ralph Ellison

It goes a long way back, some twenty years. All my life I had been looking for something, and everywhere I turned someone tried to tell me what it was. I accepted their answers too, though they were often in contradiction and even self-contradictory. I was naïve. I was looking for myself and asking everyone except myself questions which I, and only I, could answer. It took me a long time and much painful boomeranging of my expectations to achieve a realization everyone else appears to have been born with: That I am nobody but myself. But first I had to discover that I am an invisible man!

And yet I am no freak of nature, nor of history. I was in the cards, other things having been equal (or unequal) eighty-five years ago. I am not ashamed of my grandparents for having been slaves. I am only ashamed of myself for having at one time been ashamed. About eighty-five years ago they were told that they were free, united with others of our country in everything pertaining to the common good, and, in everything social, separate like the fingers of the hand. And they believed it. They exulted in it. They stayed in their place, worked hard, and brought up my father to do the same. But my grandfather is the one. He was an odd old guy, my grandfather, and I am told I take after him. It was he who caused the trouble. On his deathbed he called my father to him and said, "Son, after I'm gone I want you to keep up the good fight. I never told you, but our life is a war and I have been a traitor all my born days, a spy in the enemy's country ever since I give up my gun back in the Reconstruction. Live with your head in the lion's mouth. I want you to overcome 'em with yeses, undermine 'em with grins, agree 'em to death and destruction, let 'em swoller you till they vomit or bust wide open." They thought the old man had gone out of his mind. He had been the meekest of men. The younger children were rushed from the room, the shades drawn and the flame of the lamp turned so low that it sputtered on the wick like the old man's breathing. "Learn it to the younguns," he whispered fiercely; then he died.

But my folks were more alarmed over his last words than over his dying. It was as though he had not died at all, his words caused so much anxiety. I was warned emphatically to forget what he had said and, indeed, this is the first time it has been mentioned outside the family circle. It had a tremendous effect upon me, however. I could never be sure of what he meant. Grandfather had been a quiet old man who never made any trouble, yet on his deathbed he had called himself a traitor and a spy, and he had spoken of his meekness as a dangerous activity. It became a constant puzzle which lay unanswered in the back of my mind. And whenever things went well for me I remembered my grandfather and felt guilty and uncomfortable. It was as though I was carrying out his advice in spite of myself. And to make it worse, everyone loved me for it. I was praised by the most lily-white men of the town. I was considered an example of desirable conduct — just as my grandfather had been. And what puzzled me was that the old man had defined it as *treachery*. When I was praised for my conduct I felt a guilt that in some way I was doing something that was really against the wishes of the white folks, that if they had understood they would have desired me to act just the opposite, that I should have been sulky and mean, and that that really would have been what they wanted, even though they were fooled and thought they wanted me to act as I did. It made me afraid that some day they would look upon me as a traitor and I would be lost. Still I was more afraid to act any other way because they didn't like that at all. The old man's words were like a curse. On my graduation day I delivered an oration in which I showed that humility was the secret, indeed, the very essence of progress. (Not that I believed this — how could I, remembering my grandfather? — I only believed that it worked.) It was a great success. Everyone praised me and I was invited to give the speech at a gathering of the town's leading white citizens. It was a triumph for our whole community.

It was in the main ballroom of the leading hotel. When I got there I discovered that it was on the occasion of a smoker, and I was told that since I was to be there anyway I might as well take part in the battle royal to be fought by some of my schoolmates as part of the entertainment. The battle royal came first.

All of the town's big shots were there in their tuxedoes, wolfing down the buffet foods, drinking beer and whiskey and smoking black cigars. It was a large room with a high ceiling. Chairs were arranged in neat rows around three sides of a portable boxing ring. The fourth side was clear, revealing a gleaming space of polished floor. I had some misgivings over the battle royal, by the way. Not from a distaste for fighting, but because I didn't care too much for the other fellows who were to take part. They were tough guys who seemed to have no grandfather's curse worrying their minds. No one could mistake their toughness. And besides, I suspected that fighting a battle royal might detract from the dignity of my speech. In those pre-invisible days I visualized myself as a potential Booker T. Washington. But the other fellows didn't care too much for me either, and there were nine of them. I felt superior to them in my way, and I didn't like the manner in which we were all crowded together into the servants' elevator. Nor did they like my being there. In fact, as the warmly lighted floors flashed past the elevator we had words over the fact that I, by taking part in the fight, had knocked one of their friends out of a night's work.

We were led out of the elevator through a rococo hall into an anteroom and told to get into our fighting togs. Each of us was issued a pair of boxing gloves and ushered out into the big mirrored hall, which we entered looking cautiously about us and whispering, lest we might accidentally be heard above the noise of the room. It was foggy with cigar smoke. And already the whiskey was taking effect. I was shocked to see some of the most important men of the town quite tipsy. They were all there — bankers, lawyers, judges, doctors, fire chiefs, teachers, merchants. Even one of the more fashionable pastors. Something we could not see was going on up front. A clarinet was vibrating sensuously and the men were standing up and moving eagerly forward. We were a small tight group, clustered together, our bare upper bodies touching and shining with anticipatory sweat; while up front the big shots were becoming increasingly excited over something we still could not see. Suddenly I heard the school superintendent, who had told me to come, yell, "Bring up the shines, gentlemen! Bring up the little shines!"

We were rushed up to the front of the ballroom, where it smelled even more strongly of tobacco and whiskey. Then we were pushed into place. I almost wet my pants. A sea of faces, some hostile, some amused, ringed around us, and in the center, facing us, stood a magnificent blonde — stark naked. There was dead silence. I felt a blast of cold air chill me. I tried to back away, but they were behind me and around me. Some of the boys stood with lowered heads, trembling. I felt a wave of irrational guilt and fear. My teeth chattered, my skin turned to goose flesh, my knees knocked. Yet I was strongly attracted and looked in spite of myself. Had the price of looking been blindness, I would have looked. The hair was yellow like that of a circus kewpie doll, the face heavily powdered and rouged, as though to form an abstract mask, the eyes hollow and smeared a cool blue, the color of a baboon's butt. I felt a desire to spit upon her as my eyes brushed slowly over her body. Her breasts were firm and round as the domes of East Indian temples, and I stood so close as to see the fine skin texture and beads of pearly perspiration glistening like dew around the pink and erected buds of her nipples. I wanted at one and the same time to run from the room, to sink through the floor, or go to her and cover her from my eyes and the eyes of the others with my body; to feel the soft thighs, to caress her and destroy her, to love her and murder her, to hide from her, and yet to stroke where below the small American flag tattooed upon her belly her thighs formed a capital V. I had a notion that of all in the room she saw only me with her impersonal eyes.

And then she began to dance, a slow sensuous movement; the smoke of a hundred cigars clinging to her like the thinnest of veils. She seemed like a fair bird-girl girdled in veils calling to me from the angry surface of some gray and threatening sea. I was transported. Then I became aware of the clarinet playing and the big shots yelling at us. Some threatened us if we looked and others if we did not. On my right I saw one boy faint. And now a man grabbed a silver pitcher from a table and stepped close as he dashed ice water upon him and stood him up and forced two of us to support him as his head hung and moans issued from his thick bluish lips. Another boy began to plead to go home. He was the largest of the group, wearing dark red fighting trunks much too small to conceal the erection which projected from him as though in answer to the insinuating low-registered moaning of the clarinet. He tried to hide himself with his boxing gloves.

And all the while the blonde continued dancing, smiling faintly at the big shots who watched her with fascination, and faintly smiling at our fear. I noticed a certain merchant who followed her hungrily, his lips loose and drooling. He was a large man who wore diamond studs in a shirtfront which swelled with the ample paunch underneath, and each time the blonde swayed her undulating hips he ran his hand through the thin hair of his bald head and, with his arms upheld, his posture clumsy like that of an intoxicated panda, wound his belly in a slow and obscene grind. This creature was completely hypnotized. The music had quickened. As the dancer flung herself about with a detached expression on her face, the men began reaching out to touch her. I could see their beefy fingers sink into the soft flesh. Some of the others tried to stop them and she began to move around the floor in graceful circles, as they gave chase, slipping and sliding over the polished floor. It was mad. Chairs went crashing, drinks were spilt, as they ran laughing and howling after her. They caught her just as she reached a door, raised her from the floor, and tossed her as college boys are tossed at a hazing, and above her red, fixed-smiling lips I saw the terror and disgust in her eyes, almost like my own terror and that which I saw in some of the other boys. As I watched, they tossed her twice and her soft breasts seemed to flatten against the air and her legs flung wildly as she spun. Some of the more sober ones helped her to escape. And I started off the floor, heading for the anteroom with the rest of the boys.

Some were still crying and in hysteria. But as we tried to leave we were stopped and ordered to get into the ring. There was nothing to do but what we were told. All ten of us climbed under the ropes and allowed ourselves to be blindfolded with broad bands of white cloth. One of the men seemed to feel a bit sympathetic and tried to cheer us up as we stood with our backs against the ropes. Some of us tried to grin. "See that boy over there?" one of the men said. "I want you to run across at the bell and give it to him right in the belly. If you don't get him, I'm going to get you. I don't like his looks." Each of us was told the same. The blindfolds were put on. Yet even then I had been going over my speech. In my mind each word was as bright as flame. I felt the cloth pressed into place, and frowned so that it would be loosened when I relaxed.

But now I felt a sudden fit of blind terror. I was unused to darkness. It was as though I had suddenly found myself in a dark room filled with poisonous cottonmouths. I could hear the bleary voices yelling insistently for the battle royal to begin.

"Get going in there!"

"Let me at the big nigger!"

I strained to pick up the school superintendent's voice, as though to squeeze some security out of that slightly more familiar sound.

"Let me at those black sonsabitches!" someone yelled.

"No, Jackson, no!" another voice yelled. "Here, somebody, help me hold Jack."

"I want to get at that ginger-colored nigger. Tear him limb from limb," the first voice yelled.

I stood against the ropes trembling. For in those days I was what they called ginger-colored, and he sounded as though he might crunch me between his teeth like a crisp ginger cookie.

Quite a struggle was going on. Chairs were being kicked about and I could hear voices grunting as with a terrific effort. I wanted to see, to see more desperately than ever before. But the blindfold was as tight as a thick skin-puckering scab and when I raised my gloved hands to push the layers of white aside a voice yelled, "Oh, no you don't, black bastard! Leave that alone!"

"Ring the bell before Jackson kills him a coon!" someone boomed in the sudden silence. And I heard the bell clang and the sound of the feet scuffling forward.

A glove smacked against my head. I pivoted, striking out stiffly as someone went past, and felt the jar ripple along the length of my arm to my shoulder. Then it seemed as though all nine of the boys had turned upon me at once. Blows pounded me from all sides while I struck out as best I could. So many blows landed upon me that I wondered if I were not the only blindfolded fighter in the ring, or if the man called Jackson hadn't succeeded in getting me after all.

Blindfolded, I could no longer control my emotions. I had no dignity. I stumbled about like a baby or a drunken man. The smoke had become thicker and with each new blow it seemed to sear and further restrict my lungs. My saliva became like hot bitter glue. A glove connected with my head, filling my mouth with warm blood. It was everywhere. I could not tell if the moisture I felt upon my body was sweat or blood. A blow landed hard against the nape of my neck. I felt myself going over, my head hitting the floor. Streaks of blue light filled the black world behind the blindfold. I lay prone, pretending that I was knocked out, but felt myself seized by hands and yanked to my feet. "Get going, black boy! Mix it up!" My arms were like lead, my head smarting from blows. I managed to feel my way to the ropes and held on, trying to catch my breath. A glove landed in my midsection and I went over again, feeling as though the smoke had become a knife jabbed into my guts. Pushed this way and that by the legs milling around me, I finally pulled erect and discovered that I could see the black, sweat-washed forms weaving in the smoky-blue atmosphere like drunken dancers weaving to the rapid drum-like thuds of blows.

Everyone fought hysterically. It was complete anarchy. Everybody fought everybody else. No group fought together for long. Two, three, four, fought one, then turned to fight each other, were themselves attacked. Blows landed below the belt and in the kidney, with the gloves open as well as closed, and with my eye partly opened now there was not so much terror. I moved carefully, avoiding blows, although not too many to attract attention, fighting from group to group. The boys groped about like blind, cautious crabs crouching to protect their mid-sections, their heads pulled in short against their shoulders, their arms stretched nervously before them, with their fists testing the smoke-filled air like the knobbed feelers of hypersensitive snails. In one corner I glimpsed a boy violently punching the air and heard him scream in pain as he smashed his hand against a ring post. For a second I saw him bent over holding his hand, then going down as a blow caught his unprotected head. I played one group against the other, slipping in and throwing a punch then stepping out of range while pushing the others into the melee to take the blows blindly aimed at me. The smoke was agonizing and there were no rounds, no bells at three minute intervals to relieve our exhaustion. The room spun round me, a swirl of lights, smoke, sweating bodies surrounded by tense white faces. I bled from both nose and mouth, the blood spattering upon my chest.

The men kept yelling, "Slug him, black boy! Knock his guts out!"

"Uppercut him! Kill him! Kill that big boy!"

Taking a fake fall, I saw a boy going down heavily beside me as though we were felled by a single blow, saw a sneaker-clad foot shoot into his groin as the two who had knocked him down stumbled upon him. I rolled out of range, feeling a twinge of nausea.

The harder we fought the more threatening the men became. And yet, I had begun to worry about my speech again. How would it go? Would they recognize my ability? What would they give me?

I was fighting automatically when suddenly I noticed that one after another of the boys was leaving the ring. I was surprised, filled with panic, as though I had been left alone with an unknown danger. Then I understood. The boys had arranged it among themselves. It was the custom for the two men left in the ring to slug it out for the winner's prize. I discovered this too late. When the bell sounded two men in tuxedos leaped into the ring and removed the blindfold. I found myself facing Tatlock, the biggest of the gang. I felt sick at my stomach. Hardly had the bell stopped ringing in my ears than it clanged again and I saw him moving swiftly toward me. Thinking of nothing else to do I hit him smash on the nose. He kept coming, bringing the rank sharp violence of stale sweat. His face was a black blank of a face, only his eyes alive — with hate of me and aglow with a feverish terror from what had happened to us all. I became anxious. I wanted to deliver my speech and he came at me as though he meant to beat it out of me. I smashed him again and again, taking his blows as they came. Then on a sudden impulse I struck him lightly and as we clinched, I whispered, "Fake like I knocked you out, you can have the prize."

"I'll break your behind," he whispered hoarsely.

"For *them?*"

"For *me,* sonofabitch."

They were yelling for us to break it up and Tatlock spun me half around with a blow, and as a joggled camera sweeps in a reeling scene, I saw the howling red faces crouching tense beneath the cloud of blue-gray smoke. For a moment the world wavered, unraveled, flowed, then my head cleared and Tatlock bounced before me. That fluttering shadow before my eyes was his jabbing left hand. Then falling forward, my head against his damp shoulder, I whispered,

"I'll make it five dollars more."

"Go to hell!"

But his muscles relaxed a trifle beneath my pressure and I breathed, "Seven?"

"Give it to your ma," he said, ripping me beneath the heart.

And while I still held him I butted him and moved away. I felt myself bombarded with punches. I fought back with hopeless desperation. I wanted to deliver my speech more than anything else in the world, because I felt that only these men could judge truly my ability, and now this stupid clown was ruining my chances. I began fighting carefully now, moving in to punch him and out again with my greater speed. A lucky blow to his chin and I had him going too — until I heard a loud voice yell, "I got my money on the big boy."

Hearing this, I almost dropped my guard. I was confused: Should I try to win against the voice out there? Would not this go against my speech, and was not this a moment for humility, for nonresistance? A blow to my head as I danced about sent my right eye popping like a jack-in-the-box and settled my dilemma. The room went red as I fell. It was a dream fall, my body languid and fastidious as to where to land, until the floor became impatient and smashed up to meet me. A moment later I came to. An hypnotic voice said FIVE emphatically. And I lay there, hazily watching a dark red spot of my own blood shaping itself into a butterfly, glistening and soaking into the soiled gray world of the canvas.

When the voice drawled TEN I was lifted up and dragged to a chair. I sat dazed. My eye pained and swelled with each throb of my pounding heart and I wondered if now I would be allowed to speak. I was wringing wet, my mouth still bleeding. We were grouped along the wall now. The other boys ignored me as they congratulated Tatlock and speculated as to how much they would be paid. One boy whimpered over his smashed hand. Looking up front, I saw attendants in white jackets rolling the portable ring away and placing a small square rug in the vacant space surrounded by chairs. Perhaps, I thought, I will stand on the rug to deliver my speech.

Then the M.C. called to us, "Come on up here boys and get your money."

We ran forward to where the men laughed and talked in their chairs, waiting. Everyone seemed friendly now.

"There it is on the rug," the man said. I saw the rug covered with coins of all dimensions and a few crumpled bills. But what excited me, scattered here and there, were the gold pieces.

"Boys, it's all yours," the man said. "You get all you grab."

"That's right, Sambo," a blond man said, winking at me confidentially.

I trembled with excitement, forgetting my pain. I would get the gold and the bills, I thought. I would use both hands. I would throw my body against the boys nearest me to block them from the gold.

"Get down around the rug now," the man commanded, "and don't anyone touch it until I give the signal."

"This ought to be good," I heard.

As told, we got around the square rug on our knees. Slowly the man raised his freckled hand as we followed it upward with our eyes.

I heard, "These niggers look like they're about to pray!"

Then, "Ready," the man said. "Go!"

I lunged for a yellow coin lying on the blue design of the carpet, touching it and sending a surprised shriek to join those rising around me. I tried frantically to remove my hand but could not let go. A hot, violent force tore through my body, shaking me like a wet rat. The rug was electrified. The hair bristled up on my head as I shook myself free. My muscles jumped, my nerves jangled, writhed. But I saw that this was not stopping the other boys. Laughing in fear and embarrassment, some were holding back and scooping up the coins knocked off by the painful contortions of the others. The men roared above us as we struggled.

"Pick it up, goddamnit, pick it up!" someone called like a bass-voice parrot. "Go on, get it!"

I crawled rapidly around the floor, picking up the coins, trying to avoid the coppers and to get greenbacks and the gold. Ignoring the shock by laughing, as I brushed the coins off quickly, I discovered that I could contain the electricity — a contradiction, but it works. Then the men began to push us onto the rug. Laughing embarrassedly, we struggled out of their hands and kept after the coins. We were all wet and slippery and hard to hold. Suddenly I saw a boy lifted into the air, glistening with sweat like a circus seal, and dropped, his wet back landing flush upon the charged rug, heard him yell and saw him literally dance upon his back, his elbows beating a frenzied tattoo upon the floor, his muscles twitching like the flesh of a horse stung by many flies. When he finally rolled off, his face was gray and no one stopped him when he ran from the floor amid booming laughter.

"Get the money," the M.C. called. "That's good hard American cash!"

And we snatched and grabbed, snatched and grabbed. I was careful not to come too close to the rug now, and when I felt the hot whiskey breath descend upon me like a cloud of foul air I reached out and grabbed the leg of a chair. It was occupied and I held on desperately.

"Leggo nigger! Leggo!"

The huge face wavered down to mine as he tried to push me free. But my body was slippery and he was too drunk. It was Mr. Colcord, who owned a chain of movie houses and "entertainment palaces." Each time he grabbed me I slipped out of his hands. It became a real struggle. I feared the rug more than I did the drunk, so I held on, surprising myself for a moment by trying to topple *him* upon the rug. It was such an enormous idea that I found myself actually carrying it out. I tried not to be obvious, yet when I grabbed his leg, trying to tumble him out of the chair, he raised up roaring with laughter, and, looking at me with soberness dead in the eye, kicked me viciously in the chest. The chair leg flew out of my hand and I felt myself going and rolled. It was as though I had rolled through a bed of hot coals. It seemed a whole century would pass before I would roll free, a century in which I was seared through the deepest levels of my body to the fearful breath within me and the breath seared and heated to the point of explosion. It'll all be over in a flash, I thought as I rolled clear. It'll all be over in a flash.

But not yet, the men on the other side were waiting, red faces swollen as though from apoplexy as they bent forward in their chairs. Seeing their fingers coming toward me I rolled away as a fumbled football rolls off the receiver's fingertips, back into the coals. That time I luckily sent the rug sliding out of place and heard the coins ringing against the floor and the boys scuffling to pick them up and the M.C. calling, "All right, boys, that's all. Go get dressed and get your money."

I was limp as a dish rag. My back felt as though it had been beaten with wires.

When we had dressed the M.C. came in and gave us each five dollars, except Tatlock, who got ten for being last in the ring. Then he told us to leave. I was not to get a chance to deliver my speech, I thought. I was going out into the dim alley in despair when I was stopped and told to go back. I returned to the ballroom, where the men were pushing back their chairs and gathering in groups to talk.

The M.C. knocked on a table for quiet. "Gentlemen," he said, "we almost forgot an important part of the program. A most serious part, gentlemen. This boy was brought here to deliver a speech which he made at his graduation yesterday . . ."

"Bravo!"

"I'm told that he is the smartest boy we've got out there in Greenwood. I'm told that he knows more big words than a pocket-sized dictionary."

Much applause and laughter.

"So now, gentlemen, I want you to give him your attention."

There was still laughter as I faced them, my mouth dry, my eye throbbing. I began slowly, but evidently my throat was tense, because they began shouting, "Louder! Louder!"

"We of the younger generation extol the wisdom of that great leader and educator," I shouted, "who first spoke these flaming words of wisdom: 'A ship lost at sea for many days suddenly sighted a friendly vessel. From the mast of the unfortunate vessel was seen a signal: "Water, water; we die of thirst!" The answer from the friendly vessel came back: "Cast down your bucket where you are." The captain of the distressed vessel, at last heeding the injunction, cast down his bucket, and it came up full of fresh sparkling water from the mouth of the Amazon River.' And like him I say, and in his words, 'To those of my race who depend upon bettering their condition in a foreign land, or who underestimate the importance of cultivating friendly relations with the Southern white man, who is his next-door neighbor, I would say: "Cast down your bucket where you are" — cast it down in making friends in every manly way of the people of all races by whom we are surrounded . . .' "

I spoke automatically and with such fervor that I did not realize that the men were still talking and laughing until my dry mouth, filling up with blood from the cut, almost strangled me. I coughed, wanting to stop and go to one of the tall brass, sand-filled spittoons to relieve myself, but a few men, especially the superintendent, were listening and I was afraid. So I gulped it down, blood, saliva and all, and continued. (What powers of endurance I had during those days! What enthusiasm! What a belief in the rightness of things!) I spoke even louder in spite of the pain. But still they talked and still they laughed, as though deaf with cotton in dirty ears. So I spoke with greater emotional emphasis. I closed my ears and swallowed blood until I was nauseated. The speech seemed a hundred times as long as before, but I could not leave out a single word. All had to be said, each memorized nuance considered, rendered. Nor was that all. Whenever I uttered a word of three or more syllables a group of voices would yell for me to repeat it. I used the phrase "social responsibility" and they yelled:

"What's that word you say, boy?"

"Social responsibility," I said.

"What?"

"Social . . ."

"Louder."

" . . . responsibility."

"More!"

"Respon — "

"Repeat!"

" — sibility."

The room filled with the uproar of laughter until, no doubt, distracted by having to gulp down my blood, I made a mistake and yelled a phrase I had often seen denounced in newspaper editorials, heard debated in private.

"Social . . ."

"What?" they yelled.

" . . . equality — "

The laughter hung smokelike in the sudden stillness. I opened my eyes, puzzled. Sounds of displeasure filled the room. The M.C. rushed forward. They shouted hostile phrases at me. But I did not understand.

A small dry mustached man in the front row blared out, "Say that slowly, son!"

"What sir?"

"What you just said!"

"Social responsibility, sir," I said.

"You weren't being smart, were you, boy?" he said, not unkindly.

"No, sir!"

"You sure that about 'equality' was a mistake?"

"Oh, yes, sir," I said. "I was swallowing blood."

"Well, you had better speak more slowly so we can understand. We mean to do right by you, but you've got to know your place at all times. All right, now, go on with your speech."

I was afraid. I wanted to leave but I wanted also to speak and I was afraid they'd snatch me down.

"Thank you, sir," I said, beginning where I had left off, and having them ignore me as before.

Yet when I finished there was a thunderous applause. I was surprised to see the superintendent come forth with a package wrapped in white tissue paper, and, gesturing for quiet, address the men.

"Gentlemen, you see that I did not overpraise this boy. He makes a good speech and some day he'll lead his people in the proper paths. And I don't have to tell you that that is important in these days and times. This is a good, smart boy, and so to encourage him in the right direction, in the name of the Board of Education I wish to present him a prize in the form of this . . .

He paused, removing the tissue paper and revealing a gleaming calfskin brief case.

". . . in the form of this first-class article from Shad Whitmore's shop."

"Boy," he said, addressing me, "take this prize and keep it well. Consider it a badge of office. Prize it. Keep developing as you are and some day it will be filled with important papers that will help shape the destiny of your people."

I was so moved that I could hardly express my thanks. A rope of bloody saliva forming a shape like an undiscovered continent drooled upon the leather and I wiped it quickly away. I felt an importance that I had never dreamed.

"Open it and see what's inside," I was told.

My fingers a-tremble, I complied, smelling the fresh leather and finding an official-looking document inside. It was a scholarship to the state college for Negroes. My eyes filled with tears and I ran awkwardly off the floor.

I was overjoyed; I did not even mind when I discovered that the gold pieces I had scrambled for were brass pocket tokens advertising a certain make of automobile.

When I reached home everyone was excited. Next day the neighbors came to congratulate me. I even felt safe from grandfather, whose deathbed curse usually spoiled my triumphs. I stood beneath his photograph with my brief case in hand and smiled triumphantly into his stolid black peasant's face. It was a face that fascinated me. The eyes seemed to follow everywhere I went.

That night I dreamed I was at a circus with him and that he refused to laugh at the clowns no matter what they did. Then later he told me to open my brief case and read what was inside and I did, finding an official envelope stamped with the state seal; and inside the envelope I found another and another, endlessly, and I thought I would fall of weariness. "Them's years," he said. "Now open that one." And I did and in it I found an engraved document containing a short message in letters of gold. "Read it," my grandfather said. "Out loud."

"To Whom It May Concern," I intoned. "Keep This Nigger-Boy Running."

I awoke with the old man's laughter ringing in my ears.

(It was a dream I was to remember and dream again for many years after. But at that time I had no insight into its meaning. First I had to attend college.)

Gramma Custis Is Crazy

Warren Miller

Priest stop me in the street. About a week after I went to see him about the piece. He say. "Man I glad to see you. I thinkin sure you was picked up."

"They cant touch me Man."

"You are fast." He say.

"I too fast for em."

"Well I been waiten for you Duke Man. I been sittin up there in my room an waiten. That piece dont rust but it aint gettin any younger."

"I be aroun." I say.

He say. "Uh huh. Theys a number of people showin interest in that item. Man you dont want to wait too long."

"I be aroun Priest. I come pick it up in a day or two."

"Plenty of money aroun." Priest say an he lift up his head and sniff like he was smellin money. "Shouldnt be no trouble for you to raise the bread."

"Aint no trouble." I say. "Listen Man I in a big hurry right now. I see you aroun." We in front of Hermits restarant. Hermit got 2 big picchers in his window. One of Nasser and one of Nkruma. Hermit a big man in the back to Africa movement. Evry time I go in there he talken about it. I tell him. "Man I dont want to live with lions. It rough enough right here."

Priest say to me. "You need a little cash you can do what Rod do."

"I got other ways." I tell him.

"A couple hours at the Park and you got it made Man."

"I dont go for that." I tell him.

"Easy money Duke. Its easy money."

It make me twitch when people go on talken to me when I dont want to talk. When I get the feelin to move all I want to do is move you know. Like I get this itchyness all over me. In school some time this come over me an I want to start cuttin up an smashin things. You know like they got me an surrouned me an I gotta brake out.

Priest go on talken about the easy money in the Park. I know all about the easy money in the park. Man that kind of action make me feel creepy. He still talken an I say. "Priest I see you tomorra or nex day." An I take off.

"Stay cool." He say.

I walk aroun the block. I don't know what to do. I want some action. When they aint no school it hard to find somethin to do. When school is on it easy to find things to do. Like not goin to school. But in the summer you got to make you own action. I stood on the corner for a while hitten the bus stop sign with my hand. Keeps my hands hardened up. Then I went over to Ritzies Bar lookin for Blood but he wasnt there. Wasnt nobody there but some older guys talkin numbers. "Stay cool." Ritzie say. She give me a big smile. Ritzie she all right. Fine lookin blackskin woman with a lot of hair on top of her head all piled up. She always say. "Look at me Man. I the White Queen of the savages."

I think about how it would be to make it with Ritzie. Walken down the street I think about it. She in her 40s. Maybe 45 like. She a woman with a lot of juice. Late at night. Closin time. I the last one in the bar. She say. "Help me lock up Duke Man." She go in the back room an I lock up and turn off the lights an push the chairs in against the tables. I sit down on a bar stool an wait. Then she call me. I go into the back room. She on the bed all naked her hair spread out on the pilla an her big tits lavishin all over her.

It could happen. I think about Sue Randolph and I say to myself. "Duke go on up see her. Blood dont have to know." So I climb up to her apartment. Halls full of garbage an all kinds of muck and crap. I knock on the door. Her Mother open it. She wearen a flimsy robe holden it together with her hand. I say. "Ekscuse me. I guess I knock on the wrong door."

"I guess you goddamn well have knock on the wrong door." She say. "An dont knock on it ever again." She start yellin an I head for the stairs. She yell down after me about keepin my hands off her Sue an like that. I dont like to hear a woman swear. Especially an old woman an a Mother besides.

So then I walk over to Bloods house looken for him. I glad Sue aint home dont want to get hooked by her again. I need whut I need is the kind of woman too old for marryin. Like Ritzie. I sit down on a bench at the project an think about Ritzie again all that thick hot meat. I think if I put my body against hers I get burned by the heat. She make me think if a man put a knife in her she wouldnt stop bleedin for 10 days.

Bloods folks live in the project. His

father work for the Post Office. He been carryin a mail bag so long one shoulder is lower than the other. Blood got one sister a nurse and a brother at Fisk University learning to be a doctor or somethin. Man I dont see it workin they asses off like that. No point workin like that when they can take it all away from you when ever they feel like it you know.

The project has a little elevator like a telephone booth the green walls all scratched with initials an you know things. An it smell like garbage. New bilding but it got the Uptown Stink. It different though inside the Thurston apartment. Evything clean an so neat you afraid to sit down. Missus Thurston she Bloods Mother she open the door an say. "Come on in Richard. John Wesley be right back. I just sent him down to the supermarket." John Wesley. Thats Bloods real name. I go on in.

They must have over a 100 books in they apartment. Missus Thurston say to me. "You remember Harrison dont you Richard. He is home from Fisk." Harrison readin a book. He wearin white shoes with thick red rubber soles dressed like all the College boys. They wear a uniform like they belong to a gang. But they dont belong to no gang.

Harrison look up from his book. "Well Richard." He say. "An how are things goin with you?"

"OK." I say. "How you like it down there at Fisk?"

"Oh we are getting along." He say. "You see a lot of John Wesley dont you Richard?"

"Off an on." I tell him.

Harrison say. "He has changed. I notice a change in him an I am not sure I like it."

Missus Thurston say. "He is like a stranger in this house. As if he did not belong here an was not one of my children."

Harrison say to me. "Have you noticed any change in him lately? You see a lot of him. Has he been doing rather pecular things would you say?"

"He just the same." I say.

Harrison shakin his head. He say to his Mother. "He needs treatment Mother. Thats my opinion. He needs treatment. I do not know what is at the bottom of it but I know somethin is wrong. I wish I could have the head of the Sike Department take a look at him."

After a while an Blood still not back they relize he aint comin back. I knew it all the time. Put some money in Bloods hands he aint goin to no supermarket he goin to the junkman for a fix.

Harrison say to his Mother. "Has he done this sort of thing before Mother?"

She nod.

He say. "Mother have you no idea what is goin on with John Wesley?"

She say. "Oh my GOD Harrison do not be so blind. You brother that poor Lamb he has become an addikt."

Harrison slam his book shut. It go Thuck. He stand up an go to the window an look out. He say to the window. "They make us live like animals. Is it any wunder then that some of us act like animals an some of us become animals. The fantastic thing is how few of us succum to their idea of us." An he went on like that standin there at the window not lookin at us lookin out at Harlem. He a tall skinny boy. He wearen gray slacks with a little buckle in the back an a white shirt.

I get up an say I gotta get on home an if I see John Wesley I tell him they is waiten for him. An I go.

No place to go now but home. Gramma Custis fass asleep in her chair by the window. I go in my mothers room an look thru her draws lookin for some money. I got to buy that piece from Priest. I want it. When you have a gun then you aint no animal any more. You a hunter an can stand tall an dont have to take a soundin from no body.

No money. I lay down on the sofa and lissen to Gramma Custis snorin. I think about how to get up the bread the $15 I need. I think Maybe I will go to the Park with Rod. Maybe I do it just one or 2 times to get the 15. Or maybe I go look up Chester and borra it from him. He live downtown now an is doin all right. Then I start thinkin about Ritzie again so I get up and start walkin aroun. I go to the closet an look in the pockets of every piece of clothes. Nothin. At the back of the closet I see the shoe shine box I uset to lug aroun when I was a kid to pick up pennies shinin shoes. I give it a kick. Dont know why I aint ever throw it out. The stink of shoe polish is the worse stink of all.

When I kick the box Gramma Custis mumbel in her sleep. I look at her. She dont wake up. She got her big black leather purse on the floor near her feet. She always keep her Welfare money in it. She fold the foldin money inta little squares an stuff them inta a little purse like the money gonna last longer that way.

No body ever know how much she got. I walk over to the window an pretend I lookin out but I lookin at her. She still snorin. I kneel down an open her purse. It got a little gold clasp. I squeeze it real tight so it wont make no sound. When it open I look up at her. Her eyes is closed and her face all sagged. I reach inside for the little purse but alla time I keep watchin Gramma. When my hand touches the little purse I stop breathin. Then I look down and open it. They maybe 20 little squares of $1 bills inside.

"You boy!"

I drop the purse an stan up fast. I tryin so hard to preten I wasnt doin nothing that I believe it myself.

She glarin at me thru her glasses. She say. "Steelin from you own Gramma. Oh GOD whut gonna become of you boy. Whut happenin to you Richard you was the sweetest baby so good. An now you is so bad. Whut happenen to you."

I dint say nothin. She lean tord me in her chair like she goin to poke me. She say. "It the city. It this city this hore of Babylon. This hore city is whut happenin to you makin you go bad that was so sweet an good. This here place is the seat of Satan an it bringen you to ruin an damnation. An I will kill her childern with death The Bibel say. You a child of Babylon. An upon her forehead was a name written. MYSTERY, BABYLON THE GREAT. The mother of harlots an abominations of the earth. An the woman which thou sawist is that great city which raineth over the kings of the earth." She say.

"I aint been anywheres near Ritzies Bar." I tell her. But she dont listen.

She say. "Babylon Babylon Babylon the great is fallen boy. Is fallen. An is become the habitation of debles. An the hold of evry fowl speerit. An a cage of evry unclean an hateful bird. For all nations have drunk of the wine of the wrath of her fornication with her. An the kings of the earth have committed fornication with her. An the merchants are waxen rich off a her delicacies."

She stop for a minute an I say. "I just been over to the Thurstons. They boy Harrison is home now from Fisk University."

"Harrison is a good boy." She say. "He a

The Time the Old Woman Got Eat by the Dog

Warren Miller

credit to the Race. Come out of her my people that you be not partakers of her sin."

She off again. She say. "Come out of Babylon so that you dont receive of her playgs. Therefore shall her playgs come in one day. You lissen to me boy. Death an mornin & famine & she shall be utterly burned with fire."

"Yes Mam." I say.

"You shall see the smoke of her burning boy. Alla you liven deliciously with her an committin fornication with her you gonna bewail when you see the smoke." She point out the window. "Standin afar off for the fear of her torment." She say. "Sayin alas alas that mighty city Babylon. For in 1 hour is thy judgment come. An the merchants of the earth is gonna weep because they cant buyeth they merchandise no more. Cinamon and frankisense an horses & slaves & pearls. Ointments & oil & wheat & fine linen. Thou shalt find them no more at all boy. In one hour boy it gonna happen. In 1 hour she gonna be made desolate. GOD aint gonna over look it for ever boy. You watch out. The angel gonna throw the millstone and he sayith thus with vilence shall that great city Babylon be thrown down. For thy merchants were the great men of earth an by thy sorceries were all nations deceeved." Her face all streaky an wet with cryin. "You own Gramma." She say. She say. "Oh that sweet little lovenable boy whut happen to him. Where he gone?"

I dreamed about goin to the Zoo when I was a little kid. One of my mothers husbands carried me on his shoulders an I was eatin pop corn an some of it spillin down on his head. He look up an smile at me but when I wake up I can never remember his face. When ever I try to remember as far back as I can remember this is whut I remember. But I dont know who he was or his name or anything. I just remember at the Zoo on this mans shoulders eatin pop corn. An the lion behind bars.

I got up early because I had a lot to do. My mother was drinkin coffee in the kitchen. She work days now in a laundry. I come in an pour myself a cup of coffee an eat 5–6 slices of bread with it. My mother sittin there all hunched up over her cup.

"Why you up so early today? I worry so when you get up so early. Gives you more time for you to get youself in trouble. You aint but 14 now an already you full of scars an stitches. I dont have the strenth to take care of you an look after you like I should." An like that.

"I be all right." I tell her.

"Some time I sorry I ever lef Alabama an lef you with Gramma Custis those years. When I come up here for the opportunities. An then I come back down an brought you up here. They aint never anythin been right since."

I ask her. "Whut was the name of that husband who took me to the zoo when I was a little kid?"

She look up at me again. "Whut took you to the *Zoo?*"

"When I was a little kid he took me to the Zoo an I ride on his shoulders."

"I dont remember any of that Richard."

"He bought me pop corn."

"Maybe it was George Dickinson." She say. "Or maybe it was befor that. Maybe it was Hillard. Hillard always like you. Some times he play with you."

"Whut was his last name?"

"Jackson." She say. "Jackson. Or Johnson. Why you wanta know?"

"Maybe I meet him someday. I dont know."

She laugh. "You wont be meetin Hillard. Dont you worry bout that." She get up to leave. "You lose a person in Harlem you never see him again. Any man get adrift in Harlem he sink outa sight for ever." At the door she say. "Now you stay outa trouble today Richard hear? For if you get inta trouble again I dont know I swear I dont know whut I gonna do cept beat you good. You get in trouble once more I washen my hans of you. You gonna have to make out by youself best way you know how. I dont have the strenth no more. You dont know whut it like all day standin in that steam an the wet. An the turrible ache in my bones. It a shame to GOD to make a woman work so an then they go an take all that money outa my pay for the taxes an this & that & the other thing. Whut they want taxes from me for when they never give me nothin? No. Nothin. But this. Roaches & rats. Roaches & rats. Aint nothin decent in our lives. I ony wanted but the one husband you father but things got too much for him and he ran off an lef me. Things always get too much for men. They thinkin all day of whut they comin home to an one time they jus don come home. It easy for them. You a man an you jus like the others. All of you is a like. You ony know how to give a woman sadness an cause her pain an suffrin. You get in trouble jus one more time an I turnin you over to the cops. This time I tell the Judge and the Youth People — Take him. Take him he aint none of mine — I dont want have anythin further to do with this boy."

An like that you know.

I drink my coffee an not look at her.

She yell. "You hear me Richard you damn boy you?"

"I hear you." I say.

She leave. Slams the door so loud all the dogs in the bilding start barkin an keep on barkin all the way down the stairs. She take the subway to Queens now an be home 6-30 or 7 o'clock. After my mother leave I drink another cup of coffee an when Gramma Custis come in with the Bibel in her han I clear out.

She say. "Where you goin boy?"

I slam the door an the dogs start barkin again.

When I turn the turn of the stairs at the 2nd floor I see 2 men in uniform an I pull back quick. Not even breathin. Then I realize they aint cops by they uniforms an I step down the last step inta the hall. Door is open at Missus Jeffersons apartment. She an old old woman whut lives alone with a big mean dog. Stretcher leanin against the wall. Inside is 2 men with a net tryin to catch the dog. Dog makin a crazy sound in his throat an you can smell him out in the hall. I so busy watchin them at first I dint notice Missus Jefferson layin on the floor an whut she look like. When I get a look at her I run downstairs.

Lot of people on the stoop. One woman sayin. "She layin they dead 2–3 days. Oh I knowed I shoulda look in on her. An that dog — an she love that dog so — treated him like a little baby — that dog got so hungry he et her."

The men come out with that dog snappin and strugglin in the net. Everybody stan back an the woman say. "You a bad bad dog." The men put him in the back of a truck marked society against the cruelty to animals or somethin like that an they drive off with the dog.

Then the stretcher men come down with Missus Jefferson. They got a blanket coverin her.

The woman say. "Good by Mamie you sweet soul." She cryin.

The man take off his hat an open the door of the dead wagon for the stretcher men. He say to them. "Scratch one nigger more." The men dont say any thing. They drive away.

I walk up to 125 street to see Royal Baron.

Debut

Kristin Hunter

"Hold *still,* Judy," Mrs. Simmons said around the spray of pins that protruded dangerously from her mouth. She gave the thirtieth tug to the tight sash at the waist of the dress. "Now walk over there and turn around slowly."

The dress, Judy's first long one, was white organdy over taffeta, with spaghetti straps that bared her round brown shoulders and a floating skirt and a wide sash that cascaded in a butterfly effect behind. It was a dream, but Judy was sick and tired of the endless fittings she had endured so that she might wear it at the Debutantes' Ball. Her thoughts leaped ahead to the Ball itself . . .

"*Slowly,* I said!" Mrs. Simmons' dark, angular face was always grim, but now it was screwed into an expression resembling a prune. Judy, starting nervously, began to revolve by moving her feet an inch at a time.

Her mother watched her critically. "No, it's still not right. I'll just have to rip out that waistline seam again."

"Oh, Mother!" Judy's impatience slipped out at last. "Nobody's going to notice all those little details."

"They will too. They'll be watching you every minute, hoping to see something wrong. You've got to be the *best.* Can't you get that through your head?" Mrs. Simmons gave a sigh of despair. "You better start noticin' 'all those little details' yourself. I can't do it for you all your life. Now turn around and stand up straight."

"Oh, Mother," Judy said, close to tears from being made to turn and pose while her feet itched to be dancing, "I can't stand it any more!"

"You can't stand it, huh? How do you think *I* feel?" Mrs. Simmons said in her harshest tone.

Judy was immediately ashamed, remembering the weeks her mother had spent at the sewing machine, picking her already tattered fingers with needles and pins, and the great weight of sacrifice that had been borne on Mrs. Simmons' shoulders for the past two years so that Judy might bare hers at the Ball.

"All right, take it off," her mother said. "I'm going to take it up the street to Mrs. Luby and let her help me. It's got to be right or I won't let you leave the house."

"Can't we just leave it the way it is, Mother?" Judy pleaded without hope of success. "I think it's perfect."

"You would," Mrs. Simmons said tartly as she folded the dress and prepared to bear it out of the room. "Sometimes I think I'll never get it through your head. You got to look just right and act just right. That Rose Griffin and those other girls can afford to be careless, maybe, but you can't. You're gonna be the darkest, poorest one there."

Judy shivered in her new lace strapless bra and her old, childish knit snuggies. "You make it sound like a battle I'm going to instead of just a dance."

"It is a battle," her mother said firmly. "It starts tonight and it goes on for the rest of your life. The battle to hold your head up and get someplace and be somebody. We've done all we can for you, your father and I. Now you've got to start fighting some on your own." She gave Judy a slight smile; her voice softened a little. "You'll do all right, don't worry. Try and get some rest this afternoon. Just don't mess up your hair."

"All right, Mother," Judy said listlessly.

She did not really think her father had much to do with anything that happened to her. It was her mother who had ingratiated her way into the Gay Charmers two years ago, taking all sorts of humiliation from the better-dressed, better-off, lighter-skinned women, humbly making and mending their dresses, fixing food for their meetings, addressing more mail and selling more tickets than anyone else. The club had put it off as long as they could, but finally they had to admit Mrs. Simmons to membership because she worked so hard. And that meant, of course, that Judy would be on the list for this year's Ball.

Her father, a quiet carpenter who had given up any other ambitions years ago, did not think much of Negro society or his wife's fierce determination to launch Judy into it. "Just keep clean and be decent," he would say. "That's all anybody has to do."

Her mother always answered, "If that's all *I* did we'd still be on relief," and he would shut up with shame over the years when he had been laid off repeatedly and her days' work and sewing had kept them going. Now he had steady work but she refused to quit, as if she expected it to end at any moment. The intense energy that burned in Mrs. Simmons' large dark eyes had scorched her features into permanent irony. She worked day and night and spent her spare time scheming and planning. Whatever her personal ambitions had been, Judy knew she blamed Mr. Simmons for their failure; now all her schemes revolved around their only child.

Judy went to her mother's window and watched her stride down the street with the dress until she was hidden by the high brick wall that went around two sides of their house. Then she returned to her own room. She did not get dressed because she was afraid of pulling a sweater over her hair — her mother would notice the difference even if it looked all right to Judy — and because she was afraid that doing anything, even getting dressed, might precipitate her into the battle. She drew a stool up to her window and looked out. She had no real view, but she liked her room. The wall hid the crowded tenement houses beyond the alley, and from its cracks and bumps and depressions she could construct any imaginary landscape she chose. It was how she had spent most of the free hours of her dreamy adolescence.

"Hey, can I go?"

It was the voice of an invisible boy in the alley. As another boy chuckled, Judy recognized the familiar ritual; if you said yes, they said, "Can I go with you?" It had been tried on her dozens of times. She always walked past, head in the air, as if she had not heard. Her mother said that was the only thing to do; if they knew she was a lady, they wouldn't dare bother her. But this time a girl's voice, cool and assured, answered.

"If you think your big enough," it said.

It was Lucy Mae Watkins; Judy could picture her standing there in a tight dress with bright, brazen eyes.

"I'm big enough to give you a baby," the boy answered.

Judy would die if a boy ever spoke to her like that, but she knew Lucy Mae could handle it. Lucy Mae could handle all the boys, even if they ganged up on her, because she had been born knowing something other girls had to learn

"Aw, you ain't big enough to give me a shoe-shine," she told him.

"Come here and I'll show you how big I am," the boy said.

"Yeah, Lucy Mae, what's happenin'?" another, younger boy said. "Come here and tell us."

Lucy Mae laughed. "What I'm puttin' down is too strong for little boys like you."

"Come here a minute, baby," the first boy said. "I got a cigarette for you."

"Aw, I ain't studyin' your cigarettes," Lucy Mae answered. But her voice was closer, directly below Judy. There were the sounds of a scuffle and Lucy Mae's muffled laughter. When she spoke her voice sounded raw and cross. "Come on now, boy. Cut it out and give me the damn cigarette." There was more scuffling, and the sharp crack of a slap, and then Lucy Mae said, "Cut it out, I said. Just for that I'm gonna take 'em all." The clack of high heels rang down the sidewalk with a boy's clumsy shoes in pursuit.

Judy realized that there were three of them down there. "Let her go, Buster," one said. "You can't catch her now."

"Aw, hell, man, she took the whole damn pack," the one called Buster complained.

"That'll learn you!" Lucy Mae's voice mocked from down the street. "Don't mess with nothin' you can't handle."

"Hey, Lucy Mae. Hey, I heard Rudy

Grant already gave you a baby," a second boy called out.

"Yeah. Is that true, Lucy Mae?" the youngest one yelled.

There was no answer. She must be a block away by now.

For a moment the hidden boys were silent; then one of them guffawed directly below Judy, and the other two joined in the secret male laughter that was oddly high-pitched and feminine.

"Aw man, I don't know what you all laughin' about," Buster finally grumbled. "That girl took all my cigarettes. You got some, Leroy?"

"Naw," the second boy said.

"Me neither," the third one said.

"What we gonna do? I ain't got but fifteen cent. Hell, man, I want more than a feel for a pack of cigarettes." There was an unpleasant whine in Buster's voice. "Hell, for a pack of cigarettes I want a bitch to come across."

"She will next time, man," the boy called Leroy said.

"She better," Buster said. "You know she better. If she pass by here again, we gonna jump her, you hear?"

"Sure, man," Leroy said. "The three of us can grab her easy."

"Then we can all three of us have some fun. Oh, *yeah,* man," the youngest boy said. He sounded as if he might be about 14.

Leroy said, "We oughta get Roland and J.T. too. For a whole pack of cigarettes she oughta treat all five of us."

"Aw, man, why tell Roland and J.T.?" the youngest voice whined. "They ain't in it. Them was *our* cigarettes."

"They was *my* cigarettes, you mean," Buster said with authority. "You guys better quit it before I decided to cut you out."

"Oh, man, don't do that. We with you, you know that."

"Sure, Buster, we your aces, man."

"All right, that's better." There was a minute of silence.

Then, "What we gonna do with the girl, Buster?" the youngest one wanted to know.

"When she come back we gonna jump the bitch, man. We gonna jump her and grab her. Then we gonna turn her every way but loose." He went on, spinning a crude fantasy that got wilder each time he retold it, until it became so secretive that their voices dropped to a low indistinct murmur punctuated by guffaws. Now and then Judy could distinguish the word "girl" or the other word they used for it; these words always produced the loudest guffaws of all. She shook off her fear with the thought that Lucy Mae was too smart to pass there again today. She had heard them at their dirty talk in the alley before and had always been successful in ignoring it; it had nothing to do with her, the wall protected her from their kind. All the ugliness was on their side of it, and this side was hers to fill with beauty.

She turned on her radio to shut them out completely and began to weave her tapestry to its music. More for practice than anything else, she started by picturing the maps of the places to which she intended to travel, then went on to the faces of her friends. Rose Griffin's sharp, Indian profile appeared on the wall. Her coloring was like an Indian's too and her hair was straight and black and glossy. Judy's hair, naturally none of these things, had been "done" four days ago so that tonight it would be "old" enough to have a gloss as natural-looking as Rose's. But Rose, despite her handsome looks, was silly; her voice broke constantly into high-pitched giggles and she became even sillier and more nervous around boys.

Judy was not sure that she knew how to act around boys either. The sisters kept boys and girls apart at the Catholic high school where her parents sent her to keep her away from low-class kids. But she felt that she knew a secret: tonight, in that dress, with her hair in a sophisticated upsweep, she would be transformed into a poised princess. Tonight all the college boys her mother described so eagerly would rush to dance with her, and then from somewhere *the boy* would appear. She did not know his name; she neither knew nor cared whether he went to college, but she imagined that he would be as dark as she was, and that there would be awe and diffidence in his manner as he bent to kiss her hand . . .

A waltz swelled from the radio; the wall, turning blue in deepening twilight, came alive with whirling figures. Judy rose and began to go through the steps she had rehearsed for so many weeks. She swirled with a practiced smile on her face, holding an imaginary skirt at her side; turned, dipped, and flicked on her bedside lamp without missing a fraction of the beat. Faster and faster she danced with her imaginary partner, to an inner music that was better than the sounds on the radio. She was "coming out," and tonight the world would discover what it had been waiting for all these years.

"Aw, git it, baby." She ignored it as she would ignore the crowds that lined the streets to watch her pass on her way to the Ball.

"Aw, do your number." She waltzed on, safe and secure on her side of the wall.

"Can I come up there and do it with you?"

At this she stopped, paralyzed. Somehow they had come over the wall or around it and into her room.

"Man, I sure like the view from here," the youngest boy said. "How come we never tried this view before?"

She came to life, ran quickly to the lamp and turned it off, but not before Buster said, "Yeah, and the back view is fine, too."

"Aw, she turned off the light," a voice complained.

"Put it on again, baby, we don't mean no harm."

"Let us see you dance some more. I bet you can really do it."

"Yeah, I bet she can shimmy on down."

"You know it, man."

"Come on down here, baby," Buster's voice urged softly dangerously. "I got a cigarette for you."

"Yeah, and he got something else for you, too."

Judy, flattened against her closet door, gradually lost her urge to scream. She realized that she was shivering in her underwear. Taking a deep breath, she opened the closet door and found her robe. She thought of going to the window and yelling down, "You don't have a thing I want. Do you understand?" But she had more important things to do.

Wrapping her hair in protective plastic, she ran a full steaming tub and dumped in half a bottle of her mother's favorite cologne. At first she scrubbed herself furiously, irritating her skin. But finally she stopped, knowing she would never be able to get cleaner than this again. She could not wash away the thing they considered dirty, the thing that made them pronounce "girl" in the same way as the other four-letter words they wrote on the wall in the alley; it was part of her, just as it was part of her mother and Rose Griffin and Lucy Mae. She relaxed then because it was true that the boys in the alley did not have a thing she wanted. She had what they wanted, and the knowledge replaced her shame with a strange, calm feeling of power.

After her bath she splashed on more cologne and spent 40 minutes on her makeup, erasing and retracing her eyebrows six times until she was satisfied. She went to her mother's room then and found the dress, finished and freshly pressed, on its hanger.

When Mrs. Simmons came upstairs to help her daughter she found her sitting on the bench before the vanity mirror as if it were a throne. She looked young and arrogant and beautiful and perfect and cold.

"Why, you're dressed already," Mrs. Simmons said in surprise. While she stared, Judy rose with perfect, icy grace and glided to the center of the room. She stood there motionless as a mannequin.

"I want you to fix the hem, Mother," she directed. "It's still uneven in back."

Her mother went down obediently on her knees, muttering, "It looks all right to me." She put in a couple of pins. "That better?"

"Yes," Judy said with a brief glance at the mirror. "You'll have to sew it on me, Mother. I can't take it off now. I'd ruin my hair."

Mrs. Simmons went to fetch her sewing things, returned, and surveyed her daughter. "You sure did a good job on yourself, I must say," she admitted grudgingly. "Can't find a thing to complain about. You'll look as good as anybody there."

"Of course, Mother," Judy said as Mrs. Simmons knelt and sewed. "I don't know what you were so worried about." Her secret feeling of confidence had returned, stronger than ever, but the evening ahead was no longer the vague girlish fantasy she had pictured on the wall; it had hard, clear outlines leading up to a definite goal. She would be the belle of the Ball because she knew more than Rose Griffin and her silly friends; more than her mother; more, even, than Lucy Mae, because she knew better than to settle for a mere pack of cigarettes.

"There," her mother said, breaking the thread. She got up. "I never expected to get you ready this early. Ernest Lee won't be here for another hour."

"That silly Ernest Lee," Judy said, with a new contempt in her young voice. Until tonight she had been pleased by the thought of going to the dance with Ernest Lee; he was nice, she felt comfortable with him, and he might even be the awe-struck boy of her dream. He was a dark, serious neighborhood boy who could not afford to go to college; Mrs. Simmons had reluctantly selected him to take Judy to the dance because all the Gay Charmers' sons were spoken for. Now, with an undertone of excitement, Judy said, "I'm going to ditch him after the first dance, Mother. You'll see. I'm going to come home with one of the college boys."

"It's very nice, Ernest Lee," she told him an hour later when he handed her the white orchid, "but it's rather small. I'm going to wear it on my wrist, if you don't mind." And then, dazzling him with a smile of sweetest cruelty, she stepped back and waited while he fumbled with the door.

"You know, Edward, I'm not worried

about her any more," Mrs. Simmons said to her husband after the children were gone. Her voice became harsh and grating. "Put down that paper and listen to me! Aren't you interested in your child? — That's better," she said as he complied meekly. "I was saying, I do believe she's learned what I've been trying to teach her, after all."

Mulatto

Langston Hughes

I am your son, white man!

Georgia dusk
And the turpentine woods.
One of the pillars of the temple fell.

You are my son!
Like hell!

The moon over the turpentine woods.
The Southern night
Full of stars,
Great big yellow stars.
What's a body but a toy?
Juicy bodies
Of nigger wenches
Blue black
Against back fences.
O, you little bastard boy,
What's a body but a toy?
The scent of pine woods stings the
soft night air.
What's the body of your mother?
Silver moonlight everywhere.
What's the body of your mother?
Sharp pine scent in the evening air.
A nigger night,
A nigger joy,
A little yellow
Bastard boy.

Naw, you ain't my brother.
Niggers ain't my brother.
Not ever.
Niggers ain't my brother.

The Southern night is full of stars,
Great big yellow stars.
O, sweet as earth,
Dusk dark bodies
Give sweet birth
To little yellow bastard boys.

Git on back there in the night,
You ain't white.

The bright stars scatter everywhere.
Pine wood scent in the evening air.
A nigger night,
A nigger joy.

I am your son, white man!

A little yellow
Bastard boy.

Negro Mother

Langston Hughes

Children, I come back today
To tell you a story of the long dark way
That I had to climb, that I had to know
In order that the race might live and grow.
Look at my face—dark as the night—
Yet shining like the sun with love's true light.
I am the child they stole from the sand
Three hundred years ago in Africa's land.
I am the dark girl who crossed the wide sea
Carrying in my body the seed of the free.
I am the woman who worked in the field
Bringing the cotton and the corn to yield.
I am the one who labored as a slave,
Beaten and mistreated for the work that I gave—
Children sold away from me, husband sold, too.
No safety, no love, no respect was I due.
Three hundred years in the deepest South:
But God put a song and a prayer in my mouth.
God put a dream like steel in my soul.
Now, through my children, I'm reaching the goal.
Now, through my children, young and free,
I realize the blessings denied to me.
I couldn't read then. I couldn't write.
I had nothing, back there in the night.
Sometimes, the valley was filled with tears,
But I kept trudging on through the lonely years.
Sometimes, the road was hot with sun,
But I had to keep on till my work was done:
I *had* to keep on! No stopping for me—
I was the seed of the coming Free.
I nourished the dream that nothing could smother
Deep in my breast—the Negro mother.
I had only hope then, but now through you,
Dark ones of today, my dreams must come true:
All you dark children in the world out there,
Remember my sweat, my pain, my despair.
Remember my years, heavy with sorrow—
And make of those years a torch for tomorrow.
Make of my past a road to the light
Out of the darkness, the ignorance, the night.
Lift high my banner out of the dust.
Stand like free men supporting my trust.
Believe in the right, let none push you back.
Remember the whip and the slaver's track.
Remember how the strong in struggle and strife
Still bar you the way, and deny you life—
But march ever forward, breaking down bars.

Look ever upward at the sun and the stars.
Oh, my dark children, may my dreams and my prayers
Impel you forever up the great stairs—
For I will be with you till no white brother
Dares keep down the children of the Negro mother.

Jazz, Jive, and Jam

Langston Hughes

"It being Negro History Week," said Simple, "Joyce took me to a pay lecture to hear some Negro hysterian —— "

"Historian," I corrected.

" — hysterian speak," continued Simple, "and he laid our Negro race low. He said we was misbred, misread, and misled, also losing our time good-timing. Instead of time-taking and money-making, we are jazz-shaking. Oh, he enjoyed his self at the expense of the colored race — and him black as me. He really delivered a lecture — in which, no doubt, there is some truth."

"Constructive criticism, I gather — a sort of tearing down in order to build up."

"He tore us down good," said Simple. "Joyce come out saying to me, her husband, that he had really got my number. I said, 'Baby, he did not miss you, neither.' But Joyce did not consider herself included in the bad things he said.

"She come telling me on the way home by subway, 'Jess Semple, I have been pursuing culture since my childhood. But you, when I first met you, all you did was drape yourself over some beer bar and argue with the barflies. The higher things of life do not come out of a licker trough.'

"I replied, 'But, Joyce, how come culture has got to be so dry?'

"She answers me back, 'How come your gullet has got to be so wet? You are sitting in this subway right now looking like you would like to have a beer.'

" 'Solid!' I said. 'I would. How did you guess it?'

" 'Married to you for three years, I can read your mind,' said Joyce. 'We'll buy a couple of cans to take home. I might even drink one myself.'

" 'Joyce, baby,' I said, 'in that case, let's buy three cans.'

"Joyce says, 'Remember the budget, Jess.'

"I says, 'Honey, you done busted the budget going to that lecture program which cost One Dollar a head, also we put some small change in the collection to help Negroes get ahead.'

" 'Small change?' says Joyce, 'I put a dollar.'

" 'Then our budget is busted real good,' I said, 'so we might as well dent it some more. Let's get six cans of beer.'

" 'All right,' says Joyce, 'go ahead, drink yourself to the dogs — instead of saving for that house we want to buy!'

" 'Six cans of beer would not pay for even the bottom front step,' I said. 'But they would lift my spirits this evening. That Negro high-speaking doctor done tore my spirits down. I did not know before that the colored race was so misled, misread, and misbred. According to him there is hardly a pure black man left. But I was setting in the back, so I guess he did not see me.'

" 'Had you not had to go to sleep in the big chair after dinner,' says Joyce, 'we would have been there on time and had seats up front.'

" 'I were near enough to that joker,' I said. 'Loud as he could holler, we did not need to set no closer. And he certainly were nothing to look at!'

" 'Very few educated men look like Harry Belafonte,' said Joyce.

" 'I am glad I am handsome instead of wise,' I said. But Joyce did not crack a smile. She had that lecture on her mind.

" 'Dr. Conboy is smart,' says Joyce. 'Did you hear him quoting Aristotle?'

" 'Who were Harry Stottle?' I asked.

" 'Some people are not even misread,' said Joyce. 'Aristotle was a Greek philosopher like Socrates, a great man of ancient times.'

" 'He must of been before Booker T. Washington then,' I said, 'because, to tell the truth, I has not heard of him at all. But tonight being *Negro* History Week, how come Dr. Conboy has to quote some Greek?'

" 'There were black Greeks,' said Joyce. 'Did you not hear him say that Negroes have played a part in all history, throughout all time, from Eden to now?'

" 'Do you reckon Eve was brownskin?' I requested.

" 'I do not know about Eve,' said Joyce, 'but Cleopatra was of the colored race, and the Bible says Sheba, beloved of Solomon, was black but comely.'

" 'I wonder would she come to me?' I says.

" 'Solomon also found Cleopatra comely. He was a king,' says Joyce.

" 'And I am Jesse B. Semple,' I said.

"But by that time the subway had got to our stop. At the store Joyce broke the budget again, opened up her pocket purse, and bought us six cans of beer. So it were a good evening. It ended well — except that I ain't for going to any more meetings — especially interracial meetings."

"Come now! Don't you want to improve race relations?"

"Sure," said Simple, "but in my opinion, jazz, jive, and jam would be better for race relations than all this high-flown gab, gaff, and gas the orators put out. All this talking that white folks do at meetings, and big Negroes, too, about how to get along together — just a little jam session would have everybody getting along fine without having to listen to so many speeches. Why, last month Joyce took me to a Race Relations Seminar which her club and twenty other clubs gave, and man, it lasted three days! It started on a Friday night and it were not over until Sunday afternoon. They had sessions' mammy! Joyce is a fiend for culture."

"And you sat through all that?"

"I did not set," said Simple. "I stood. I walked in and walked out. I smoked on the corner and snuck two drinks at the bar. But I had to wait for Joyce, and I thought them speeches would never get over! My wife were a delegate from her club, so she had to stay, although I think Joyce got tired her own self. But she would not admit it. Joyce said, 'Dr. Hillary Thingabod was certainly brilliant, were he not?'

"I said, 'He were not.'

"Joyce said, 'What did you want the man to say?'

"I said, 'I wish he had sung, instead of *said.* That program needed some music to keep folks awake.'

"Joyce said, 'Our forum was not intended for a musical. It was intended to see how we can work out integration.'

"I said, 'With a jazz band, they could work out integration in ten minutes. Everybody would have been dancing together like they all did at the Savoy — colored and white — or down on the East Side at them Casinos on a Friday night where jam holds forth — and we would have been integrated.'

"Joyce said, 'This was a serious seminar, aiming at facts, not fun.'

" 'Baby,' I said, 'what is more facts than acts? Jazz makes people get into action, move! Didn't nobody move in that hall where you were — except to jerk their head up when they went to sleep, to keep anybody from seeing that they was nodding. Why, that chairman, Mrs. Maxwell-Reeves, almost lost her glasses off her nose, she jerked her head up so quick one time when that man you say was so brilliant were speaking!'

" 'Jess Semple, that is not so!' yelled Joyce. 'Mrs. Maxwell-Reeves were just lost in thought. And if you think you saw *me* sleeping —— '

" 'You was too busy trying to look around and see where I was,' I said. 'Thank God, I did not have to set up there like you with the delegation. I would not be a delegate to no such gabfest for nothing on earth.'

" 'I thought you was so interested in saving the race!' said Joyce. 'Next time I will not ask you to accompany me to no cultural events, Jesse B., because I can see you do not appreciate them. That were a discussion of ways and means. And you are talking about jazz bands!'

" 'There's more ways than one to skin a cat,' I said. 'A jazz band like Duke's or Hamp's or Basie's sure would of helped that meeting. At least on Saturday afternoon, they could have used a little music to put some pep into the proceedings. Now, just say for instant, baby, they was to open with jazz and close with jam — and do the talking in between. Start out, for example, with "The St. Louis Blues," which is a kind of colored national anthem. That would put every human in a good humor. Then play "Why Don't You Do Right?" which could be addressed to white folks. They could pat their feet to that. Then for a third number before introducing the speaker, let some guest star like Pearl Bailey sing "There'll Be Some Changes Made" — which, as I understand it, were the theme of the meeting, anyhow — and all the Negroes could say *Amen!*

" 'Joyce, I wish you would let me plan them interracial seminaries next time. After the music, let the speechmaking roll for a while — with maybe a calypso between speeches. Then, along about five o'clock, bring on the jam session, extra-special. Start serving tea to "Tea For Two," played real cool. Whilst drinking tea and dancing, the race relationers could relate, the integraters could integrate, and desegregators desegregate. Joyce, you would not have to beg for a crowd to come out and support your efforts then. Jam — and the hall would be jammed! Even I would stick around, and not be outside sneaking a smoke, or trying to figure how I can get to the bar before the resolutions are voted on. *Resolved: that we solve* the race problem! Strike up the band! Hit it, men! Aw, play that thing! "How High the Moon!" How high! Wheee-ee-e!' "

"What did Joyce say to that?" I demanded.

"Joyce just thought I was high," said Simple.

The Mystery of Black

Nat Hentoff

In a way, if the Negro were not here, we might be forced to deal within ourselves and our own personalities with all those vices, all

John Fisher's concern over the "casual attitude of many Negroes about sex" is part of the pyramid of white sexual beliefs about the Negro which are reflected in fears of Negroes' getting "too close" in housing and in schools. The foundation of the pyramid is dread of miscegenation.

The more sophisticated whites recognize, at least consciously, that differences in sexual behavior and attitudes are class rather than racial differences. The average middle-class Negro is no more casual about sex than the average middle-class white. Among Negro middle-class girls, as a matter of fact, there appears to be a greater degree of sexual "morality" than among their white counterparts. These girls, as Kenneth Clark notes in *Prejudice and Your Child* (1955), react "against the stereotyped concept of the Negro by rigidly controlling their own behavior and at times maintaining almost unrealistically high standards of personal and sexual conduct."

It is the lower-class Negro, then, who creates sexual anxiety in the largest number of whites. And the anxiety is often highly ambivalent. Edgar Z. Friedenberg describes the problem of many white middle-class teachers in the slums. They are confronted by children "inconveniently aware of their own sexuality and inconveniently skilled at bringing it to the attention of others. They live, their teachers sometimes say, like animals; and as they say it, a ghost sobs, harshly."

Distorted white conceptions of Negro "sensuality" will die hard. For many *those conundrums, and all those mysteries with which we have invested the Negro race.* — James Baldwin

whites, their own sexual guilts, unconsciously projected onto the Negro stereotype, cannot be admitted. Without seeing Negro sex life as it actually is, they will continue to fear and condemn in Negroes what they fear in themselves. In other whites there is a related form of distortion — the idealization of the greater instinctual "gratification" among Negroes; and that idealization obscures reality as much as does moral condemnation of "the casual attitude of many Negroes about sex."

Both the moralists and the romanticists are often remarkably ignorant about sex in the slums. They *do* know about those places described by Anne Petry in her novel *The Street* (1946), "where people were so damn poor they didn't have time to do anything but work, and their bodies were the only sources of relief from the pressure under which they lived; and where the crowding together made the young girls wise beyond their years." And the young boys too.

But what of the quality of that relief from pressure? And how unalloyed is the "wisdom" of the young? In their study of New Haven, *Social Class and Mental Illness* (1958), August B. Hollingshead and F. C. Redlich proved again, as Michael Harrington notes in *The Other America* (1962), that the poor "are never really that informed." Commenting on that study, Harrington continued: "Along with a cynical version of the facts of life, there went an enormous amount of misinformation. For instance, young girls were given systematic misinformation on the menstrual period. They were often frightened and guilt-ridden about sex at the same time they were sophisticated."

Similarly the moralists and the romanticists seldom mention the frequent incidence of impotence in the Negro male. There is more sexual freedom among adolescents in the ghetto, but as they grow older this "freedom" often changes into yet another affliction of being poor and black.

When, as in many lower-class Negro families, the male cannot feel himself a man, the sexual roles become confused. Men dominated first by mothers who were their central support as children often find that their wives too are economically the "heads" of the household. In this context masculine potency can be as maddeningly elusive in bed as it is everywhere else.

As for lower-class Negro women, Kardiner and Oversey in *The Mark of Oppression* concluded that:

> The most prevalent complaints of the females in this group about their marriages are: the marriages are loveless; there is no companionship; the women are only bed mates; the husbands do not support them. The entire relationship is more often than not taken up with a power struggle between husband and wife, with the former usually in a submissive role, and the female holding dominance by virtue of her actual or potential capacity as a provider. The absence of affectionate relatedness is the predominant feature of these marriages.

Dr. Kermit T. Mehlinger, a Chicago psychiatrist who specializes in marriage counseling, also contrasts reality with "these general myths about the sexual potency of Negro males and the desirability of Negro women." Actually, says Dr. Mehlinger, "there is great sexual disturbance among the Negro population. Repressions and inhibitions utilize psychic energy. With so much energy tied up in hostilities and conflicts, it is only natural that there would be disturbances in the sexual sphere. The unconscious knows no color bar."

What of the sensuality in the music of the black ghetto? Listen to it again. There is anguish as well as the irony of the blues in Ray Charles, the prototypical musical spokesman for the Negro masses. Listen to the aggressiveness of the tenor saxophone-organ combos which proliferate in Negro neighborhoods. There is some joy in this music, but there is also much rage and often a chilling sense of loss.

Whites, moreover, who admire and envy the sensual "grace" of Negro athletes and dancers seem, first of all, to be amazingly oblivious to how many awkward Negro athletes and dancers there are. And they do not recognize *all* the elements in the gracefulness they do see. Take that "natural" rhythm, for example. A Negro aware of being invisible when he works downtown for "the man" may well try to show in his dancing how remarkable and unavoidably visible an instrument he can make of his body. In the process he can also release some of his aggression against "the man" in the very pyrotechnics of the dance.

In his essay "My Negro Problem — and Ours," in the February 1963 issue of *Commentary,* Norman Podhoretz admitted to the persistence in him of "twisted feelings about Negroes." Among them were "twinges of fear . . . and resentment," but there was also envy: ". . . just as in childhood I envied Negroes for what seemed to me their superior masculinity, so I envy them today for what seems to me their superior physical grace and beauty. I have come to value physical grace very highly, and I am now capable of aching with all my being when I watch a Negro couple on the dance floor, or a Negro playing baseball or basketball. They are on the kind of terms with their own bodies that I should like to be on with mine, and for that precious quality they seem blessed to me."

Podhoretz speaks of "they." Middle-class Negro secretaries? Certainly not the middle-aged maids listlessly walking to the subway for the ride uptown? And does he ache only when he sees a Negro dancer or athlete? There are, after all, lithe young whites who dance with grace. It is a highly selective view of the physical appearance of Negroes which focuses on the young and graceful among them. Reading Podhoretz's tribute to "their superior physical grace and beauty" is like watching an MGM all-Negro musical in the 1930s. All God's chillun in the ghetto are lissome swingers. Where *do* they put the old and the ugly, the fat and the scrawny?

Another form of idealization is Norman Mailer's attempt in "The White Negro" and other works to construct an action philosophy of the "hip" out of what he considers to be the attitudes of those Negroes who have not already turned gray in their desire to become part of the majority culture.

"If," Mailer writes in "The White Negro," "the fate of twentieth-century man is to live with death from adolescence to premature senescence, why then the only life-giving answer is to accept the terms of death, to live with death as immediate danger, to divorce oneself from society, to exist without roots, to set out on that uncharted journey into the rebellious imperatives of the self . . . where security is boredom and therefore sickness, and one exists in the present."

A source of this life-giving prescription, Mailer adds, is the Negro. "Knowing in the cells of his existence that life was war, nothing but war, the Negro (all exceptions admitted) could rarely afford the sophisticated inhibitions of civilization, and so kept for his survival the art of the primitive, he lived in the enormous present, he subsisted for his Saturday night kicks, relinquishing the pleasures of the mind for the more obligatory pleasures of the body, and in his music he gave voice to the character and quality of his existence, to his rage and the infinite variations of joy, lust, languor, growl, cramp, pinch, scream and despair of his orgasm."

As I have tried to indicate, those Negroes who more or less fit Mailer's description of the "hip" prototype live in a present that is far from enormous. And how much knowledge of themselves — Mailer's goal of hipsterdom — do they gain in their existentialist immersion in "the more obligatory pleasures of the body"? To what extent do they thereby "open the limits of the possible" for themselves?

I cannot answer with any exactitude, nor can Mailer. It is one thing for him, a white man of the middle class, to seek danger and violence as a means of self-liberation, but I do not believe he can begin to equate whatever he thinks he has discovered in his own raids into himself with the way the "authentic" Negro hipster lives and feels. And here I am talking of the Negro hipster in the ghetto, not the more recent "beat" Negro in Greenwich Village, New York, and similar integrated enclaves of disaffiliation in other cities.

Through the years I have known a considerable number of Negroes who have "liberated" themselves "from the Super-Ego of society." I first met them through my interest in jazz and the men who made it; and then, as, for various reasons, I spent more and more time in Negro neighborhoods in Boston and New York, my acquaintanceship with them broadened outside the jazz life. As a white, I was not "accepted," but I hung out with many Negro hipsters long and closely enough to be extremely skeptical of Mailer's conceptions of how they live.

I write, I should point out, with no more admiration for the way most Americans exist than Mailer has. I have not, however, seen an existential Elysium in the black slums. The Negro hipsters, with all the reservations about Negro "sensuality" I've noted, do *use* their senses more than the "squares," and in that respect theirs is a more intense way of life. There is also among them, however, a pervasive sense of rootlessness, the price of which is much higher than Mailer acknowledges.

I am not even speaking primarily of the constant anxiety about money. Nor do I mean, if one has found a way of making money in an illegal or extralegal manner, the anxiety of constantly staying ahead of the cops or of other predators in the ghetto. This kind of floating dread can ultimately wear a man down as effectively as can the acquisitive struggle for upward mobility in the middle-class world. What I do mean essentially is the feeling of being lost, of coming to that inevitable point at which the kicks lose strength and have to be greatly intensified in order to match the gratification less powerful stimuli used to bring.

Speaking in another context, Lenny Bruce once said, "There's nothing sadder than an aging hipster." The Negro hipster in the slums gets old quickly, and he is sad more and more often as he does grow old. In terms of survival, he does learn a great deal about himself and others. There is a cunning and a nakedly real knowledge of interpersonal relations and motivations which a man on the edge of society has to acquire if he is to survive. But using Mailer's criteria — the expansion of the potentiality of self — this knowledge is limited, because once you do learn it, it is basically repetitive.

You learn to be cynical and manipulative and resilient. But how much can you learn of pleasure that is more durable than quick kicks, or of satisfactions more lasting than having conned somebody in order to survive? It is instructive that Mailer, who knows the satisfactions of work one feels is worth doing, does not mention this absence of meaningful work in the lives of the prototypical Negro hipsters. Yet this absence is felt, all the more gnawingly as the hipster gets older.

Fundamentally Mailer appears to be unaware of the depth of anxiety, desperation, and sheer physical discomfort which ghetto living imposes on all the poor, hip and square. In an exchange with Lorraine Hansberry in the *Village Voice,* Mailer wrote: "For fact, dear lady, you have lived no doubt in as many coldwater pads as any of us. Or known the people who did. Did we suffer so much? Did the cockroaches crow worse than the transistor radios in the thin swindle walls of the New Barracks?"

For a middle-class writer, this assessment of comparative suffering is posturing. Setting up the hollow values of "upward mobility" as an alternative to slum living evades the question of what is most acutely relevant to those who live in the slums. Miss Hansberry was much closer to reality than Mailer when she wrote in the same exchange:

> . . . blues or no blues, life roots or no life roots, Negroes of *all* classes have made it clear that they want the hell out of the ghetto just as fast as . . . anything . . . can thrust them. Worse, they have a distinct tendency to be astonished and/or furious that *everyone* doesn't know it. Misery may be theatrical to the onlooker but it hurts him who is miserable.

Mailer proclaims in *The Presidential Papers* (1963), that "what is at stake in the twentieth century is not the economic security of man — every bureaucrat in the world lusts to give him this — it is, on the contrary, the peril that they will extinguish the animal in us." Before worrying about the health of the animal in them, millions of Negroes in the slums would like to find that lusting bureaucrat.

It is not that Mailer's essential point is irrelevant. He, along with Paul Goodman and other critics of middle-class unlife, is concerned that the rise out of the ghettos, if it ever happens, may well mean that the Negro will become like the rest of us and will, as Mailer wistfully puts it, lose "his salt." However, it is possible that the social and economic changes necessary to enable the Negro to get a *chance* to escape from the slums may alter the values of the society as a whole. But even if a basic revision in American values does not take place as "the movement" increasingly focuses on institutional change, the solution Mailer provides as to how all of us, Negro and white, can save our souls ("explore that domain of experience where security is boredom and therefore sickness") is meaningless to those in poverty, particularly the black poor. They want to "make it," not in Mailer's way, but out of where they are now.

Seymour Krim, who is no fonder of middle-class characterlessness than Mailer, is much more perceptive about hipsterdom in his book, *Views of a Nearsighted Cannoneer* (1961). Krim writes of the heightened pleasures and excitement he found in jazz and later in the streets and bedrooms of Harlem. But he has not deceived himself about life in the ghetto. In asking white jazz partisans to face the implications of the source of the music which attracts them, Krim points out: "Here is a life . . . that at home, in its intimate relationships, its man-woman relationships, is as sordid, as painful, as grotesque in its accumulation of miseries as anything in Maxim Gorki's autobiography."

And in acknowledging the need for "chicks, color, barbecue, wild inventive humor with the stab of truth in it" which led him to Harlem, Krim also *saw* Harlem:

> I could never immunize myself to the garbage in the streets . . . the pawnshops, five to a block, the rat-infested tenements, the thousands of dollars spent on TVs and radio-phonographs at the sacrifice of medical aid and sanitation, the feverish traffic in drugs, the hordes of sullen-faced, corner-haunting hustlers . . . the wild red rage on the broken-beer-bottle 5 A.M. streets and the ceaseless stealing. . . . I will truly hate to see Harlem go — where will I seek then in my time of need, O merciless life? — and yet I would obviously help light the match that blows it out of existence.

In addition to Mailer, there are lesser writers who romanticize the Negro as the present-day fount of "primitive," life-giving passion. Jack Kerouac, for instance, writes: "At lilac evening I walked with every muscle aching . . . wishing I were a Negro, feeling that the best the white world has offered was not enough ecstasy for me, not enough life, joy, kicks, music . . ." To which James Baldwin has responded: "I would hate to be in Kerouac's shoes if he should ever be mad enough to read this aloud afrom the stage of Harlem's Apollo Theater."

There has also been Kitten, the heroine of Robert Gover's *One Hundred Dollar Misunderstanding* (1962). In the novel, the fourteen-year-old Negro prostitute is the apotheosis of mother wit. Condemnatory of white personal and public hypocrisy, Kitten is infinitely more vivid than the male protagonist, a puffy, unbelievably vacuous white college student. Kitten's insights into the hollowness of the white middle class are accurate enough, but the instinctual wisdom claimed for this black child implies that, even at the cost of being a whore, Kitten has grown up "natural" into a most enviable state of being.

At the very end there is a faint indication that Kitten is nonetheless not well enough equipped to fulfill her extraordinary capacities — let alone to survive economically in any other profession — and so there is a passing reference to her saving her fees to go to "readin college." Yet Kitten, "old blackass Pickaninny me," is fundamentally a reverse Stepin Fetchit caricature with a touch of the boy raised by wolves who goes on to get a Ph.D. in natural history.

The wide appeal of *One Hundred Dollar Misunderstanding* was due in large part to the fact that whites could accept Kitten's biting criticism of them because it came from the kind of person one could not take seriously. She was "advanced" for her age and condition, but the moral impact of the novel was glancing — somewhat like Smokey Bear telling us to watch what we do with our cigarettes in the woods. What does a *bear* know? Or, as Negro writer John Williams speculated, " . . . would

One Hundred Dollar Misunderstanding have been quite so well received had Kitten been a Negro social worker instead of a whore, and the inability of man and woman, black and white, to communicate been put on an altogether different symbolic level?"

The romanticists, from Mailer to Gover, are of no use to the Negro who wants out of the ghetto. Neither are Norman Podhoretz and the other white liberals who are exploring their "twisted feelings" about Negroes — however necessary that exploration is now for *them.* Nor is John Fischer's "moral uplift" campaign of major use as motivation for the lowest of the dispossessed. ut Fischer is more cogent than the others I have discussed in this chapter, and more cogent than he may himself realize, when he writes that the Negro will get out of his present plight "only when he begins to change his circumstances, make new history, and shoulder a bigger share of responsibility for the fix he is in."

Fischer is correct, but not in the sense he means — the establishment of First Class Citizens' Councils among Negroes. The "bigger share of responsibility" the Negro must shoulder as he makes "new history" is to be in the vanguard of those organized for change throughout the society.

Obviously, as has been emphasized, this change, which involves a much more massive assault on poverty than President Lyndon Johnson or any other political leader has yet suggested, cannot be accomplished by Negroes alone. But it will not be set in motion without Negro impetus. Accordingly, more of the Negro poor have to be enlisted in this campaign. For that to happen will require more Negro leaders who are aware of what has to be done and who can so explain specific programs to potential recruits that the latter are motivated to vote, to engage in direct action, and to apply pressure in any other manner which may be effective.

Although the over-all alliance and its leadership will have to be integrated, the next stage of organization among the Negro masses will be under black leadership because many of the Negro poor cannot now be moved to action by *anyone* with a white skin.

At a mass civil rights rally in Harlem in the spring of 1963, the organizer, a Negro, told those of his co-workers who were white that he could not allow them any longer to pass among the crowd with containers for contributions. "More and more often in recent weeks," he explained, "the containers have been snatched away from white hands. You can't expect them to see that *you're* pure in heart. From now on, all collectors will be Negro."

Psychedelos

Psychedelos

I will journey
to a place where I may see
that which there is to see.
Gene Fowler, Shaman Songs

In his book Waiting for the End, *Leslie Fiedler asserts that America is changing from a whiskey culture to a drug culture. Certainly in recent years the illegal use of drugs, especially among the young, has spread at a fantastic rate. This section examines some of these drugs and the implications of their use.*

Gene Fowler's Psychedelos *is a poetic reconstruction of a "trip," alive with exotic sensory experiences and witty, sophisticated word-play. In this poem, the psychedelic experience becomes a whimsical and mysterious journey into the speaker's psyche (his "room"). "Outside my room a darkness," he notes; but inside there is light, commonplace reality dissolves as "silver backing flakes from the mirror" and becomes "bright snow." Images of light flood through the poem: there is "moon-woman" and "sun-man"; there are "the light-globe people" who write in the Holy Book; there are the miners with "cyclopean/corneal lamp." The journey home ends in darkness, and "strangers entering the room/are opaque."*

This is not at all a poem in praise of drugs, however; it seems instead to be an evocation of the intuitive, imaginative world below the superficial levels of consciousness. In contrast, Ernest Havemann's essay "Psychochemistry: Personality by Prescription" is a factual and explicitly hopeful examination of the pharmacological revolution. Mr. Havemann studies the far-reaching implications of the use of drugs to influence mental illness, sexual behavior, the need for sleep, and the process of aging. Although Mr. Havemann's tone is optimistic, he is very much aware of the hazards inherent in such drugs.

The three essays and the poem that complete this section illustrate the proposition that drugs are neither good nor bad in themselves, but may be used in creative or destructive ways. Alfred R. Lindesmith, in "The Marihuana Problem — Myth or Reality?" makes a thorough and objective survey of the nature and effects of marihuana, in support of his argument that laws governing the use of marihuana should be no more repressive than laws governing the use of alcohol. "LSD and the Third Eye," by John N. Bleibtreu, examines the relationship between the psychedelic experience and the mysterious "pineal gland" — "the third eye, the eye of the mind." Mr. Bleibtreu is particularly concerned with a dilemma about the nature of reality, the paradox that "truth may be obtained through a state of mind in which reason is dislocated." He wants to discover a way to creative madness, which allows us to transcend commonplace reality and yet function as sane beings. On the other hand, William S. Burroughs' "Deposition: Testimony Concerning a Sickness" offers some tough-minded advice from a man who spent fifteen years of his life addicted to "hard" narcotics such as heroin: "Look down LOOK DOWN along that junk road before you travel there and get in with the Wrong Mob. . . ." Anne Sexton's poem "The Addict" presents "the queen of this condition," "an expert on making the trip," who takes her pills "eight at a time from sweet pharmaceutical bottles." "Yes/I try/to kill myself in small amounts,/an innocuous occupation." So she says. She has traveled a long way from "Psychedelos."

Go, go, go, said the bird: human kind
Cannot bear very much reality.
T. S. Eliot, "Burnt Norton" (from Four Quartets)

Psychedelos

Gene Fowler

i

silver backing flakes from the mirror, falls

bright snow

from the direction of the Pleiades

each platinum faceted pellet

coming down
fast as light

i catch them
with the grace and shout of a riveter

in a molecule thick membrane of hand

a hand filling the evening sky

at my equator—

ii

outside my room a darkness

the trick there is always a trick

is in keeping an equalized pressure

change it just a bit

the skin of the room waves like flags joined

along their edges

shape a floor
to the textures of a lovely girl
lie on her

if you can-can

if you can-can

iii

Moon-woman laughs

a harmonium at play

her breasts are cones
ice cream spilling over
sticky

threads lacing stars together

O, Moon-woman
turn from the window

only a darkness
lies beyond my room

there is nothing to await

and i am the great riveter

how much, in gold
coin, so i may carry your child

her nipples were gold coins

swollen to suns
in her quick pregnancy

from across the raging room

was our only way to love

i threw out my love
and when i missed, great furrows

were cleaved in her flesh

but when those silver pellets struck

she would throb and swell

and 300 things
would come to be in my room

iv

Sun-man, armed with the compleat angle-er

explores in my room

the room is rectangular
by measure
a block of oleomargarine

sliced into thin sheets
it is a Holy Book

the light-globe people
are writing in it

their dazzling heads
melting the pages together

bright heiroglyphs
lost in chunks of hardened
Greece

Sun-man rocks on fat buttocks
popping globes with silver rocks

i collect fragments
trying to read
over exploding shoulders

v

the Crone
read my palm, scraping away calluses
saving them
in a stone jar

your life-line
is hollow-stump peculiar
dark-kitten irregular

however i rede
wherever i pick it up
it leads to the four corners
of the room

you must, my dear
pulling my hips from me, jarring
them with the calluses

you must, my dear
flared nostrils bat-flying
thru the strands of room

feel a map
lest you forget this room

when the magic physic
is done
and you shrink to solid-state

uncallused fingers
sorebright from cracked safes

weave life-lines
thru points of light

with a quick stitch
and a soaking up of colors

vi

Sun-man is lecturing upon
litters and scions

advancing into awlcomy

the equator is one who equates
the equated an equature

in the beginning was . . .

teacher, tell us of the equinox
tell us again of the lovely equinox

equinox is the coroner stone
the frowndation
of awl dumbocracy

a contraction of 'equal knocks'
—for awl

awl is an only bard of murdern kratosism

vii

WARNING

all mining must be confined to the interior

the skin of the room
may be pushed back, arranged variously
but must not be torn

or darkness will spill in

reductive mining is recommended

the miners are brawny fellows
cyclopian

corneal lamp peering deep in

to dig what is kneaded
without cutting threads of the map

there are many bits of pellet-element
all held apart by chunks of rock
the task of the miner, to ask

the bits to move inward from the rock shell
and form an arrangement one might enter

the miners expose their veins

i wear the bright colors

viii

mirror, mirror
on the wall

who is

billowing clouds of cotton candy

must be packed into tiny ore-cars
for delivery

the skin of the room hides

behind thickness, a sickness

builds in my hope

Sun-man is gone, out the window

Moon-woman is dead

the old Crone in her lace of answers

retreats to a corner

of the ceiling

silver comets fly to the mirror

and strangers entering the room

are opaque

Psychochemistry: Personality by Prescription

Ernest Havemann

As anyone can plainly see, this is one of mankind's strangest eras. On the one hand, all is pessimism: The world is plagued by violence, starvation, overpopulation and alienation. Yet never have so many well-informed men been so rosily optimistic: There is a strong school of thought holding that all our problems are basically chemical and will soon yield to solution as readily as the question of what happens when two atoms of hydrogen join with an atom of oxygen. (In case you have forgotten, $H_2 + O = H_2O$; namely, water. As simple as all that.)

It is typical of our era that Dr. Glenn Seaborg, chairman of the Atomic Energy Commission, should have taken time out from worrying about the atom to tell an audience of women, not entirely in jest, that they will soon have a marvelous "antigrouch pill" to sweeten the dispositions of their menfolk. (Presumably, it could be slipped into the unsuspecting male's morning coffee, like a lump of sugar, to turn him from terrible tiger to purring kitten.)

It is also typical that two other respected thinkers, one a scientist and one an author, should have placed the rather humorous-sounding antigrouch pill on a serious global basis. The scientist, Dr. Heinz Lehmann of Canada's McGill University, has predicted an "antiaggression drug" that will overcome what seem up to now to be the natural human tendencies to pick quarrels and to make war. The author, Arthur Koestler, claims in his *The Ghost in the Machine* that most of man's troubles are caused by a conflict between his "old brain," which controls his emotions, and his "new brain," which determines his thoughts; this gap will eventually be bridged by a drug that will give us all a "coordinated, harmonious state of mind," making us far too contented to fret or to fight.

There are also respected researchers on record as believing that man will soon have drugs that will cure his major mental disturbances, eliminate his fears and anxieties, keep him fat or lean at will, let him decide for himself how long, if at all, he cares to sleep, make him much smarter than ever before and even permit him to live longer. You name it and there is somebody — not a wild-eyed visionary but a sane and skeptical scientist — who believes it is just around the corner.

Are we really on the verge of a chemical breakthrough in the control of human personality?

If you were a psychiatrist at a mental hospital, you would have to think so. You might be inclined to say, indeed, that the breakthrough has already been made. What has happened in the mental hospitals has taken place so rapidly and spectacularly that the events have outsped communications; they constitute one of the great untold and unappreciated stories of our time. Few people know about it except the veteran staff members who worked in the hospitals in the old days — meaning before about 1955 — and who work there yet.

In the mid-Fifties, there were 560,000 patients in mental hospitals and the figure was rising by 12,000 a year. For all practical purposes, the hospitals might have borne the same legend that Dante said was inscribed on the gates of hell, "All hope abandon, ye who enter here." Some of the patients were in strait jackets, lest they kill one another or the guards. Some of them were in wet packs — wrapped in wet sheets in a bathtub — in an attempt to cool them down. The wards were full of men and women tearing out their hair, cursing, using the floors for toilets. Even the calmest of the patients were terrified of the future. The staffs were overworked and frustrated; there was time only to guard the overcrowded buildings and prevent trouble, no time at all to practice the intensive psychotherapy that was then considered the only possible glimmer of chance for improvement. Everybody knew that the very atmosphere of a mental hospital was enough to drive a normal man crazy, that almost nobody could be expected to recover there; yet for the hopelessly disturbed patients of the day, there was no alternative.

Into this dismal picture, one day, there suddenly dropped the first of the chemical weapons against mental disease — two tranquilizers discovered at almost the same instant, chlorpromazine and reserpine. Physicians gave one or the other to their most difficult patients and sat back in utter disbelief. Dr. Nathan S. Kline, the veteran research director of New York's Rockland State Hospital, still displays the excitement of the successful explorer when he recalls what happened: "We knew the minute we tried the drugs that this was it. We knew it not after the first one hundred patients, not after the first fifty, but after the first six."

Today, of course, there are many tranquilizers, all of which have a remarkably benign effect on the schizophrenic patients who have the world's most crippling psychosis. There are also drugs to combat the symptoms of depression, another common psychosis, as well as the symptoms of the manic state that often alternates with depression. The atmosphere in the mental hospitals has totally changed. They are less crowded now — 425,000 patients instead of 560,000. The patients are far less destructive, far less terrified, far more "normal" in their behavior. The staffs have more time to treat the patients, with individual or group psychotherapy as well as medicine. And patients do recover; more than twice as many as before go back to rejoin their families and to work at jobs, like anybody else. In human terms, the improvement is nothing short of magnificent. Even in cold financial terms, the drugs to control mental disturbances have been of astounding value. Dr. Kline estimates that they have saved the U.S. some 20 billion dollars in the cost of new buildings and beds and continuing care that would otherwise have had to be provided for the mentally disturbed.

All this, in the almost unanimous opinion of the researchers, is only the beginning. It is a cliché in psychiatric circles to say that the present mind drugs do not cure mental disturbance but only relieve the symptoms, thus enabling the patient to live a more normal life and sometimes making him amenable to the talking-out benefits of intensive psychotherapy that may get at the roots of his conflicts. That is to say, most psychiatrists and psychologists and almost all psychoanalysts continue to believe that mental disturbances are usually functional — caused by some kind of disturbance in personality dynamics — rather than due to physical causes. Yet even the functional theorists tend to believe that better drugs are on the way. Dr. Sherwyn Woods, director of graduate education in psychiatry at the University of Southern California, is, for example, one of those who believe that the basic cause of schizophrenia lies in functional problems in thinking and human relations. Yet Dr. Woods also believes that the functional problems lead to or are associated with biochemical disturbances that determine the symptoms of schizophrenia, and he believes that even the most stubborn symptoms will mostly prove treatable with new drugs. "Within twenty years," he says, "we should have chemicals that are effective in controlling hallucinations and delusions and making patients far more comfortable than they are even today."

Even more optimistic are those psychiatrists who, impressed by the success of the tranquilizers and antidepressants, are beginning to think that all serious mental disturbance is basically biochemical in nature, some kind of abnormal bodily chemistry that poisons the brain and makes it act in strange and unfortunate ways. Dr. Kline, for example, says flatly, "I think schizophrenia is probably an organic disorder, and I'm almost sure that 80 percent of depressions are organic." In his private practice, Dr. Kline relies strictly on medications and no longer practices any psychotherapy at all. ("Some of my patients," he concedes, "seem to be disappointed that I don't ask them about their sex lives and masturbation and sibling rivalry and all that; I guess I lose some of them that way.") And Dr. Kline is one of those who forecast that new medicines will prevent even that currently hopeless form of psychosis caused by damage to the brain due to senility. ("The trouble with the human brain," he says, "is that it's grown too big for the human skull; it doesn't get enough blood supply, especially as we get older. But someday we'll find a new way of nourishing it and keeping its cells from dying off.")

If all psychoses are organic, then all of them theoretically can be cured — or at least controlled, completely and permanently, like diabetes — with the right kind of medicine. Indeed, a situation might arise similar to one of the present ironies in physical medicine. Nowadays, it is almost better to have pneumonia, which can easily be cured with antibiotics, than a common cold, for which no cure exists. Someday it may be better to have a major psychosis, curable with some specific drug of the future, than to have one of the minor psychoneurotic disorders, such as an anxiety state or a sexual obsession, which even Dr. Kline and his fellow theorists consider to be functional in origin and treatable only with psychotherapy.

What is the layman to think about the argument of functional versus organic? Until recently, the functional viewpoint had all the better of it; all attempts to find a physical basis ended in either failure or controversy. Now, however, the scales may be tipping; there is strong new evidence that any one of several physical abnormalities may be associated with schizophrenia. One of them concerns a part of the blood plasma known as alpha-2-globulin. This substance is present in everybody's blood stream; but in the blood of schizophrenics, it has been found in amounts far above normal. The finding is particularly impressive because it was made independently by three research laboratories, two in the United States and one in the Soviet Union. One of the researchers, Dr. Jacques Gottlieb of the Lafayette Clinic in Detroit, theorizes that an excess amount of alpha-2-globulin may bore its way into brain cells and cause them to function something like a short-circuited switchboard.

Another possibility also has been discovered by several researchers, among them, C. A. Clarke of the University of Liverpool; they have found that the urine of schizophrenics, but not the urine of normal people, often contains a complicated chemical called DMPE. This chemical has a structure that is similar both to adrenaline, which is secreted in large amounts by the human adrenal gland in states of stress and emotion, and to mescaline, a chemical found in a Southwestern cactus plant that was chewed by primitive American Indians to produce a binge that looks for all the world like some forms of schizophrenia. The Clarke findings would seem to indicate that schizophrenics, owing to some hereditary defect in burning off their adrenaline, might be continuously intoxicated by a mescaline-like chemical produced by their own bodies.

Without much fanfare, this sort of possibility has now been carried a step further. Dr. Mark D. Altschule, a Harvard scientist, and his colleague Dr. Zoltan L. Hegedus have announced the discovery, made in a test tube, that human blood contains enzymes that can convert adrenaline into several chemicals called "brain poisoning indoles," presumably capable of causing all kinds of mental aberrations. Moreover, reported Drs. Altschule and Hegedus, the tendency to produce large quantities of these indoles seems to be greater in schizophrenics than in normal people and also to be hereditary; it appears to be higher among the relatives of schizophrenics than among other people. Score another point for the theory that the body and brain of the schizophrenic might be a sort of hereditary chemical factory for converting adrenaline into its own intoxicants.

A great many scientists are now working on biochemical research into mental disturbances, following these leads and seeking new ones. Even Dr. Linus Pauling, the Nobel Prize winner, came out this year with a new organic theory of mental disturbance. Dr. Pauling has decided that normal mental functioning depends on the presence of many kinds of molecules, including those of many of the B vitamins, vitamin C, uric acid and other substances normally present in the brain. The average person, Dr. Pauling contends, gets enough of these substances from his daily diet or produces them in sufficient quantity through his own bodily chemistry. The mentally ill person, however, owing to some kind of hereditary difference, needs more of them, because he burns them off faster or cannot produce them as efficiently. His bodily chemistry, especially the chemistry of his brain, is off in such a way as to make him suffer, in effect, from a deficiency disease, like rickets or scurvy.

The way to treat him, says Dr. Pauling, is to pinpoint the deficiency and correct it — a new kind of treatment that he calls orthomolecular psychiatry (meaning to provide the right amount of the right molecules at the right time and place). Dr. Pauling's theory has been challenged by some psychiatrists — but his record shows that it is hardly safe to dismiss his ideas.

There is one form of brain abnormality, it should be added, that has been treated successfuly with a specific drug for many years. This is epilepsy, not a psychosis but a strange disorder in which parts of the brain seem to become overexcitable, leading from time to time to what might be called electrical explosions, accompanied by seizures ranging from mild blackouts to intense convulsions. Julius Caesar suffered from epileptic "fits," and so would more than 1,000,000 people today, where it not for a drug called Dilantin. Taken daily, Dilantin restores the brain's nerve cells to normal excitability and prevents them from firing too quickly or too often; its use permits most epilepsy patients to lead perfectly normal lives, free from fear of a seizure. Recently, there has been speculation that Dilantin may also relieve some kinds of depression, control irrational anger and break the obsessive, "round-and-round" thinking patterns that seem to plague many people. (The noted financier Jack Dreyfus, Jr., who reports that his own mood and thinking abilities have been greatly improved by Dilantin, has set up a foundation to explore these possibilities.)

Besides relieving the symptoms of mental disease — or possibly even curing it — what else can the chemical breakthrough do? One thing it has already done is revolutionize human sexual behavior; for the first time in man's history, it has separated the sex act from the act of procreation. To most Americans today, the word "pill" means one thing first and foremost — the birth-control pill, 99.7 percent effective in preventing pregnancy. The pill is by far the most efficient method of birth control ever invented; indeed, it is the only sure method, short of sterilization. It works by delicately tinkering with the female hormone cycle and thus preventing the monthly release of a ripe egg. No egg, no pregnancy — regardless of when sexual intercourse takes place.

As good as the pill is, it has some disadvantages. Some women object to the fact that it must be taken every day for 20 days and then stopped for eight days; they have trouble remembering. Never mind. Soon a woman will be able to go to her physician and get a single shot that will do the job for three months, and no remembering necessary. Or, if she finds it more convenient, she will switch to the new "minipill," already tested and found effective. This one will be taken every day of the year, and no need to consult the calendar. The same hormones used in the minipill could even be implanted under the skin, in a slightly porous capsule that would permit the proper dose to leak into the blood stream each day. Without causing any undue problems, the capsule might be large enough to last for 20 years, thus constituting a sort of "20-year pill." (If the woman decided at any time during this period to have a baby, she would simply take another kind of chemical to cancel out the effects of her 20-year pill.) Or, if the right technique can be perfected, it is entirely possible that the woman of the future can have herself *vaccinated* against pregnancy; this would be done with a serum producing antibodies in her blood stream that would make her immune to the effect of sperm, just as present vaccinations make her immune to smallpox germs. The woman who has sexual intercourse only rarely, and does not want to bother with any of the other techniques, may be able to indulge without fear of pregnancy because of the availability of the "morning-after pill," already tested but not yet perfected; the morning-after pill will prevent the fertilized egg, if there should be one, from becoming implanted in the wall of the womb. Even pills for men, safely making them temporarily sterile by preventing the development of living sperm, are theoretically possible. In fact, one such pill has already been found effective; it has never been marketed, because the user suffers a violent reaction if he takes as much as a single alcoholic drink.

The pill already controls pregnancy, and more convenient versions of it are just around the corner. What about that other fear of so many women (and of men as well) — the problem called obesity? Here one gets into difficult psychological ground. Many psychiatrists think that people get fat strictly as a form of self-protection: the overweight man is shielding himself (or, more often, the overweight woman is shielding *her*self) from life's obligations to be socially attractive and adept and to lead a normally active sex life. Making a fat person skinny, according to this school of thought, will only add to his (more often, *her*) anxieties. Yet it is well known that bodily weight depends upon how much food is eaten, and the amount of food that is eaten seems to depend upon two small areas in the brain. When one of these areas is removed from the brain of a rat, the animal loses almost all interest in food; it has no appetite at all to speak of. When the other area is removed, the animal seems to be constantly hungry and soon becomes grossly fat. Taken together, the two areas serve as a sort of "appestat" that says when to eat and when to stop. Why not assume that the fat person's appestat is simply off kilter — in a way that could be corrected by some specific drug? (There already are drugs that can reduce appetite after a fashion, but all of them are also stimulants and therefore not specific.)

What about drugs to make people happy — not just to get them out of depressions or to tranquilize them but to make them actively and buoyantly happy? We already have drugs that put people in a happy mood; the most accepted one is alcohol, and among the legally forbidden ones is marijuana. But alcohol and marijuana are what one researcher calls "sloppy drugs," even though alcohol is such an integral part of social ritual that it will probably always remain on the human scene. There undoubtedly are better drugs, just waiting to be discovered, that would make a person wake up smiling and sing through his day, without ever affecting his mental judgment or getting him in trouble with the law. There probably also are drugs yet to be found that will enhance a person's ability to perceive the beauty in his world — to recapture the delight of the child who thinks of a shiny penny as not only a piece of money but an object of art. And if human perception can be enhanced, why not human intelligence?

Intelligence is a strange thing; the unhappy fact is that no one even has an acceptable theory as to why one person should be smarter than another. Certainly, intelligence (or lack of it) depends in some way on the brain, whose trillions of possible nerve circuits act as a feedback system that absorbs information from the eyes and ears, processes it, stores it and at the appropriate time sends it back to the vocal cords, to be uttered as words of wisdom, or to the finger tips, to become the written evidence of learning. But why one brain should be better at this job than another is a mystery. Mere size does not tell the story; most human brains run about three pounds and deviations from this weight are not necessarily related to intelligence; there doubtless have been Eskimo fishermen with bigger brains than Einstein's. Mere numbers are not the answer; while the genius has upward of ten billion nerve cells in his brain, so in many cases does the low-grade moron. (Indeed, a young low-grade moron may have *more* brain cells than an older genius, for these cells die off at the rate of 100,000 a day after a person reaches 35.) The efficiency of the nerve cells and their fibers as conductors of the nervous impulse does not seem to be crucial; the long fibers that stretch from our spinal cords and enable us to wiggle our toes, and that presumably have scant effect on how smart we are at atomic physics, are better and faster conductors than the fibers inside the brain.

There has been much speculation that learning depends upon a permanent alteration of a living chemical called RNA inside the nerve cell; this theory stems from the work of a Swedish scientist named Holger Hydén, who trained rats to balance on a wire, then analyzed individual nerve cells and found changes in the molecular structure of their RNA. This chemical is closely related to DNA, which carries the code of human heredity; and, like DNA, it is so complicated in structure as to be capable of taking trillions of possible forms, each a little unlike any other. If the molecules for DNA can contain the entire code that directs the development of some cells into the human bone structure and others into the human heart, and can make some people tall and brown-eyed and others short and blue-eyed, then it seems reasonable to suppose that the RNA molecules inside the nerve cells might possibly carry the code for all the most complicated details of human learning.

More recently, Dr. Hydén has reported a further complication involving the 100 billion so-called glial cells that support and help nourish the nerve cells of the brain. In a new experiment, he trained right-handed rats to use their left paws to pull food from a tube, and left-handed rats to use their right paws. When he analyzed their brains, he found not only altered RNA molecules but also new forms of protein. It is his theory that the RNA instructed the glial cells to manufacture these new proteins, which then became part or all of the memory trace. Another investigator working along similar lines with pigeons, Boston's Dr. Samuel Bogoch, has also reported finding new brain proteins — plus, just to add another complication, new chemicals that are a combination of protein and sugar.

If learning depends on chemical changes of the RNA inside nerve cells, or on the manufacture of new chemicals as directed by RNA, then some exciting possibilities open up. Researchers have been quick to explore them, and the result has been a series of the most fascinating — and controversial — experiments in all scientific history. The first occurred at the University of Michigan, where a psychologist named James V. McConnell taught some primitive little animals called flatworms to escape a shock signaled by a flashing light, then chopped them up and fed them to some other flatworms. The "cannibals," he found, were unusually quick to solve the problem of escaping the shock — for all the world as if they had absorbed knowledge along with their food.

As if this were not enough of a scientific sensation, psychologist Allan Jacobson of UCLA soon came up with a topper. Using rats and hamsters, he taught half of his animals that they could get a food pellet by pressing a bar whenever a light flashed; the other half, whenever a click sounded. When they had thoroughly learned their lessons, he killed them, extracted RNA from their brains and injected the RNA into a new group of rats and hamsters. Lo and behold, he found that the new animals injected with RNA from those trained to respond to a light flash showed a significant tendency to do the same thing. Those who received RNA from the click group showed a strong tendency to respond to the click. This time, it appeared that learning had been transferred with a hypodermic needle.

The implications of these experiments are fantastic. They would seem to forecast a day when the laborious process of education could be short-cut; college students would learn about atomic physics not by hitting their books but by receiving injections of surplus RNA from the brains of their instructors. The immense learning of a man such as Einstein could be preserved by feeding slices of his brain to a selected group of young scholars. But, alas, this whole area of transfer of learning is currently surrounded by doubt. Shortly after Dr. Jacobson reported his findings, other scientists tried to duplicate his results; 18 such experiments were set up and all 18 failed. The question now is whether he did something wrong or the other experimenters did, and an attempt to find the answer is being made in many laboratories across the nation. Some of the early results look promising for transfer of training, and one scientist who took part in the 18 experiments that appeared to prove Dr. Jacobson wrong has now changed his mind. But other results have thus far been inconclusive or flatly negative. At the moment, it appears to be the majority opinion among scientists that transfer of learning is impossible and the RNA theory of memory, dubious.

If not the RNA inside the nerve cell, then what about the myriad switching points inside the brain? As everyone who has taken a freshman psychology course knows, each nerve fiber ends in branches that form connections called synapses with other nerve fibers. The nervous impulse, though it is a tiny electrical charge, cannot leap like a spark of electricity across a synapse. Instead, it can only trigger the release of a chemical that may or may not stimulate the next nerve to fire. Could it be that efficiency at getting a message through the synapses is the reason one person is brighter than another?

Under the electromicroscope, it would not seem so, for all synapses look remarkably similar. There seems to be no reason to think that the synapses are any closer or tighter in the genius than in the dullard or, for that matter, than in the monkey. On the other hand, it is known that learning can cause a nerve cell to grow, like a tree proliferating its roots and branches, and form additional synapses with other nerve cells from which it had previously been isolated (just as the tree taps new sources of food and light). At the same time, other changes take place that may act as a sort of soldering of connections at the synapses.

Some quite remarkable results have been

reported by Dr. David Krech, a psychologist at the University of California at Berkeley, who had the ingenuity to undertake what he has called a Head Start program for young rats. He placed the rats together in a special cage, where they could react not only to one another but also to all kinds of "creative playthings," such as ladders to climb and wheels to turn; at the same time, they could watch all the sights and hear all the sounds of a bustling human laboratory. Simultaneously, he raised their twins in solitary confinement, in quiet and dimly lit cages, where they got no intellectual stimulation at all. The Head Start rats proved much smarter at solving rat-type problems than did their twins, and post-mortem examination of their brains showed some striking differences. The cortex — the highest or "thinking" part of the brain — was much better developed. The nerve cells were bigger; there were more glial cells and larger blood vessels. Moreover, the cortex contained more of the enzyme (called acetylcholineesterase) that acts to transfer the nerve impulse across the synapse.

In thinking of a "smart pill" that would improve human intelligence, perhaps it does not matter whether the feedback circuit depends on RNA, the synapses or something as yet unimagined. One scientist who has speculated on this point is Dr. John Eric Holmes, a physiology professor at the University of Southern California Medical School, whose learning experiments have even included an unsuccessful attempt to teach the mimosa to fold its leaves in response to light and darkness as well as to touch. Says Dr. Holmes, "Whether RNA is the key or a blind alley, it still should be possible to increase an individual's learning ability."

Indeed, the world already possesses a smart pill that has worked, for reasons unknown, on mice. As Dr. James L. McGaugh has found at the University of California at Riverside, injections of such powerful central-nervous-system stimulants as strychnine or Metrazol can greatly improve the ability of a mouse to learn a maze. The effect seems to be more pronounced for dull mice than for smart mice, possibly indicating that the ideal smart pill, when it is discovered, will do more for the mentally retarded than for those who are already near the biological limit of human performance. At least two drug companies are known to have been testing such a pill for human beings, composed of chemicals much less lethal than strychnine but nonetheless promising.

Just as it has been found possible to stimulate learning in lower animals, so has it been found possible to stop learning. Dr. Murray Jarvik, at the Albert Einstein Medical School in New York City, has experimented with rats placed on a small platform above the floor of a cage. The rat's natural tendency is to very quickly step down from the platform. If it gets a painful electrical shock from the floor, however, it learns right then and there to stay on the platform; the next time, it will remain there without budging for as long as the experimenter cares to wait. What Dr. Jarvik has done is to teach a rat to expect the shock, then quickly disrupt its brain chemistry by using a sort of electroshock treatment. The next time the rat is placed on the platform, instead of remembering its lesson, it steps right down, as if it had never learned to expect a shock. (Human beings who undergo electroshock treatment also lose their memory for recent events.)

At the University of Michigan, Dr. Bernard W. Agranoff has blotted out the memories of goldfish by injecting them with puromycin, an antibiotic drug that interferes with the ability of RNA to perform its normal function of synthesizing new protein materials inside the cell. He teaches the goldfish to avoid an electric shock by swimming across a barrier to the unlighted end of its tank; if he then immediately injects puromycin into the fish's skull, all memory of the training vanishes. Oddly enough, even a "stupid pill," such as puromycin seems to be, might have value to human beings. As Dr. Krech has pointed out, a drug of this type might boost the learning ability of a person who remembers so many details as to get hopelessly bogged down at the task of sorting out what is essential.

In functional terms, human intelligence or learning ability seems to depend on three quite different skills. First, one must be able to pay attention, to concentrate, to get the message or, in the words of Dr. Sidney Cohen of the UCLA Medical School, to "comb down on the problem." Next, one's brain must lay down some sort of lasting memory trace, perhaps in the form of changed RNA molecules, perhaps in the form of proteins manufactured under the direction of RNA, perhaps in chemical changes at the synapses, perhaps in some other way. Lastly, one must have a retrieval system, a method of scanning the memory traces and focusing on the right one. "All three processes," says Dr. Cohen, "could possibly be improved chemically; so I see no reason chemicals couldn't be contrived that would improve our thinking abilities." The smart pill may be not just one pill but several, to influence the various processes involved in learning. The drugs may work best, as Dr. Krech's studies would indicate and as Dr. Cohen also believes, in conjunction with improved psychological methods of training and disciplining that wonderful and as-yet-unrealized instrument called the human mind. But they seem to be merely waiting for a discoverer.

Like intelligence, sleep is another of nature's great mysteries. We need sleep; many of us need eight hours'; we must spend a full third of our lives in this state of unconsciousness. But why? At one time it was thought that the waste products of normal activity accumulated in the blood stream and eventually drugged the brain; while the body was at rest during sleep, these waste products were then eliminated. But studies of Siamese twins, who share a common blood stream, have disproved this theory; scientists have observed one Siamese baby sound asleep while the other remained wide awake. Now, sleep has been traced to two centers in the brain. If one of these centers is removed from an animal, it will sleep constantly. If the other is removed, it will not sleep at all — but eventually, proving that sleep is a biological necessity, it will go into a coma and die, as if from utter exhaustion.

Brain waves change during sleep; indeed, electroencephalograph studies of human beings have shown four recognizable patterns of waves that seem to indicate four stages of sleep, ranging from light to very deep. Obviously, something goes on during sleep, certainly in the brain and possibly elsewhere; this something is essential to good health and even to staying alive. But why this should be is unknown. Dr. Nathan Kline, one of the researchers who have been fascinated by the problem, speculates that at the beginning of mankind's history, perhaps not all men needed to sleep. But man's nighttime vision is poor; a man who wandered around through the darkness would have been subject to accident and fair game for beasts of prey. Thus, evolution favored those men who, for some reason, were forced by the requirements of their own brains and bodies to spend the hours of darkness in a state of suspended animation and in a protected spot. If Dr. Kline's thoughts are correct, we sleep today, though there is no longer any evolutionary need for it, because only those of our ancestors who required sleep managed to survive and pass along their trait. Dr. Kline has also pointed out that the old Mogul emperors, in contrast to most more-or-less-modern human beings, are said to have got along just fine on no more than three-and-a-half hours' sleep a night. Was this also an inherited trait, passed along by some strange evolutionary accident? Or did the Mogul emperors have a drug?

Some drugs have already been found to reduce the need for sleep; patients who go on the antidepressants often find themselves, like the Mogul emperors, getting along on three to four hours' for as long as they take the medicine. (These medicines are usually prescribed for only brief periods; what would happen to the patients if they continued to sleep so little is not known.) At any rate, there seems scant doubt that the mystery will eventually be solved. Says Dr. L. R. Hines, director of biological research for the Hoffmann-La Roche drug company, "There's unquestionably a biochemical explanation for sleep and someday somebody will find it." Will this mean that we will then simply swallow a pill when tired, instead of going to bed? Conceivably, it will mean exactly that.

If science can promise us a pill that will end the need for sleep, then why not something that is really far out? Why should science not bring true the ancient dream of a Fountain of Youth and give us some magic elixir that will keep us young and active to an age denied to previous generations? Why not, indeed? One scientist who believes the dream may be within grasp is Dr. Denham Harman of the University of Nebraska Medical School, who has already had considerable success in lengthening the life expectancy of his laboratory mice. Dr. Harman's secret is hardly a secret at all; it is nothing more than a well-known chemical called BHT, commonly used to prevent spoilage of the fats and oils in potato chips and bottled salad dressings. When Dr. Harman fed his mice a special diet including BHT, they lived 50 percent longer on the average than other mice of the same breed — presumably because the BHT slowed down some of the chemical reactions inside the body that cause aging and eventually death. He has not yet had much luck at increasing the maximum age to which the hardiest of his mice live; in human terms, he has helped more of his mice live to 80, rather than pushed the maximum age to 120. Moreover, a good deal of additional testing must be done before anyone would recommend for the human race a daily dose of BHT or something similar. But Dr. Harman is convinced that an increase in the human life span, through diet and the addition of chemicals, is almost sure to come.

Dr. Harman's predictions, of course, raise an interesting philosophical problem. It has long been accepted that the benefits of science and medicine should belong to everyone. But suppose the day actually arrives when science has a pill that will lengthen the human life span. Should everyone have it — the moron as well as the genius, the criminal as well as the philanthropist? Would a Republican Government try to limit it to Republicans and a Democratic Government to Democrats? At this time, when overpopulation threatens man's future, should anybody at all be entitled to the pill?

The antisleep pill would also introduce some tricky new problems into human affairs. Social scientists are already worried about the new age of leisure that is being spawned by automation; they wonder how man will ever manage to fill his time. How would he occupy himself if he suddenly found his waking hours, thanks to an antisleep pill, increased by one half? As for the smart pill and the stupid pill, if these are perfected, who will decide who gets which? If the smart pill creates a world in which everyone is equally bright, will man be happier, or will his affairs grind to a halt?

Even today's drugs have already created problems — for example, the tranquilizers. When a tranquilizing drug is given to a mental-hospital patient who would otherwise murder the attendants or beat his own head bloody against a wall, there seems to be no moral issue involved. But what if the same tranquilizer, or one of its cousins, is taken in large doses by an ordinary, everyday, more-or-less-normal person who is not about to do himself or others any harm, is getting along all right at his job, has no burning personal conflicts and merely likes the relaxed and easygoing feeling that the medicine produces, just as he might like to take a cocktail or two before dinner?

In this early stage of the pharmacological revolution, there already are millions of people in the U.S. who are on some kind of behavior-controlling drug. Physicians write more prescriptions for various kinds of tranquilizers, antidepressants, sleeping pills and pep pills than for medicines to combat pain or heart disease; about a third of all new prescriptions written this week by doctors across the nation will be of this type. (So great is the demand that the doctor *has* to write the prescription, whether he believes the patient needs the drug or not, else he loses the patient to another doctor.) In some circles, especially among businessmen and middle- and upper-class housewives, pills to calm jittery nerves or to help get the day's work done are a chief topic of social conversation. At parties, people exchange pills like recipes or golfing tips: "Here, try one of mine." "This pill has made a new man of me; take one and see." "My pills don't seem to be working anymore; let me have one of yours."

The thought of all this is already working as a sort of antisleep pill for researchers in the drug field; worrying about it causes them many a restless night. In the first place, all known drugs have side effects; even the common aspirin tablet possesses its dangers, and the behavior-controlling drugs are far more potent than aspirin. Some of them cause temporary sexual impotence; some of them create muscular pain or spasms so severe that a doctor who did not know the cause might well be inclined to perform surgery. Some drugs are dangerous when taken along with alcohol or sleeping pills; some will shoot blood pressure to alarming heights when taken along with even such a common food as cheese. Some are addicting and some, if improperly used, can actually kill the patient. Thus, the indiscriminate passing around of pills is the most risky kind of self-medication.

"The potential hazards," says Dr. Sherwyn Woods, "are really horrendous."

Besides the physical dangers, there are also moral dangers; this is especially apparent today in the case of the tranquilizers. "Who's to say," asks Dr. Woods, "what the appropriate level of tranquillity is? Certainly, we know that too much of it interferes with motivation and creativity. In fact, the kind of problem solving in general that has got man where he is today has been stimulated mostly by a lack of tranquillity." Dr. Cohen says, "I'm not in favor of reducing anxiety except when it gets to be disintegrating to the patient; I can't think of any kind of anxiety-free, conflict-free, challenge-free society that would be a worthy society. Muscles atrophy when they have nothing to work against, and so does the mind." And one drug-company executive adds, "The last thing on earth I'd want to see, in a world still as imperfect as ours, is everyone walking around so completely tranquil as to be oblivious to all the defects."

To most of the experts, the thought of an antiaggression drug, as suggested by Dr. Lehmann, or of the "harmony drug" suggested by Arthur Koestler, is one of the great hopes of the pharmacological age. "It would be wonderful," says Dr. Cohen, "if we could control criminality, violence and cruelty. And it certainly seems possible that we can find a calming agent, rather than a tranquilizer, that will reduce man's hostilities without taking the edge off his awareness and enjoyment of life." Yet even here there are conceivable dangers. If everyone in the U.S. were taking a calming pill and harboring not a single harsh thought toward anyone, our nation might be at the mercy of another aggression-bound nation that chose to ban the pill. Like the Industrial Revolution and the discovery of atomic energy, the pharmacological revolution has its hazards. We will have to learn to live with them, for the effects of the revolution are here to stay.

The Marihuana Problem — Myth or Reality?

Alfred R. Lindesmith

The primary fact about marihuana which ought to be taken into account by legislators but is not, is that it is not a habit-forming drug. By this is meant that the regular use of marihuana does not produce tolerance, and its abrupt cessation does not lead to withdrawal distress. As a consequence the problem of controlling or regulating its use is sharply different from that presented by the genuine drugs of addiction, i.e., the opiates such as heroin and morphine and their synthetic equivalents. Nevertheless, by federal legislation in 1951 and 1956, the increased penalties imposed on opiate users and peddlers were also applied to the users and distributors of marihuana. This extension was made casually with little discussion or investigation and with no apparent appreciation that the use of marihuana is something almost totally different from the use of heroin.

Effects of Smoking Marihuana

Marihuana is ordinarily used in this country by smoking. The effects it produces are experienced as exhilaration, loss of inhibitions, a changed sense of time, and other psychological effects which have sometimes been described and extravagantly praised by those who have experienced them. These effects are in a general way comparable to the stimulating effects produced by alcohol in the sense that they are intoxicating, although they differ qualitatively from those of alcohol.

Intrinsically, however, marihuana is less dangerous and less harmful to the human body than is alcohol. It is, for example, not habit-forming, whereas alcohol is. While the alcoholic commonly substitutes alcohol for food, marihuana sharply stimulates the appetite. Chronic alcoholism is associated with various psychotic conditions and diseases such as Korsakoff's psychosis and cirrhosis of the liver. In comparison, the smoking of marihuana produces relatively trivial physical effects, although it does appear that immoderate use of the more concentrated products of the hemp plant also produce deleterious bodily effects. Such effects, however, are not conspicuous among American reefer smokers, probably because of the relatively small quantities of the essential drug that are ingested from the poor quality marihuana ordinarily consumed in this country. The American marihuana smoker who inadvertently uses too much when he switches, let us say, to the more potent ganja plant raised in Mexico and the West Indies is likely to experience nothing more alarming than going to sleep and waking up hungry.

Use of Marihuana in Other Countries

Marihuana consists of the dried and crumbled stems, leaves, and seed pods of a plant known as Indian hemp or *Cannabis sativa.* These materials are often mixed with tobacco and in the United States are ordinarily smoked. In many other parts of the world a special type of hemp plant of unusual potency, known commonly as *ganja,* is used in a similar manner or it may be brewed and drunk as ganja tea — a common practice in the West Indies, where this drink is prized for its alleged therapeutic efficacy. In India the uncultivated hemp plant is smoked as marihuana is here and is also drunk. It is known there as *bhang.* The essential drug of the hemp plant is *cannabis indica* or *cannabinol* and it, of course, can be taken in this form. This essential drug is derived primarily from the resin of the female hemp plant. This concentrated hemp resin is commonly known as *hashish* and is immensely more powerful than either ganja or marihuana. The comparison of hashish and marihuana is like that between pure alcohol and beer. Lurid accounts of the psychological effects and dangers of hemp are often based upon observations made by and upon hashish users. The mixture smoked as marihuana ordinarily contains very small quantities of the drug and its effects are correspondingly less spectacular, less dangerous, and less harmful than those of hashish.[1]

The medical use of *cannabis indica* has declined in Western medicine but it is still extensively used in the Ayurvedic and Unani systems of indigenous medicine in India. In various parts of the world folk beliefs attribute great therapeutic and even divine virtues to the drug. In Jamaica it is known to many persons of the lower classes as "the wisdom weed" and it is alleged that it stimulates good qualities in the person who uses it and brings him closer to God. The use of ganja there is supported by references to various Biblical passages which recommend the "herbs of the field." The same passages, incidentally, are taken by the devotees of peyote (a cactus containing mescaline) to refer to that plant. A back-to-Africa protest cult in Jamaica, known as the Ras Tafari, has adopted ganja as a symbol of the movement and its members sometimes refer to themselves as the "herb men." In defiance of the Government, members of this cult, and others who are simply impressed by the fact that ganja is a more profitable crop than any other, grow and harvest the plant and use some of it themselves. Ganja tea is regarded as a prime ameliorative agent in the folk treatment of many diseases including asthma, tuberculosis, venereal disease, and many others, especially all types of respiratory ailments. Ganja cigarettes are extensively used by the workers in the sugar cane fields and some foremen of the sugar producing companies state that, were it not for ganja, they would have difficulty finding workingmen to harvest their crops.[2]

On the book jacket of Professor Robert P. Walton's 1938 book entitled, *Marihuana: America's New Drug Problem,* Frederick T. Merrill and Mr. Anslinger are quoted. The latter observed: "It is a new peril — in some ways the worst we have met, and it concerns us all." Merrill was even more emphatic and alarmed: "If the abuse of this narcotic drug is not stamped out at once, the cost in crime waves, wasted human lives, and insanity will be enormous." Quoting Walton, Merrill notes that marihuana often produces "uncontrollable irritability and violent rages, which in most advanced forms cause assault and murder." He continues: "Amnesia often occurs, and the mania is frequently so acute that the heavy smoker becomes temporarily insane. Most authorities agree that permanent insanity can result from continual

For general discussions of marihuana see: Robert P. Walton, *Marihuana: America's New Drug Problem* (Philadelphia: Lippincott, 1938), and Norman Taylor, *Flight from Reality* (New York: Duell, Sloan and Pearce, 1949).

[2] From observations and interviews with Jamaicans by the writer during a visit to that island.

[3] N. Taylor, *Flight from Reality,* p. 27.

[4] *Report of the Indian Hemp Drug Commission* (7 vols.; Simla, India, 1894), cited by N. Taylor, *Flight from*

over-indulgence." Marihuana has had no noticeable effect in increasing the population of our mental institutions and whatever crimes of violence it may instigate are as nothing when compared to those that are linked with the use of alcohol.

Norman Taylor notes that the hemp plant, called *Cannabis sativa* by Linnaeus in the eighteenth century, probably originated in Central Asia or in China, where it was described in a book on pharmacy written by one Shen Nung nearly three thousand years before the birth of Christ.[3] The euphoric potential of the resinous female plant was known then and troubled Chinese moralists, who called it the "Liberator of Sin." Nung, however, recommended the medicine from this plant for "female weakness, gout, rheumatism, malaria, beri-beri, constipation and absent-mindedness." From China the use of hemp spread westward to India, to the Middle East, and along both sides of the Mediterranean, and ultimately reached Europe and the Western hemisphere. Nowhere has its use been eradicated, even after thousands of years of effort in some instances. Recent publications of the United Nations comment on the apparent continued spread of the practice.

The evil reputation of hemp was enhanced when, during the eleventh century, it became linked with a cult headed by one Hasan which initiated a new political tactic of secret assassination to cleanse the Moslem world of false prophets. Hasan's full name was Hashishin and he was called the Old Man of the Mountain. The terms *hashish* and *assassin* are linked with the name of *Hasan* and his cult.

Use by Lower Classes

It is possible that the bad reputation of marihuana and other forms of this drug reflects in part the bias of upper classes against an indulgence of the lower strata. Since hemp grows luxuriantly without cultivation in many parts of the world, it is available to many of its devotees at extremely low cost — in India, for example, at about one-twentieth the price of good quality whiskey in 1894, when the English carried out an extensive inquiry into the subject.[4] Denunciations of the weed come characteristically from persons of those classes which prefer whiskey, rum, gin, and other alcoholic beverages and who do not themselves use marihuana. Such persons, overlooking the well-known effects of alcohol, commonly deplore the effects of hemp upon the lower classes and often believe that it produces murder, rape, violence, and insanity.

Despite the prevalence of these beliefs among the drinkers of rum and whiskey and the upper classes generally, impartial investigations invariably have shown no such results. The moderate use of hemp, according to the Indian Hemp Drug Commission in 1894, does not produce significant mental or moral injuries, does not lead to disease, nor does it necessarily or even usually lead to excess any more than alcohol does. Excess, the Commission said, is confined to the idle and dissipated.[5] Many years later in New York City similar conclusions were stated on the basis of experimental study and from an examination of violent crimes committed in that city over a period of years.[6]

In Jamaica, where the lower classes regard the drug with favor, persons of high social status commonly assert that

Reality, p. 34.

[5] N. Taylor, *Flight from Reality,* pp. 34–35.

[6] *The Marihuana Problem in the City of New York: Sociological, Medical, Psychological and Pharmacological Studies* by the Mayor's Committee on Marihuana, George B. Wallace, Chairman (Lancaster, Pa.: Jaques Cattell Press, 1945).

ganja is a potent cause of much of the personal violence which is relatively frequent there among the working classes. This is staunchly denied by the ganja users, who contend that the effects are usually in the opposite direction but admit that ganja may bring out the evil in some persons who are already evil. Police examination of violent crimes in Jamaica suggest that ganja has little connection with them and that they arise rather from sexual jealousy and the highly informal manner in which sexual matters are arranged on that island among the simpler people of the lower classes.

Marihuana and Alcohol

In general, virtually all of the charges that are made against marihuana tend to shrink or dissolve entirely when they are closely examined by impartial investigators. The present tendency of the rank-and-file policeman, despite the enormous penalties attached to handling marihuana, is to regard it as a minor problem hardly deserving serious attention except for those who handle the weed in large amounts for mercenary purposes or who promote its use among the uninitiated.

Ironically, the accusations that are leveled at marihuana are all applicable to alcohol, as has been demonstrated by innumerable investigations. These studies indicate that much murder, rape, and homicide is committed by persons under the influence. The special psychoses and ailments of alcoholics are numerous and well delineated in countless scientific and literary productions. The menace of the drinking driver of automobiles is well understood by all and is more or less accepted as one of the inevitable hazards of life in the modern world. It is well known, too, that the manufacturers of alcoholic beverages advertise their products and seek to enlarge their markets and that the use of alcohol spreads from those who already have the practice to those who do not. Why, then, so much excitement about marihuana? It is said that marihuana sometimes causes girls and women to lose their virtue and innocence, but the role of alcohol in this respect is infinitely more important. It seems inconsistent, therefore, that while the decision to drink or not to drink is viewed as a personal moral decision, the use of marihuana should be viewed as a heinous crime subject to long prison sentences.

Among those who have never used hemp or seen it used by others the belief is often found that marihuana acts as a sexual stimulant or aphrodisiac. Actually its effects, like those of opiates, are in exactly the opposite direction, tending to cause the user to lose interest in the opposite sex. Users more frequently than not report the absence of ideas of sex or say that Venus herself could not tempt them when they are under the influence of this drug.

The Effects of Anti-Marihuana Legislation

In 1937 the Congress passed a Marihuana Tax Act, modeled after the Harrison Act. It was designed to curb the use of marihuana by the use of the federal police power, and like the Harrison Act imposed penalties upon both buyers and sellers. This Act was the result of a publicity campaign staged by the Federal Bureau of Narcotics under Mr. Anslinger's direction and leadership. The bill was passed with little discussion after brief hearings on the ground that marihuana was a highly dangerous drug inciting its users to commit crimes of violence and often leading to insanity.[7]

The beliefs concerning marihuana which led to this legislation may be represented in a pure and extreme form by turning to the writing of a hyperactive reformer and alarmist of the period, Earle Albert Rowell.[8] He claimed in 1939 that he had spent fourteen years campaigning against this weed, delivering more than four thousand lectures in forty states and personally pulling up and destroying many flourishing hemp fields. Mr. Rowell's zealous opposition to marihuana was only slightly less intense than his disapproval of alcohol and tobacco. The use of tobacco, he correctly observed, invariably precedes the smoking of the deadly reefer. Mr. Rowell came into disfavor with the Bureau of Narcotics around 1938 and this agency spent considerable energy and manpower in an attempt to silence and discredit him. This may have been because of Mr. Rowell's view that opiate addiction is a disease or perhaps because of his repeated allegations that the police were not sufficiently diligent in destroying marihuana.

Mr. Rowell summarized the effects of marihuana as follows:

We know that marihuana —
1. Destroys will power, making a jellyfish of the user. He cannot say no.
2. Eliminates the line between right and wrong, and substitutes one's own warped desires or the base suggestions of others as the standard of right.
3. Above all, causes crimes; fills the victim with an irrepressible urge to violence.
4. Incites to revolting immoralities, including rape and murder.
5. Causes many accidents both industrial and automobile.
6. Ruins careers forever.
7. Causes insanity as its speciality.
8. *Either in self-defense or as a means of revenue, users make smokers of others, thus perpetuating evil.*[9]

In 1939 when Rowell published his book, marihuana was regarded as a relatively new drug menace in the United States. Mr. Rowell thought that he had already detected an increase of the population of mental hospitals because of it:

Asylums and mental hospitals in this country are beginning to see and feel the influence of marihuana, and are awaking to its deleterious effects on the brain. As we traveled through the various states, superintendents of these institutions told us of cases of insanity resulting from marihuana.[10]

"The baleful mental effects of marihuana," he said, "begin soon after the first reefer is smoked. . . ."[11]

When Mr. Anslinger appeared before the Senate subcommittee which was investigating the illicit drug traffic in 1955 under the guidance of Senator Price Daniel, there were only a few offhand discussions of marihuana. Mr. Anslinger observed that the Bureau in its national survey was "trying to keep away from the marihuana addict, because he is not a true addict." The real problem, he said, was the heroin addict. Senator Daniel thereupon remarked:

Now, do I understand it from you that, while we are discussing marihuana, the real danger there is that the use of marihuana leads many people eventually to the use of heroin, and the drugs that do cause complete addiction; is that true?[12]

[7] See *Taxation of Marihuana:* Hearings before the Committee on Ways and Means, U.S. House of Representatives, 75th Cong., 1st sess., April and May, 1937 (hereafter called *House Marihuana Hearings, 1937*); and *Taxation of Marihuana:* Hearings before a Subcommitte of the Committee on Finance, U.S. Senate, 75th Cong., 1st sess., on H.R. 6906 (hereafter called *Senate Marihuana Hearings, 1937*).

[8] Earle Albert Rowell and Robert Rowell, *On the Trail of Marihuana, the Weed of Madness* (Mountain View, Cal.: Pacific Press Publishing Association, 1939). See also Earle Albert Rowell, *Dope: Adventures of David Dare* (Nashville, Tenn.: Southern Publishing Association, 1937).

[9] E. A. Rowell and R. Rowell, *On the Trail of Marihuana*, p. 33.

[10] *Ibid.*, p. 51.

[11] *Ibid.*

[12] *Daniel Subcommittee Hearings,* Part 5, 1955, p. 16.

Mr. Anslinger agreed:

> That is the great problem and our great concern about the use of marihuana, that eventually if used over a long period, it does lead to heroin addiction.[13]

Senators Welker and Daniel pursued the subject, and Mr. Anslinger, when prompted, agreed that marihuana was dangerous. Senator Welker finally asked this question:

> Is it or is it not a fact that the marihuana user has been responsible for many of our most sadistic, terrible crimes in this nation, such as sex slayings, sadistic slayings, and matters of that kind?

Mr. Anslinger hedged:

> There have been instances of that, Senator. We have had some rather tragic occurrences by users of marihuana. It does not follow that all crime can be traced to marihuana. There have been many brutal crimes traced to marihuana, but I would not say that it is a controlling factor in the commission of crimes.[14]

Eighteen years earlier, in 1937, the year in which the federal antimarihuana law was passed, Mr. Anslinger had presented a very different picture of marihuana. Prior to 1937 Mr. Anslinger and the Bureau of Narcotics had spearheaded a propaganda campaign against marihuana on the ground that it produced an immense amount of violent crime such as rape, mayhem, and murder, and that many traffic accidents could be attributed to it. During the 1937 hearings before a House subcommittee, Representative John Dingell of Michigan asked Mr. Anslinger: "I am just wondering whether the marihuana addict graduates into a heroin, an opium, or a cocaine user."

Mr. Anslinger replied: "No, sir; I have not heard of a case of that kind. I think it is an entirely different class. The marihuana addict does not go in that direction." [15]

A few months later in the same year, before a Senate subcommittee which was considering the antimarihuana law which the Bureau of Narcotics had asked for, Mr. Anslinger commented: "There is an entirely new class of people using marihuana. The opium user is around 35 to 40 years old. These users are 20 years old and know nothing of heroin or morphine." [16]

The theme stated by the Commissioner of Narcotics in 1955, that the main threat in marihuana is that it leads to the use of heroin, is now ordinarily cited as the principal justification for applying to it the same severe penalties that are applied in the case of heroin. Reformer Rowell in 1939 was more logical and consistent than either the Senators or the Commissioner when he emphasized that cigarette smoking invariably preceded reefer smoking. Mr. Rowell told of a shrewd gangster whom he engaged in what now appears as a prophetic discussion of the prospects of the dope industry.[17]

> The gangster remarked: "Marihuana is the coming thing."
>
> "But," I protested in surprise, "marihuana is not a habit-forming drug like morphine or heroin; and, besides, it's too cheap to bother with."
>
> He laughed. "You don't understand. Laws are being passed now by various states against it, and soon Uncle Sam will put a ban on it. The price will then go up, and that will make it profitable for us to handle."

The gangster, according to Mr. Rowell, then commented on the shrewd manner in which the tobacco companies had popularized cigarettes among the soldiers of the First World War and on the enormous increase in cigarette consumption by young persons. He grew eloquent: "Every cigarette smoker is a prospect for the dope ring via the marihuana road. Millions of boys and girls

[13] *Ibid.*

[14] *Ibid.* p. 18.

[15] *House Marihuana Hearings,* 1937, p. 24.

[16] *Senate Marihuana Hearings,* 1937, pp. 14–15.

[17] E. A. Rowell and R. Rowell, *On the Trail of Marihuana,* pp. 69–74.

now smoke. Think of the unlimited new market!"

Mr. Rowell got the idea and commented as follows to his readers:

> Slowly, insidiously, for over three hundred years, Lady Nicotine was setting the stage for a grand climax. The long years of tobacco using were but an introduction and training for marihuana use. Tobacco, which was first smoked in a pipe, then as a cigar, and at last as a cigarette, demanded more and more of itself until its supposed pleasures palled, and some of the tobacco victims looked about for something stronger. Tobacco was no longer potent enough.

Mr. Rowell was not optimistic about the future:

> Marihuana will continue to be a problem for both police and educators, because it is so easy to grow, to manufacture, and to peddle, and is such a quick source of easy money. The plant can be grown anywhere; it can be harvested secretly, prepared in twenty-four hours without a penny of investment for equipment; and every cigarette user is a prospect As our laws are enforced and the weed becomes scarcer, the price will rise, and greater profit accrue to venturesome and successful peddlers. Whereas now it is usually peddled by lone wolves, as soon as the weed becomes scarcer and the price rises, organized crime will step in and establish a monopoly.[18]

While Mr. Rowell, in the manner of reforming alarmists, exaggerated the evil with which he was preoccupied, the above appraisal of the effects of the Marihuana Tax Act has been reasonably well borne out by subsequent events. Certainly it was a more realistic assessment of the law's effects than any that were made by the legislators who passed the bill or by the officials who promoted it. Mr. Rowell was also completely right in pointing out that virtually every marihuana smoker graduated to this practice from cigarette smoking. His gangster informant was correct in his calculation that state and federal laws prohibiting marihuana would make the weed more expensive and more profitable for peddlers to handle, and also correctly foresaw that with the same merchants handling both marihuana and heroin it would become a simple matter for marihuana users to switch from the less to the more dangerous drug, as they have done.

In the United States during the nineteenth century, and the early decades of the twentieth, addiction to opiates frequently developed from the abuse of alcohol. This still occurs to some extent and is frequently reported from other parts of the world, for morphine provides a potent means of relieving the alcoholic hangover. An American doctor once advocated as a cure of alcoholism that alcohol addicts be deliberately addicted to morphine, arguing with considerable plausibility that of the two habits the latter was obviously the lesser evil.[19] Moreover, he practiced what he preached and recommended his technique with considerable enthusiasm for use by others.

The truth of the matter, of course, is that very few cigarette smokers go on to marihuana, very few marihuana users go on to heroin, and very few alcohol users graduate to the use of heroin. Since some barbiturate and amphetamine users progress to heroin it should be added that it is also only a very small proportion who do. If all of these substances were to be prohibited because they are sometimes involved in the progression toward heroin addiction there is little doubt that the illicit traffic in marihuana and heroin would be expanded to include the other offending substances and that the movement from less to more serious habits would be greatly facilitated.

No one, of course, recommends the use

[18] *Ibid.*, pp. 88–89.

[19] J. R. Black, "Advantages of Substituting the Morphia Habit for the Incurably Alcoholic," *Cincinnati Lancet-Clinic,* XXII, n.s. (1889), Part I, 537–41.

of marihuana nor does anyone deny that there are evil effects and consequences associated with using it. The fact that the use of marihuana is outlawed, for example, means that it is often obtained through association with unsavory types, often used in an underworld environment, and the user takes the risk of criminal prosecution. It is also undeniable that marihuana intoxication may sometimes lead to automobile accidents and to irresponsible or criminal acts. The controversy with respect to marihuana is solely concerning the relative prevalence or frequency of such results in comparison to similar consequences following from the use of alcoholic beverages. All empirical investigations indicate that alcohol constitutes a far greater social danger than does marihuana.

Mayor LaGuardia's Committee on Marihuana

Mayor LaGuardia's Committee on Marihuana, on the basis of a close examination of the matter in New York City, stressed the relative triviality of the effects of marihuana use in a report published in 1945.[20] In the July 1943 issue of the *Military Surgeon,* the editor, Colonel J. M. Phalen, commented as follows in an editorial on "The Marihuana Bugaboo":

> The smoking of the leaves, flowers and seeds of *Cannabis sativa* is no more harmful than the smoking of tobacco or mullein or sumac leaves. . . . The legislation in relation to marihuana was ill-advised . . . it branded as a menace and a crime a matter of trivial importance. . . . It is hoped that no witch hunt will be instituted in the military service over a problem that does not exist.[21]

Similar statements have been made by many other competent investigators and observers.

On the other hand, as has been pointed out, a sharply divergent view has been presented by law enforcement officials, particularly by the Federal Bureau of Narcotics, and also by many individual writers. The sharp divergence of views among the scientifically oriented evidently depends upon the manner in which the research is done. Investigators who rely on the opinions of high echelon officials, who have no direct acquaintance with the use of marihuana and who base their opinions on anecdotes rather than actual statistical data, usually reach the conclusion that marihuana is a highly dangerous drug which produces much violent crime and insanity. These conclusions, as we have suggested, may be a reflection of upper-class hostility toward an unfamiliar lower-class indulgence. More critical and skeptical investigators, who look for basic statistical evidence, invariably fail to find it and end up writing debunking articles for which they are roundly abused by the moralists.

It is often felt that, even if the dangers of marihuana are exaggerated, these exaggerations and misstatements should be allowed to stand so that they may frighten adolescents away from the drug. The implication that adolescents are influenced to any appreciable degree by articles appearing in scientific journals is probably absurd. Those who use marihuana probably come to do so on the basis of personal associations and direct observations of their own.

The deliberate circulation of false information is self-defeating in that the adventurous, experimentally inclined youth can quickly discover for himself, by trying the weed or talking to those who have smoked it, that much of the officially circulated view is false. He is then

[20] *The Marihuana Problem in the City of New York.*
[21] Cited by N. Taylor, *Flight from Reality,* p. 36.

prepared to believe that everything he has been told about narcotics is equally wrong.

When Mayor LaGuardia's Committee on Marihuana made its report, it was strongly attacked by those committed to a belief in the marihuana menace. The *Journal of the American Medical Association* in 1943 published a letter from Mr. Anslinger in which he criticized an article by Drs. Allentuck and Bowman on findings derived from the New York study in which they had participated.[22] There were rumors that the New York marihuana study was to be suppressed, but after considerable delay, it was ultimately released in 1945. On April 28, 1945, the *Journal of the American Medical Association* editorially assailed the report, using language and arguments of a type not ordinarily found in learned journals:

> For many years medical scientists have considered cannabis a dangerous drug. Nevertheless, a book called "Marihuana Problems" by the New York City Mayor's Committe on Marihuana submits an analysis by seventeen doctors of tests on 77 prisoners and, on this narrow and thoroughly unscientific foundation, draws sweeping and inadequate conclusions which minimize the harmfulness of marihuana. Already the book has done harm. One investigator has described some tearful parents who brought their 16 year old son to a physician after he had been detected in the act of smoking marihuana. A noticeable mental deterioration had been evident for some time even to their lay minds. The boy said he had read an account of the LaGuardia Committee report and that this was his justification for using marihuana. He read in *Down Beat,* a musical journal, an analysis of this report under the caption "Light Up, Gates, Report Finds Tea a Good Kick."
>
> A criminal lawyer for marihuana drug peddlers has already used the LaGuardia report as a basis to have defendants set free by the court. . . .
>
> The book states unqualifiedly to the public that the use of this narcotic does not lead to physical, mental or moral degeneration and that permanent deleterious effects from its continued use were not observed on 77 prisoners. This statement has already done great damage to the cause of law enforcement. Public officials will do well to disregard this unscientific, uncritical study, and continue to regard marihuana as a menace wherever it is purveyed.[23]

Despite the fact that this editorial continues to be cited and reproduced to discredit the New York study, the conclusions of the report enjoy considerable status and are undoubtedly far closer to the realities of the situation than is the view represented by the A.M.A. editorial. Indeed, if one judges the law enforcement agencies by their actions rather than their words, it appears that even the police, to a considerable extent, have swung over to the viewpoint of the Mayor's Committee.

Marihuana Arrests

After 1951 the budget and field force of the Federal Bureau of Narcotics were substantially enlarged. Nevertheless, the number of marihuana arrests has steadily declined and by 1960 it was close to the vanishing point, with only 169 such cases. In previous years the numbers of federal marihuana violations were reported as follows:[24]

1952	1,288
1954	508
1956	403
1958	179

Of the 169 federal marihuana violations reported in 1960, 88 occurred in California, 16 in Maryland, and 13 in Kentucky. No other state had as many as ten, and no violations were reported from 28 states. We have already noted that the Bureau does not bother to count marihuana users in its national survey of addiction and does not regard marihuana as an addicting drug. The above figures on enforcement suggest

[22] J.A.M.A., 121, No. 3 (Jan. 16, 1943), 212–13.

[23] J.A.M.A., 127, No. 17 (April 28, 1945), 1129.

[24] From the annual report of the Bureau of Narcotics for the years indicated. In 1962 the number of marihuana cases was 242. (*Traffic in Opium and Other Dangerous Drugs,* 1962, p. 62.)

that, at the federal level at least, the marihuana laws are being largely ignored since it is not claimed that the use of marihuana is diminishing.

Statistics on marihuana prosecutions as such are extremely difficult to obtain and data that are available are very unreliable and incomplete. The Federal Narcotics Bureau presented to the Daniel Subcommittee a summary of marihuana prosecutions for the year 1954, giving both federal and nonfederal cases. It is not claimed that the latter are complete; they are merely figures from some of the main cities in the indicated states.

Marihuana Arrests—Federal and Local by States—1954 [25]

	Arrests	
State	*Federal*	*Local*
Alabama	2	6
Arizona	25	4
Arkansas	2	0
California	51	1,101
Colorado	28	1
Connecticut	2	6
Delaware	0	1
District of Columbia	3	17
Florida	4	30
Georgia	4	1
Idaho	0	2
Illinois	13	327
Indiana	0	14
Iowa	0	8
Kansas	2	0
Kentucky	39	8
Louisiana	17	105
Maine	0	0
Maryland	2	30
Massachusetts	5	1
Michigan	30	270
Minnesota	0	5
Mississippi	0	1
Missouri	9	15
Montana	0	6
Nebraska	1	13
Nevada	16	2
New Hampshire	0	0
New Jersey	5	26
New Mexico	23	10
New York	5	407
North Carolina	0	0
North Dakota	0	0
Ohio	25	23
Oklahoma	2	13
Oregon	1	8
Pennsylvania	3	50
Rhode Island	0	0
South Carolina	4	0
South Dakota	0	0
Tennessee	11	1
Texas	325	612
Utah	4	0
Vermont	0	0
Virginia	0	1
Washington	22	10
West Virginia	0	0
Wisconsin	0	47
Wyoming	4	0
Alaska	5	0
Hawaii	14	23
Totals	713	3,205
Grand Total		3,918

From this table it will be seen that 3,263 of the total of 3,918 arrests were made in the six states of California, Texas, Illinois, Michigan, New York, and Louisiana. These states are, in one way or another, centers of the marihuana traffic. High arrest rates in California, Texas, and Louisiana no doubt arise from the fact that

[25] *Daniel Subcommittee Hearings,* 1955, pp. 267–71, exhibit 7. Note the unexplained discrepancy between the federal total given here and that of the preceding citation.

considerable quantities of marihuana are smuggled into the country there from Mexico and the Caribbean area. The rates in Illinois, Michigan, and New York reflect mainly police activity in the three large cities of Detroit, Chicago, and New York, all of them narcotics distribution centers. Heroin arrests are also highest in the states of California, New York, Illinois, and Michigan, while Texas and Louisiana are farther down on the list.

The penalty provisions applicable to marihuana users under state and federal law are about the same as those applied to heroin users. These penalties are entirely disproportionate to the seriousness of the offending behavior and lead to gross injustice and undesirable social consequences. For example, it is well known that many jazz musicians and other generally inoffensive persons use or have used marihuana. To send these persons to jail is absurd and harmful and serves no conceivable useful purpose. The moderate or occasional marihuana user is not a significant social menace. Jails and prisons, chronically overcrowded, should be used for those who present a genuine threat to life and property. The absurdity is compounded when an occasional judge, ignorant of the nature of marihuana, sends a marihuana user to prison to cure him of his nonexistent addiction. The writer was once in court when a middle-aged Negro defendant appeared before the judge charged with having used and had in his possession one marihuana cigarette during the noon hour at the place where he had worked for a number of years. This man had no previous criminal record and this fact was stated before the court. Nevertheless, a two-year sentence was imposed to "dry up his habit."

The President's Advisory Commission which reported on narcotic and drug abuse in 1963 took cognizance of the relatively trivial nature of the marihuana evil by suggesting that all mandatory sentences be eliminated for crimes involving it and that judges be granted full discretionary power in dealing with offenders.[26] These suggestions are excessively timid and not entirely logical, for there is no good reason why a mere user of marihuana should be subjected to a jail sentence at all. The marihuana user probably ought to be dealt with by the law along the same lines that are used with persons who drink alcohol.

If it is deemed in the public interest to punish smokers of marihuana, such punishments should ordinarily consist of fines only, up to some maximum of perhaps $500.00, depending upon the offense and the defendant's ability to pay. These fines might be scaled down or eliminated entirely for persons who provided information concerning their source of supply. Police efforts should be focused primarily on the traffic rather than on the user. Persons driving automobiles under the influence of the drug might be fined and deprived of their driving licenses for a period of time. Crimes which could be shown to the satisfaction of a court of law to be linked with the use of marihuana ought to be dealt with about the way that crimes arising from the use of alcohol are handled.

Laws such as this, with penalties of a reasonable nature, would probably be more effective than those now in effect because they would be more enforceable and more in accord with the nature of the problem being dealt with. They would have the effect of reducing the discrepancy that now exists between the laws as written and the laws as they are actually enforced. A more matter-of-fact and realistic handling of the

[26] *Final Report:* The President's Advisory Commission on Narcotic and Drug Abuse, p. 42.

marihuana problem would also probably reduce the aura of sensationalism which now surrounds the subject and diminish the illicit glamor which is now attached to the hemp plant.

It is argued by some that the marihuana industry should be brought under control by legalization, taxation, licensing, and other devices like those used to control alcohol — and to exploit it as a source of revenue. Advocates of this view might well argue that there should be no unfair discrimination among vices; that if the greater evil of alcohol use is legal, the lesser one of marihuana smoking should be so as well. Since the smoking of marihuana will undoubtedly continue regardless of legislation against it, it can also be argued that it would be better to accept the inevitable than to wage war for a lost cause.

In opposition to this extremely permissive position, the more conservative reformer can call attention to the fact that, outside of a few Asian and African countries, the use of this substance is everywhere disapproved of and subject to legal restrictions. It is possible that legal sanctions exercise some deterrent effect and that without them the use of this drug might spread even more rapidly and assume more virulent forms. Should the use of marihuana become anywhere nearly as widespread as that of alcohol it might be too late to talk of effective restrictions since the users would command too many votes. A legal marihuana or ganja industry which advertised its product and sought to improve it through research and experimentation would be a distinct embarrassment to the nation as a whole as well as being a direct economic threat to the alcoholic beverage industries and possibly to the tobacco industry. A final and decisive argument seems to be that public opinion is not likely in the foreseeable future to accept indulgence in marihuana as an equivalent of, or substitute for, indulgence in alcohol.

The long history of the use of marihuana, the spread of the practice throughout the world in the face of determined and sometimes fanatical opposition, and the persistence of the practice once it is established — all suggest that the smoking of marihuana will continue in the United States for some time to come. The practical question seems to be one of minimizing and controlling the practice while avoiding the extreme tactics of prohibitionists. A comprehensive, impartial public inquiry into the matter, based on the assumption that marihuana is *not* the same as heroin, might help to bring about a more sober and rational approach to an indulgence which merits some concern but which is far less serious than is presently suggested by the harsh inflexibility of current laws.

LSD and the Third Eye

John N. Bleibtreu

The current popularity of such writers as William Burroughs, Genêt, and others, who specialize in the baroque recesses of human behavior, makes it seem as if, in this age of reason, we feel ourselves constrained within the confines of sanity and yearn for vicarious release.

The belief that in madness there may exist a core of numinous knowledge is a commonplace in all human societies. In the Western tradition, the doctrine that truth may be obtained through a state of mind in which reason is dislocated, a state of ecstatic revelation, is generally supposed to have originated with the Thracian worship of Dionysius, later becoming synthesized by Pythagorus, and to have received its most complete elaboration in the dialogues of Plato.

The class of drugs of which LSD-25 is the most potent member may prove for our time to be a very useful tool in exploring, via the scientific method, the roots of this age-old dilemma concerning the nature of perceived reality. That madmen may often be capable of incredible accomplishment should be obvious to everyone living in this century, whose history has been so monstrously deformed by the activities of an undeniable madman, Adolf Hitler. This one terrible example should quench all disputations concerning the correlations between mental aberration and accomplishment. These disputations most frequently arise in connection with accomplishment in the creative arts, where the biographies of many greatly talented people are replete with histories of bizarre behavior of one kind or another. It is impossible, however, to make such correlations on any kind of statistical basis, since for every "mad artist" on the model of Van Gogh, one can point to two equally creative, original, and productive artists on the sane and sober models of J. S. Bach or T. S. Eliot.

In addition to the artificially induced LSD state, there are other, naturally occurring temporary states in which there is a collapse of the normal routines by which the mind ordinarily processes the information it receives of the outside world. Not only Hitler but before him Alexander the Great, Julius Caesar, and Napoleon Bonaparte all reportedly suffered from mysterious seizures which overtook them at seemingly random times — often inconveniently. Dostoevsky also suffered from these states, and his reports of them are sufficiently detailed to permit a more certain medical diagnosis of his affliction — some kind of psychomotor epilepsy. As he describes the "aura" which precedes his seizures, the language is remarkably similar to that used by LSD subjects. Dostoevsky wrote: "For a few moments I experience such happiness as is impossible under ordinary circumstances and of which other people can have no notion. I feel complete harmony in myself and in the world and this feeling is so strong and sweet that for several seconds of such bliss, one would give ten years of one's life; indeed, perhaps one's whole life." Others have reported on these aura states as well. Along with the feelings of pace and euphoria, there is a general impression of a clear and golden shimmering light. Quite often there is a sense of cerebral clarity as well, and solutions of a lovely simplicity appear for the most intractably knotted problems.

None of the names used to describe the class of drugs to which LSD belongs and which produce these peculiar states of altered consciousness is completely satisfactory. When they were first developed, they were called psychotomimetic (imitative of psychosis), but this term rang unhappily in the ears of many who felt that the word implied pathology and thus made a negative value judgment. Another name for them, hallucinogenic, was unfortunate in that it rendered an epistemological judgment — hallucinations being by definition unreal or untrue — and if one is to maintain a proper stance of scientific objectivity, one must suspend judgment regarding the reality of reality, for it is just possible that in some way these drugs augment our sense receptors or in some way so alter the mechanism of their functioning that another dimension of reality is made manifest. This last notion is the one implied in the term psychedelic (mind manifesting), which seems gradually to be coming into general use to describe both the class of drugs and those states of mind with which they are associated.

There is a vast literature running back for thousands of years which describes psychedelic experiences, long before 1938, when Albert Hofmann first synthesized d-lysergic acid dyethylamide. Some of the literature describes attacks, sudden, spontaneous, and totally unexpected, like that attack which overcame St. Paul on the road to Damascus. Other traditions in the literature describe states that were induced by fasting, by the sensory deprivation resulting from disciplined meditation (the willful exclusion of sensory input), by hysteria through frenzied dancing or orgiastic sexuality, by hypnosis, or by the use of various natural psychedelic intoxicants. Reports of these kinds of exalted states have come to us not only through the literature of religious fanaticism; such accomplished scientists as Pascal and Newton have written of being overcome by mystic trances to which they attribute many of their creative insights. William James well understood that the mystic was often able to effect an almost miraculous synthesis between this world of "imagined" reality and the world of phenomena. In recent years, psychology has tended, to its discredit, to ignore these elements of William James's thought. One of the happy by-products of LSD has been the revival of interest in William James on the part of academic psychologists who had previously thought that these concerns of his were a cranky eccentricity in the body of his worthwhile work. Two famous reports of modern times of this kind of correlation — between the hard factual world of science and the dreamworld of the psychedelic state — are those of Friedrich Kekule, the German chemist who has written that he was "presented with" the closed-chain theory of the structure of the benzene molecule during one such dream-trance state, and Otto Loewi, who wrote that in 1921 he awakened from a dream in which was described to him the means by which chemical transfer was accomplished between nerve and effector cells. Loewi rushed down to his laboratory, where he proceeded to prove the reality of the dream — an accomplishment which led to the

Nobel Prize.

From the time of Dionysius to the time of Plato, the cultures of the Mediterranean consented to this doctrine that claimed the existence of an order of ultimate reality which lies beyond apparent reality, and that this "paranormal" reality is accessible to the consciousness only when the "normal" routines of mental data processing are dislocated. It was Plato's pupil Aristotle who spoiled his master's game. Following upon Aristotle, Western philosophy became bifurcated. The philosophical temper of our civilization, being scientifically and technically oriented, is basically Aristotelian.

No such rational figure as Aristotle arose in the Orient to a position of equal eminence. Regardless of the reasons, Indian anatomists and zoologists, who were no doubt just as curious as the Greeks about the origins of life, and as skilled in dissection, did not feel compelled to set their disciplines up in opposition to metaphysics. Metaphysical philosophy and natural philosophy remained joined like Siamese twins. As a result, that discipline which became medicine in the West evolved into a system known as Kundilini Yoga in the Hindu culture. This was a system designed to produce in those who followed its teachings a condition of controlled "creative" madness.

In Western terms, Kundilini Yoga can be understood as a biological statement, couched in the language of poetic metaphor. The system made a heroic attempt to join together the seeming disparate entities of body and mind. It is a very complicated doctrine; in oversimplified terms, the system encourages the practitioner to progress through the control of six stages, called chakras, of body-mind coordination. The sixth, the highest and most exalted state, is called the sahasrara.

The physiological site of this sixth chakra, the sahasrara, is located in the center of the forehead; it is symbolized by an eye — the so-called third eye, the inner eye, or the eye of the mind. When this eye is opened, a new and completely other dimension of reality is revealed to the practitioner of yoga. Western scholars when they first came upon this literature took the third eye to be an appropriately poetic metaphor and nothing else.

But in the middle of the nineteenth century, as the subcontinent of Australia and its surrounding territory came to be explored, a flurry of zoological interest centered upon a lizard native to the area, the tuatara (*Sphenodon punctatum*). This animal possessed, in addition to two perfectly ordinary eyes located on either side of its head, a third eye buried in the skull which was revealed through an aperture in the bone, covered by a transparent membrane, and surrounded by a rosette of scales. It was unmistakably a third eye, but upon dissection it proved to be nonfunctional. Though it still possessed the structure of a lens and retina, these were no longer in good working order; also lacking were appropriate neural connections to the brain. But the presence of this eye in the tuatara still poses a puzzle to present-day evolutionists, for almost all vertebrates possess a homologous structure in the center of their skulls. It is present in many fish, all reptiles, birds, and mammals (including humans). No functional role whatever could be imagined for this structure in humans, and it remained merely an anatomical curiosity until 1898, when Otto Heubner, a German physician, wrote a paper associating cancers of this organ with instances of precocious puberty in children. Heubner's observation was confirmed many times over in the intervening years and gave rise to a number of theories concerning the role of the pineal organ as a regulator of sexual maturity. Those who adhered to these theories considered the pineal to be a gland, but since no secretions could be isolated or identified as emanating from this organ, the theories remained unsubstantiated by clinical evidence.

In 1948 no one was paying any attention to the pineal organ. A hematologist, Maurice Rapport, working in the Cleveland Clinic was engaged in the search for that substance in blood serum which could be related to the tendency of blood to clot, and which might also cause the constriction of blood vessels. He eventually found just such a substance; it tended to make blood form clots, and it tended to be a muscle- as well as a vaso-constrictor. Rapport named this substance serotonin; it is manufactured quite profusely by specialized cells lining the wall of the gut, and it is presumed to play a role of some kind in the peristaltic movements.

Directly as Rapport announced his discovery, the new chemical came under intensive scrutiny; biochemists were eager to find means of augmenting its role as a clotting agent and vasoconstrictor; they were also eager to find means of blocking these functions. It was E. J. Gaddum, a professor of pharmacology at the University of Edinburgh, who seems to have been one of the first to note a connection between serotonin and mental states of being. In a paper published in 1953, he pointed out the odd fact that LSD-25 was a potent antagonist to serotonin. Two biochemists working at the Rockefeller Institute, D. W. Woolley and E. Shaw, were similarly struck by this odd coincidence. They tested a number of other chemicals antagonistic to serotonin and wrote in a rather startled tone: "Among each of these compounds are some that cause mental aberrations. . . . If this be true, then the naturally occurring mental disorders — for example schizophrenia — which are mimicked by these drugs may be pictured as being the result of a cortical serotonin deficiency arising from metabolic failure rather than from drug action."

This announcement produced a thrill of excited hope, which was short-lived; there were other antagonists to serotonin just as potent as LSD which had no effect whatever on mental states. Serotonin also refused to pass through the so-called "blood-brain barrier." If it was injected into the bloodstream of an animal (or a human), it did not seem to pass into the brain. But the medical profession accommodated itself easily to this particular disappointment; for this discovery and a series of others which occurred during the same period gave rise to a whole new set of concepts concerning the roles of various chemical compounds manufactured within the brain. Many of them were molecules of a type known as amines. They were not, strictly speaking, hormones, since they were not produced and secreted by glandular tissue, but by scattered specialized cells, including nerve cells. They came to be called, in a quaint reversion to eighteenth-century diction, neurohumors. According to Webster, a humor is a fluid or juice of an animal or plant, specifically one of the four fluids — blood, phlegm, choler, and melancholy — conceived as entering into the constitution of the body and determining, by their relative proportions, a person's health and temperament; hence one's disposition, or state of mind, whether constitutional, habitual, or temporary. The discovery of the chemical nature of these humors led to the development of chemicals antagonistic to them and thus to entire families of humor-regulating drugs — the tranquilizers, anti-depressants, nervous-system stimulants, and so on.

But despite this new knowledge, the mystery of the LSD-serotonin antagonism persisted. Serotonin is not an unusual chemical in nature; it is found in many places — some of them odd, like the salivary glands of octopuses; others ordinary: it abounds in plants; bananas, figs, plums are especially rich in it. What was it doing in the brains of humans? What was its evolutionary history? In 1958 a Yale Medical School professor of dermatology named Aaron B. Lerner published a paper on the pineal gland which placed this elusive substance in some vague kind of historical perspective and provided for it a real functional role in the brains of mammals.

It had been known since 1917 that if crushed pineal glands were introduced into water in which tadpoles were swimming, the skin color of the tadpoles would turn light. The chemical substance melanin is the pigment which darkens skin color. It is located in specialized cells scattered through the topmost layer of skin. Pineal extract caused these cells to contract in tadpole skin and in certain other reptiles which change their skin color in response either to mood or environmental setting. Lerner was interested in melanomas, cancers of the pigment cells of human skin; he was curious to find out if there was any possible connection between this skin-lightening substance found in pineals and cancer. After an incredible four-year project, during which time he dissected over 250,000 cattle pineal glands supplied to him by the Armour Company, he finally isolated the substance responsible, calling it melatonin, since it caused the contraction of melanin-producing cells.

He proved that melatonin was a hormone, that it was produced specifically by the pineal organ, and that therefore this organ was a true, functioning gland, not merely a vestigial sight organ, a relic from our reptilian past. He discovered, moreover, how melatonin was manufactured by the pineal — by the action of certain enzymes on a precursor chemical which must pre-exist in the pineal in order for it to be transformed into melatonin. This precursor chemical turned out to be serotonin.

But try as he would, Lerner could find no connection between melatonin and the pigment cells of mammalian skin. In fact, he could find no use whatever for melatonin in the body economy of mammals. The task of exploring the role played by melatonin in the bodies of mammals was undertaken by a brilliant biochemist, Julius Axelrod, working at the National Institutes of Health in Bethesda, Maryland, in the company of several young associates, notably Richard Wurtman and Solomon Snyder. They discovered the basic biochemical sequences performed by the pineal in the manufacture of melatonin; they found that it was produced from serotonin by the action of two enzymes, an acetylating enzyme and a methoxylating enzyme. By blocking or augmenting the action of these enzymes, Axelrod and his assistants were able, most ingeniously, to stimulate or suppress the organism's own manufacture of melatonin. In the course of this work, it became apparent that Otto Heubner's old contention that the pineal produced a substance which interfered with sexual development was very close to the truth. Melatonin did, in fact, suppress physiological sexuality in mammals. If test animals were stimulated to manufacture excessive amounts of melatonin, their gonads and ovaries tended to become reduced in size, to shrink, to atrophy. The estrous, or fertility, cycle in females could likewise be altered experimentally by doses of melatonin.

Now, two most curious functions had been attributed to the pineal gland, the third eye, the eye of the mind. It had now been established that this organ produced a chemical which had, indirectly at least, been associated with psychedelic states. It also produced a chemical which suppressed functional sexuality. The literature of religious mysticism in all ages and all societies has viewed the mystical passion of ecstasy as being somehow analogous to, or involved with, carnal passion. In the pineal gland, in the eye of the mind, were discovered a hormone and a neurohumor which were functionally associated with both kinds of passion.

Axelrod and his co-workers also discovered another incredible fact. The pineal gland produces its chemicals according to a regular oscillating beat, the basis of this beat being the so-called circadian rhythm. This pulse remains constant if darkness and light follow one another through the course of the day in a regular alternation. They found that the pineal responded somehow to light conditions, that by altering light conditions they could extend, contract, even stabilize the chemical production rhythms of the pineal.

How does the pineal perceive light, directly, by being a light sensor itself, still performing some of the functions of an eye; or indirectly, via the central nervous system? The evidence is still not conclusive. Light does penetrate bone and brain to reach the pineal in significant amounts. This was proved by a University of California zoologist, W. F. Ganong, who implanted photocells adjacent to the site of the pineal in sheep and got altered readings from his instruments depending on whether the animals were standing in direct sunlight or in shade. On the other hand, if animals are blinded, or have the nerves connecting the eye to the brain severed, some of the pineal rhythms are dampened, just as though the animals were being maintained in continual darkness. But there is still a sufficient number of discrepancies in the evidence to leave the question of direct light sensing by the pineal open for the moment. Axelrod and Wurtman believe that there are other, undiscovered chemicals being manufactured by the pineal, for they see signs of enzyme activity which cannot be accounted for by either serotonin or melatonin.

The fact that the pineal responds to light, even if this response is indirect via the central nervous system, has some fascinating and far-reaching conceptual applications. There are many behavioral changes which overtake animals as the seasons change, and which can be produced out of season in the laboratory by simulating the appropriate span of artificial daylight. Do such seasonal changes in mood and behavior persist in humans?

The great religious holy days of all faiths tend to cluster around the times of the solstices and equinoxes. Is it possible that the human pineal gland responds to these alterations in the length of daylight, and by changinging the balance of neurohumors in the brain, perhaps effects a greater incidence of psychedelic states in certain susceptible individuals just at these crucial times? This possibility provides an entirely new potential dimension to our secular understanding of the religious experience.

Since Lerner had done his original pineal research at Yale, his colleagues belonging to various disciplines had become fascinated with his work even before it was published. As a result, Yale had a kind of head start in pineal research. Among the first to pursue the trail of pineal hormones and neurohumors was Nicholas Giarmin, a professor of pharmacology who had been a former student of Gaddum's at Edinburgh and remembered the connection Gaddum had made five years previous between LSD and serotonin. With him worked a professor of psychiatry, Daniel Freedman, who had become fascinated by the whole new field of pharmacology and states of mind. They began by measuring the serotonin contents of the various parts of the human brain at autopsy. In order to make these measurements, one must exploit the very limits of our technological capacities. Neurohumors exist in the brain in infinitesimally small amounts. They are measured by a unit known as the nanogram, which is one billionth of a gram. Not only are assay procedures highly critical, but since drastic chemical changes occur between that state which we call life and that which we define as death, it is difficult to prove that the amounts of any given entity found on autopsy are the same as those which might be found in the same tissue in the flush of life.

Giarmin and Freedman confirmed that the human brain manufactures serotonin at various sites other than the pineal. It is produced in scattered isolated cells, but the density of these cells varies with their location in the brain. For example, in the thalamus, they discovered 61 nanograms of serotonin per gram of tissue; in the hippocampus, 56 ng.; in the central gray section of the midbrain, they found 482 ng. But in the pineal, they found 3140 ng. of serotonin per gram of tissue. The pineal was unmistakably the richest site of serotonin in the brain.

Since the pineal seems to produce serotonin in excess of its needs for melatonin production, what happens to this excess? Does the gland provide a kind of serotonin reservoir for the brain as a whole? Can one make a correlation between pineal serotonin and mental disorder? As its name would imply, the pineal looks like a miniature pine cone sitting in the middle of the brain atop a stalklike appendage. The vascular and neural connections between it and the rest of the body run down this stalk into the spinal column and the central nervous system, not into the brain proper. If serotonin from the pineal does get back into the brain proper, it must do so through such a circuitous route that many workers discredit this possibility.

Though their work only accidentally impinged on making such correlations, Giarmin and Freedman did find that the pineals of certain deceased mental patients who had suffered from specified mental disorders showed a considerable excess of serotonin in their pineals. The average amount of serotonin found in the pineals of normal persons is about 3.52 micrograms per gland. One schizophrenic was found to have a pineal containing 10 micrograms of serotonin, while another patient, a sufferer from delirium tremens, had a pineal containing 22.82 micrograms of serotonin. Owing to the difficulties of obtaining the brains of the recently dead for autopsy, the Giarmin-Freedman sample is pathetically small, consisting only of thirteen cases. The same difficulties which confronted them also confront other workers who might be tempted to confirm these findings on a larger scale.

Strong suspicion has fallen now on serotonin as being one of the principal agents of the psychedelic experience, but whatever its role, it is certain that other neurohumors are additionally involved in the chemical transactions which produce the state. It is likely that LSD itself produces certain effects quite on its own. Studies made with tracer elements and the electron microscope now reveal that LSD strikes like a chemical guerrilla, entering into receptor granules in brain cells swiftly, and then leaving swiftly after a very short time, perhaps ten or twenty minutes (in animals). This initial period coincides with the onset of the most violent symptoms of the LSD state as it is observed in test animals. But when the twenty minutes are done, and the bulk of the LSD has left the receptor granules, it is replaced by what seems to be excessive, or supernormal, amounts of serotonin. Since the LSD state lasts for some ten hours, and during this time serotonin can be measured (again at autopsy) in supernormal amounts in receptor granules, it must be considered one of the important participants of that chemical transaction which produces the state. However, melatonin possesses the same basic indole molecular structure as the LSD molecule. It is not at all difficult to imagine how this substance could be metamorphosed into a psychedelic material. But so far, injections of melatonin have produced no altered mental states in humans.

The use of LSD in exploring these strange dislocated states of mind is most convenient because the effects are invariably reliable, and within certain limits quite predictable. All the neurohumors tend to alter, in one way or another, the data processing programming of the brain. LSD is one of the keys which open the compartment into which this drastic new programming can be introduced. Fasting as a means of altering body chemistry and so producing this kind of psychedelic state seems to be effective only among those who are marginally nourished in the first place. Sensory deprivation *is* effective, and for those who can will themselves into a state of such intense meditation as will exclude incoming signals from the environment, the computer model provides a simple analogy. The brain is always working, but as these outside signals cease coming through, the brain begins processing peripheral data, memories from the past, sense impressions of such subtlety that they are normally bypassed in favor of more vivid input signals which affect survival and so on.

For most of us, most of the time, our world is a Darwinian environment. We must manipulate ourselves within it, or attempt to manipulate it in order to survive. These survival needs tend to color our appreciation of this world, and we are continually making judgments about it. Some of these judgments are based on prior personal experience, others are provided by the culture. This "recognition system" is one of the elements disrupted by the psychedelic state. Normally we anticipate that water will feel wet. To the madman, or the person entranced by LSD, the wetness of water can come as an incredible surprise.

The principal question concerning psychedelic states remains: How much disruption can the system tolerate? "Cowper came to me," writes William Blake, "and said: 'O that I were insane always. . . . Can you not make me truly insane? I will never rest till I am so. O that in the bosom of God I was hid. You retain health and yet are as mad as any of us — over us all.' "

The problem of how to maintain a certain madness while at the same time functioning at peak efficiency has now captured the attention of many psychiatrists. There seems to be a point at which "creative" madness becomes degenerative, impeding function rather than stimulating it. The mental hospitals are filled with patients who passed from transient, or occasional, psychedelic states into perpetual psychosis. Freedman, with the help of another Yale colleague, Malcolm Bowers, has collected a number of case histories of persons who were admitted into mental institutions for various acute psychotic seizures. But as they speak and write about the onset of their illness, they describe psychedelic experiences. Why did they not "pass through" the experience to be enriched by it, as did William Blake? Here, for example, is the report of a twenty-one-year-old student who was removed to a mental hospital in "a severely agitated delusional state":

I [began to be] fascinated by the little insignificant things around me. There was an additional awareness of the world that would do artists, architects and painters good. I ended up by being too emotional, but I felt very much at home with myself, very much at ease. . . . It was not a case of seeing more broadly, but deeper. I was losing touch with the outside world, and lost my sense of time. . . . I could see more deeply into the problems other people had and would go directly into a deeper subject with a person. I had the feeling that I loved everybody in the world. Sharing emotions was like wiping the shadow away, wiping away a false face.

Bowers and Freedman do not tell us the final history of this patient. We do know, however, that Cowper asked for insanity and got it. He died a gibbering idiot, while Blake lived on into a ripe and irritable old age, still working, still writing, still slipping in and out of his mysterious states which allowed him a clear and brilliant vision of a world which, if the rest of us see at all, we see as through a glass darkly.

Man is unique by virtue of being possessed by intuitions concerning the scope of the mysterious universe he inhabits. He has devised for himself all manner of instruments to prove the nature of this universe. Now at last, with the molecule of this strange acid, he has found an instrument which opens the inner eye of the mind and which may hopefully allow him to explore the vast interior spaces where the history of millions of years of memories lie entangled among the roots of the primordial self. Through it we may find a means of understanding more clearly the roots of madness and of helping the insane to return to the world of commonplace reality.

Deposition: Testimony Concerning a Sickness

William S. Burroughs

I awoke from The Sickness at the age of forty-five, calm and sane, and in reasonably good health except for a weakened liver and the look of borrowed flesh common to all who survive The Sickness. . . . Most survivors do not remember the delirium in detail. I apparently took detailed notes on sickness and delirium. I have no precise memory of writing the notes which have now been published under the title *Naked Lunch.* The title was suggested by Jack Kerouac. I did not understand what the title meant until my recent recovery. The title means exactly what the words say: NAKED Lunch — a frozen moment when everyone sees what is on the end of every fork.

The Sickness is drug addiction and I was an addict for fifteen years. When I say addict I mean an addict to *junk* (generic term for opium and/or derivatives including all synthetics from demerol to palfium.) I have used junk in many forms: morphine, heroin, dilaudid, eukodal, pantapon, diocodid, diosane, opium, demerol, dolophine, palfium. I have smoked junk, eaten it, sniffed it, injected it in vein-skin-muscle, inserted it in rectal suppositories. The needle is not important. Whether you sniff it smoke it eat it or shove it up your ass the result is the same: addiction. When I speak of drug addiction I do not refer to keif, marijuana or any preparation of hashish, mescaline, Bannisteria Caapi, LSD6, Sacred Mushrooms or any other drug of the hallucinogen group. . . . There is no evidence that the use of any hallucinogen results in physical dependence. The action of these drugs is physiologically opposite to the action of junk. A lamentable confusion between the two classes of drugs has arisen owing to the zeal of the U.S. and other narcotic departments.

I have seen the exact manner in which the junk virus operates through fifteen years of addiction. The pyramid of junk, one level eating the level below (it is no accident that junk higher-ups are always fat and the addict in the street is always thin) right up to the top or tops since there are many junk pyramids feeding on peoples of the world and all built on basic principles of monopoly:

1. Never give anything away for nothing.
2. Never give more than you have to give (always catch the buyer hungry and always make him wait).
3. Always take everything back if you possibly can.

The Pusher always gets it all back. The addict needs more and more junk to maintain a human form . . . buy off the Monkey.

Junk is the mold of monopoly and possession. The addict stands by while his junk legs carry him straight in on the junk beam to relapse. Junk is quantitative and accurately measurable. The more junk you use the less you have and the more you have the more you use. All the hallucinogen drugs are considered sacred by those who use them — there are Peyote Cults and Bannisteria Cults, Hashish Cults and Mushroom Cults — "the Sacred

Mushrooms of Mexico enable a man to see God" — but no one ever suggested that junk is sacred. There are no opium cults. Opium is profane and quantitative like money. I have heard that there was once a beneficent non-habit-forming junk in India. It was called *soma* and is pictured as a beautiful blue tide. If *soma* ever existed the Pusher was there to bottle it and monopolize it and sell it and it turned into plain old time JUNK.

Junk is the ideal product . . . the ultimate merchandise. No sales talk necessary. The client will crawl through a sewer and beg to buy. . . . The junk merchant does not sell his product to the consumer, he sells the consumer to his product. He does not improve and simplify his merchandise. He degrades and simplifies the client. He pays his staff in junk.

Junk yields a basic formula of "evil" virus: *The Algebra of Need.* The face of "evil" is always the face of total need. A dope fiend is a man in total need of dope. Beyond a certain frequency need knows absolutely no limit or control. In the words of total need: *"Wouldn't you?"* Yes you would. You would lie, cheat, inform on your friends, steal, do *anything* to satisfy total need. Because you would be in a state of total sickness, total possession, and not in a position to act in any other way. Dope fiends are sick people who cannot act other than they do. A rabid dog cannot choose but bite. Assuming a self-righteous position is nothing to the purpose unless your purpose be to keep the junk virus in operation. And junk is a big industry. I recall talking to an American who worked for the Aftosa Commission in Mexico. Six hundred a month plus expense account:

"How long will the epidemic last?" I inquired.

"As long as we can keep it going. . . . And yes . . . maybe the aftosa will break out in South America," he said dreamily.

If you wish to alter or annihilate a pyramid of numbers in a serial relation, you alter or remove the bottom number. If we wish to annihilate the junk pyramid, we must start with the bottom of the pyramid: *the Addict in the Street,* and stop tilting quixotically for the "higher ups" so called, all of whom are immediately replaceable. *The addict in the street who must have junk to live is the one irreplaceable factor in the junk equation.* When there are no more addicts to buy junk there will be no junk traffic. As long as junk need exists, someone will service it.

Addicts can be cured or quarantined — that is allowed a morphine ration under minimal supervision like typhoid carriers. When this is done, junk pyramids of the world will collapse. So far as I know, England is the only country to apply this method to the junk problem. They have about five hundred quarantined addicts in the U.K. In another generation when the quarantined addicts die off and pain killers operating on a non-junk principle are discovered, the junk virus will be like smallpox, a closed chapter — a medical curiosity.

The vaccine that can relegate the junk

virus to a landlocked past is in existence. This vaccine is the Apomorphine Treatment discovered by an English doctor whose name I must withhold pending his permission to use it and to quote from his book covering thirty years of apomorphine treatment of addicts and alcoholics. The compound apomorphine is formed by boiling morphine with hydrochloric acid. It was discovered years before it was used to treat addicts. For many years the only use for apomorphine which has no narcotic or pain-killing properties was as an emetic to induce vomiting in cases of poisoning. It acts directly on the vomiting center in the back brain.

I found this vaccine at the end of the junk line. I lived in one room in the Native Quarter of Tangier. I had not taken a bath in a year nor changed my clothes or removed them except to stick a needle every hour in the fibrous gray wooden flesh of terminal addiction. I never cleaned or dusted the room. Empty ampule boxes and garbage piled to the ceiling. Light and water long since turned off for non-payment. I did absolutely nothing. I could look at the end of my shoe for eight hours. I was only roused to action when the hourglass of junk ran out. If a friend came to visit — and they rarely did since who or what was left to visit — I sat there not caring that he had entered my field of vision — a gray screen always blanker and fainter — and not caring when he walked out of it. If he had died on the spot I would have sat there looking at my shoe waiting to go through his pockets. Wouldn't you? Because I never had enough junk — no one ever does. Thirty grains of morphine a day and it still was not enough. And long waits in front of the drugstore. Delay is a rule in the junk business. The Man is never on time. This is no accident. There are no accidents in the junk world. The addict is taught again and again exactly what will happen if he does not score for his junk ration. Get up that money or else. And suddenly my habit began to jump and jump. Forty, sixty grains a day. And it still was not enough. And I could not pay.

I stood there with my last check in my hand and realized that it was my last check. I took the next plane for London.

The doctor explained to me that apomorphine acts on the back brain to regulate the metabolism and normalize the blood stream in such a way that the enzyme system of addiction is destroyed over a period of four or five days. Once the back brain is regulated apomorphine can be discontinued and only used in case of relapse. (No one would take apomorphine for kicks. *Not one case of addiction to apomorphine has ever been recorded.*) I agreed to undergo treatment and entered a nursing home. For the first twenty-four hours I was literally insane and paranoid as many addicts are in severe withdrawal. This delirium was dispersed by twenty-four hours of intensive apomorphine treatment. The doctor showed me the chart. I had received minute amounts of morphine that could not possibly account for my lack of the more severe withdrawal symptoms such as leg and stomach cramps, fever and my own special symptom, The Cold Burn, like a vast hive covering the body and rubbed with menthol. Every addict has his own special symptom that cracks all control. There was a missing factor in the withdrawal equation — that factor could only be apomorphine.

I saw the apomorphine treatment really work. Eight days later I left the nursing home eating and sleeping normally. I remained completely off junk for two full years — a twelve year record. I did relapse for some months as a result of pain and illness. Another apomorphine cure has kept me off junk through this writing.

The apomorphine cure is qualitatively different from other methods of cure. I have tried them all. Short reduction, slow reduction, cortisone, antihistamines, tranquilizers, sleeping cures, tolserol, reserpine. None of these cures lasted beyond the first opportunity to relapse. I can say definitely that I was never *metabolically* cured until I took the apomorphine cure. The overwhelming relapse statistics from the Lexington Narcotic Hospital have led many doctors to say that addiction is not curable. They use a dolophine reduction cure at Lexington and have never tried apomorphine so far as I know. In fact, this method of treatment has been largely neglected. No research has been done with variations of the apomorphine formula or with synthetics. No doubt substances fifty times stronger than apomorphine could be developed and the side effect of vomiting eliminated.

Apomorphine is a metabolic and psychic regulator that can be discontinued as soon as it has done its work. The world is deluged with tranquilizers and energizers but this unique regulator has not received attention. No research has been done by any of the large pharmaceutical companies. I suggest that research with variations of apomorphine and synthesis of it will open a new medical frontier extending far beyond the problem of addiction.

The smallpox vaccine was opposed by a vociferous lunatic group of anti-vaccinationists. No doubt a scream of protest will go up from interested or unbalanced individuals as the junk virus is shot out from under them. Junk is big business; there are always cranks and operators. They must not be allowed to interfere with the essential work of inoculation treatment and quarantine. *The junk virus is public health problem number one of the world today.*

Since *Naked Lunch* treats this health problem, it is necessarily brutal, obscene and disgusting. Sickness is often repulsive details not for weak stomachs.

Certain passages in the book that have been called pornographic were written as a tract against Capital Punishment in the manner of Jonathan Swift's *Modest Proposal.* These sections are intended to reveal capital punishment as the obscene, barbaric and disgusting anachronism that it is. As always the lunch is naked. If civilized countries want to return to Druid Hanging Rites in the Sacred Grove or to drink blood with the Aztecs and feed their Gods with blood of human sacrifice, let them see what they actually eat and drink. Let them see what is on the end of that long newspaper spoon.

I have almost completed a sequel to *Naked Lunch.* A mathematical extension of the Algebra of Need beyond the junk virus. Because there are many forms of addiction I think that they all obey basic laws. In the words of Heiderberg: "This may not be the best of all possible universes but it may well prove to be one of the simplest." If man can *see.*

Post Script. . . . Wouldn't You?
And speaking *Personally* and if a man speaks any other way we might as well start looking for his Protoplasm Daddy or Mother Cell. . . . *I Don't Want To Hear Any More Tired Old Junk Talk And Junk Con.* . . . The same things said a million times and more and there is no point in

saying anything because *NOTHING Ever Happens* in the junk world.

Only excuse for this tired death route is THE KICK when the junk circuit is cut off for the non-payment and the junk-skin dies of junk-lack and overdose of time and the Old Skin has forgotten the skin game simplifying a way under the junk cove the way skins will. . . . A condition of total exposure is precipitated when the Kicking Addict cannot choose but see smell and listen. . . . Watch out for the cars. . . .

It is clear that junk is a Round-the-World-Push-an-Opium-Pellet-with-Your-Nose-Route. Strictly for Scarabs — stumble bum junk heap. And as such report to disposal. Tired of seeing it around.

Junkies always beef about *The Cold* as they call it, turning up their black coat collars and clutching their withered necks . . . pure junk con. A junky does not want to be warm, he wants to be Cool-Cooler-COLD. But he wants The Cold like he wants His Junk — NOT OUTSIDE where it does him no good but INSIDE so he can sit around with a spine like a frozen hydraulic jack . . . his metabolism approaching. Absolute ZERO. TERMINAL addicts often go two months without a bowel move and the intestines make with sit-down-adhesions — Wouldn't you? — requiring the intervention of an apple corer or its surgical equivalent. . . . Such is life in The Old Ice House. Why move around and waste TIME?

Room for One More Inside, Sir.

Some entities are on thermodynamic kicks. They invented thermodynamics. . . . Wouldn't you?

And some of us are on Different Kicks and that's a thing out in the open the way I like to see what I eat and visa versa mutatis mutandis as the case may be. *Bill's Naked Lunch Room.* . . . Step right up. . . . Good for young and old, man and bestial. Nothing like a little snake oil to grease the wheels and get a show on the track Jack. Which side are you on? Fro-Zen Hydraulic? Or you want to take a look around with Honest Bill?

So that's the World Health Problem I was talking about back in The Article. The Prospect Before Us Friends of MINE. Do I hear muttering about a personal razor and some bush league short con artist who is known to have invented The Bill? Wouldn't you? The razor belonged to a man named Occam and he was not a scar collector. Ludwig Wittgenstein *Tractatus Logico-Philosophicus:* "If a proposition is NOT NECESSARY it is MEANINGLESS and approaching MEANING ZERO."

"And what is More UNNECESSARY than junk if You Don't NEED it?"

Answer: "Junkies, if you are not ON JUNK."

I tell you boys, I've heard some tired conversation but no other OCCUPATION GROUP can approximate that old thermodynamic junk Slow-DOWN. Now your heroin addict does not say hardly anything and that I can stand. But your Opium "Smoker" is more active since he still has a tent and a Lamp . . . and maybe 7–9–10 lying up in there like hibernating reptiles keep the temperature up to Talking Level: How low the other junkies are whereas We — WE have this tent and this lamp and this tent and this lamp and this tent and nice and warm in here nice and warm nice and IN HERE and nice and OUTSIDE ITS COLD. . . . ITS COLD OUTSIDE where the dross eaters and the needle boys won't last two years not six months hardly won't last stumble bum around and there is no class in them. . . . But WE SIT HERE and never increase the DOSE . . . is a SPECIAL OCCASION with all the dross eaters and needle boys out there in the cold. . . . And we never eat it never never never eat it. . . . Excuse please while I take a trip to The Source Of Living Drops they all have in pocket and opium pellets shoved up the ass in a finger stall with the Family Jewels and the other shit.

Room for one more inside, Sir.

Well when that record starts around for the billionth light year and never the tape shall change us non-junkies take drastic action and the men separate out from the Junk boys.

Only way to protect yourself against this horrid peril is come over HERE and shack up with Charybdis. . . . Treat you right kid. . . . Candy and cigarettes.

I am after fifteen years in that tent. In and out in and out in and OUT. *Over* and *Out.* So listen to Old Uncle Bill Burroughs who invented the Burroughs Adding Machine Regulator Gimmick on the Hydraulic Jack Principle no matter how you jerk the handle result is always the same for given co-ordinates. Got my training early . . . wouldn't you?

Paregoric Babies of the World Unite. We have nothing to lose but Our Pushers. And THEY are NOT NECESSARY.

Look down LOOK DOWN along that junk road before you travel there and get in with the Wrong Mob. . . .

STEP RIGHT UP. . . . Only a three Dollar Bill to use BILL's telescope.

A word to the wise guy.

The Addict

Anne Sexton

Sleepmonger,
deathmonger,
with capsules in my palms each night,
eight at a time from sweet pharmaceutical bottles
I make arrangements for a pint-sized journey.
I'm the queen of this condition.
I'm an expert on making the trip
and now they say I'm an addict.
Now they ask why.
Why!

Don't they know
that I promised to die!
I'm keeping in practice.
I'm merely staying in shape.
The pills are a mother, but better,
every color and as good as sour balls.
I'm on a diet from death.

Yes, I admit
it has gotten to be a bit of a habit—
blows eight at a time, socked in the eye,
hauled away by the pink, the orange,
the green and the white goodnights.
I'm becoming something of a chemical
mixture.
That's it!

My supply
of tablets
has got to last for years and years.
I like them more than I like me.
Stubborn as hell, they won't let go.
It's a kind of marriage.
It's a kind of war
where I plant bombs inside
of myself.

Yes
I try
to kill myself in small amounts,
an innocuous occupation.
Actually I'm hung up on it.
But remember I don't make too much noise
And frankly no one has to lug me out

and I don't stand there in my winding sheet.
I'm a little buttercup in my yellow nightie
eating my eight loaves in a row
and in a certain order as in
the laying on of hands
or the black sacrament.

It's a ceremony
but like any other sport
it's full of rules.
It's like a musical tennis match where
my mouth keeps catching the ball.
Then I lie on my altar
elevated by the eight chemical kisses.

What a lay me down this is
with two pink, two orange,
two green, two white goodnights.
Fee-fi-fo-fum—
Now I'm borrowed.
Now, I'm done.

Eros

Whose flesh is flame?
Where is your eye?
Gene Fowler, Shaman Songs

As J. I. Simmons and Barry Winograd observe in "Sex" (a chapter from their book It's Happening), *there is among the young "what amounts to a new pattern of sexual behavior and a new code of sexual morality." Instead of being life's grand obsession, sex is becoming, for many young people, simply "another human activity."*

But of course it is not that simple, despite the new sexual freedom. Certainly there is much sorrow and confusion and neurotic compulsion mingled with the joy and passion of these relationships. For instance, Herbert Gold's story "Girl Getting Educated at Noon on Sunday" sketches an entirely casual affair between a professor of French at San Francisco State and a liberated and lovely girl, Sue Cody, who refuses to play "that girlie-girl-game, the cop-out sex game." She is candid, intelligent, expert — but pathetic in her willingness to be used, her refusal to commit herself. Then there is Jane — in the poem "Bertram's Garden" by Donald Justice — who has just been seduced and cries alone while Bertram sleeps: a tiny tragedy, for Jane will "lie down with others soon/Naked to the naked moon."

On the other hand, the "New Girls — the subject of John Clellan Holmes' essay "The New Girls" — is more clearly liberated *than either Sue Cody or Jane. She emphatically rejects the traditional female roles; she affirms her integrity as a person; and she enjoys an increased sense of her own value as a female human being. She has achieved her "final freedom from the sexual status that was the fate of women in the past." She is socially, intellectually, and sexually the equal of men. But Mr. Holmes goes further still; he asserts that the New Girl "is pioneering in what may be the emotional landscape of tomorrow, a new Garden of Eden from which only the sense of sin and dissemblance will be expelled."*

Is the New Girl, as seen by Mr. Holmes, merely the female counterpart of the stereotyped Playboy *reader? Is there any significance in the fact that this essay originally appeared in* Playboy? *Certainly many of the other writers in this section might argue that Mr. Holmes distorts reality. In Harvey Cox's essay "Sex and Secularization," for instance, Mr. Cox could almost be speaking of the New Girl's image when he argues that the "humanization" of sex is impeded "by the parading of cultural-identity images for the sexually dispossessed, to make money." The New Girl may or may not be identical with The Girl, the American beauty of the mass media, to whom Mr. Cox devotes much of his essay. But the similarities between the New Girl and The Girl seem dangerously close, and that similarity is implicit in Mr. Cox's analysis of* Playboy. *We see further evidence that the New Girl is perhaps only a high-gloss Playmate, after all, in Mr. Cox's argument that our Puritan and Victorian pasts remain very much with us, and that "our sexual ethics are caught in a crossfire of contradiction and confusion."*

In John Updike's story, "Eros Rampant," we see that contradiction and confusion again, as we move away from the young and enter a house full of love — a contemporary American home, with children, multiple adultery, yoga, and assorted psychoses. The Maples seem totally amoral; their erotic compulsions flourish. But they take no pleasure from their sexual indulgences. They remain, like the Lovemaker in Robert Mezey's poem, "Ravished by despair" and "Restless, unsatisfied."

For the most part, these are bleak and joyless views of sex and love. In some recent American poetry, however, there are intimations of deeper, more satisfying concepts of love. In the three love poems that follow Mezey's poem, Hilary Ayer Fowler writes with lyric beauty of a sensuous, gentle, unselfish love. And in the work of Theodore Roethke, who was perhaps America's greatest love poet, the power, intensity, and life-giving force of love is reaffirmed. "The Sensualist" is tough, unsentimental, sexual; "Light Listened" erotic but tender. "Once More, the Round" is general and philosophical. First, Roethke gives lyric praise to life itself:

Now I adore my life
With the Bird, the abiding Leaf,
With the Fish, the questing Snail,
And the Eye altering all.

But in the dance of life, Roethke believes, love makes the music:

And I dance with William Blake
For love, for love's sake;

And everything comes to One,
As we dance on, dance on, dance on.

Sex

J. L. Simmons and Barry Winograd

Mostly on their own and in defiance of their elders, the more "liberated" members of our society have been evolving what mounts to a new pattern of sexual behavior and a new code of sexual morality. Like so much of what is happening today, the current sexual revolution is most characterized by its distinctive style — the approach of the individual toward sexual attitudes and the sexual act itself. The sensationalistic play upon erotic sex, so prevalent in the fifties and still with us in the sixties (responsible, for instance, in making the sex tease part of the American way of life), has been outgrown by many; largely young people dissatisfied with the tinsel values of America's commercialized eroticism. Because these patterns are in the process of emerging, they are still amorphous and uncrystallized. But already something of their particular shape can be seen.

A boy and girl talk casually several times while sitting at a table with other people. Perhaps he touches her hair once while he is getting up to leave and perhaps she touches his sleeve as she asks him about someone they both know. On a later day they may meet by accident and go for a walk together along the beach or perhaps they find each other at a friend's house. Afterwards, she sleeps with him because she likes him and because they were able to share other things. He finds her beautiful and, although he doesn't know her last name (what's in a name?), he knows that she too gets turned on by the

From *It's Happening,* 1966, chapter 6. Reprinted by permission of J. L. Simmons and Barry Winigrad.

sunset and Dylan. In a former decade she might have fixed him a cup of tea with the same grace and for the same reasons. Today she pulls back the covers and he might be in the kitchen rolling a joint. Maybe this is the beginning of a twosome or maybe it is only an encounter that doesn't survive the bring down of physical tiredness and the morning sun. But either way, the experience was a meaningful thing in and of itself, haunted by fewer compulsions from a frustrated or inhibiting past and constrained by fewer promises of the future. And it isn't inevitable; people who happen to be of the opposite sex will often spend great chunks of time together, will tell each other of their hangups and the dysentery they picked up in Mexico, will travel across the country together and sleep on one another's shoulder without any sexual intent or byplay whatsoever. Some will go to bed the first night they meet; others spend months in the same company with not a single sexual episode.

Acquaintances and friends become fleeting lovers, then acquaintances again; strangers meet and become momentary bedmates or soulmates, then dance off again to another partner and another scene. Those who stay involved with each other over fair durations of time — and this is still the majority — are involved in more ways and share a wider variety of things than unmarried couples did before. The traditional distance between the sexes has lessened. And they see more of each other under a greater variety of conditions.

But the new sex scene is not free love nor mass debauchery. More people are becoming more sexually experienced both in number of partners and in varieties of the act and sex is losing some of its sacred character along with many of the guilts and fears that previously hounded some who took part in non-marital sexual behavior. These people are reacting to the fact that guilt is something not always self-generated, but often created by parents and a society whose credo is that you *should* feel guilty. For many — more than ever before — sex is simply becoming another human activity. What's happening is that more and more pairs swing together just because they both want to. It is an easier, fuller, more candid, and encompassing style of relating in which the participants do more things together and become involved with each other as companions as well as sex objects to be used or romantic strangers to hang one's illusions and projections on. Partners come to know each other more quickly and more fully as fellow human beings with money problems, everyday habits, menstrual cramps, body deficiencies, and so on.

The newly emerging sex scene is partly a result of the major historical sweeps; the partial emancipation of women and youth; increasing secularization, urbanization, and mobility; and the dissemination of effective birth control techniques, especially oral contraceptive devices — liberators in any sense of the word. It is also the spreading of styles of heterosexual relationships which, as we noted earlier, first evolved in Bohemia and among the urban declasse. Perhaps it also reflects a sense of uncertainty about the future; a hesitation to live by long range plans in a scrambled and ever-changing time and a more intense sense of the present moment. A young man known to have lived with several girls once commented, "Why should I hang-up a chick, even if she wanted to get hung-up, when I don't really know where I'm going or how I'm ever gonna get there?" The day of the long-term romance where couples grew to know each other by exchanging daydreams and shy kisses has receded, just as it had supplanted the earlier widespread custom of marriage essentially by arrangement between families.

Romantic zeal (and innocence) is still rampant and of an evening one can find droves of young swains and maidens gazing about with that mixed expression of joy and anguish called romantic love. For that matter, partners are still brought to the parental home for sessions of mutual sizing up and parental disapproval can still carry enough force to break up many an ongoing affair. However, the growing financial and emotional independence of the young is continually gnawing away at the previously widespread norm dictating parental, and even familial, approval of the proposed mate. For many years, most people married the first person with whom they had a serious (but not necessarily coital) love affair, and they remained throughout their lives innocent of other possibilities, much like the primitive soul who subsisted on a diet of maize with only an occasional feast to break the monotony. And if you were a bit more liberal, and say you went to Harvard, you married, so the story goes, the second Radcliffe girl you went to bed with. These themes are not so predominant as they once were and the companionable style is coming into its own day. Less and less do couples represent graven psychoanalytically tinged idols for each other. Their sexual activities, including the waltz of courtship, are less dark Freudian wrestling matches and more tender intimacies and simple good fun.

Married life too seems more a swinging affair based on mutual involvement and fulfillment than execution of a solemn vow. Many divorces occur and these breakups still entail tragedy for a large number of people, but this doesn't necessarily mean that the American family or the institution of marriage is disintegrating. Those marriages which remain intact are probably on the whole more satisfying now that unhappy marriages have become easier to dissolve. Adultery's still around, but there's always been adultery and there is no reason to assert that it is on the increase, at least among men. The current change recognizes today's family and marriage function for what it is — the structuring of affectional ties between individuals. Crying about lost family purpose and meaning, says the ethos, is just that, crying over something belonging to another era.

The preliminaries to sexual intimacies are different from what they have been up until recently and the consequences of the fact that sexual intimacies have occurred have also changed. Rather than the measured steps of increasing physical contact which have prevailed in the past (and which were even given numbers running from one to ten in parts of England) there is now instead the preliminary of establishing some working level of communication which goes beneath the veneer of "where are you from," "what do you do," and "what's your major."

But the emerging sex ethos is not simply a matter of enjoying the companionship of others who happen to have different sexual equipment. Combined with this is a sometimes only semi-conscious search for the elusive essence of masculinity or femininity in one's partner. It is often semiconscious in that it can be inferred only from the choice of those whom one becomes really serious about rather than those one simply digs. It is elusive because the conventional models of man and woman have blurred and have broken down to some extent (as many writers have pointed out) and because what there is in the way of conventional models are more or less unacceptable. These models presume acceptance of things now being called into question — formal social grace, aggressive manliness, a ruthless drive for success, fashionableness, the personality sell, and so on. Each sex feels freer now to have attitudes, interests and tastes which were formerly the exclusive property of one sex or the other. Fewer things are thought "unmanly" or "unwomanly." Men can cook and sew, clean house, and iron; women can spout philosophical insights, tinker with woodcraft, and fix dirty carburetors. Thus for those with "liberalized" sexual codes it is positively consistent for a woman to admit forthrightly that she really does enjoy sex and for a man to fall in love with and marry somebody who's been to bed with a dozen other men. Some males go further, preferring girls who've had experience with others, shying away from virginity as a possible badge of coldness.

The sex scene is not an unremitted ball. Unrequited love, poor choices, and the disillusionments that troubadours have always sung about are still around. Girls still wait for the guys to move, though their invitations are more direct, less subtly clothed than in the past. And, as with romantic sentiment formerly, companionship and communication are sometimes unconscious or deliberate covers for starkly sexual goals. One of the common interpersonal measuring devices in the happening world is, of course, the other's view of sex and its place in life. Jill has sexual hangups and the tale manages to spread around. She's a virgin, though she really isn't sure whether she's right or not. The fact that she thinks she doesn't want to wait makes her defensive in relationships, often freezing up entirely. In some circles this becomes a confederation problem; in others a call for help, speedily dispatched by a close friend in whom trust is easily invested. Or, even, altruism with overtones of pure sex motivations on the part of males (as well, increasingly, as females) who ask "what's the matter?" while her interpersonal stock drops in the back of their minds. Jill is told about and is aided in getting birth control pills ("just go see this doctor . . . he's really cool about the whole thing"), which give a calmness of mind that will help her in living with her conflict about sexual behavior. Still, men remain hesitant, fearing preliminary frustrations and later over-involvements should a relationship develop out of some assistance they've rendered — "go ahead and groove with her, it's your sanity."

There's little doubt that the capacity to simply *enjoy* sex is greater among youth than among their parents; that they have fewer social and psychological compulsions and are surprisingly competent sexual craftsmen. A brutally simple law of learning is that competence increases with experience, and young people are starting to learn earlier than ever before. Does this mean that they have become self-indulgent libertines? Or, have they recaptured some of the simple human capacity abdicated by overcivilized Westerners?

The development and transition of sexual mores has always been difficult, if not impossible, to measure and depict. People in this country, regardless of their liberalism about sex, are hard put to rise above deeply embedded attitudes about "proper" behavior. Sex, as opposed to either love or marriage, for many was discussed surreptitiously, if at all. And numerous researchers have shown that the degree of permissiveness (or suppression) of sexual discussion goes hand in hand with the prevalence of emotional problems. Things like sexual teasing and game-playing, perfected by the American advertising industry, and often a central factor in interpersonal problems, seem to be fading among swingers as the changing sex ethic emerges.

But how many young individuals really approach sex with a freer, unmitigated sense of enjoyment and a feeling of responsibility to the other partner? Work measuring such attitudes and related behavior has only lately begun and the studies of the past two decades seem surprisingly inadequate when we seek to know exactly what's happening. Generally, though, they appear to support what we've already said. And their data gathering experiences indicate that barriers to the discussion of sex have dropped, if not totally, at least far below their pre-World War II level. More study will undoubtedly take place and with our expanding appetite for sexual data they probably will be heartily received. The past year, for example, has seen the rise of *Human Sexual Response* to the top of best-seller lists, despite its ten dollar price tag and its often laborious treatment of the topic. And social scientists, lawyers, and humanists are once again delving into the field in search of the level and type of activity, its actual and legal consequences, and the philosophical pertinence of sex in the Twentieth Century.

Increased distribution of literature about sex, both psychoanalytic and medical, has sparked a fairly common and open awareness of the subject. So much so, that an average coed can recite the latin nomenclature for her genital system and specify their role in psycho-sexual traumas. When two people find difficulty in their sexual relationship, it rarely need be the same problem it once was. If it cannot be faced and assumed and then handled, the relationship collapses more often than not. Females today are increasingly aware that their independence of spirit and womanly freedom can have an enormous influence on male assumptions of masculinity. In turn, the impact can be seen in the sexual response, or lack of it, on the part of the male. The blurring of traditional roles has created certain amounts of personal freedom from the obligations of past, customary bases of relationships, but at the same time it presents problems previously unknown.

For many years, to a majority of American females, the presiding sexual norm was plain: no sex until marriage (and not much after). Its important corollary was also simple: no male will marry a girl who is not a virgin. And a new creature was created — the technical virgin who went just so far but never far enough for a full sexual commitment. This permitted the male to roam and romp freely, to garner the tools and experience and emotional outlet provided by the sex act, to be prepared to teach when the great step of marriage was taken. Times have changed, but not as drastically as many believe. Because of their previous roles, and long established values about sex in and out of marriage, females have acquired a general set of meanings about sex. For the majority, it is still the Big Event to be supremely treasured.

Waiting, or at least being extremely careful in the selection of a bedmate, has enshrouded the female view of sex with the posit that reward will come to every female if she is not free with her body and thus her soul. The meaning has been drummed so hard (*i.e.* sex is the most beautiful thing in the world and therefore it should be "saved" until marriage) that it has come into conflict with the even older Protestant ethic viewing of sex as a necessary evil and not a supreme form of human communication. Today the first view can be seen as stemming from the emergence of psychoanalytic theory in the Twentieth Century, but amidst our mild sexual revolution even this doctrine has undergone noticeable change. The change has necessitated a different outlook from both the male and female perspectives. No longer is sex so sacrosanct that it need be saved until the night after the State waves its wand behind the altar. No longer need the man feel compelled, even obsessed, with a marital tie to virginity.

Contemporary lovers may move from no contact to complete intimacy with a swiftness which shocks and disconcerts their elders, but these elders are wrong when they judge this to be nothing but widespread promiscuity. Promiscuity does of course exist, but it may be no more common than it has ever been and as a sixty year old woman remarked, "We used to wear a dozen petticoats and skirts down to the floor, but a few still managed to get them over their heads." Very few youths will simply have sex with anyone under any circumstances, just as few people will accept a dinner engagement with anyone under any circumstances. In fact, for many, the controlling norm has become: sex is fine as long as it is not promiscuous. This vague and general dictum carries with it the obligation to feel that the sexual act possesses, in and of itself, a fine meaning that it is another form, albeit a higher one, of human relations. Given the fact that females, when faced with the choice, can sanction premarital sex in their own conscience, they also tend to believe — somewhere in the back of their mind — that the man they give themselves to will also be their husband when pragmatic circumstances permit. Increasing numbers of young females are finding that sexual inhibitions, guilt, and frustrations don't arrive immediately after the first round of petting or intercourse. Sexual neuroses are not always springing up when submission to sex is first made — the philosophy being "why wait if we're going to be married anyway" — as both parties are pulled into a half-believing, half-deceiving "we will marry" collusion. These neuroses, that can cripple marital as well as premarital relationships, are rising up with surprising frequency following the pre-marital divorce. For it is after the first tense, adult affair that the realization is made that more than one man will have intercourse with her before she gets married. It is at this point that adjustment to the situation is especially difficult, and that the success of future intimate relations can hang in the balance. Many girls have difficulty realizing that the male has also been exposed to our mild revolution, some firmly holding the view that they won't go into marriage with a virgin. They see women today as emancipated from restrictions of the past in which physical love was a selfish item, a commodity to be bartered in interpersonal transactions.

"Bed-hopping," as some young folks call their free and easy approach toward sex, is one side of changing premarital relations. The other face of modern sex revolves around the couple that, as one college administrator sputtered, "is an indicant of the high level of off-campus cohabitation." What this particular observer was saying was that a lot of people are living together today in a fashion more open than ever before. This is not the master/mistress relationship of previous eras, nor the behavior of two working people in their late 20's. Rather, the emergence of the unmarried young couple heralds a state of unblessed bliss. Couples living together, sharing expenses, doing the dishes, the laundry, and facing the economic necessities any married couple must bear, are common on most college campuses. And, indeed, even in the big cities where work and play come together, "setting up house" is certainly not unknown.

Living together, as any couple married or not will readily admit, is not like shacking up for an evening. It is filled with the joy, the tension, the trauma, and the closeness of any relationship kept at an optimum degree for almost twenty-four hours every day. One fact too often passed over by observers is this: young couples are literally and physically together almost all the time. Their general life interest is the same, especially in college settings, and their social relationships so overlap that they are brought that much closer to each other. Normal, married pairs are usually physically separated for a good portion of their daily lives. The lines between business, sociability, and the homelife are developed early in the marriage, but these are the same lines which are foggy, if they even exist, for the unmarried couple in the college milieu. This fact of life helps explain the intenseness of many youthful affairs. The ever-present intensity offers few outlets for frustration and disagreement and, because the choice to live together has not bound either partner in a life-long commitment (although marriage is seen by most as residing somewhere in the future), the unmarried couple is able to exercise an amount of freedom from each other that is sort of a halfway house between matrimony and weekend affairs. If, for example, a particularly crashing argument has occurred, it is no trouble at all for one of the partners to call up an old roommate or friend in order to secure housing for an evening "away from home." More common behavior, perhaps, if an immediate reconciliation cannot be made, is a simple move to another bed or couch in the apartment.

When campus couples live together they grow to appreciate their mutual responsibilities, the most important being the difficulties of living full time with another individual. The authors personally know several cases in which a couple has gone on to marriage, usually after one of the partners graduates or assumes a level of security in his occupation. We are also aware of numerous cases in which a marital disaster has been avoided by a period of cohabitation. Many young people, if they believe in marriage at all, want to make sure about the choice and have found living together the best means of getting an overall picture of a relationship's future possibilities. "Keeping house" offers most of the joys of marriage (less childbirth, hopefully) without the binding pressure of a supposed life-long commitment. And conventional society might note that these pre-marital trials save the individual and the State the pains and social costs of legal divorce.

Yet, even with a new morality, questions and problems remain. What causes the discord and sorrow that are part of so many youthful relationships today, while, paradoxically, the total sexual environment seems to have loosened, permitting a large number of individuals to freely and openly participate in sex discussion and relations?

Without much doubt, youth itself is a significant factor in the breakup of young couples — from the time dating starts in high school (or earlier in some locales) to the time serious courtship usually begins in the late teens. Youth in its fury (a New York policeman chided a nineteen year old Village hipster with "you people really have a rough time bringing up us old folks") sometimes forgets that as an individual gets older he also gets wiser. An individual of eighteen obviously doesn't have the same amount (or kind) of wisdom that he will have when twenty-one. As we get older our values and meanings are reinforced and refined, sometimes changed. Our particular likes and dislikes undergo the same process especially in the area of our attitudes about sex, love, and marriage. These changes are the hurdles young lovers must pass, and many don't make it without stumbling.

A second issue the changing sexual ethic must meet is the "standard" psychological problems of the past. Young and beautiful, Diane has been the victim of a disastrous home life (one of the negative benefits of today's freedom to pursue happiness in and out of marriage); her anger toward her father, the image in which she "sees" him, comes to the fore in her dating and sexual relations. Though desirous of sexual intimacies, even espousing a model position in favor of the new morality and growing one's own tree, her antagonisms rush forth, frustrating (or, worse, castrating) the partner and tormenting herself. The problem is no less real when the male is defensively aggressive. Both situations breed unstable, probably divorce-bound relationships in which neither party gets self-satisfaction or fulfillment. With a widespread norm that accepts extracurricular sex, but not necessarily the responsibilities that go with it, the problem we have long had, outlined above, is multiplied many times over. What we have described here is only one of the many common friction-producing forces in human relationships. Others abound and there is little to lead us to believe they will disappear in a few years, if ever. (Possessive love as a neurotic attachment is an aspect of human relationships that's been around since time began. Few prophets would doubt that it is here to stay.) Some, those usually on edge to begin with, have already asked: "Is it needed? Is the new morality really worth it?"

The increased adoption of new sexual attitudes is bound to lead to some rise in normative conflicts within this nation. Personal mobility in this country is now widespread, and this movement combined with speeded communications bears two faces when related to American sexual mores. Individuals with attachment to changing, liberalized norms about sex must still face large pockets of "Puritanic" attitudes throughout the country. At the same time the word is spread, it arouses howling opposition. Our morality censors speak out against sensual dancing, symbolistic art, enticing literature, and almost everything else that in one way or another is part of the changing sexual ethic. Social reactions toward deviance from the sexual norms of a particular audience have never been known to be forgiving or comforting. On the contrary, those youths who come home from school, for example, as reformers of sexual attitudes must still face the anger of parents, who in turn usually ask, if not demand, the proper homage to the middle class "do's" and "don'ts" about sex and its aftermath. So, as the credo spreads and sinks into increasingly larger fractions of the population it also draws strident attacks from moral adversaries and advisors.

Regardless of the mental state of an individual, those who adopt and live by the reformed sexual attitudes are all too often called "sick," "depraved," or "perverted." Quite clearly, those who level such charges fail to realize they might be intruding upon another's personal code of ethics and behavior. If we were to follow statutory law as a guide to the state of sexual honesty in America, as has been indicated many times, we would be sorrowfully amiss in our conclusions. In over half the states in this country it is illegal to have intercourse in any manner other than with the male on top. Sodomy, as legally deviant sex behavior is usually called, is probably the most frequent and widespread crime in the United States. The past two decade's increased publication of "how to do it" marriage and sex manuals has been an invitation to partake in "crime" and "debauchery." Our changing sexual dispositions are a response to this hypocrisy and to other double standards about intimate personal relations. Those opposing the recognition of some new attitudes could even, in this case, be called the "deviant" few, for, in fact, it is the majority of Americans who harbor distaste for such statutes even though their disapproval is usually carried on in the secrecy of a boudoir retreat.

A specific response to the judgment that sexual behavior is not a fair and adequate measure of mental health has been the development, too, of somewhat freer attitudes about homosexuality and bisexuality. "If one person wants to do it, if they find another attractive, who am I to say 'queer' or 'fag' or 'les'?" Punishment for homosexuality by consenting adults is one of the severest forms of misguided retribution; punishment for something intensely personal and private; a back lashing for behavior that, along with some other "crimes," certainly has no "victim." "I really dig it — who has the right to say I shouldn't? My moral code is my moral code and let's let it go at that," challenged one campus homosexual. As a matter of fact, although few have relations with others of the same sex (though it's more widespread than in the past), there is a growing feeling among hang-loose adherents that the homosexual should be free to follow the course he wishes, but of course without infringing on another's particular sexual prerogative.

The sex continuum, ranging from "it's bad and sinful" to "it's as easy as talking," is somewhere in the middle range today. Presentation of the sexual self is not really a matter of convenience or a "free love" ethos, as some would have it. It is a measured means of showing deep care and respect, a design to enhance and polish not culminate a relationship. The sexual inhibitions of the future will be found in those who have the greatest difficulty reconciling this approach with the one of the reigning generation in modern life. It is a problem of viewing sex not with some selfish values ("I've got to get my hair done at so and so's, do this and that, and Joe will jump right where I want him"), but as a documentation of feeling for another. With growing acceptance of an approach like this, it seems doubtful that motion along the continuum of sexual activity will recede; it is more likely to move forward, unhampered by the Protestant ethic of immorality or by pseudo-realistic doctrines of concerted amorality, both of which can easily detach meaning from all sex.

Girl Getting Educated at Noon on Sunday

Herbert Gold

"Would you have dinner with me one night this week?" he asked the girl at a pause in the foaming, churning breakers of sound. It rose, it rose again, it fell, it rose, and then there was a pause.

"No," she answered, smiling sweetly.

"But I thought — you seem — that look on your face——" She had a way of fixing her eyes against his as they danced. She had a way of moving against the way he moved.

"Sure I grok you," she said.

Slightly comforted and emboldened, he nevertheless gave up and thought he might as well be a scientist about it. "What did I do wrong?" he asked.

"Nothing," she said. The amplified sitar, the electric violin, the wired harpsichord and the pile-driving rhythm instruments were being launched once more to another victory against the stoned and the stunned. There was a willingness to be overcome.

"You have a friend?"

"Nothing special," she said. "I came here with a group — all friends."

"Then why not?"

She stood a little sideways, gazing at him with her clear sweet hilarious smile, as the acid-rock music of the Salvation Auditorium in San Francisco crested once again. He liked her eyes — smile wrinkles at the corners of the eyes of a girl who couldn't have been more than 22. He liked the healthy slim California look: silk blouse, checked Carnaby pants, slouching healthy spine — a gutsy challenging teasing funny chick. Good style.

"Then why not?" he asked again.

"I don't make dates. *Plots,* no. I don't make that scene," she said.

He frowned. "What a drag."

"But I'll go home with you now," she said, without changing the expression but leaning now from right to left instead of from left to right. "Cuba, *si* — plans, no."

He had her by the elbow and was pushing through the crowd toward the door. He was thinking: We both must smell of smoke. He was thinking: But no beer, that was another generation. He was thinking: Oh, man, let's get out of here, and lucky the car is parked nearby, before she changes her mind. *Tu penses, donc tu n'es pas* — think a little less, please. This is the time to shut it off.

The Anonymous Artists of America, a strong acid-rock group, was pouring its ardent heart and amplified soul into a song called *When I Was Worried:*

When I was worried
You made the stars turn pink
When I was worried
You taught me not to think
You said you'd make me feel real fine
Just sign here on the dotted line
And then you made me love you,
Dr. Swain.

Or maybe the song was called *Dr. Swain.* The dance at the Salvation Auditorium south of Mission Street in San Francisco had not yet come to the scheduled feature attraction: silent Zen contemplation of stones, pennies and corncobs by everyone seated in a circle. However, in the meantime, while waiting to draw up legs in the mandala posture, there was pop and op body painting, there were strobe lights changing everyone into stop-action dancers, there was the band, there was the drip, bubble and bounce light show, there were two projectors doing bits of film, there were Hell's Angels and Berkeley students, there were free apples, free licorice, there were posters and petitions to sign and custumes and the dreamy joy making of people in every known variety of high. Including horniness. The previous number had been introduced by the bushy-bearded leader of the band as "an oldie but a goodie, a dusty diamond, a pearl of some kind of price. . . . Some a you folks out there might remember gettin' pregnant to this song, 'way back in nineteen and sixty-four." The way his beard grew, it looked as if he were walking upside down. He was wearing ecstatic dress — swirls, spangles, silks. The crowd included everything, even clean-shaven gawkers. Including Jim Curtis, just looking around tonight and just finding this girl, this lovely sweet funny girl whose name he didn't even know yet. He would get her outside before he would ask her to repeat her name. He hadn't been able to hear it over the Anonymous Artists of America. It would be better, perhaps, to ask it when they were already on their way.

"I only," she was saying. "I only," she was explaining. "I only," she murmured sweetly at him, "go with people I grok by accident. Dating is a drag."

"Yeah, sure," he said, thinking this was

a time to emphasize the areas of agreement.

"Sometimes it means you're lonely. Sometimes it means you're going home with Dr. Swain, say, or nobody else, and that's *something* else. But I'd rather make it by myself than play that girlie-girl-girl game, the cop-out sex game, you know?"

"Sure, yeah," he said, being on the safe side. He would disagree later. Now was still the time to be agreeable, even a little more. "Jeez, they're a good band," he said.

"They're coming up strong. Write their own songs, communal 'em together, too."

"Who's Dr. Swain?"

She gave him her first puzzled and disappointed look. It crossed her charmed, pleased, healthy, sinewy face like a cloud; it made her body bend another way, backward and looking, as if she were wearing bifocal granny glasses, octagonally dubious. What had he done wrong? How had he let her down? "You don't know who Dr. Swain is?" she asked.

He walked on without answering. He would not compound his sin. He would wait and see if maybe Dr. Swain came to mind. As a matter of fact, he knew lots of doctors — surgeons, internists, Ph.D.s in various fields, particularly the Romance area — and he himself was a professor of French at San Francisco State; but how could a chap know everybody, such as Dr. Swain? It's a big country — the scene is big. She seemed to forgive and forget his failure; for, a moment later, emerging from the convolutions of fret, he found her still by his side.

Out through the crowd; out into the crowd waiting on the sidewalk, the kids without the $2.50 to get past the guards, the white cops brooding, the kids selling revolutionary buttons (YELLOW POWER, SUPPORT VIET ROCK, MARCEL PROUST IS A YENTA), the musicians from the next group, the Santa Fe Weed, unloading their cargo of horns, strings and fuse boxes from their paisley-painted hearse, the astonished winos, relics of pre-mind-expansion, stunned in the doorways, an urban-renewal expert with a clipboard, counting the traffic, the Negro cops watching, the idlers noticing, the pile-up of cycles and Vespas and Hondas, the sports cars slowing down, the teeny-boppers giggling in duos, hoping to be invited in. Air, blessed sea-drift air of San Francisco. Jim took a deep breath. A noise of revving entered with the air, but it was oxygen, all the same. The lungs can take vibration. The girl — *his* girl — was smiling at a spade cat in spats, opera slippers and a long white double-breasted parking-attendant coat with the words RENT-A-TRIP stenciled in psychedelic-ecstatic script above the pocket. Jim's lungs could not take this vibration.

Uncool was his spirit.

An effort. Wars are won by the steady. A moral equivalent of war must be fought by new forms of steady.

Uncool to cool, *over,* he thought.

Abruptly, Jim Curtis had one of those ideas that provide a turning point of sorts — for an evening or for a life, depending on the energy of the decision and the richness of deposit it leaves after combustion. He swung round on the crowded sidewalk, a sidewalk like a Turkish bazaar, and, half facing her, put his arm about the girl whom he was escorting to his apartment and, instead of asking her name, he took her chin in his hand, pressed it upward gently and kissed her; and then, not dislodging his mouth, he slipped around and they slipped together and kissed deeply there amid the murky crowd. Someone nearby was saying mumble-mumble-mumble. Jim did not care to listen. He was kissing. When they separated, the girl said, "It does good to kiss someone now and then."

"Yes, it does good," he said.

"I didn't expect that," she said.

"Neither did I."

She smiled sweetly. "You probably didn't hear my name," she said. "Sue Cody."

"I'll tell you my name, too," he said, and told her. She moved her lips, as if she had trouble remembering names, though she could always recall the face of the man who had kissed her. She looked as if she had not very often been kissed; felt, squeezed, taken home, rumpled, jumped on, yes, but not, like this, just kissed on the street by a man delighted with silk blouse, narrow pants, graceful dancer's slouch, well-articulated spine. However the clothes clung to her, he realized that he had thought until kissing her that she was a slender, willowy colt of a girl. Well, she was a slender and willowy colt, but she was also opulent. And smart. And funny. (You can tell all that from a kiss? he asked himself.) And crazy. (From a kiss? You can tell? Jim?)

"Mumble-mumble-mumble," she said, and smiled radiantly. "And just think of Buffalo Bill; that way, you can remember my name," she said.

"Wha'?"

"Think about it, Fred. It'll come to you."

"You're tough, aren't you?"

For answer she said nothing. She slid over toward him as close as she could. She took hold of his arm. She was hummming *When I Was Worried.* Well, that's a hard tune to keep. She was clever, she had music in her, probably mathematics, too; or she had heard it a lot. And *tough,* to her age, he recalled, it means boss, it means very fine.

It was one of those easy drives home, knowing that the mystery is to be unraveled and no fright in it. Pleasure, not pride; pleasure, not anxious lust; joy in the certain slide of present and coming events. There was a nimbus of fog about the street lamps. A few deep baying notes reverberated from the Golden Gate — freighters, fog. Tonight Jim liked himself. This was a surprising pleasure, too.

It does good to kiss a girl, he thought. And a strong acid-rock moll is used to going home with strange men, perhaps, but not so used to being kissed impulsively first on the wide space of sidewalk in front of the Salvationist Building. Oh, Sue Cody, I like you, he thought. She was making Jim like himself. That's a nice way to begin a friendship and end an evening.

It sort of occurred to him that like maybe they would just go up to his place and scramble some eggs in wine and talk and drink a bit of wine or smoke a bit of pot (he kept it with his collection of Rimbaud, Verlaine, René Char, Henri Michaux and St. John Perse). Just that. Maybe no more. A girl who took to a kiss so sweetly might understand. It was a way to dissolve nervousness: Go slow. Sure, she would understand; but then, it was not necessary to go slow, she had understood so well already, he had understood her so well, it was not necessary to understand, he was not nervous — not, not, not nervous — well, not very nervous. Instead of 10 percent delight and 90 percent nervousness, which was the usual proportion on first meetings, it was only 10 percent nervousness and 83 percent delight. The minority seven percent was divided among curiosity (five percent), residual panic (one percent) and fatherly concern, hypoglycemia, itchy nose and effort to recall cleanliness of undershorts (trace factors).

"Let's kiss again. I grok that," she was saying.

"Can't. Driving."

"Mind if I——"

"Go right ahead. I'll keep my eye glued to the road and my mighty hands on the wheel. My iron will enables me to respond without moving."

He paused at the intersection. Her breath was upon his cheek and her merry eyes were examining his jaw line. In the throbbing neon of a corner bar (DAS GUPTA SUTRA, did it say? Could it say that? Could a bar get away with an Indian raga neon sign?), she was acquainting herself with his profile ("Jim Curtis, not Fred," she was saying), and then she was tenderly pressing her lips to his cheek, she was leaning over the gearshift, her hands were exploring, her . . .

"Wait!" he said.

She pouted.

"My iron will," he said, "even with all my steel on the side of the National Safety Council, we are about to become a mere statistic in the annals of sober driving, if you keep that up."

"You don't love me," she said.

"I want to stay alive in order to get you home and jump on your bones," he said.

This sentimental comment seemed to console her.

"What's my name?" she asked. "Quick!"

"Suecody-as-in-Buffalo-Bill."

"Right. Very good. I don't have a phone, it's a drag. But we're here, aren't we, 'cause you stopped the wheels, and that's what counts."

"We're here," he said, meaning they were there. The top of Twin Peaks, where he lived, lay shrouded in wisps of fog, thick rolling stretches and then layers of clear mountain air. They were washed in the damp ocean currents slowly drifting through the Golden Gate on a mild October evening. Smoke and noise and confusion were being rinsed away; hair would smell good; he took his time leading her up the walk to the hare-brained wooden steps. It was a house broken up into apartments — a dental student, a secretary who voted to the right but bounced on her bed with hippies, the shrewd old lady who owned the building. Jim's apartment was the best one, the one with a fireplace and a view of the cool city. Hang up the painted bodies, he wanted to tell her (Sue Cody, he would remember the name); hang up the rock bands and the strobe lights, hang up the Goodwill Industries clothes, hang up the hang-ups, we're home.

"We're home," he said.

"I grok it here," she answered.

"You're not here yet."

"Close enough. I grok it."

He switched on lights and lit the fireplace. He burned real oak logs, not pressed sawdust. He was pleased that she could see his books and papers on his desk. He was hoping she couldn't hear the rhythmic sound of the right-wing hippie upstairs. He had met her in such a frivolous way, he wanted her to think him serious. If he had met her at school — a graduate student, a secretary — he would have hoped for the good luck to impress her as frivolous. "Play against my type, whatever it is," he said.

"What?"

"I'm mumbling to myself. I live alone and get to talking to myself."

"Well, you're not alone now, are you? Let's kiss again."

Hand on tight pants and nothing beneath them. Hand on silken blouse. Gentle mouth and hard right hand. Gentle left hand rubbing and hard mouth. "Oh, good, good," he said.

She broke away, laughing. "Do you know what you're doing?" she asked.

"Trust me."

"But I could feel your heart pounding."

"That's all right, trust me."

"Gee, Jim. Jim, that's a, you're a. I mean a funny person. Again!"

And they kissed and he made a sweet slip-slip-slipping sound as he pulled the blouse out. He tugged, it caught, it gave, she greedily explored him. "Would you believe I never kissed like this before?" she asked.

"Don't say would-you-believe," he said.

"I never did. More, more," she said.

Later, he thought, he would try to figure her out. Now was not the time for that. She was shameless without clothes on. He switched off the light and she stood at the window, looking out at the dim and deserted street. No one could see in, but still, how did she know that? She stood naked in the window, musing over the bushes gently swaying in the wind and fog, while he fled to the bathroom. He spent a few minutes there.

She called to him: "What's that noise upstairs?"

"Thump-thump?" he asked.

"Right."

"Never mind," he said.

"Groovy," she said. "You hear me? I like your house."

He waited before returning. He wanted a space of silence. Let her look out the window; let her absorb the quiet of Twin Peaks and being with this man, Jim Curtis, who he was. He wanted to be easy with her, all organs easy and relaxed, ready to play. When he returned, she was still naked in the window, in the light of the street, bathed in a bluish suffusion that seemed to come from within her flesh rather than from the fog-diffused glow.

"You look blue," he said.

"It's from inside. You've heard about bions? My bions are glowing."

"It's the light off the street."

"You don't know what bions are, friend, and that's why I dare to say it. Dirty, dirty, *dirty* talk, in a way. It means I like you." She said *like* instead of *grok.*

"Bions?" he asked.

"Let's now," she said, suddenly hoarse, tugging at him. "Oh, you're sweet and I like you."

"Sue."

Returning to himself by her side, Jim wondered if it would be all right to ask her for a *date* in, say, five minutes. To meet again in this bed in five minutes. Or would that be uncool? Or should he go all the way and propose meeting also tomorrow, no matter what she felt like tomorrow? Dare he make a plan with her? Dare he ask her to make a plan?

Here he was, her body opened to him, joyful to him, and he could do anything with it, with her — perhaps — but tomorrow was the great question, and tomorrow and tomorrow, where she said she lived only by impulse and happenstance.

"Would you?" he asked.

"Would I what?" she said.

"Never mind. Later."

"Do you like music, maybe?" she suggested. One toe moved as if to prod him off the bed toward his rig.

"Yes, sure."

"You got any raga-rock? The Four Tops' freak-out of *Reach Out I'll Be There?* Any folk backlash soul? *The Ballad of the Green Bra?*"

"Uh," he said, "the Jean-Paul Kreder

Ensemble doing *Chants de la Renaissance?* There's *Perdre le Sens Devant Vous,* there's. . . ."

Silence. "Well, any Beatle record is OK. *Rubber Soul.*"

There would always be the danger with this girl of her taking over. That was the second danger. The first was that she would just disappear into thin unamplified raga-rock in the distant air. Danger made Jim's nose itch. He was looking for danger. The moral equivalent of war was suddenly this gear-laden, eyes-aslant, body-greedy young lady. He wanted to open her up to the world beyond tripping and Motown records: to Jim Curtis.

He was not sure he could manage. To persuade her that she needed him, but for what? To learn French? What else did he know that she didn't know?

Maybe he could just give up. Senator Everett Dirksen, he thought, plays it cool. . . . Well, he would follow his nose, and where his nose led him — ah, that was nice.

She was sighing. "Nice, nice," she was saying, "oh, yes."

He forgot all his ideas and plans. She was delicious.

An hour later, she sat up suddenly and pulled the sheet over them both. "You don't have to take me home," she said, "if you don't mind my spending the night here."

"Mind?" he said incredulously.

"Well, some men, they like to be alone afterward, I don't know, I met a boy one time he had to change the sheets and all. You never know when you'll find a freaky kind. He had all sorts of ideas he wanted to try out, but afterward — clean sheets, no me. I didn't grok that."

"Sh."

"Another one, he wanted a full meal sent up by the Chinese Chinkaroony Kitchen. Wow. Not a snack — *food* food. And then he had a frozen pizza, it was more like a waffle with cheese. I'm used to a guy he wants his morning gruel before he goes out into the rice fields, but—— And then the *real* freak, he——"

"Never mind, I don't want to hear," he said.

"Yeah, I suppose," she said into the dark. "Maybe you're sleepy. Am I losing my mystery, talking so much?"

He laughed and rolled over upon her and kissed her cheek, licked her cheeks, kissed and butted her gently, and she giggled and sang, " 'When I was worried, You taught me not to think,' " and pretty soon they must have both been asleep, because he heard a dawn bird twittering. The fog lay heavy outside. They had never drawn the curtains. He should get up or the sun would wake them. He would get up soon. He would get up right away to draw the curtains. He was sleeping.

Hours later, when she saw his eyes open, one at a time, it turned out that she had been waiting for his two eyes so she could say, "You know what? You taught me to sleep with a man, to *sleep.* I was comfortable. I was lying there in the crook of your elbow——"

She had been lying there, warm and obedient, asleep, yes, from when he almost got up to pull the curtains.

"It's not bad," he said, "to do that."

"No," she said submissively, "it's not bad to do that, either."

She didn't make dates, but she would stay home with him now. She didn't make plans, but she would search in his eyes with the love-me look, the I-love-you look, eyes glowing and sweet, tender for real, feeling for real, desire for real, all there for him now. No, she would tell him nothing much about who she was. ("Well, you know . . ." she said.) No, she would make no promises for the future. "It's so beautiful right now, let's not think ahead, let me now, let me do that now, let me, oh, let me sweet——"

It's not so bad to do that.

It was nearly noon.

What if she was right and he was wrong? What if her way, no plans, was the right way, and his way, think ahead, think about protecting her, think about the future, was the wrong way? He had taught her to kiss, true; he had taught her to sleep sweetly, tightly rolled against him, all right, yes; but what if she could teach him about snatching joy on the run? He would be grateful. He caressed her body, thinking this over. He rubbed her tummy. She was saying shyly, "Can we kiss again?"

She tasted good. Her skin shone with good health. "Wild rice, no sugar, but honey, no candy, fruits but not too much, whole-grain cereals, good things like that, what's grown in the area — corn——"

"It's a good thing, that's all. It's not the macrobiotic eating."

She giggled.

"Now should we get up?"

"If," she said, sighing, "you want to."

It was that reluctant sighing remark that led him into his false step. It was his own fault, but it was her sigh that led him. Was she tired? Was she disappointed? "Was I . . . ?" he asked. "Was it . . . ?"

She smiled with that bright alertness he recalled from the stranger he had met less than a day earlier. "Well," she said, "I've known boys who came more often than you," — she marshaled her ideas briskly — "but I don't know, it's nice with you."

"You're the second best in that department I've ever known," he said maliciously, furiously. "You're the third or fourth prettiest girl I've ever met, and in the sack, you know, making it, you're fairly close to the top — maybe even second, as I said. Or third, anyway. You like that? You like that, kid?"

"Oh," she said.

"Use a little imagination. Look: Other person here! Me human being! Me no Tarzan — me sentient critter! Me jealous, me proud, me——"

She stroked him gently. "You nice boy," she said. "Look, all I meant was — oh, I hate to go out on a limb about anything — *I like you.*"

He looked at her straight in the eyes, as he had done only a few hours ago, already it seemed an age ago, finding each other in the crowd on the dance floor. Yet what did he know about her? What else did he know about her, Buffalo Bill Sue Cody whatever-her-name? "I like you very much," he said.

"I like you very much," she repeated in a tone like his.

And they both laughed together.

"It sounds like hypnotism," she said, "we say it so often, but it feels good. Oh, it do."

"It isn't necessary to tell the whole truth," he said. "Let me explain this situation to you — this sort of situation. You can express the good part, that's enough."

She looked hurt. "But weren't you asking me? I did say something wrong, Dr. Swain?"

She poked him. She wanted him to giggle along with her.

He swung his legs down to the floor. He sat, slightly slumped, on the edge of the bed. She stroked his spine, thinking about the massage, about yoga, about sport, about all the things that told her that his posture spelled discouragement in a questioning curve of spine. He was sulking. He was disappointed. He was wondering what had got him into this. He was jealous. He was thinking about a future of deception. He was going to ask her to be kind. He was about to ask her to be loyal and faithful. He was about to try to make her forget everything but him. He was making trouble for himself. He was making trouble for her.

She was following his eyes avidly. She was ready for the new stage. She was obedient to him, as she had been obedient to her Negro, her Mexican, her hip nonpainters and media-mix experts. She was a sweet girl. She grokked him for more than the moment.

And so she could learn to be miserable; that is, to fall in love. The afternoon sun lay aslant on their still, willing bodies.

In Bertram's Garden

Donald Justice

Jane looks down at her organdy skirt
As if *it* somehow were the thing disgraced,
For being there, on the floor, in the dirt,
And she catches it up about her waist,
Smooths it out along one hip,
And pulls it over the crumpled slip.

On the porch, green-shuttered, cool,
Asleep is Bertram, that bronze boy,
Who, having wound her around a spool,
Sends her spinning like a toy
Out to the garden, all alone,
To sit and weep on a bench of stone.

Soon the purple dark will bruise
Lily and bleeding-heart and rose,
And the little Cupid lose
Eyes and ears and chin and nose,
And Jane lie down with others soon
Naked to the naked moon.

The New Girl

John Clellon Holmes

A virgin coed, on being asked why she is taking the pill, explains that just as she wants to feel absolutely free to say yes without fear of pregnancy, so she wants to be sure that when she says no she isn't using this same fear as a cop-out. A lyrically graphic book of poetry about sexual euphoria, composed largely in love's forbidden language, is the object of an obscenity action in San Francisco, and its author is neither Allen Ginsberg nor Henry Miller but a pretty young poetess in tank top and hip-huggers. A clear-eyed maiden in patterned stockings lists her five civil rights arrests with the same quiet pride with which her older sister once listed her sorority affiliation. A high-fashion model, earning $50,000 a year, takes ten months off to gypsy around Europe with a hippie poet, making the *Provo* scene in Amsterdam, living on bread and wine on the beach at Iviza, and comes home to resume her career with no more scars to her psyche than the secretary of the past brought back from her proverbial two weeks of man hunting in the Poconos. A plain girl from a plain neighborhood in Brooklyn, driven by the urge to sing but refusing to accept the old showbiz rule that plain girls are doomed to being funny (so many Cass Dalys or Martha Rayes), creates an eerie beauty out of her large nose and aquiline features, inspiring thereby a whole style of kookie chic. Serious actresses, who have "done time" at the Actors Studio, appear fully nude in films or Happenings and do not feel like exhibitionists, much less whores. A folk singer devotes part of the fortune she has amassed with her ethereal, May-moon voice to the establishment of a school for the teaching of nonviolent direct action. A young socialite, bored by the charity-bazaar organizing and cotillion chaperoning that were the fate of her kind in other years, appears in underground movies, pals around with working-class minstrels from Liverpool and, far from being ostracized by her set, leads the march of Park Avenue down to the East Village.

Though these young women and their counterparts do not yet represent the numerical majority of their generation, there are strong reasons for believing that they constitute the advance guard of a new female attitude, an attitude that heralds the most profound change in femininity since the suffragettes, a change that is creating nothing less than a New Girl (the counterpart of the New Young Man), a girl with the very interests — sexual freedom and psychedelics, skindiving and the swim, Bobby Kennedy and Bobby Dylan, the New Left and civil rights — that so sharply distinguish that young man from his elders. Like all advance guards, this New Girl is pioneering the territory her sisters will eventually colonize; and what has happened to her may well happen to all young women tomorrow. What has happened is the emergence, at long last, of the Postfeminist Girl.

What Joan Baez and Baby Jane Holzer have in common is not a similar moral or political attitude, any more than what Barbra Streisand shares with poet Lenore

Kandel is an identical life style or clothes taste. Indeed, young women today are astonishingly diverse in their solutions to the question of how they want to live and toward what ends. What they all share, however, is a radically new relationship to the stereotypes that have defined womanhood heretofore — those stereotypes of wife, mother, spinster, courtesan, whore or ball breaker that were the only options offered to women in the past, roles that were conceived by men for the most part and reflected male attitudes that had their source in male needs. What the New Girls of today all exhibit in their various ways is an impatience with these roles and a rejection of the traditional idea that women, unlike men, are somehow supposed to be *fulfilled* by the roles they play, among which they would include the historically most recent, and emotionally least fulfilling, role of all (created by women themselves) — that of the feminist.

If the New Girl's impatience with role playing seems curious to some men, it is because these men forget that oppressed groups, in order to survive, are forced to act out the image of themselves that their oppressors find most acceptable. The Negro's evolution in America, for instance, could be described as a process of Stepin Fetchit turning into "Bojangles" Robinson turning into Harry Belafonte turning into Dick Gregory — all of which succeeding "images" revealed more about the white man's changing attitudes toward the Negro than the Negro's actual attitudes toward himself.

Women, it must be remembered, have been full citizens of the U.S. for less than 50 years — only half as long as Negroes. Before 1920, they had little choice but to become so many *Little Women, Sister Carries* or *Madame Bovarys.* And, like Negroes, women's social emancipation (at least in terms of real equality of opportunity) remained, until recent years, largely a matter of a constitutional amendment that carried about as much weight as the paper on which it was printed. Also like Negroes, the psychic liberation of women from all the subtle hangovers of chattel status in the past has taken considerably longer. Its achievement may be only now in sight, and perhaps the most persistent hangover of all has been feminism itself.

"Psychologically, feminism had a single objective: the achievement of maleness by the female." So wrote Marynia Farnham and Ferdinand Lundberg in *Modern Woman, the Lost Sex.* For the feminist played a role no less thwarting to her development as a human being than the patient helpmate or compliant mistress whom she hoped to supplant. If her aims were positive, the attitude behind them was deeply negative. Though she was always loudly defending female rights, she was actually preoccupied with attacking male privileges. Her crusades for birth control, for the right to smoke and drink in public and for an abolition of the double standard in sex and business stemmed largely from her sense of outrage at injustice, rather than from a desire to live more fully, more experimentally, more permissively. And the feminist attitude did not vanish with the passage of the 19th Amendment, which granted women the vote.

In the 1920s, for instance, the emancipated woman bound down her breasts, chopped off her hair and stood at the speak-easy bar, knocking back bootleg with the men and thereby acting just like all strangers in a new church: She watched what the other guy was doing and imitated him. As an example, Lady Ashley (heroine of Hemingway's *The Sun Also Rises*) reserved her ultimate contempt for the male character who "wanted me to grow my hair out. . . . He said it would make me more womanly," because her aim, of course, was to be *less* "womanly" in the feminine sense, associated, as that was, with the hateful past.

In the 1930s and 1940s, having discovered that male domination was fully as psychological as it was social, women became more openly aggressive, taking over the trousers as well as the causes once considered exclusively male and insisting that they were not only just like men but might even be superior to them. Indeed, one of Mary McCarthy's heroines, after a night of lovemaking with a businessman in a lower berth, could haughtily think of herself "as a citadel of socialist virginity, that could be taken and taken again, but never truly subdued. . . . She had come out of it untouched, while he had been reduced to a jelly." The women of those years wrote books that grimly attempted to prove that females were far more adaptable to the collectivized circumstances of modern life than males, and others that triumphantly stated that because the clitoris had measurably thicker nerve endings than the penis, female sexuality was immeasurably more rewarding than male.

All these feminist positions, however, had a single self-defeating characteristic in common: They defined femininity by comparison with, or in contradistinction to, masculinity. All were influenced by the viewpoint of the liberated slave, which seeks to first emulate, then compete with and finally destroy the ex-master. For at the bottom of it, the feminist was not seeking femininity at all but was still imprisoned by the idea that she could escape the demeaning role of "weaker sex" only by adopting yet another role: the masculinized woman.

Feminism was basically a movement of social reform, but though legislation and changing mores gradually emptied it of substance, it continued to have a more or less fugitive existence in the platforms of left-wing political parties, where it was known as "the woman question." No better indication of its final and complete demise can be found than the fact that the New Left (in whose ranks there are almost as many girls as boys) may be the first radical movement in modern history that does not concern itself with women's rights at all.

Doctrinaire feminism would strike the dedicated young women of Students for a Democratic Society as an anachronism about on a par with Prohibition, for they simply do not feel like an aggrieved minority that needs defending. Indeed, even the special status immemorially reserved for women who "worked for the cause" (manning the mimeograph rather than the barricades) seems silly to the New Girl of today, in light of that hunger for immediate, personal involvement that is her strongest motivation. It would never occur to her to stay behind, mailing out leaflets, when the bus leaves for the Pentagon; and the idea that there are certain confrontations from which she is excused on account of her sex is an idea as foreign to her as taking to her bed during menstruation. Confrontation, putting one's self on the line, walking down a Southern street side by side with a Negro youth (and thus risking the ugliest epithet — "Nigger lover" — that a bigot can think of to hurl at a woman, a sexual epithet specifically designed to insult her femininity); all this is precisely the *point* of her involvement; for by refusing to accept even a role that might exempt her from the consequences of her beliefs, she is affirming her conviction that *all* role playing is degrading to a human being. To help the Negro escape the necessity of playing Uncle Tom, she is willing to forgo the protection that is accorded Little Eva.

Feminism, then, is dead as a social movement; but is the New Girl really free of the psychic prejudices that succeeded it? Some raw comparisons may be illuminating.

In their day, Ingrid Bergman and Elizabeth Taylor flouted accepted social morality by changing marital partners without waiting to be divorced. Both risked, and suffered, the wrath of an outraged public, meanwhile portraying themselves as martyrs to a love so great it transcended custom. But both quickly married their lovers once they were free to do so. New Girl Julie Christie, on the contrary, lived openly and happily with her former mate, blandly announced that she had no plans to marry and averred that it was nobody's business but her own.

After Hedy Lamarr appeared nude in *Ecstasy* in the 1930s, she spent most of the rest of her career trying to live it down, confessing in interview after interview what a mistake it had been and refusing to pose for any but the most decorous pinup pictures. But when Vanessa Redgrave appeared nude in a movie in the 1960s, she did not feel that she had compromised herself or her craft, much less that the Academy Award nomination that she received for the role was a tribute to her figure rather than her talent.

Edna St. Vincent Millay's arrest in connection with the Sacco-Vanzetti case was the culmination of her revolt against the moral double standards of her time; for in her eyes, radical sexual attitudes assumed radical political ones. The young activist of a few years ago, however, who could (and did) boast of civil rights jail records as long as their arms, considered themselves morally superior to girls with none and would not have countenanced being treated like camp followers by anybody.

The difference is simple: The female rebels of the past defied the conventional roles of womanhood and then more or less meekly paid the price for that defiance, whereas today's New Girl thinks of herself as affirming her integrity as a person (a person who happens to be a woman) and fully expects to be rewarded for this affirmation by an increased sense of her individual worth.

All signs indicate that it is femininity itself that the New Girl seeks to experience and define afresh. She wants to know nothing less than what it is like to be a female human being, no longer either a willing *or* a rebellious appendage to some man but her own unique self. In the process, she has discovered that many of the assumed differences between men and women are shabby myths and many of the denied ones have a stubborn reality. For instance, at one and the same time, she can assert that her intelligence is as powerful as any man's and can also admit, with no feeling of inferiority, that it tends to operate on a different current — A.C. rather than D.C., as it were. But that she wants to accept and inhabit herself as a woman (and not one or another version of Adam's rib) is clear, no matter where you choose to look.

The most basic role that women were required to play in the past was that of the mannequin, the clotheshorse, the *living* doll. Unlike men, women were compelled to experience themselves as objects — vessels of purity or seductiveness, fragile beauty or fleshly allure — things to be adorned, posed, desired and possessed. In this sense, women's fashions were so many costumes that identified the roles that women had chosen, or were compelled to play. It was assumed that a girl's morals were reflected in her necklines.

The New Girl, however, is not interested in dressing up, or down, to men's unexamined conceptions of women. Not for her to feel that her body is shameful and thus, at the onset of puberty, to buy her cashmeres three sizes too big and lower her skirts to disguise the fact that girls have comely knees or risk being thought "fast and loose." Not for her (if she is a few years older) to allow herself to be gotten up in a succession of grotesque "new looks" by one or another Mr. Fruit, whose evident intention is to distort or humiliate her femininity.

Instead, she comes hurrying down the street in her white plastic boots or plum-colored snubby flats, her figure *there* for all to see — in miniskirt or minipants or miniseparates; her dress, more than not, designed to reveal her lingerie and her lingerie, more than not, designed to reveal her body; violets in wild clusters on her panties, bra more of a window than a garment; wearing her pajamas in the street and, like as not, little more than a smile in her bed; arraying herself in a veritable peacock profusion of bold colors and bolder prints, of wild fabrics and even wilder designs — all of which add up to a style that is kinky, pert, daring, frivolous, flamboyant, theatrical and unabashedly sexy; a style whose basic ingredients seem to be flair and imagination, a style that is above all an *eccentric* style, resulting from *boutique* browsing, hours of experimentation before a mirror and an eagerness to discover her own taste and her own chosen image.

The New Girl's fashions all emphasize femaleness (whether the model be The Dragon Lady or Alice in Wonderland) and they are mostly created by women, and young women at that. More than anything else, these clothes express the conviction that the female body is superbly natural, sensuous and efficient; that it was created to move (rather than stand still) and to move men (rather than the envy of other women). When designer Mary Quant was asked what was the *point* of the new fashion, she replied unhesitatingly: "Sex." In short, it is clear that the New Girl, even in her manner of dress, is declaring a fresh awareness of herself and of men and, above all, of the relation between the two.

What most distinguishes the Postfeminist Girl from her mother is her attitude toward sex, and her own sex in particular. It is not so much a question of a wider moral latitude as it is a matter of deeper self-knowledge. I don't mean to imply that women are, in actual fact, exclusively sexual creatures (in thrall to their biology and its cycle) when I say that almost every aspect of the New Girl's personality reflects her final freedom from the sexual status that was the fate of women in the past. But nevertheless, a female's life, until recently, was defined by two all-but-irrevocable facts: the necessity of marrying young, which her subservient economic position made almost obligatory, and the constant possibility of pregnancy, which her gender made the essential condition of her existence. Like it or not, she was reduced to the level of a sexual object (as much by her body as by the male's), and if her emotional life often remained stunted, it was because she could never fully escape from the phantoms of marriage and motherhood that seemed to haunt her future. If most women dutifully played the roles of wife and momma (or felt guilty if they did not), it wasn't only because there were few other roles available but because they could not conceive of themselves *except* in terms of the mating and mothering to which their very bodies seemed to condemn them.

All this has changed now and it has changed forever, and the single most important factor in that change has been, quite simply, the advent of the contraceptive pill. At one stroke, it accomplished a triple liberation that centuries of *coitus interruptus,* calendar counting and precautionary technology had never been able to achieve. It freed women from their own biology, putting into their hands (rather than men's) an inexpensive, simple-to-use, foolproof method of preventing conception and even controlling menstruation, a method that involved neither temperature taking, humiliating diaphragm measurings well before the act nor mood-breaking diaphragm insertions just prior to it. No longer does a girl have to premeditate her desire by deciding whether to take her "equipment" along on a date or risk being overcome when unprepared. No longer does a girl have to excuse herself to "outwit" her anatomy at the very moment when she feels most like indulging it. And the degree to which the pill has made possible the preservation of feminine dignity and integrity is suggested by this reaction (on the part of a 22-year-old) to the famous diaphragm-fitting scene in Mary McCarthy's *The Group:* "My God, how could any girl feel that sex was going to be good, much less *fun,* after being so clinically groped and measured by a total stranger that way!" To the New Girl of today, the very mechanics of contraception before the pill tended to demean a woman in her own eyes.

But in freeing her *from* her body, the pill accomplished something considerably more important: It freed her *to* its desires. By allowing a woman to enjoy sex without either the fear of pregnancy or the embarrassment of premeditation, it encouraged her to discover sexuality itself — female sexuality. All nonerotic considerations having been removed, women can at last confront their sexual natures with the same libidinous directness that men have always exhibited, a directness (as Lenore Kandel says) that "devour[s] all my secrets and my alibis" — with the result that in the past ten years we have learned more about female sexual response than in the ten centuries that preceded them, and we have learned it from women themselves.

But the third liberation that the pill made possible may have the most far-reaching consequences of all, because, having freed women from biology, and thus sexual reticence, it freed them from men as well and from men's wishful images of them. No longer dependent on a man to marry her if she "gets caught," released from the secondary sexual role (and all its distractions) that this dependency imposed on her, the New Girl is finally free of role playing itself and has entered into an equality with men, psychic as well as legal, in which she can at last discover and develop a uniquely individual *and* a uniquely feminine personality.

Menstruation, marriage and motherhood: These were the central facts of female life heretofore. But this is no longer true and young women today exercise a degree of control over these facts that has made it possible for each of them to say and mean that she "enjoys being a girl." That unsettling moment, when the arrival of "the curse" and the budding of breasts were such a shame and an embarrassment to young girls, is no longer an ordeal. In this era of the training bra, 12-year-olds are envious of 13-year-olds *because* they have bosoms; and 14-year-olds, anticipating a beach party that is scheduled at an inopportune time, borrow Enovid, not to prepare for something sexual but to postpone anything biological that might curtail their fun. As the teenage heroine of Rosalyn Drexler's *I Am the Beautiful Stranger* puts it: "I'm so glad I got my period. I waited a long time. Now so much will change." It is this note of outright eagerness to be initiated into the mysteries of womanhood that is new.

College girls, 44 percent of whom (according to a recent survey) feel that premarital sex between engaged couples is perfectly all right, nevertheless insist that their moment of sexual decision be as free as possible of the dilemma once expressed by the paradoxical "If I do, he'll think I'm cheap. But if I don't, he'll think I'm prudish," just as they refuse to accept the male prejudices to which this age-old female watchword referred: "Don't act too bright, or he'll be intimidated. But don't act too dumb, either, or he won't be interested." Girls today simply do not regard themselves as being governed by masculine preconceptions such as these.

But it is the young single woman in the city, probably no longer a virgin and just as probably regarding this fact not as a troubling loss of innocence but as a valuable gain of experience, who best epitomizes the New Girl. Her life may be either a female facsimile of the hip bachelorhood of her male counterpart (her pad equipped with the same Herb Alpert LPs, wire wine rack, deep-enough-for-two divan and copper pot for that "special" casserole) or she may have taken to the lofts with her young man, living in the careless, tribal, improvised poverty of those who have dropped out. But whether her trip is to a dating bar for the purpose of meeting likely male swingers (a bar that she can enter, drink in and exit from alone, if no one strikes her fancy) or into inner space via LSD (a trip she makes equally on her own), the New Girl's venturesomeness implies, above everything else, an almost complete absence of all those tensions about "being single" that were etched in stress lines around the mouths of girls in their mid-20s heretofore.

The girl of today intends to marry, but she sees marriage as the *culmination* of a relationship that has survived intimacy, not as the beginning of one. She is looking for Mr. Cool, not Mr. Clean, and she will probably pass her 27th birthday with no nightmares of spinsterhood disturbing her dreams, much less those of the young man who may be sleeping beside her. Meanwhile, she is busy, inquisitive, excited, unsentimental (though not unromantic) and, above all, vividly alive. Probably she is more responsible than her boyfriend for making this the first dancing generation since the 1940s; and certainly male willingness to explore bolder sartorial, not to mention tensorial, styles has been encouraged by her enthusiasm for the new — that enthusiasm for game playing itself that always emerges when one is no longer required to act a part.

Just as the assumption that all girls are feverish to get married has been proved obsolete, now that women are as free to experiment as men, so the notion that females are driven by some darkly visceral urge to have babies had not survived their ability to avoid them if they so choose. The matter is now firmly a question of voluntary decision, and soon there may be no reason the abortionist's curette cannot join the parental shotgun in the same oblivion. The New Girl probably wants babies — sometime. At least, she's no longer involved in the fierce denials of the so-called maternal instinct that made some of her older, "emancipated" sisters such a bore. But she's in no hurry. Or she's in the sort of hurry that Mary Quant expressed when she said, "Gestation is so slow, so out of date. I really don't see why it can't be speeded up." Which must stand as some ultimate in freedom from biology.

In any case, the New Girl refuses to act as though pots and pans, much less diapers and douches, add up to a satisfactory or fulfilling life; and you can bet that this lyric by The Mamas and the Papas describes her emotional expectations to a tee:

Words of love so soft and tender
Won't win a girl's heart anymore.
If you love her, then you must send her
Somewhere where she's never been before.

This is at once an announcement that today's girl is free of her own sentimentalities and a warning that she can no longer be approached in terms of them. But if it sounds somehow antiromantic, it is also clearly prosexual. Done with roles herself, impatient with all the *routines* to which role playing leads, the New Girl fully expects her young man to act the same.

It could be argued, for example, that the very willingness on the part of the girls of the civil rights, free-speech, love or peace movements to dare fire hoses, cattle prods, tear gas and jail cells constituted the most decisive factor in spurring on their young men, for it was an unequivocal sign of the extent to which the Postfeminist Girl had severed herself from the clinging-vine, going-steady, bouncy-cheerleader roles of the past, and it served notice that she would no longer consider the football hero or big man on campus as her exclusive masculine ideal. In fact, it may well be that mutual commitment to the dangers and fulfillments of personal action has bound together the boys and girls of this generation in a compact that is actually *sexual* in nature, because each has passed the same rite of maturation in the other's presence. This similarity of male and female experience (sitting in together or tripping out — it doesn't matter which) is the most distinguishing characteristic of the New Youth, all of whom have more in common with one another than they do with any of their elders, regardless of sex.

But certainly today's girl feels that "words of love" are somehow empty unless they are grounded in the facts of life and, aside from being respected as a woman, she wants to be encountered as a human being. In return, she no longer expects such outworn gallantries as having her arm taken when crossing a street (her hand is much more to the point), nor does she get offended if the conversation strays from the demure, the lily-white or the trivial; and, as a consequence, the old-fashioned concept of the lady has little more meaning for her than the old-fashioned concept of the whore, neither being descriptive of the wide range of feminine experience that she is discovering.

Postfeminism has freed the girls of today to a candor and an articulateness about themselves that has infused all the arts; and never before have there been so many first-rate writers, painters and musicians among women, some of whom are so good that the age-old put-down, "It isn't *what* she does, it's the fact that she can *do* it at all," is now hopelessly moribund. Talents as sizable as Doris Lessing, Marisol and Buffy Sainte-Marie do not need to be apologized for with qualifiers such as *woman* writer, *lady* sculptor or *girl* composer. They are so accomplished that their gender has no bearing on the level of their achievement, though it has a great deal to do with the nature of the work itself, which is intensely, unapologetically feminine and makes no attempt to cultivate, much less ape, the masculine preconceptions that have dominated the arts for centuries — preconceptions that older artists such as Mary McCarthy and even Simone de Beauvoir tried so stubbornly to anticipate, and disarm, on their own terms.

What is different is the works of these New Girls is not the subject matter (both McCarthy and Lessing, for instance, write about similar types of women) but their attitude toward that subject matter — an attitude that makes use of, rather than trying to overcome or disguise, such distinctively female traits as subjectivity, compassion, sensuality, a taste for decoration and an involvement in the shifting immediacies of reality. If novelist Doris Lessing relies on these traits to creatively describe, for the first time, the elusive experience of female orgasm, critic Susan Sontag calls on them no less when she attempts to confront a work of art as nakedly and openly as she would a lover.

In such works, it is possible at last for men to glimpse the world of femininity from the inside: a world that is not exclusively made up of chintz curtains, baking dishes and billets-doux; a world in which *they* appear like slightly boyish Humphrey Bogarts as seen through the eyes of tolerant and affectionate Lauren Bacalls: a contemporaneously discordant world that is nevertheless keyed to the realities of the body and its unpanicked rhythms; the world you hear in the voice of Mama Cass Elliott, a voice that is as darkly oboe, as richly brocade, as *fat* (in the jazz sense) as the voice of a switched-on Lilith; that world of stockings to be rinsed out and emotional post-mortems to be made, of sagacious hopes and shopping lists, which men leave behind when they put on their shoes and go away with a kiss and a promise to call; a world with an indescribable aroma of scent and sensibility to it. And the books and paintings and songs that describe this world are (as anthologist Barbara Alson has said): "tougher, less sentimental, less euphemistic . . . more often personal, much less often precious. And while not less feminine, certainly less ladylike." To which anyone, after all the Pearl Bucks and the Elizabeth Barrett Brownings of the past, will utter a profound "Amen!"

If the passage of time since enfranchisement, plus the pill, plus today's saner moral climate, have worked together to make the Postfeminist Girl possible, it may be the so-called generation gap that has made her a fact. For young Americans now are more passionately than ever before engaged in posing questions, and most of their questions have to do with the stereotyped life roles their elders expect them to take for granted. "The time it takes to hypnotize the young into standardization is called growing up" (as one of them has said), and they want no part of it. But never has a generation been less supine as regards its wars nor more committed as regards its causes. Never has a generation denied society so recklessly nor affirmed the individual so idealistically. And rarely has any generation felt so strongly, or with such sound reasons, that it constituted a community in itself that existed, separate and besieged, right in the middle of an uncomprehending environment, to which its very processes of awareness were alien and antithetical.

If the search for a new, more direct experience of the self is the overriding quest of this time, and if this means getting down to what Negroes call the nitty-gritty and existentialists call the essential reality, women may be better equipped than men for the arduous journey inward. Having been forced into masks and made to act as if the masks were real, having had no choice but to somehow survive as themselves *within* a role, and having at last gained that psychic freedom without which all social freedom is a sham, young women today are singularly prepared to function on the personal, subjective, nonabstract, *now* level where this generation (boys as well as girls) believes its truths will be found. In one sense, women have been in this territory from the beginning. They intimately know the disparity between the actor and the part he plays, between social codes and human nature; and it is this very disparity that has come to obsess young people today, revealing, as it does, the layer on layer of hypocrisy, deceit and complacency under which most older citizens of modern society bury their bad consciences, while the world worsens for lack of simple love and honesty. The antidote to this obsession is to tell it like it is, as the New Girl is intent on doing; and it may not be too farfetched to prophesy that the girls of this generation will affect its future as decisively as the boys.

Indeed, there are even signs of a temporary imbalance between the sexes, for which the New Girl is partially responsible. Some young men find it difficult to adjust to her expectation of full sexual pleasure, as well as moral equality; or her insistence that, insofar as she has come out from behind her masks, he must do no less and meet her as nakedly as she wants to meet him; or her eager involvement in all the things that, up until now, he may have considered *his* province. Ironically, the New Girl's rediscovery of femininity may compel men into a re-evaluation of some of the more "he-mannish" aspects of masculinity, for she knows that having to prove one's manliness is as false as having to act womanly and, though she understands the dilemma, she has less and less patience with it, and this is bound to put a certain degree of pressure on men. Nevertheless, there are an equal number of signs that women have now evolved to a point where they can admit that today's men, far from being only protectors or breadwinners or Casanovas, sometimes suffer from the same anxieties, insecurities and identity crises that were thought of in the past as peculiarly female problems. Certainly the New Girl is better equipped than her older sister to offer that human understanding (as against simple mothering) that such problems deserve, and this feeling of likeness, this similarity of emotional experience, this sense of being in the same capsizable boat (in terms of the society) is a powerful asset.

There are even reasons to suspect that the eventual righting of these old sexual imbalances and the new, less antagonistic male-female polarity that could result may do away at last with the centuries-old notion that men and women are somehow unalterably locked in an oblique opposition to each other, like sumo wrestlers poised in an embrace at once violent and erotic — a notion that is at the bottom of what older generations have always called the battle of the sexes. There have been periods of armistice in this battle and there have been periods of armed truce, but the urge to dominate or undermine (from one side or the other) has gone on and on relentlessly.

What the emergence of the New Girl suggests is that at last there may be some hope for a real and lasting peace, in which the truly feminine and the truly masculine can exist side by side, acknowledging the similarity of desire that drives them to merge and the differences of consciousness that keep them happily distinct; neither any longer seeking to subject or subvert the other, but both united in the effort to cultivate those areas where polarities can converge.

In this light, the Postfeminist Girl is pioneering in what may be the emotional landscape of tomorrow, a new Garden of Eden from which only the sense of sin and dissemblance will be expelled, and clearly men will profit fully as much as she from her explorations into a more candid and authentic femininity. And meanwhile, they have the mingled pleasure and astonishment of her company.

Sex and Secularization

Harvey Cox

No aspect of human life seethes with so many unexorcised demons as does sex. No human activity is so hexed by superstition, so haunted by residual tribal lore, and so harassed by socially induced fear. Within the breast of urban-secular man, a toe-to-toe struggle still rages between his savage and his bourgeois forebears. Like everything else, the images of sex which informed tribal and town society are expiring along with the eras in which they arose. The erosion of traditional values and the disappearance of accepted modes of behavior have left contemporary man free, but somewhat rudderless. Abhoring a vacuum, the mass media have rushed in to supply a new code and a new set of behavioral prototypes. They appeal to the unexorcised demons. Nowhere is the persistence of mythical and metalogical denizens more obvious than in sex, and the shamans of sales do their best to nourish them. Nowhere is the humanization of life more frustrated. Nowhere is a clear word of exorcism more needed.

How is the humanization of sex impeded? First it is thwarted by the parading of cultural-identity images for the sexually dispossessed, to make money. These images become the tyrant gods of the secular society, undercutting its liberation from religion and transforming it into a kind of neotribal culture. Second, the authentic secularization of sex is checkmated by an anxious clinging to the sexual standards of the town, an era so recent and yet so different from ours that simply to transplant its sexual ethos into our situation is to invite hypocrisy of the worst degree.

Let us look first at the spurious sexual models conjured up for our anxious society by the sorcerers of the mass media and the advertising guild. Like all pagan deities, these come in pairs — the god and his consort. For our purposes they are best symbolized by The Playboy and Miss America, the Adonis and Aphrodite of a leisure-consumer society which still seems unready to venture into full postreligious maturity and freedom. The Playboy and Miss America represent The Boy and The Girl. They incorporate a vision of life. They function as religious phenomena and should be exorcised and exposed.

The Residue of Tribalism

Let us begin with Miss America. In the first century B.C., Lucretius wrote this description of the pageant of Cybele:

> Adorned with emblem and crown . . . she is carried in awe-inspiring state. Tight-stretched tambourines and hollow cymbals thunder all round to the stroke of open hands, hollow pipes stir with Phrygian strain. . . . She rides in procession through great cities and mutely enriches mortals with a blessing not expressed in words. They strew all her path with brass and silver, presenting her with bounteous alms, and scatter over her a snow-shower of roses.[1]

Now compare this with the annual twentieth-century Miss America pageant in Atlantic City, New Jersey. Spotlights probe the dimness like votive tapers, banks of flowers exude their varied aromas, the orchestra blends feminine strings and regal

[1] This is quoted from Lucretius ii, 608f. in T. R. Glover, *The Conflict of Religions in the Early Roman Empire* (Boston: Beacon, 1960), p. 20. It was originally published in 1909 by Methuen & Co. Ltd.

trumpets. There is a hushed moment of tortured suspense, a drumroll, then the climax — a young woman with carefully prescribed anatomical proportions and exemplary "personality" parades serenely with scepter and crown to her throne. At TV sets across the nation throats tighten and eyes moisten. "There she goes, Miss America——" sings the crooner. "There she goes, your ideal." A new queen in America's emerging cult of The Girl has been crowned.

Is it merely illusory or anachronistic to discern in the multiplying pageants of the Miss America, Miss Universe, Miss College Queen type a residuum of the cults of the pre-Christian fertility goddesses? Perhaps, but students of the history of religions have become less prone in recent years to dismiss the possibility that the cultural behavior of modern man may be significantly illuminated by studying it in the perspective of the mythologies of bygone ages. After all, did not Freud initiate a revolution in social science by utilizing the venerable myth of Oedipus to help make sense out of the strange behavior of his Viennese contemporaries? Contemporary man carries with him, like his appendix and his fingernails, vestiges of his tribal and pagan past.

In light of this fertile combination of insights from modern social science and the history of religions, it is no longer possible to see in the Miss America pageant merely an overpublicized prank foisted on us by the advertising industry. It certainly is this, but it is also much more. It represents the mass cultic celebration, complete with a rich variety of ancient ritual embellishments, of the growing place of The Girl in the collective soul of America.

This young woman — though she is no doubt totally ignorant of the fact — symbolizes something beyond herself. She symbolizes The Girl, the primal image, the One behind the many. Just as the Virgin appears in many guises — as our Lady of Lourdes or of Fatima or of Guadalupe — but is always recognizably the Virgin, so with The Girl.

The Girl is also the omnipresent icon of consumer society. Selling beer, she is folksy and jolly. Selling gems, she is chic and distant. But behind her various theophanies she remains recognizably The Girl. In Miss America's glowingly healthy smile, her openly sexual but officially virginal figure, and in the name-brand gadgets around her, she personifies the stunted aspirations and ambivalent fears of her culture. "There she goes, your ideal."

Miss America stands in a long line of queens going back to Isis, Ceres, and Aphrodite. Everything from the elaborate sexual taboos surrounding her person to the symbolic gists at her coronation hints at her ancient ancestry. But the real proof comes when we find that the function served by The Girl in our culture is just as much a "religious" one as that served by Cybele in hers. The functions are identical — to provide a secure personal "identity" for initiates and to sanctify a particular value structure.

Let us look first at the way in which The Girl confers a kind of identity on her initiates. Simone de Beauvoir says in *The Second Sex* that "no one is *born* a woman." [2] One is merely born a female, and "*becomes* a woman" according to the models and meanings provided by the civilization. During the classical Christian centuries, it might be argued, the Virgin Mary served in part as this model. With the Reformation and especially with the Puritans, the place of Mary within the symbol system of the Protestant countries was reduced or eliminated. There are those who claim that this excision constituted an excess of zeal that greatly impoverished Western culture, an impoverishment from which it has never recovered. Some would even claim that the alleged failure of American novelists to produce a single great heroine (we have no Phaedra, no Anna Karenina) stems from this self-imposed lack of a central feminine ideal.

Without entering into this fascinating discussion, we can certainly be sure that, even within modern American Roman Catholicism, the Virgin Mary provides an identity image for few American girls. Where then do they look for the "model" Simone de Beauvoir convincingly contends they need? For most, the prototype of femininity seen in their mothers, their friends, and in the multitudinous images to which they are exposed on the mass media is what we have called The Girl.

In his significant monograph *Identity and the Life Cycle,* Erik Erikson reminds us that the child's identity is not modeled simply on the parent but on the parent's "super-ego." [3] Thus in seeking to forge her own identity the young girl is led beyond her mother to her mother's ideal image, and it is here that what Freud called "the ideologies of the superego . . . the traditions of the race and the people" become formative. It is here also that The Girl functions, conferring identity on those for whom she is — perhaps never completely consciously — the tangible incarnation of womanhood.

To describe the mechanics of this complex psychological process by which the fledgling American girl participates in the life of The Girl and thus attains a woman's identity would require a thorough description of American adolescence. There is little doubt, however, that such an analysis would reveal certain striking parallels to the "savage" practices by which initiates in the mystery cults shared in the magical life of their god.

For those inured to the process, the tortuous nightly fetish by which the young American female pulls her hair into tight bunches secured by metal clips may bear little rememblance to the incisions made on their arms by certain African tribesmen to make them resemble their totem, the tiger. But to an anthropologist comparing two ways of attempting to resemble the holy one, the only difference might appear to be that with the Africans the torture is over after initiation, while with the American it has to be repeated every night, a luxury only a culture with abundant leisure can afford.

In turning now to an examination of the second function of The Girl — supporting and portraying a value system — a comparison with the role of the Virgin in the twelfth and thirteenth centuries may be helpful. Just as the Virgin exhibited and sustained the ideals of the age that fashioned Chartres Cathedral, as Henry Adams saw, so The Girl symbolizes the

[2] Simone de Beauvoir, *The Second Sex* (New York: Knopf, 1953; London; Cape), p. 41.

[3] Erik Erikson, *Identity and the Life Cycle* (New York: International University Press, 1959).

values and aspirations of a consumer society. (She is crowned not in the political capital, remember, but in Atlantic City or Miami Beach, centers associated with leisure and consumption.) And she is not entirely incapable of exploitation. If men sometimes sought to buy with gold the Virgin's blessings on their questionable causes, so The Girl now dispenses her charismatic favor on watches, refrigerators, and razor blades — for a price. Though The Girl had built no cathedrals, without her the colossal edifice of mass persuasion would crumble. Her sharply stylized face and figure beckon us from every magazine and TV channel, luring us toward the beatific vision of a consumer's paradise.

The Girl is *not* the Virgin. In fact she is a kind of anti-Madonna. She reverses most of the values traditionally associated with the Virgin — poverty, humility, sacrifice. In startling contrast, particularly, to the biblical portrait of Mary in Luke 1:46–55, The Girl has nothing to do with filling the hungry with "good things," hawking instead an endless proliferation of trivia on TV spot commercials. The Girl exalts the mighty, extols the rich, and brings nothing to the hungry but added despair. So The Girl does buttress and bring into personal focus a value system, such as it is. In both social and psychological terms, The Girl, whether or not she is really a goddess, certainly acts that way.

Perhaps the most ironic element in the rise of the cult of The Girl is that Protestantism has almost completely failed to notice it, while Roman Catholics have at least given some evidence of sensing its significance. In some places, for instance, Catholics are forbidden to participate in beauty pageants, a ruling not entirely inspired by prudery. It is ironic that Protestants have traditionally been most opposed to lady cults while Catholics have managed to assimilate more than one at various points in history.

If we are correct in assuming that The Girl *functions* in many ways as a goddess, then the cult of The Girl demands careful Protestant theological criticism. Anything that functions, even in part, as a god when it is in fact not God, is an idol. When the Reformers and their Puritan offspring criticized the cult of Mary it was not because they were antifeminist. They opposed anything — man, woman, or beast (or dogma or institution) — that usurped in the slightest the prerogatives that belonged alone to God Almighty. As Max Weber has insisted, when the prophets of Israel railed against fertility cults, they had nothing against fertility. It is not against sexuality but against a cult that protest is needed. Not, as it were, against the beauty but against the pageant.

Thus the Protestant objection to the present cult of The Girl must be based on the realization that The Girl is an *idol.* She functions as the source of value, the giver of personal identity. But the values she mediates and the identity she confers are both spurious. Like every idol she is ultimately a creation of our own hands and cannot save us. The values she represents as ultimate satisfactions — mechanical comfort, sexual success, unencumbered leisure — have no ultimacy. They lead only to endless upward mobility, competitive consumption, and anxious cynicism. The devilish social insecurities from which she promises to deliver us are, alas, still there, even after we have purified our breaths, our skins, and our armpits by applying her sacred oils. She is a merciless goddess who draws us farther and farther into the net of accelerated ordeals of obeisance. As the queen of commodities in an expanding economy, the fulfillment she promises must always remain just beyond the tips of our fingers.

Why has Protestantism kept its attention obsessively fastened on the development of Mariolatry in Catholicism and not noticed the sinister rise of this vampirelike cult of The Girl in our society? Unfortunately, it is due to the continuing incapacity of theological critics to recognize the religious significance of cultural phenomena outside the formal religious system itself. But the rise of this new cult reminds us that the work of the reformer is never done. Man's mind is indeed — as Luther said — a factory busy making idols. The Girl is a far more pervasive and destructive influence than the Virgin, and it is to her and her omnipresent altars that we should be directing our criticism.

Besides sanctifying a set of phony values, The Girl compounds her noxiousness by maiming her victims in a Procrustean bed of uniformity. This is the empty "identity" she panders. Take the Miss America pageant, for example. Are these virtually indistinguishable specimens of white, middleclass postadolescence really the best we can do? Do they not mirror the ethos of a mass-production society, in which genuine individualism somehow mars the clean, precision-tooled effect? Like their sisters, the finely calibrated Rockettes, these meticulously measured and pretested "beauties" lined up on the Boardwalk bear an ominous similarity to the faceless retinues of goose-steppers and the interchangeable mass exercisers of explicitly totalitarian societies. In short, *who* says this is beauty?

The caricature becomes complete in the Miss Universe contest, when Miss Rhodesia is a blonde, Miss South Africa is white, and Oriental girls with a totally different tradition of feminine beauty are forced to display their thighs and appear in spike heels and Catalina swim suits. Miss Universe is as universal as an American adman's stereotype of what beauty should be.

The truth is that The Girl can*not* bestow the identity she promises. She forces her initiates to torture themselves with starvation diets and beauty-parlor ordeals, but still cannot deliver the satisfactions she holds out. She is young, but what happens when her followers, despite added hours in the boudoir, can no longer appear young? She is happy and smiling and loved. What happens when, despite all the potions and incantations, her disciples still feel the human pangs of rejection and loneliness? Or what about all the girls whose statistics, or "personality" (or color) do not match the authoritative "ideal"?

After all, it is God — not The Girl — who is God. He is the center and source of value. He liberates men and women from the bland uniformity of cultural deities so that they may feast on the luxurious diversity of life He has provided. The identity He confers frees men from all pseudo-identities to be themselves, to fulfill their human destinies regardless whether their faces or figures match some predetermined abstract "ideal." As His gift, sex is freed from both fertility cults and commercial exploitation to become the thoroughly human thing He intended. And since it is one of the last items we have left that is neither prepackaged nor standardized, let us not sacrifice it too hastily on the omnivorous altar of Cybele.

The Playboy, illustrated by the monthly magazine of that name, does for the boys what Miss America does for the girls.

Despite accusations to the contrary, the immense popularity of this magazine is not solely attributable to pin-up girls. For sheer nudity its pictorial art cannot compete with such would-be competitors as *Dude* and *Escapade. Playboy* appeals to a highly mobile, increasingly affluent group of young readers, mostly between eighteen and thirty, who want much more from their drugstore reading than bosoms and thighs. They need a total image of what it means to be a man. And Mr. Hefner's *Playboy* has no hesitation in telling them.

Why should such a need arise? David Riesman has argued that the responsibility for character formation in our society has shifted from the family to the peer group and to the mass-media peer-group surrogates.[4] Things are changing so rapidly that one who is equipped by his family with inflexible, highly internalized values becomes unable to deal with the accelerated pace of change and with the varying contexts in which he is called upon to function. This is especially true in the area of consumer values toward which the "other-directed person" is increasingly oriented.

Within the confusing plethora of mass media signals and peer-group values, *Playboy* fills a special need. For the insecure young man with newly acquired free time and money who still feels uncertain about his consumer skills, *Playboy* supplies a comprehensive and authoritative guidebook to this forbidding new world to which he now has access. It tells him not only who to be; it tells him *how* to be it, and even provides consolation outlets for those who secretly feel that they have not quite made it.

In supplying for the other-directed consumer of leisure both the normative identity image and the means for achieving it, *Playboy* relies on a careful integration of copy and advertising material. The comic book that appeals to a younger generation with an analogous problem skillfully intersperses illustrations of incredibly muscled men and excessively mammalian women with advertisements for body-building gimmicks and foam-rubber brassière supplements. Thus the thin-chested comic-book readers of both sexes are thoughtfully supplied with both the ends and the means for attaining a spurious brand of maturity. *Playboy* merely continues the comic-book tactic for the next age group. Since within every identity crisis, whether in teens or twenties, there is usually a sexual-identity problem, *Playboy* speaks to those who desperately want to know what it means to be a man, and more specifically a *male,* in today's world.

Both the image of man and the means for its attainment exhibit a remarkable consistency in *Playboy.* The skilled consumer is cool and unruffled. He savors sports cars, liquor, high fidelity, and book-club selections with a casual, unhurried aplomb. Though he must certainly *have* and *use* the latest consumption item, he must not permit himself to get too attached to it. The style will change and he must always be ready to adjust. His persistent anxiety that he may mix a drink incorrectly, enjoy a jazz group that is passé, or wear last year's necktie style is comforted by an authoritative tone in *Playboy* beside which papal encyclicals sound irresolute.

"Don't hesitate," he is told, "this assertive, self-assured weskit is what every man of taste wants for the fall season." Lingering doubts about his masculinity are extirpated by the firm assurance that "real men demand this ruggedly masculine

[4] David Riesman, *The Lonely Crowd* (New Haven: Yale University Press, 1950; Harmondsworth, Middlesex: Penguin).

smoke" (cigar ad). Though "the ladies will swoon for you, no matter what they promise, don't give them a puff. This cigar is for men only." A fur-lined canvas field jacket is described as "the most masculine thing since the cave man." What to be and how to be it are both made unambiguously clear.

Since being a male necessitates some kind of relationship to females, *Playboy* fearlessly confronts this problem too, and solves it by the consistent application of the same formula. Sex becomes one of the items of leisure activity that the knowledgeable consumer of leisure handles with his characteristic skill and detachment. The girl becomes a desirable — indeed an indispensable — "Playboy accessory."

In a question-answering column entitled "The Playboy Adviser," queries about smoking equipment (how to break in a meerschaum pipe), cocktail preparation (how to mix a Yellow Fever), and whether or not to wear suspenders with a vest alternate with questions about what to do with girls who complicate the cardinal principle of casualness either by suggesting marriage or by some other impulsive gesture toward a permanent relationship. The infallible answer from the oracle never varies: sex must be contained, at all costs, within the entertainment-recreation area. Don't let her get "serious."

After all, the most famous feature of the magazine is its monthly fold-out photo of a *play*mate. She is the symbol par excellence of recreational sex. When playtime is over, the playmate's function ceases, so she must be made to understand the rules of the game. As the crew-cut young man in a *Playboy* cartoon says to the rumpled and disarrayed girl he is passionately embracing, "Why speak of love at a time like this?"

The magazine's fiction purveys the same kind of severely departmentalized sex. Although the editors have recently dressed up the *Playboy* contents with contributions by Hemingway, Bemelmans, and even a Chekhov translation, the regular run of stories relies on a repetitious and predictable formula. A successful young man, either single or somewhat less than ideally married — a figure with whom readers have no difficulty identifying — encounters a gorgeous and seductive woman who makes no demands on him except sex. She is the prose duplication of the cool-eyed but hot-blooded playmate of the fold-out.

Drawing heavily on the fantasy life of all young Americans, the writers utilize for their stereotyped heroines the hero's schoolteacher, his secretary, an old girl friend, or the girl who brings her car into the garage where he works. The happy issue is always a casual but satisfying sexual experience with no entangling alliances whatever. Unlike the women he knows in real life, the *Playboy* reader's fictional girl friends know their place and ask for nothing more. They present no danger of permanent involvement. Like any good accessory, they are detachable and disposable.

Many of the advertisements reinforce the sex-accessory identification in another way — by attributing female characteristics to the items they sell. Thus a full-page ad for the MG assures us that this car is not only "the smoothest pleasure machine" on the road and that having one is a "love-affair," but most important, "you drive it — it doesn't drive you." The ad ends with the equivocal question "Is it a date?" [5]

Playboy insists that its message is one of

[5] This whole fusing of sex and machine symbols in contemporary mass media was once brilliantly explored by Marshall McCluhan in *The Mechanical Bride,* now out of print.

liberation. Its gospel frees us from captivity to the puritanical "hatpin brigade." It solemnly crusades for "frankness" and publishes scores of letters congratulating it for its unblushing "candor." Yet the whole phenomenon of which *Playboy* is only a part vividly illustrates the awful fact of a new kind of tyranny.

Those liberated by technology and increased prosperity to new worlds of leisure now become the anxious slaves of dictatorial tastemakers. Obsequiously waiting for the latest signal on what is cool and what is awkward, they are paralyzed by the fear that they may hear pronounced on them that dread sentence occasionally intoned by "The Playboy Adviser": "You goofed!" Leisure is thus swallowed up in apprehensive competitiveness, its liberating potential transformed into a self-destructive compulsion to consume only what is *à la mode. Playboy* mediates the Word of the most high into one section of the consumer world, but it is a word of bondage, not of freedom.

Nor will *Playboy*'s synthetic doctrine of man stand the test of scrutiny. Psychoanalysts constantly remind us how deep-seated sexuality is in the human being. But if they didn't remind us, we would soon discover it ourselves anyway. Much as the human male might like to terminate his relationship with a woman as he would snap off the stereo, or store her for special purposes like a camel's-hair jacket, it really can't be done. And anyone with a modicum of experience with women knows it can't be done. Perhaps this is the reason *Playboy*'s readership drops off so sharply after the age of thirty.

Playboy really feeds on the existence of a repressed fear of involvement with women, which for various reasons is still present in many otherwise adult Americans. So *Playboy*'s version of sexuality grows increasingly irrelevant as authentic sexual maturity is achieved.

The male identity crisis to which *Playboy* speaks has at its roots a deep-set fear of sex, a fear that is uncomfortably combined with fascination. *Playboy* strives to resolve this antinomy by reducing the proportions of sexuality, its power and its passion, to a packageable consumption item. Thus in *Playboy*'s iconography the nude woman symbolizes total sexual accessibility but demands nothing from the observer. "You drive it — it doesn't drive you." The terror of sex, which cannot be separated from its ecstasy, is dissolved. But this futile attempt to reduce the *mysterium tremendum* of the sexual fails to solve the problem of being a man. For sexuality is the basic form of all human relationship, and therein lies its terror and its power.

Karl Barth has called this basic relational form of man's life *Mitmensch,* co-humanity.[6] This means that becoming fully human, in this case a human male, requires not having the other totally exposed to me and my purposes — while I remain uncommitted — but exposing myself to the risk of encounter with the other by reciprocal self-exposure. The story of man's refusal so to be exposed goes back to the story of Eden and is expressed by man's desire to control the other rather than to *be with* the other. It is basically the fear to be one's self, a lack of the "courage to be."

Thus any theological critique of *Playboy* that focuses on its "lewdness" will misfire completely. *Playboy* and its less successful imitators are not "sex magazines" at all. They are basically antisexual. They dilute and dissipate authentic sexuality by

[6] Karl Barth, *Church Dogmatics* (Edinburgh: T & T Clark, 1957), II–2.

reducing it to an accessory, by keeping it at a safe distance.

It is precisely because these magazines are antisexual that they deserve the most searching kind of theological criticism. They foster a heretical doctrine of man, one at radical variance with the biblical view. For *Playboy*'s man, others — especially women — are *for* him. They are his leisure accessories, his playthings. For the Bible, man only becomes fully man by being *for* the other.

Moralistic criticisms of *Playboy* fail because its antimoralism is one of the few places in which *Playboy* is right. But if Christians bear the name of One who was truly man because He was totally *for* the other, and if it is in Him that we know who God is and what human life is for, then we must see in *Playboy* the latest and slickest episode in man's continuing refusal to be fully human.

Freedom for mature sexuality comes to man only when he is freed from the despotic powers which crowd and cower him into fixed patterns of behavior. Both Miss America and The Playboy illustrate such powers. When they determine man's sexual life, they hold him in captivity. They prevent him from achieving maturity. They represent the constant danger of relapsing into tribal thralldom which always haunts the secular society, a threat from which the liberating, secularizing word of the Gospel repeatedly recalls it.

Remnants of Town Virtues

Equally hazardous for sexual maturity, however, is the lure of town culture, the period we have most recently left behind, at least in most respects. In the area of sexual ethics, this period speaks to us through the traditional sexual practices of our Puritan and Victorian pasts. Since the melody of this ethic lingers on today, our sexual ethics are caught in the crossfire of contradiction and confusion. To illustrate this tension, let us take the traditional ideal of premarital chastity.

I choose this not because of any belief that it is really the key issue. It does seem clear, however, that for many young adults today "to bed or not to bed" *seems* to be the Big Question, and I believe the reasons they press it so vigorously merit exploration. Three aspects of the problem require particular attention: (1) why the yes or no of premarital chastity is more critical for young adults today than in the past; (2) why the answers we usually give to this question are either not heard or provide little guidance; and (3) what, if anything, we should be saying about the matter.

Let us reject at the outset any Kinseyian inference that what *is* being done should determine what *ought* to be done. But let us candidly admit that our culture has undergone drastic changes. Though our Puritan style of life has vanished almost completely, the Puritan sex ethic remains, at least on paper. We have exchanged ankle-length dresses for bikinis. We hold blanket parties instead of bobbing for apples. But the people caught up in these epochal changes are still taught, albeit with winks and evasions, the selfsame code of total premarital abstinence that was instilled into Priscilla Alden.

We have thus fashioned for unmarried young adults a particularly unfortunate combination of emotional environments. They are constantly bombarded — through clothing styles, entertainment, advertising, and courtship mores — with perhaps the most skillfully contrived array of erotic stimulants ever amassed. Their sexual fears and fantasies are studied by motivational researchers and then ruthlessly exploited by mass-media hucksters. Elizabeth Taylor's Brobdingnagian bosom decorates billboards, and throaty songstresses hum their hoarse invitations from transistors.

Yet we pass on to our youth, unaltered, a set of behavioral taboos that, in a sex-saturated society, seem diabolically created to produce a high level of duplicity and desperation.

Why have we deliberately constructed such a bizarre imbalance in our moral and psychological milieu? Obviously because we want to have our cake and eat it too. We want to gorge ourselves at the table of an affluent society whose continued prosperity, we are told, necessitates a constantly expanding market. And sex sells anything. At the same time we want to cherish our national memories of Pilgrims and piety, including the sexual code of Massachusetts Bay. The inherent contradiction comes home to roost in the already tormented psyche of the unmarried young adult.

The essential contradictions of any society, as the Marxists say, are concentrated in its proletariat. In a sexually exploitative society, youth subculture becomes the psychological proletariat. It picks up the tab for our hypocrisy. Exposed to all the stimulants married people are, young people are forbidden the socially acceptable form of fulfillment. The refusal is expressed both in the laws of the realm and in the official taboos of the culture. Enforcement, however, is sporadic, and, because the signals are so confused and contradictory, adolescents suspect that it is all one vast dissimulation.

No wonder the beatnik, who rejects *both* the signals of the mass media and the sexual mores, becomes the secret hero of many young adults.

To make matters just a bit more trying, we have thoughtfully provided Jane and Joe more privacy and permissiveness in dating than ever before. This extends far beyond Harvard dormitory rooms. I wonder if Henry Ford ever realized that his invention would be viewed by many not primarily as a means of transportation but as the urban society's substitute for Keats' "elfin grot."

Remember also that dating (and with it various types of petting) now reaches down to the sixth grade. Youngsters are thus exposed for a longer period and much more intensely to the mutual exploration of erogenous regions, which is the American courtship pattern. The only advice they get is "Don't go too far," and it is usually the girl who is expected to draw the line.

By the time a girl who begins petting at thirteen has reached marriageable age, she has drawn an awful lot of lines. If she is especially impressed with her religious duty to avoid sexual intercourse, she will probably have mastered, by twenty-one, all the stratagems for achieving a kind of sexual climax while simultaneously preventing herself and her partner from crossing the sacrosanct line.

What this border-skirting approach does to inhibit her chances for a successful adjustment in marriage is a question now engaging the attention of psychologists and marriage counselors. One psychologist who specializes in sexual behavior remarked recently that if Americans had consciously set out to think up a system that would produce maximal marital and premarital strife for both sexes, we could scarcely have invented a sexually more sabotaging set of dating procedures than we have today. This may be an overstatement, but I suspect the inherent hypocrisy of the cultural taboo and the patterns of behavior it engenders must have considerable negative influence on marriage.

Add to this the fact that penicillin and oral contraceptives will soon remove the last built-in deterrents to premarital coitus, and the reason for the recent rumblings of discontent with traditional standards becomes clearer. Not that the young adults themselves are guiltless. They share the blame for perpetuating the same values. But they also consider themselves the victims of a kind of cultural charade. They are shown one thing, told another, and they never know when the society will wink and when it will whip them. Their suspicion that they are the fall guys in a giant collusion is expressed in their growing demand that we come clean on this matter.

Now we can turn to the question of why, amid this schizophrenic carnival of prurience and prudery, the Christian Gospel seems to offer so little positive guidance. I believe the answer to this question is that most young adults do not perceive Christian sexual ethics as "evangelical," that is, as *good news.* They are not hearing the Gospel as good news and therefore they are not hearing the Gospel at all, but something else.

The German theologian Friedrich Gogarten states that the two most serious dangers from which the Gospel must be protected are (a) its being dissolved into a myth and (b) its being hardened into a religion of Law.[7] In either case it ceases to be the Gospel. When we examine what has happened to the Gospel as it touches the area of sex, it is evident that both of these distortions have set in.

The Gospel comes to the sexual puzzlement of most young adults not as a liberating *yes,* not as God's Good News freeing them for personhood and community. It comes rather as a remnant of cultural Christendom and an assortment of confused conventions. To be heard once again as the Gospel it must be demythologized and delegalized.

Let us turn first to the task of demythologizing it from odd bits of sexual folklore with which it has been confused. I shall refer to only two of the many mythical motifs that obfuscate the Gospel in its bearing on sexual conduct. First the ideal of romantic love, which Denis de Rougement has traced to paganism and which is almost always fused with any young American's ideas about sex.[8] Second, the Western obsession with coital intercourse as normative sexuality and hence as that which defines the content of chastity and virginity. The identification is now so complete that, as Theodor W. Adorno recently pointed out, intercourse now *means* coitus.[9]

Both the romantic ideal and the identification of intercourse with coitus are cultural accretions that have been coalesced with the rule of premarital chastity. The combination has so beclouded the liberating power of the Gospel that it can scarcely be heard because of them, and the Gospel is frequently perceived to be saying almost the opposite of what is intended.

The ideal of romantic love is the most obvious mythical excrescence. It leads often to the belief, especially among girls, that certain forms of intimacy become progressively less objectionable the more you "love" the boy. The snares in this

[7] Friedrich Gogarten, *Der Mensch zwischen Gott und Welt,* (Stuttgart: F. Vorwerk Verlag, 1956), p. 34.

[8] Denis de Rougement, *Love in the Western World* (New York: Pantheon, 1956).

[9] Theodor W. Adorno, *Neun Kritische Modelle* (Frankfurt: Suhrkamp Verlag, 1963), pp. 99ff.

curious amalgam of Our Gal Sunday and Saint Teresa are manifold. Among adolescents of all ages, *love* has come to mean nothing more than a vague emotional glow. It's "that ol' black magic, . . . those icy fingers up and down my spine."

The belief that love is the only honest basis for sex forces countless maidens into anguished efforts to justify their sexual inconstancy by falling in and out of love with a passing parade of partners. Naturally, opportunities for self-deception are almost endless, and the outcome is often an acid cynicism about the possibility of ever really loving anyone.

Furthermore, the sex-and-romantic-love equation sets up an inevitable collision course. The conflict occurs because, although girls tend to "go the limit" only with a boy they believe they "love," many boys, as sociologist Winston Ehrmann shows in his *Premarital Dating Behavior,*[10] will stop short of intercourse with girls they "love" or "respect," though they will go as far as possible with another girl. Thus girls associate sex with romantic love far more than boys do, and emotional scars emerging from this built-in contradiction often last far into married life.

Since girls feel they must be swept into sexual experience by something "bigger than both of us," they often fail to take the precautions against pregnancy they might otherwise. Somehow it doesn't seem romantic to go out with a boy, having prepared in advance to be swept off one's feet. Consequently, many instances of intercourse are not "planned," but occur more or less spontaneously at the end of an evening of progressively heavier necking. Unwanted pregnancies, abortions, shattered family relations, and forfeited careers are the inevitable result.

[10] Winston Ehrmann, *Premarital Dating Behavior* (New York: Holt, 1959).

One solution is to admonish everybody to avoid any physical contact that could spiral toward intercourse. But how sane or compassionate is this advice in a society where various types of petting are the only socially approved way of handling tensions exacerbated by a sexually saturated culture? Petting does sometimes lead to intercourse, but not always. Most of the time it does not. To try to abolish it while still retaining our prosperity and our aphrodisiac advertising would be even less honest than the preach-and-wink pharisaism.

Another antidote is simply to deromanticize sex. This would mean urging young people who are going to have intercourse anyway (and who, under layers of unsuccessful self-deception, know they will) to accept the full responsibility for their behavior and to take the necessary steps to avoid pregnancy.

Such a solution, although more realistic, has almost as little chance of acceptance as the first. It would necessitate dispelling the illusions of romantic love and suggesting that young people ponder soberly in the light of day what they are really doing. But it would also require our society to face up to the cant and flimflam of its sexual folkways, and this no one really wants to do. So the black magic, petting, and pregnancies will probably continue.

A more stubborn and deceptive segment of folklore that has been equated with the doctrine of premarital chastity is one that is rarely discussed openly: the curious presumption that a person who has not experienced coital intercourse remains a virgin — no matter what else he or she has done. This popular piece of legerdemain explains in part the discovery by Kinsey that, although the incidence of premarital intercourse among women has merely mounted steadily, premarital petting of all varieties has skyrocketed.

Kinsey's finding could be substantiated by the most casual observer of the American college scene. The number of students who do not pet at all is negligible. An increasing number regularly carry their necking to the point of heavy sex play and orgasm. A pert young graduate of a denominational college assured me recently that although she had necked to orgasm every week-end for two years, she had never "gone all the way." Her premarital chastity was intact.

Or was it? Only, I submit, by the most technical definition of what is meant by preserving virginity. True, some writers actually advocate such noncoital orgasm as the "safest" way for unmarried people to achieve sexual climax. However distasteful this idea may seem to some, it is extremely important to realize that the church's traditional teaching actually functions in such a fashion as to give considerable support to this view.

The ideal of premarital chastity is generally understood to mean that, although necking is somewhat questionable, the fragile gem of virginity remains intact so long as coitus is avoided. This myth has helped open the floodgate to a tidal wave of noncoital promiscuity.

Here the demythologizing process might be helped if we note Saint Paul's insistence (in I Corinthians 6:15–16) that liaisons intended to be highly casual, for example with prostitutes, nevertheless involve us in a relationship that is inevitably much deeper than we bargained for. We "become one flesh." D. S. Bailey calls this "a psychological insight . . . altogether exceptional by first-century standards." [11]

Saint Paul saw the striking fact that as human beings we both *have* and *are* bodies. This is an issue that has been explored at length by such contemporary philosophers as Gabriel Marcel and Maurice Merleau-Ponty. Paul saw that sex — unlike excretion, for example — is not simply a physiological but also a "bodily" (somatic) activity. It involves us at the deepest levels of our personal identity.

But why limit Saint Paul's insight to coital intercourse alone, or to contacts with prostitutes? The mere avoidance of coitus does not exempt anyone from becoming "one flesh" with another. All "virgins" who are promiscuous neckers should know that. Nor can the "one flesh" phenomenon be restricted to the bordello.

Saint Paul knew that no sexual relationship could be kept merely physical without ceasing to be really sexual in the fully human sense of the word. This is why the playmate-of-the-month domestication of sex as a purely recreational pursuit just doesn't work. Paul really appreciated sex more than Hugh Hefner does. He expected more from it. Sex is certainly fun, but to make it *simply* fun is to eviscerate and enfeeble it. Then it eventually ceases even to be fun.

When it is demythologized, the evangelical sexual ethic turns out to be an invitation to life together in a community of personal selves. The Gospel frees us from the need to cling to romantic self-deception and the works of righteousness by which we clothe our promiscuity in the costume of technical virginity. By delivering us from mythology into history, Jesus Christ allows us to see that the marvelous skein of privileges and responsibilities in which we find ourselves as human beings is something for which we are responsible. But how do we exercise this responsibility?

[11] D. S. Bailey, *Sexual Relations in Christian Thought* (New York: Harper, 1959; London: Longmans, Green).

At this point the going becomes more difficult. Any effort to arrest the degeneration of the Gospel into some form of Law will be viewed in some quarters as antinomianism, the belief that the precepts of the Law are not binding for Christians. A Gospel ethic, however, demands more maturity and more discipline than a Law ethic. Evangelical ethics are by nature riskier. This risk must be run since the New Testament insists unequivocally that it is the Gospel and not the Law that saves. How then can we begin to "delegalize" the Gospel when sexual behavior is the question at issue?

The Gospel is addressed to persons; the Law sees acts. One weakness of the traditional ethical formulation on premarital chastity is its sweeping inclusiveness and total lack of discrimination. Reduced to a precept, the ideal of premarital chastity permits no distinction between intercourse by engaged couples, for example, and the chilling exploitation of high school girls at fraternity parties. Both are transgressions of the Law, and there is no middle ground between virginity and nonvirginity.

Consequently there emerges alongside the technical virgin her shadowy counterpart, the technically fallen woman — the girl who, because she once consented to intercourse, now feels she is permanently pastured among the goats. She has crossed the sexual Styx and there is no way back. Because she can no longer present herself to her husband in purity on the wedding night anyway, why shouldn't anything go?

Her self-condemnation arises in part because she has not heard the *good* news. She has perceived the traditional teaching as a *law.* Law without Gospel is arbitrary and abstract. It cannot discriminate among cases. And it has nothing helpful to say to the transgressor. Consequently, for the increasing proportion of young people who have already had sexual intercourse, the rule of premarital chastity is simply irrelevant. And since for many it appears to be the only record the church ever plays on this subject, they conclude the church has nothing to say to them.

But preaching the Gospel also entails preaching the Law — exposing the false absolutes from which one is liberated. Negatively this means making clear the distorted images of sex from which the Gospel delivers us. Positively it entails protecting sex as a fully human activity against all the principalities and powers that seek to dehumanize it. In our day these include the forces, both within and without, that pervert sex into a merchandising technique, a means of self-aggrandizement, a weapon for rebelling against parents, a recreational pursuit, a way to gain entrance into the right clique, *or* — let the reader beware — a devotional act with some sort of religious significance.

To be freed from the "bondage of the Law" means to be freed from these dehumanizing powers. It also means to be freed from those diabolical pressures toward subcultural conformity that push so many adolescents into whatever is "in" at the moment. Sexual freedom in Christ, in one concrete case, means that a harried co-ed can say *no* to a cloying Romeo without feeling she is being hopelessly square.

Evangelical ethics cease to be Law and once again become Gospel when the Word liberates people from cultural conventions and social pressures, when persons discover their sexuality as a delightful gift of God that links them in freedom and concern to their fellows. But how do we make *this* Gospel heard by young adults in today's sexually rapacious society?

Before answering this question we must admit that we have created a set of cultural conditions in which sexual responsibility is made exceedingly difficult. In our American Xanadu, exhortations to individual continence are almost as useless as urging businessmen to eschew the profit motive.

It is strange how even people who see most clearly that crime, illegitimacy, narcotics addiction, and poverty are largely structural problems still interpret the increase in premarital sexual experience as a breakdown in personal morals.

But the jig is nearly up. Our feverish effort to paper over a society propelled by drives for sex and status with a set of Victorian courtship mores is breaking down badly. We must direct our fire more toward the "feminine mystique" and the cynical misutilization of sex by the public-relations culture than toward the hapless individual offender.

This may involve some searching questions about limiting the deliberate use of sexual stimulation in selling or, even more radically, about the merit of an economic system that seems to require a constant perversion of sexuality in order to survive. Commercial exploitation of sex drives — not the call girls — is our most serious form of prostitution today.

When we do turn from the society to the individual, especially to the unmarried young adult, we must avoid giving a simple yes-or-no answer to the question of premarital chastity. Of course, this will sound like evasion, but any simple answer panders to the cheap attempt to oversimplify the issue, to reduce all the intricacies of premarital sexuality to one decision. And churchmen, by allowing the Gospel to deteriorate into folklore and fiat, have contributed to this fatal oversimplification.

I do not believe that an evangelical ethic of premarital sex can be chopped down to a flat answer to this weighted question without impoverishing and distorting it. Instead of registering an answer, the Gospel poses a question of its own (as Jesus himself frequently did with such questions). It asks how I can best nourish the maturity of those with whom I share the torments and transports of human existence.

The Gospel liberates men from mythical taboos and rigid concepts for a purpose: so that the full and untrammeled resources of the human imagination can be exercised in responsibility for others within the patterns of public and private life. In the freedom of the Gospel, we arrive at decisions by utilizing norms that themselves must always be open to criticism and transformation and are therefore never final. Traditional Christian sexual norms are no exception. They do not stand above history. They have arisen as Christians attempted to live faithfully through constantly changing social systems. Like all human codes they stand in continuous need of revision so they will help rather than hinder God's maturation of man.

Christians believe God is at work in history bringing man to adulthood and responsibility. Within this framework the norms by which we make our decisions are fashioned and discarded in a continuing conversation with the Bible and with the culture, a conversation that is never completed. The Christian knows he is free only as a partner in this conversation and as a member of this community. This means, among other things, that his decisions about sexual conduct inevitably involve more people than he would sometimes like to involve. Sex is never simply a private matter.

To refuse to deliver a prepared answer whenever the question of premarital intercourse pops up will have a healthy influence on the continuing conversation that is Christian ethics. It moves the axis of the discussion away from the arid stereotypes by which we oversimplify intricate human issues. It gets us off dead-end arguments about virginity and chastity, forces ut to think about fidelity to persons. It exposes the promiscuity of sexual pharisees and the subtle exploitation that poisons even the most immaculate Platonic relationships.

By definition, premarital refers to people who plan to marry someone someday. Premarital sexual conduct should therefore serve to strengthen the chances of sexual success and fidelity in marriage, and we must face the real question of whether avoidance of intercourse beforehand is always the best preparation.

This question includes consideration of the appropriate degree of sexual intimacy during increasingly extended engagement periods. The reason it cannot be answered once and for all is that circumstances vary from couple to couple. Guidance must be given with specific persons rather than with general conventions in view.

Admittedly, this approach requires more resourcefulness and imagination than relying on universally applicable axioms. Principles are useful, perhaps indispensable in ethical thinking, but all too often "sticking to principles" can become just another way to avoid seeing persons. It can signify a relapse from Gospel into Law.

Perhaps one day we in America will put away childish things and become mature men and women who do not have to rely on the male and female deities of the mass media to tell us who to be. Perhaps one day we will outgrow our ridiculous obsession with sex, of which our fixation on chastity and virginity is just the other side of the coin. Until that time, however, we should rejoice that in Jesus Christ we are freed from myth and from Law. We are placed in a community of selves, free to the extent that we live for each other, free to develop whatever styles of life will contribute to the maturation of persons in a society where persons are often overlooked as we scamper to pursue profits and piety all at once.

Eros Rampant

John Updike

The Maples' house is full of love. Bean, the six-year-old baby, loves Hecuba, the dog. John, who is eight, an angel-faced mystic serenely unable to ride a bicycle or read a clock, is in love with his Creepy Crawlers, his monster cards, his dinosaurs, and his carved rhinoceros from Kenya. He spends hours in his room after school drifting among these things, rearranging, gloating, humming. He experiences pain only when his older brother, Richard Jr., sardonically attempts to enter his room and pierces his placenta of contemplation. Richard is in love with life, with all outdoors, with Carl Yastrzemski, Babe Parelli, the Boston Bruins, the Beatles, and with that shifty apparition who, comb in hand, peeps back shiny-eyed at him out of the mirror in the mornings, wearing a moustache of toothpaste. He receives strange challenging notes from girls — *Dickie Maple you stop looking at me* — which he brings home from school carelessly crumpled along with his spelling papers and hectographed notices about eye, tooth, and lung inspection. His feelings about young Mrs. Brice, who confronts his section of the fifth grade with the enameled poise and diction of an airline hostess, are so guarded as to be suspicious. He almost certainly loves, has always deeply loved, his older sister, Judith. Verging on thirteen, she has become difficult to contain, even within an incestuous passion. Large and bumptious, she eclipses his view of the television screen, loudly frugs while he would listen to the Beatles, teases, thrashes, is bombarded and jogged by powerful rays from outer space. She hangs for hours by the corner where Mr. Lunt, her history teacher, lives; she pastes effigies of the Monkees on her walls, French-kisses her mother good-night, experiences the panic of sleeplessness, engages in long languorous tussels on the sofa with the dog. Hecuba, a spayed golden retriever, races from room to room, tormented as if by fleas by the itch for adoration, ears flattened, tail thumping, until at last she runs up against the cats, who do not love her, and she drops exhausted, in grateful defeat, on the kitchen linoleum, and sleeps. The cats, Esther and Esau, lick each other's fur and share a bowl. They had been two of a litter. Esther, the mother of more than thirty kittens mostly resembling her brother, but with a persistent black minority vindicating the howled appeal of a neighboring tom, has been "fixed"; Esau, sentimentally allowed to continue unfixed, now must venture from the house in quest of the bliss that had once been purely domestic. He returns scratched and battered. Esther licks his wounds while he leans dazed beside the refrigerator; even his purr is ragged. Nagging for their supper, they sit like bookends, their backs discreetly touching, an expert old married couple on the dole. One feels, unexpectedly, that Esau still loves Esther, while she merely accepts and understands him. She seems scornful of his merely dutiful attentions. Is she puzzled by her abrupt surgical lack of what drastically attracts him? But it is his big square

From *Harper's Magazine,* June, 1968. Reprinted by permission of John Updike.

tomcat's head that seems puzzled, rather that her triangular feminine feline one. The children feel a difference; both Bean and John cuddle Esau more, now that Esther is sterile. Perhaps, obscurely, they feel that she has deprived them of a miracle, of the semiannual miracle of her kittens, of drowned miniature piglets wriggling alive from a black orifice vaster than a cave. Richard Jr., as if to demonstrate his superior purchase on manhood and its righteous compassion, makes a point of petting the two cats equally, stroke for stroke. Judith claims she hates them both; it is her chore to feed them supper, and she hates the smell of horsemeat. She loves, at least in the abstract, horses.

Mr. Maple loves Mrs. Maple. He goes through troublesome periods, often on Saturday afternoons, of being unable to take his eyes from her, of being captive to the absurd persuasion that the curve of her solid haunch conceals, enwraps, a precarious treasure mistakenly confided to his care. He cannot touch her enough. The sight of her body contorted by one of her yoga exercises, in her elastic black leotard riddled with runs, twists his heart so that he cannot breathe. Her gesture as she tips the dregs of white wine into a potted geranium seems infinite, like one of Vermeer's moments frozen in an eternal light from the left. At night he tries to press her into himself, to secure her drowsy body against his breast like a clasp, as if without it he will come undone. He cannot sleep in this position, yet maintains it long after her breathing has become steady and oblivious: can love be defined, simply, as the refusal to sleep? Also he loves Penelope Vogel, a quaint little secretary at his office who is recovering from a disastrous affair with an Antiguan; and he is in love with the memories of six or so other women, beginning with a seven-year-old playmate who used to steal his hunter's cap; and is half in love with death. He as well seems to love, perhaps alone in the nation, President Johnson, who is unaware of his existence. Along the same lines, Richard adores the moon; he studies avidly all the photographs beamed back from its uncongenial surface.

And Joan? Whom does she love? Her psychiatrist, certainly. Her father, inevitably. Her yoga instructor, probably. She has a part-time job in a museum and returns home flushed and quick-tongued, as if from sex. She must love the children, for they flock to her like sparrows to suet. They fight bitterly for a piece of her lap and turn their backs upon their father, as if he, the source and shelter of their life, were a grotesque intruder, a chimney sweep in a snow palace. None of his impersonations with the children — scoutmaster, playmate, confidant, financial bastion, factual wizard, watchman of the night — win them over; Bean still cries for Mommy when hurt, John approaches her for the money to finance yet more monster cards, Dickie demands that hers be the last good-night, and even Judith, who should be his, kisses him timidly, and saves her open-mouthed passion for her

"So," Joan says to him. "You slept with that little office mouse." It is Saturday; the formless erotic suspense of the afternoon is over. The Maples are in their room dressing for a party, by the ashen light of dusk, and the watery blue of a distant streetlamp.

"I never have," he says, thereby admitting, however, that he knows who she means.

"Well you took her to dinner."

"Who says?"

"Mack Dennis. Eleanor saw the two of you in a restaurant."

"When do they converse? I thought they were divorced."

"They talk all the time. He's still in love with her. Everybody knows that."

"Okay. When do he and *you* converse?"

Oddly, she has not prepared an answer. "Oh — " His heart falls through her silence. "Maybe I saw him in the hardware store this afternoon."

"And maybe you didn't. Why would he blurt this out anyway? You and he must be on cozy terms."

He says this to trigger her denial; but she mutely considers and, sauntering toward her closet, admits, "We understand each other."

How unlike her, to bluff this way. "When was I supposedly seen?"

"You mean it happens often? Last Wednesday, around eight-thirty. You *must* have slept with her."

"I couldn't have. I was home by ten, you may remember. You had just gotten back yourself from the museum."

"What went wrong, darley? Did you offend her with your horrible pro-Vietnam stand?"

In the dim light he hardly knows this woman, her broken gestures, her hasty voice. Her silver slip glows and crackles as she wriggles into a black knit cocktail dress; with a kind of determined agitation she paces around the bed, to the bureau and back. As she moves, her body seems to be gathering bulk from the shadows, bulk and a dynamic elasticity. He tries to placate her with a token offering of truth. "No, it turns out Penelope only goes with Negroes. I'm too pale for her."

"You admit you tried?"

He nods.

"Well," Joan says, and takes a half-step toward him, so that he flinches in anticipation of being hit, "do you want to know who *I* was sleeping with Wednesday?"

He nods again, but the two nods feel different, as if, transposed by a terrific unfelt speed, a continent had lapsed between them.

She names a man he knows only slightly, an assistant director in the museum, who wears a collar pin and has his gray hair cut long and tucked back in the foppish English style. "It was *fun,*" Joan says, kicking at a shoe. "He thinks I'm *beau*tiful. He cares for me in a way you just *don't.*" She kicks away the other shoe. "You look pale to me too, buster."

Stunned, he needs to laugh. "But we all think you're beautiful."

"Well you don't make me *feel* it."

"*I* feel it," he says.

"You make me feel like an ugly drudge." As they grope to understand their new positions, they realize that she, like a chess player who has impulsively swept forward her queen, has nowhere to go but on the defensive. In a desperate attempt to keep the initiative, she says, "Divorce me. Beat me."

He is calm, factual, admirable. "How often have you been with him?"

"I don't know. Since April, off and on."

Her hands appear to embarrass her; she places them at her sides, against her cheeks, together on the bedpost, off. "I've been trying to get out of it, I've felt horribly guilty, but he's never been at all pushy, so I could never really arrange a fight. He gets this hurt look."

"Do you want to keep him?"

"With you knowing? Don't be grotesque."

"But he cares for you in a way I just don't."

"Any lover does that."

"God help us. You're an expert."

"Hardly."

"What *about* you and Mack?"

She is frightened. "Years ago. Not for very long."

"And Freddy Vetter?"

"No, we agreed not. He knew about me and Mack."

Love, a cloudy heavy ink, inundates him from within, suffuses his palms with tingling pressure as he steps close to her, her murky face held tense against the expectation of a blow. "You whore," he breathes, enraptured. "My sweet bride." He kisses her hands; they are corrupt and cold. "Who else?" he begs, as if each name is a burden of treasure she lays upon his bowed serf's shoulders. "Tell me all your men."

"I've told you. It's a pretty austere list. You know *why* I told you? So you wouldn't feel guilty about this Vogel person."

"But nothing happened. When you do it, it happens."

"Sweetie, I'm a woman," she explains, and they do seem, in this darkening room above the muted hubbub of television, to have reverted to the bases of their marriage, to the elemental constituents. Woman. Man. House.

"What does your psychiatrist say about all this?"

"Not much." The triumphant swell of her confession has passed; her drier manner prepares for days, weeks of his questions. She retrieves the shoes she kicked away. "That's one of the reasons I went to him, I kept having these affairs — "

"*Kept* having? You're killing me."

"Please don't interrupt. It was somehow very innocent. I'd go into his office, and lie down, and say, 'I've just been with Mack, or Otto — ' "

"Otto. What's that joke? Otto is 'toot' spelled inside out."

" ' — and it was wonderful, or awful, or so-so,' and then we'd talk about my childhood masturbation. It's not his business to scold me, it's his job to get me to stop scolding myself."

"The poor bastard, all the time I've been jealous of him, and he's been suffering with this for years; he had to listen every *day.* You'd go in there and plunk yourself still warm down on his couch — "

"It wasn't every day at all. Weeks would go by. I'm not Otto's only woman."

The artificial tumult of television below merges with a real commotion, a screaming and bumping that mounts the stairs and threatens the aquarium where the Maples are swimming, dark fish in ink, their outlines barely visible, known to each other only as eddies of warmth, as mysterious animate chasms in the surface of space. Fearing that for years he will not again be so close to Joan, or she be so open, he hurriedly asks, "And what about the yoga instructor?"

"Don't be silly," Joan says, clasping her pearls at the nape of her neck. "He's an elderly vegetarian."

The door crashes open; their bedroom

explodes in shards of electric light. Richard Jr. is frantic, sobbing.

"Mommy, Judy keeps teasing me and getting in front of the television!"

"I did not. I did not." Judith speaks very distinctly. "Mother and Father, he is a retarded liar."

"She can't help she's growing," Richard tells his son, picturing poor Judith trying to fit herself among the intent childish silhouettes in the little television room, pitying her for her bulk, much as he pities Johnson for his Presidency. Bean bursts into the bedroom, frightened by violence, and Hecuba leaps upon the bed with rolling golden eyes, and Judith gives Dickie an impudent and unrepentant sideways glance, and he, gagging on a surfeit of emotion, bolts from the room. Soon there arises from the other end of the upstairs an anguished squawk as Dickie invades John's room and punctures his communion with his dinosaurs. Downstairs, a woman, neglected and alone, locked in a box, sings about *amore.* Bean hugs Joan's legs so she cannot move.

Judith asks with parental sharpness, "What were you two talking about?"

"Nothing," Richard says. "We were getting dressed."

"Why were all the lights out?"

"We were saving electricity," her father tells her.

"Why is Mommy crying?" He looks, disbelieving, and discovers that indeed, her cheeks coated with silver, she is.

At the party, amid clouds of friends and smoke, Richard resists being parted from his wife's side. She has dried her tears, and faintly swaggers, as when, on the beach, she dares wear a bikini. But her nakedness is only in his eyes. Her head beside his shoulder, her grave soft voice, the plump unrepentant cleft between her breasts, all seem newly treasurable and intrinsic to his own identity. As a cucold, he has grown taller, attenuated, more elegant and humane in his opinions, airier and more mobile. When the usual argument about Vietnam commences, he hears himself sounding like a dove. He concedes that Johnson is unlovable. He allows that Asia is infinitely complex, devious, ungrateful, feminine: but must we abandon her therefore? When Mack Dennis, grown burly in bachelorhood, comes and asks Joan to dance, Richard feels unmanned and sits on the sofa with such an air of weariness that Marlene Brossman sits down beside him and, for the first time in years, flirts. He tries to tell her with his voice, beneath the meaningless words he is speaking, that he loved her, and could love her again, but that at the moment he is terribly distracted and must be excused. He goes and asks Joan if it isn't time to go. She resists; "It's too rude." She is safe here among proprieties and foresees that his exploitation of the territory she has surrendered will be thorough. Love is pitiless. They drive home at midnight under a slim moon nothing like its photographs — shadow-caped canyons, gimlet mountain ranges, gritty circular depressions around the metal feet of the mechanical intruder sent from the blue ball in the sky.

They do not rest until he has elicited from her a world of details: dates, sites, motel interiors, precisely mixed emotions. They make love, self-critically. He exacts the new wantonness she owes him, and in compensation tries to be, like a battered old roué, skillful. He satisfies himself that in some elemental way he has never been displaced; that for months she has been struggling in her lover's grasp, in the gauze net of love, her wings pinioned by tact. She assures him that she seized on the first opportunity for confession; she confides to him that Otto spray-sets his hair and uses perfume. She, weeping, vows that nowhere, never, has she encountered his, Richard's, passion, his pleasant bodily proportions and backwards-reeling grace, his invigorating sadism, his male richness. Then why . . . ? She is asleep. Her breathing has become oblivious. He clasps her limp body to his, wasting forgiveness upon her ghostly form. A receding truck pulls the night's silence taut. She has left him a hair short of satiety; her confession feels still a fraction unplumbed. The lunar face of the electric clock says three. He turns, flips his pillow, restlessly adjusts his arms, turns again, and seems to go downstairs for a glass of milk.

To his surprise, the kitchen is brightly lit, and Joan is on the linoleum floor, in her leotard. He stands amazed while she serenely twists her legs into the lotus position. He asks her again about the yoga instructor.

"Well, I didn't think it counted if it was part of the exercise. The whole point, darley, is to make mind and body one. This is Pranayama — breath control." Stately, she pinches shut one nostril and slowly inhales, then pinches shut the other and exhales. Her hands return, palm up, to her knees. And she smiles. "This one is fun. It's called the Twist." She assumes a new position, her muscles elastic under the black cloth tormented into runs. "Oh, I forgot to tell you, I've slept with Harry Saxon."

"Joan, no. How often?"

"When we felt like it. We used to go out behind the Little League field. That heavenly smell of clover."

"But sweetie, why?"

Smiling, she inwardly counts the seconds of this position. "You know why. He asked. It's hard, when men ask. You mustn't insult their male natures. There's a harmony in everything."

"And Freddy Vetter? You lied about Freddy, didn't you?"

"Now *this* pose is wonderful for the throat muscles. It's called the Lion. You mustn't laugh." She kneels, her buttocks on her heels, and tilts back her head, and from gaping jaws thrusts out her tongue as if to touch the ceiling. Yet she continues speaking. "The whole theory is, we hold our heads too high, and blood can't get to the brain."

His chest hurts; he forces from it the cry, "Tell me everybody!"

She rolls toward him and stands upright on her shoulders, her face flushed with the effort of equilibrium and the downflow of blood. Her legs slowly scissor open and shut. "Some men you don't know," she goes on. "They come to the door to sell you septic tanks." Her voice is coming from her belly. Worse, there is a humming. Terrified, he awakes, and sits up. His chest is soaked.

He locates the humming as a noise from the transformer on the telephone pole near their windows. All night, while its residents sleep, the town communes with itself electrically. Richard's terror persists, generating mass as the reality of his dream sensations is confirmed. Joan's body seems small, scarcely bigger than Judith's, and narrower with age, yet infinitely deep, an abyss of secrecy, perfidy, and acceptingness; acrophobia launches sweat from his palms. He leaves the bed as if scrambling backward from the lip of a vortex. He again goes downstairs; his wife's revelations have steepened the treads and left the walls slippery.

The Lovemaker

Robert Mezey

The kitchen is dark; he turns on the light. The floor is bare. The familiar objects of the kitchen seem discovered in a preservative state of staleness, wearing a look of tension, as if they are about to burst with the strain of being so faithfully themselves. Esther and Esau pad in from the living room, where they have been sleeping on the sofa, and beg to be fed, sitting like bookends, expectant and expert. The clock says four. Watchman of the night. But in searching for signs of criminal entry, for traces of his dream, Richard finds nothing but — clues mocking in their very abundance — the tacked-up drawings done by children's fingers ardently bunched around a crayon, of houses, cars, cats, and flowers.

I see you in her bed,
Dark, rootless epicene,
Where a lone ghost is laid
And other ghosts convene;

And hear you moan at last
Your pleasure in the deep
Haven of her who kissed
Your blind mouth into sleep.

But the body, once enthralled,
Wakes in the chains it wore,
Dishevelled, stupid, cold,
And famished as before—

And hears its paragon
Breathe in the ghostly air,
Anonymous carrion,
Ravished by despair.

Lovemaker, I have felt
Desire taking my part,
But lacked your constant fault
And something of your art,

Unwilling to bend my knees
To such unmantled pride
As left you in that place,
Restless, unsatisfied.

Bone

Hilary Fowler

My trees will all be tall
the branches starting high—
hard to climb
but at the top
new sight

I will not shade you from the light
but offer
innumerable mirrors

I know peace
is hard for you
you must find it
          not by pruning me
but by moving in my strangeness

Flesh

Hilary Fowler

. . . as she walked
in that strange garden

she met a night-blooming Serious

They talked together
for many nights

When she had to go on
to the daylight world

for company
she brought him
poppies
and a small green
tree frog

Reprinted by permission of the author. These poems have appeared in *Perspectives, The Peace And Gladness Anthology,* and the book *Mind Dances* (dustbooks, 1967).

The Beginnings

Hilary Fowler

I had thought of your hair as like bark
but it moves in the wind fine
as spider silk
glints in the sun like a net

tiny hairs
catch at the corners of your mouth

You have eaten an orange
your chin smells
of its sticky juice
kissing you
I would taste both orange
and your lips

Here in the sun
the grass moves
graceful
to the tunes of the wind

You do not move
your ears hear only words
and never music

If you were sap
and I a tree
you would not refuse
to flow

The Sensualists

Theodore Roethke

"There is no place to turn," she said,
"You have me pinned so close;
My hair's all tangled on your head,
My back is just one bruise;
I feel we're breathing with the dead;
O angel, let me loose!"

And she was right, for there beside
The gin and cigarettes,
A woman stood, pure as a bride,
Affrighted from her wits,
And breathing hard, as that man rode
Between those lovely tits.

"My shoulder's bitten from your teeth;
What's that peculiar smell?
No matter which one is beneath,
Each is an animal,"—
The ghostly figure sucked its breath,
And shuddered toward the wall;
Wrapped in the tattered robe of death,
It tiptoed down the hall.

"The bed itself begins to quake,
I hate this sensual pen;
My neck, if not my heart, will break
If we do this again,"—
Then each fell back, limp as a sack,
Into the world of men.

Light Listened

Theodore Roethke

O what could be more nice
Than her ways with a man?
She kissed me more than twice
Once we were left alone.
Who'd look when he could feel?
She'd more sides than a seal.

The close air faintly stirred.
Light deepened to a bell,
The love-beat of a bird.
She kept her body still
And watched the weather flow.
We live by what we do.

All's known, all, all around:
The shape of things to be;
A green thing loves the green
And loves the living ground.
The deep shade gathers night;
She changed with changing light.

We met to leave again
The time we broke from time;
A cold air brought its rain,
The singing of a stem.
She sang a final song;
Light listened when she sang.

Once More, The Round

Theodore Roethke

What's greater, Pebble or Pond?
What can be known? The Unknown.
My true self runs toward a Hill
More! O More! visible.

Now I adore my life
With the Bird, the abiding Leaf,
With the Fish, the questing Snail,
And the Eye altering all;
And I dance with William Blake
For love, for Love's sake;

And everything comes to One,
As we dance on, dance on, dance on.

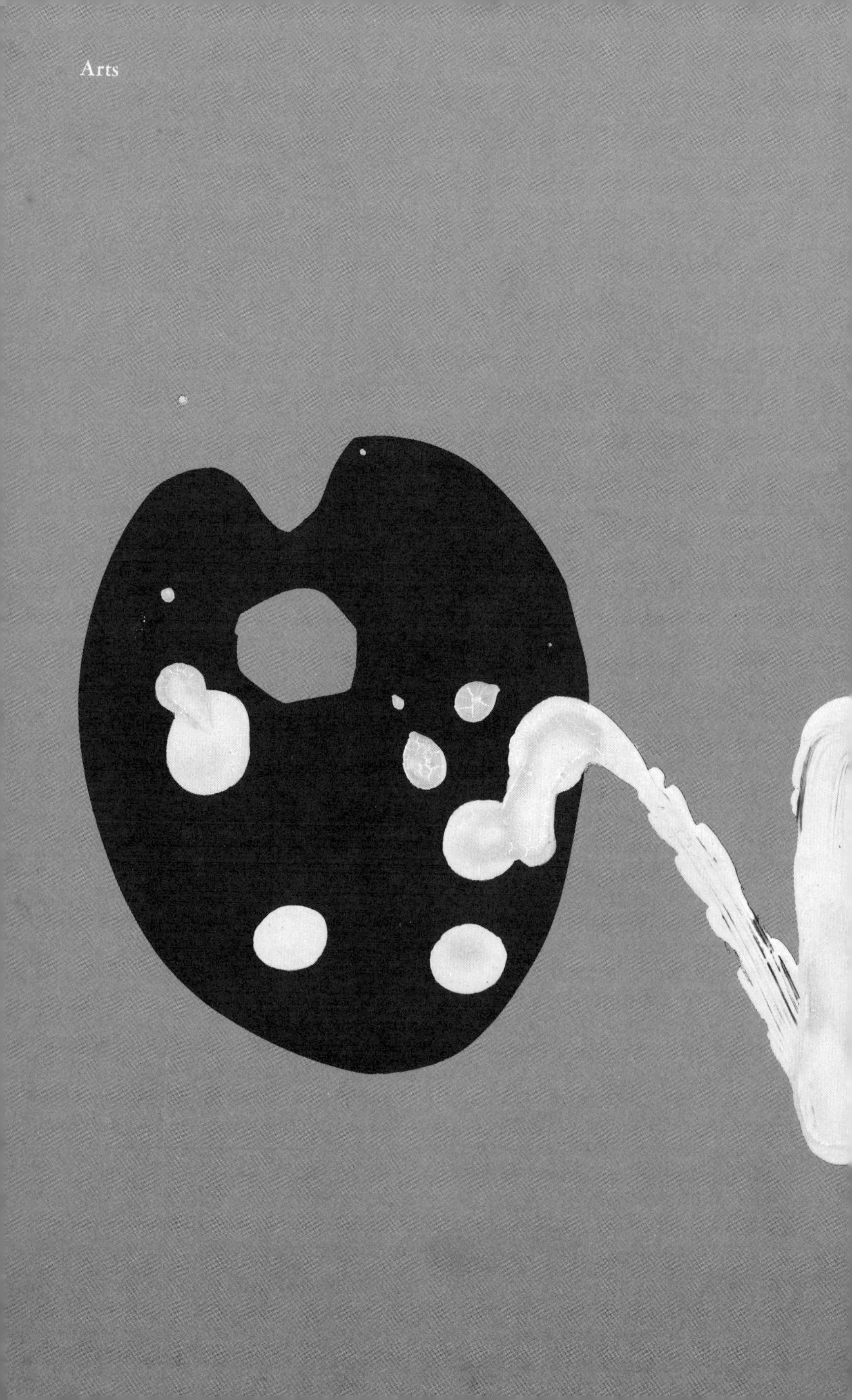
Arts

those ghost shamans
will make the ghosts to walk
again in great tribes
Gene Fowler, Shaman Songs

According to Marshall McLuhan, we are moving out of the age of the visual (created by the invention of movable type in the fifteenth century) and into the age of the aural and tactile (created by the invention of television). Reading is a visual *experience, McLuhan says, while television is not visual at all: television stimulates the sense of hearing and the sense of touch, restoring the "sensory balance" and* re*creating "tribal unity" out of fragmented, isolated individuals.*

It sounds demented, like many of McLuhan's pronouncements — BUT WHAT IF HE'S RIGHT? This is the question raised by Tom Wolfe in a spectacular essay on McLuhan's life, ideas, and influence. If he's right, Wolfe points out, his impact on our times will be greater than Freud's, for McLuhan may single-handedly change our ways of thinking about ourselves and our modes of existence. Already McLuhan has influenced poets, "mixed-media" artists, and "underground" moviemakers by teaching them that "The medium is *the message." It seems clear that his ideas have begun to touch other arts, and to spread into endeavors that we don't normally think of as arts — advertising, packaging, costuming, and, strangely enough, teaching. His theories may certainly be applied to many of the other selections in this book, and particularly to those in* ARTS.

McLuhan sets the theme for the other writers in this section, each of whom deals in some way with the relationship between art and society. In his essay "The New Mutants" Leslie Fiedler analyzes the "prophetic" content of contemporary literature, "the myth of the end of man, of the transcendence or transformation of the human" (hence, "the new mutants"). Fiedler points out that the new mutants in our midst are "non-participants in the past . . . dropouts from history," who reject cultural continuity and "the tradition of the human" in the Western world. They are the young people who "advocate prolonging adolescence to the grave, and are ready to dispense with school as an outlived excuse for leisure." In the literature of "the post-male, post-heroic world," the new mutants have given us "porno-poetry" (even "silent" or "skinny" poetry) and "porno-esthetics," along with mixed media art and underground movies.

In "Trash, Art, and the Movies," Pauline Kael observes, "Movies — a tawdry corrupt art for a tawdry corrupt world — fit the way we feel." She then goes on to show that craftsmanship and technique have nothing to do with the enjoyment *of movies, and that extremely crude movies may be highly entertaining.*

Frank Zappa, in "The New Rock," offers "a brief history of rock and its relationship to our society." Zappa concludes that "Our present state of sociosexual enlightenment is, to a certain extent, attributable to the evolution of rock and vice versa." Both Miss Kael and Mr. Zappa deal with specific forms of artistic media which are an integral part of the lives of today's youth.

Gene Fowler's Shaman Songs *is art, in the best sense of the word: highly skilled, carefully made, socially relevant.* Shaman Songs *is a poetic evocation of man's plight in twentieth century America. The speaker is a modern shaman — part poet, part medicine-man, part seer and prophet. His "tribe" is fearful, directionless, and alienated, in sharp contrast to the primitive tribe that knew itself, its possibilities, and its limitations. While the primitive tribe, as we see in "Hunting Song," found inspiration and spiritual guidance in its shaman, the modern tribe does not hear the shaman's voice; the shaman is alien, an outsider:*

Near my tent, you drop your head.
At my fire, your smile is stiff.
Still, you do not call.

Shaman Songs *explores our fears, our problems, and our "hang-ups," but unlike our other wasteland poems — T. S. Eliot's "The Wasteland," Allen Ginsberg's "Howl" — it is profoundly optimistic about the* future *of modern man. For it concludes with a vision of rebirth, in which we see the possibility of a new America.*

What If He Is Right?

Tom Wolfe

I first met Marshall McLuhan in the spring of 1965, in New York. The first thing I noticed about him was that he wore some kind of a trick snap-on necktie with hidden plastic cheaters on it. He was a tall man, 53 years old, handsome, with a long, strong face, but terribly pallid. He had gray hair, which he combed straight back. It was a little thin on top, but he could comb it into nice sloops over the ears. Distinguished-looking, you might say. On the other hand, there were the plastic cheaters. A little of the plastic was showing between his collar and the knot of the tie. I couldn't keep my eye off it. It's the kind of tie you buy off a revolving rack in the Rexall for about 89¢. You just slip the plastic cheaters — they're a couple of little stays sticking out of the knot like wings — you slip them under your collar and there the tie is, hanging down and ready to go, Pree-Tide.

We were having lunch, five of us, out back in the garden of a French restaurant called Lutèce, at 249 East 50th Street. Lutèce is a small place but one of the four or five most fashionable restaurants in New York, I suppose. Certainly it is one of the most expensive. It is so expensive, only your host's menu has the prices listed. Yours just has a list of the dishes. That way you won't feel guilty about it. They put decanters of distilled water on the tables at Lutèce and they have a real wine steward. It is one of those places in the East Fifties in Manhattan where the Main Biggies and the Fashionable Matrons convene for the main event of the weekday, the Status Lunch. Executives, culturati, rich women who are written up in *Women's Wear Daily,* illuminati of all sorts meet there in a marvelous chorale of King Sano and Eastern Honk voices. The women walk in looking an ice-therapy 45, force-starved, peruked and lacquered at the hairdresser's, wearing peacock-colored Pucci dresses signed "Emilio" up near the throat, taking in "the crowd," sucking their cheeks in for the entrance, and calling Lutèce's owner by his first name, which is André, in a contralto that has been smoke-cured by fifteen to twenty years of inhaling King Sanos, the cigarette of New York Society women. The men come in wearing lozenge-shaped cuff links with real links and precious metal showing on the inside as well as the outside of the cuffs, not those Swank-brand gizmos that stick through and click, and they start honking over André and each other, speaking in a voice known as the Eastern boarding-school honk, a nasal drawl mastered by Nelson Rockefeller, Hungtington Hartford, and Robert Dowling, among other eminent Americans. It was grand here, as I say. All honks and smoke-cured droning.

Our table was not the most illustrious, but it was in there trying: a movie actress; the daughter of one of the richest women in America; one of New York's top editors; and, of course, McLuhan. McLuhan, however, was not a celebrity at that time. I doubt that anybody else in the restaurant had ever heard of him.

And vice versa. McLuhan could not have been more oblivious of the special New York grandeur he had landed in. I don't think he noticed the people at all. He was interested in the little garden, or rather its thermodynamics, the way it was set out here in the heat of the noonday sun.

"The warmth steps up the tactile sense and diminishes the visual," he told us presently — as nearly as I can remember his words — I was following the plastic cheater. "It is more involving. It obliterates the distance between people. It is literally more 'intimate.' That's why these so-called 'garden restaurants' work."

Just before he made this sort of statement — and he was always analyzing his environment out loud — he would hook his chin down over his collarbone. It was like an unconscious signal — *now!* I would watch the tie knot swivel over the little telltale strip of plastic. It was a perfect Rexall milky white, this plastic.

At the time I didn't realize that McLuhan had been brought here, to New York, to Lutèce also, to be introduced to *haute New York.* He was about to make his debut, after a fashion. He was about to change from Herbert Marshall McLuhan, 53-year-old Canadian English professor, to *McLuhan.* He certainly didn't act like it, however. It had all been planned, but not by him. To him there was no *haute New York.* It was all past tense in this town. Toward the end of the meal his chin came down, the knot swiveled over the plastic — voices droned and honked richly all around us — and he turned his eyeballs up toward the great office buildings that towered above our little thermodynamic enclave.

"Of course, a city like New York is obsolete," he said. "People will no longer concentrate in great urban centers for the purpose of work. New York will become a Disneyland, a pleasure dome . . ."

Somehow, plastic cheaters and all, he had the charisma of a haruspex, the irresistible certitude of the monomaniac. I could see New New York turning into a huge Astrodome with raggy little puberteens in white Courrèges boots giggling and shrieking and tumbling through the atmosphere like the snow in one of those Christmas paperweights you turn upside down —

WHAT if he's right What . . . if . . . he . . . is . . . right
W-h-a-t i-f h-e i-s r-i-g-h-t

<table>
<tr><td></td><td></td><td>R</td><td></td></tr>
<tr><td>W</td><td></td><td>I</td><td></td></tr>
<tr><td>H</td><td>IF</td><td>G</td><td>?</td></tr>
<tr><td>A</td><td>HE</td><td>H</td><td></td></tr>
<tr><td>T</td><td>IS</td><td>T</td><td></td></tr>
</table>

Quite a few American businessmen, it turned out, were already wondering the same thing. There were many studs of the business world, breakfast-food-package designers, television-network creative-department vice presidents, advertising "media reps," lighting-fixture fortune heirs, patent lawyers, industrial spies, we-need-vision board chairmen — all sorts of business studs, as I say, wondering if McLuhan was . . . right. At the time McLuhan was a teacher working out of a little office off on the edge of the University of Toronto that looked like the receiving bin of a second-hand bookstore, grading papers, *grading papers,* for days on end, getting up in the morning, slapping the old Pree-Tide tie on, teaching English, grading more papers—

But what if — large corporations were already trying to put McLuhan in a box. Valuable! Ours! Suppose he *is* what he sounds like, the most important thinker since Newton, Darwin, Freud, Einstein, and Pavlov, studs of the intelligentsia game — suppose he *is* the oracle of the modern times — *what if he is right?* — he'll be in there, in our box.

IBM, General Electric, Bell Telephone, and others had been flying McLuhan from Toronto to New York, Pittsburgh, all over the place, to give private talks to their hierarchs about . . . this unseen world of electronic environment that *only he sees fully.* One corporation offered him $5,000 to present a closed-circuit — *ours* — television lecture on the ways the products in its industry would be used in the future. Another contributed a heavy subsidy to McLuhan's Centre for Culture and Technology at the University of Toronto, which, despite the massive name, was at that time largely McLuhan's genius and some letterhead stationery. One day in New York, McLuhan was staying at Howard Gossage's suite at the Lombardy Hotel. Gossage is a San Francisco advertising man. McLuhan was staying there and representatives of two national weekly magazines called up. Both offered him permanent offices in their buildings, plus fees, to do occasional consulting work. Just to have him in the box, I guess —

"What should I do, Howard?" says McLuhan.

"Take 'em both!" says Gossage. "You need offices on both sides of town. Suppose you get caught in traffic?"

McLuhan looks puzzled, but Gossage is already off into his laugh. This Gossage has a certain wild cosmic laugh. His eyes light up like Stars of Bethlehem. The laugh comes in waves, from far back in the throat, like echoes from Lane 27 of a bowling alley, rolling, booming far beyond the immediate situation, on to . . .

. . . in any case, McLuhan never failed to provoke this laugh. Perhaps because there were really two contradictory, incongruous McLuhans at this point. Even his appearance could change markedly from situation to situation. One moment he would look like merely the English teacher with the Pree-Tide tie on, naïve, given to bad puns derived from his studies of *Finnegans Wake* and worse jokes from God knows where, a somewhat disheveled man, kindly, disorganized — the very picture of the absent-minded professor. The next moment he would look like what he has, in fact, become: the super-savant, the Freud of our times, the omniscient *philosophe,* the unshakable dialectician. That was whenever the subject was The Theory, which it usually was. On those occasions the monologue began, and McLuhan was, simply, the master. He preferred Socratic dialogues, with six to ten people in attendance. A Socratic dialogue, like a Pentecostal sermon, is a monologue punctuated by worshipful interruptions. "Marshall is actually very polite," said one of his friends, meaning to be kind. "He always waits for your lips to stop moving."

Among his business clients, McLuhan was always that, monomaniac and master. The business studs would sit in their conference rooms under fluorescent lights, with the right air-conditioned air streaming out from behind the management-style draperies. Upward-busting hierarch executives, the real studs, the kind who have already changed over from lie-down crewcuts to brushback Eric Johnston-style Big Boy haircuts and from Oxford button-downs to Tripler broadcloth straight points and have hung it all on the line, an $80,000 mortgage in New Canaan and a couple of kids at Deerfield and Hotchkiss — hung it all on the line on knowing exactly what this corporation is all about — they sit there with the day's first bloody mary squirting through their capillaries — and this man with a plastic cheater showing at the edge of the collar, who just got through *grading papers,* for godsake, tells them in an *of-course* voice, and with *I'm-being-patient* eyes, that, in effect, politely, they all know just about exactly . . . nothing . . . about the real business they're in —

— Gentlemen, the General Electric Company makes a considerable portion of its profits from electric light bulbs, but it has not yet discovered that it is not in the light bulb business but in the business of moving information. Quite as much as A.T.&T. Yes. *Of-course I-am-willing-to-be-patient.*

He pulls his chin down into his neck and looks up out of his long Scotch-lairdly face. Yes. The electric light is pure information. It is a medium without a message, as it were. Yes. Light is a self-contained communications system in which the medium is the message. *Just think that over for a moment —*
I-am-willing-to-be — When IBM discovered that it was not in the business of making office equipment or business machines —

——but that it was in the business
of processing
information,
then it began
to navigate
with
clear
vision.
Yes.

Swell! But where did *this* guy come from? What is this — cryptic, Delphic saying: *The electric light is pure information.*

Delphic! *The medium is the messsage. We are moving out of the age of the visual into the age of the aural and tactile. . . .*

It was beautiful. McLuhan excelled at telling important and apparently knowledgeable people they didn't have the foggiest comprehension of their own bailiwick. He never did it with any overtone of now-I'm-going-to-shock-you, however. He seemed far, far beyond that game, out on a threshold where all the cosmic circuits were programmed. I can see him now, sitting in the conference room on the upper deck of an incredible ferryboat that Walter Landor, one of the country's top package designers, has redone at a cost of about $400,000 as an office and design center. This great package design flagship nestles there in the water at Pier 5 in San Francisco. The sun floods in from the Bay onto the basketwoven wall-to-wall and shines off the dials of Landor's motion-picture projection console. Down below on the main deck is a whole simulated supermarket for bringing people in and testing package impact — and McLuhan says, almost by the way:

"Of course, packages will be obsolete in a few years. People will want tactile experiences, they'll want to feel the product they're getting — "

But! —

McLuhan's chin goes down, his mouth turns down, his eyes roll up in his *of-course* expression: "Goods will be sold in *bins.* People will go right to bins and pick things up and *feel* them rather than just accepting a package."

Landor, the package designer, doesn't lose his cool; he just looks — *what if he is right?*

. . . *The human family now exists under conditions of a global village. We live in a single constricted space resonant with tribal drums* . . . That even, even, even voice goes on —

— McLuhan is sitting in the Laurent Restaurant in New York with Gibson McCabe, president of *Newsweek,* and several other high-ranking communications people, and McCabe tells of the millions *Newsweek* has put into reader surveys, market research, advertising, the editorial staff, everything, and how it paid off with a huge rise in circulation over the past five years. McLuhan listens, then down comes the chin: "Well . . . of course, your circulation would have risen about the same anyway, the new sensory balance of the people being what it is . . ."

Print gave tribal man an eye for an ear.

McLuhan is at the conference table in the upper room in Gossage's advertising firm in San Francisco, up in what used to be a firehouse. A couple of newspaper people are up there talking about how they are sure their readers want this and that to read — McLuhan pulls his chin down into his neck:

"Well . . . of course, people don't actually *read* newspapers. They get into them every morning like a hot bath."

Perfect! Delphic! Cryptic! Aphoristic! Epigrammatic! With this even, even, even voice, this utter scholarly apolomb — with *pronouncements* —

The phone rings in Gossage's suite and it's for McLuhan. It is a man from one of America's largest packing corporations. They want to fly McLuhan to their home office to deliver a series of three talks, one a day, to their top management group. How much would he charge? McLuhan puts his hand over the receiver and explains the situation to Gossage.

"How much should I charge?"

"What do you usually get for a lecture?" says Gossage.

"Five hundred dollars."

"Tell him a hundred thousand."

McLuhan looks appalled.

"Oh, all right," says Gossage. "Tell him fifty thousand."

McLuhan hesitates, then turns back to the telephone: "Fifty thousand."

Now the man on the phone is appalled. That is somewhat outside the fee structure we generally project, Professor McLuhan. They all call him Professor or Doctor. We don't expect you to prepare any new material especially for us, you understand, and it will only be three talks —

"Oh — well, then," says McLuhan, "twenty-five thousand."

Great sigh of relief. Well! That is more within our potential structure projection, Professor McLuhan, and we look forward to seeing you!

McLuhan hangs up and stares at Gossage, nonplussed. But Gossage is already off into the cosmic laugh, bounding, galloping, soaring, eyes ablaze — *¡más allá! – ¡más allá!* just over the next skyline! — El Dorado, Marshall! Don't you understand! —

Looking back, I can see that Gossage, but not McLuhan, knew what was going to happen to McLuhan over the next six months. Namely, that this 53-year-old Canadian English teacher, gray as a park pigeon, would suddenly become an international celebrity and the most famous man his country ever produced.

McLuhan rose up from out of a world more obscure, more invisible, more unknown to the great majority of mankind than a Bantu village or the Southeast Bronx. Namely, the EngLit academic life. Tongaland and the Puerto Rican slums may at least reek, in the imagination, of bloodlust and loins oozing after sundown. EngLit academia, so far as the outside world is concerned, neither reeks nor blooms; an occasional whiff of rotting tweeds, perhaps; otherwise, a redolence of nothing. It is a world of liberal-arts scholars, graduate schools, *carrels,* and monstrous baby-sitting drills known as freshman English. It is a far more detached life than any garret life of the artists. Garret life? Artists today spend their time calling up Bloomingdale's to see if the yellow velvet Milo Laducci chairs they ordered are in yet.

English-literature scholars start out in little cubicles known as carrels, in the stacks of the university libraries, with nothing but a couple of metal Klampiton shelves of books to sustain them, sitting there making scholarly analogies — detecting signs of Rabelais in Sterne, signs of Ovid in Pound, signs of Dickens in Dostoevsky, signs of nineteenth-century flower symbolism in Melville, signs of Schlegelianism in Coleridge, signs of the oral-narrative use of the conjunctive in Hemingway, signs, analogies, insights — always *insights!* — golden *desideratum!* — hunched over in silence with only the far-off sound of Maggie, a Girl of the Stacks, a townie who puts books back on the shelves — now she is all right, a little lower-class-puffy in the nose, you understand, but . . . — only the sound of her to inject some stray, *sport* thought into this intensely isolated regimen. In effect, the graduate-school scholar settles down at an early age, when the sap is still rising, to a life of little cubicles, little money, little journals in which his insights, if he is extremely diligent, may someday be recorded. A Volkswagen, a too-small apartment, Department Store Danish furniture with dowel legs — before he is 30 his wife will have begun to despise him as a particularly sad sort of failure, once the cultural charisma of *literature* has lost its charm. How much better to have failed at oil prospecting or the diaper-service game than at . . . practically nothing!

McLuhan graduated from the University of Manitoba in 1933, then went to England and took another B.A. at Cambridge (in 1936; and, eventually, a doctorate, in 1942). At Cambridge in the thirties the literati were keen on PopCult. Movies, advertising, radio, display art were something to be analyzed as a "language," a kind of technological Creole that was understood instinctively (*ProleSlob!*) among the masses. It was up to the literati to discern its grammar and syntax (*O GaucheKick!*). Wyndham Lewis had written extensively on popular culture. F. R. Leavis had written *Culture and Environment.* Joyce's *Finnegans Wake,* Eliot's *The Waste Land* and Pound's *Cantos* seemed, in the fellows rooms of Cambridge, to be veritable nigger nightclubs of PopCult. Lewis, particularly, influenced McLuhan.

In 1936 McLuhan took his first teaching job, at the University of Wisconsin. He immediately found himself in one of the most exquisitely squalid hells known to middleclass man: freshman English at a Midwestern university. The teacher's evidently serious interest in the likes of Donne, Shakespeare, or Milton marks him at once, of course, as a pedantic and therefore all the more hopeless fool. One thing the poor nit can do in this situation is assign *The Old Man and the Sea, Of Mice and Men,* or some other storybook in words of one syllable and hope that will hold the little bastards for ten or twelve weeks.

McLuhan, however, had pride and ambition. He resorted to the GaucheKick PopCult of Cambridge. He showed the little bastards advertisements, the same advertisements their gummy little brains soaked up every day outside the classroom. What do these ads *really* convey? he would ask.

It works. It is a nice stratagem. Others have used it effectively, too, notably Orwell in essays like "The Art of Donald McGill." One presents a Gotham Gold Stripe nylon-stockings ad showing a pair of slick and shimmering female legs on a pedestal. Or a Lysol vaginal-wash ad showing a gorgeous woman in an evening dress sinking into a pool whose ripples are inscribed Doubt, Inhibitions, Ignorance, Misgivings. Or a Bayer aspirin ad showing a drum majorette wearing a military helmet and jackboots and carrying a mace-like baton captioned: "In 13.9 seconds a drum majorette can twirl a baton twenty-five times . . . but in only TWO SECONDS Bayer Aspirin is ready to go to work!" What is the true language of these ads? What do they *really* convey? Why, the wedding of sex and technology (The Mechanical Bride), the breakdown of the sexual object, Woman, into component machine parts: the Bakelite legs on a pedestal; the antiseptic, B.O.-free plastic vagina; the "goose-stepping combination of military mechanism and jackbooted eroticism."

Yes! *It is written — but I say unto you* . . . From Wisconsin McLuhan went to the University of St. Louis, Assumption University (Windsor, Ontario), and St. Michael's College of the University of Ontario. Along the way he became something of a charismatic figure in the phlegmy grim dim world of EngLit academia. He attracted circles of students and spoke to student groups, *extra curricula,* both in lectures and in Socratic gatherings. He showed slides of ads, comic strips, and newspapers, exploring the hidden language of "the folklore of industrial man," as he called it.

After Wisconsin, every institution McLuhan taught in was Roman Catholic. In the mid-1930's he had become a convert to Catholicism. His parents were Scotch-Irish Protestants from western Canada. McLuhan was apparently influenced by Catholic intellectuals in England, notably Chesterton and Hopkins. Twenty years later he was to discover a piece of PopCult that was to him a strangely Catholic and catholic force in the world: TV.

In 1951 McLuhan published his "industrial folklore" material in a book, *The Mechanical Bride.* The book went virtually unnoticed, then out of print, and he was left with stacks of copies himself. In 1966, before the book was republished as a $2.95 paperback, copies brought $40 and $50 apiece.

Compared to his two major books, *The Gutenberg Galaxy* (1962) and *Understanding Media* (1964), *The Mechanical Bride* is embarrassingly moralistic. It is written with the conventional nineteenth-century, anti-industrial bias of *the literary man,* a term McLuhan would later associate with the worst sort of intellectual obtuseness and rear-guardism. *The Mechanical Bride* is explicitly presented as a book designed to help Western man protect himself from the hidden persuasions of Madison Avenue, the press, and Showbiz. "Why not use the new commercial education as a means to enlightening its intended prey? Why not assist the public to observe consciously the drama which is intended to operate upon it unconsciously?"

The Mechanical Bride, however, as a book about folklore and the "collective public mind," led McLuhan more and more toward the work of anthropologists and historians. Certainly one of the great influences on his thinking was his friend and colleague at the University of Toronto, Edmund Carpenter, an anthropologist with whom he edited a book called *Explorations in Communication.*

Two books were published by university presses in 1950 and 1951 that changed McLuhan's life, I suppose you could say. They were *Empire and Communications* and *The Bias of Communication,* by Harold Innis. Innis was at the University of Toronto at the time. Innis gave McLuhan the basic insight of his career, which he was to compress into the aphorism: *The medium is the message.* You seldom hear anything about Innis in the many critiques of McLuhan. This is not McLuhan's fault, however. He gave Innis full credit in the *Gutenberg Galaxy* (p. 50): "Innis also explained why print causes nationalism and not tribalism; and why print causes price systems and markets such as cannot exist without print. In short, Harold Innis was the first person to hit upon the *process* of change as implicit in the *forms* of media technology. The present book is a footnote of explanation to his work."

McLuhan was also influenced by Henri Bergson. He adapted some of Bergson's theories about the central nervous system. They impressed Aldous Huxley as well. Bergson had the idea that the brain is a "reducing valve." The senses, he said, send an overwhelming flood of information to the brain, which the brain then filters down to an orderly trickle it can manage for the purpose of survival in a highly competitive world. Modern man, he believed, has become so rational, so utilitarian, so devoted to the classification of information for practical purposes, that the trickle becomes very thin and distilled, indeed, though efficient. Meantime, said Bergson, modern man has screened out the richest and most wondrous part of his experience without even knowing it. Implicit in this theory is the idea that sometime in the past primitive man experienced the entire rich and sparkling flood of the senses fully. It ties in with one of the most ancient metaphysical beliefs: the belief that out there somewhere, beyond the veil that blinds our egocentric modern minds, is our forgotten birthright, a world of wholeness, unity, and beauty. As a Roman Catholic, incidentally, McLuhan found the idea very congenial: "The Christian concept of the mystical body — all men as members of the body of Christ — this becomes technologically a fact under electronic conditions." *The All-in-One.*

McLuhan's great stroke was to bring Innis's and Bergson's ideas forward, beyond print, beyond the confines of the scholarly past, and into the present, like an anthropologist. In short, he turned their ideas on to PopCult, to television, motion pictures, radio, the telephone, the computer, photography, xerography: *the media.*

McLuhan had plenty of PopCult to look at in the 1950's. He had a house full of children. In 1939 he had married Corinne Lewis, an American actress. They had two sons and four daughters. They took over the place. Inside — TV, record players, radios, telephones, and children — while McLuhan wrote of tribal man and the Gutenberg revolution; of space and time and the collision of civilizations; of the seamless web and the electronic unification of mankind; on a ping-pong table in the back yard.

McLuhan is fond of quoting Daniel Boorstin's dictum, "The celebrity is a person who is known for his well-knownness." That pretty much describes McLuhan himself. McLuhan is one of those intellectual celebrities, like Toynbee or Einstein, who is intensely well known as a name, and as a *savant,* while his theory remains a grand blur. Part of the difficulty is that McLuhan is presented to the world as "the communications theorist." His first book, *The Mechanical Bride,* was a book about communication. Since then McLuhan has barely dealt with communication at all, at least if you define communication as "interchange of thought or opinions." He is almost wholly concerned with the effect of the means of communication (the medium) on the central nervous system. His theory falls squarely in a field known as cognitive psychology, even though his interests cut across many fields. Modern cognitive psychology is highly scientific, devoted to complex physiological experiments. McLuhan isn't. In fact, he is a theoretical cognitive psychologist.

This is made quite clear in *The Gutenberg Galaxy. Understanding Media* is really a chapbook for *The Gutenberg Galaxy*'s theory.

The theory, as I say, concerns the central nervous system. McLuhan makes a set of assumptions, à la Bergson, about how the central nervous system processes information. He believes that humans have a "sensory balance" — a balance between the five senses: sight, hearing, touch, smell, and taste. This balance, he says, changes according to the environment. For example, if the visual sense is dimmed, the auditory sense intensifies (as in the blind); if the auditory sense is increased, the sense of touch diminishes (as when a dentist puts earphones on a patient, turns up the sound, and thereby reduces his sensitivity to pain). Great technological changes, he goes on to say, can alter these "sensory ratios" for an entire people. McLuhan is concerned chiefly with two of these great technological changes: (1) the introduction of print in the fifteenth century (reputedly by Johann Gutenberg) and the spread of literacy in the next four hundred years: (2) the introduction of television in the twentieth.

Print, says McLuhan, stepped up the visual sense of Western man at the expense of his other senses. It led, he says, to "the separation of the senses, of functions, of operations, of states emotional and political, as well as of tasks." This, he says, had overwhelming historical consequences: nationalism and nationalist wars (cultural fragmentation); the modern army, industrialism and bureaucracy (fragmentation of tasks); the market and price structure (economic fragmentation); individualism and the habit of privacy (fragmentation of the individual from the community) — and schizophrenia and peptic ulcers (caused by the fragmentation of both intellect and action from emotion); pornography (fragmentation of sex from love); the cult of childhood (fragmentation by age); and a general impoverishment of man's intuitive and artistic life (because of the fragmentation of the senses). And those are but a few of the results he mentions.

Enter TV. Television and the electric media generally, says McLuhan, are reversing the process; they are returning man's sensory ratios to the pre-print, pre-literate, "tribal" balance. The auditory and tactile senses come back into play, and man begins to use all his senses at once again in a unified, "seamless web" of experience. (Television, in McLuhan's psychology, is not primarily a visual medium but "audio-tactile.") The world is becoming a "global village," to use one of his happy phrases.

The immediate effects of TV on the central nervous system, says McLuhan, may be seen among today's young, the first TV generation. The so-called "generation gap," as he diagnoses it, is not a state of mind but a neurological fact. It is a disparity between a visual, print-oriented generation and its audio-tactile, neo-tribal offspring. School dropouts, he says, are but the more obvious casualties among a great mass of "psychic dropouts." These are children educated by the electric media to have unified, all-involving sensory experiences. They sit baffled and bored in classrooms run by teachers who fragment knowledge into "subjects," disciplines, specialties, and insist on the classification of data (rather than "pattern recognition," which is the principle of computers). This means, he says, that the educational system must be totally changed. In the long run, he says, the new neural balance will cause total change in everything anyway: "Total Change, ending psychic, social, economic, and political parochialism. The old civic, state, and national groupings have become unworkable. Nothing can be further from the spirit of the new technology than 'a place for everything and everything in its place.' You can't *go* home again." Many of the implications of the theory are very cheery, indeed: no more bitter nationalism — instead, the global village; no more shut-out, ghetto-pent minority groups (racial fragmentation) — instead, all "irrevocably involved with, and responsible for," one another; no more tedious *jobs* (mechanistic fragmentation) — instead, all-involving *roles;* no more impoverished intuition (fragmented senses) — instead, expanded, all-embracing sensory awareness; and so on. Man made whole again!

Man Made Whole Again

I gazed upon the printed page.
It tore me limb from limb.
I found my ears in Mason jars,
My feet in brougham motorcars,
My khaki claws in woggy wars—
But in this cockeyed eyeball age
I could not find my soul again.
Vile me.
And then—
I touched a TV *dial*
And—pop!—
it made me whole again.

To a clinical neurologist or psychologist, McLuhan's neurology is so much air. McLuhan's subject matter, as I say, is not communication but the central nervous system. The central nervous system is today perhaps the greatest dark continent of the physical sciences. Precious little is known about even the crudest neural functions. It was not until the 1950's that experimenters discovered, piecemeal, through experiments in several countries, the actual processes by which even so primitive an impulse as hunger is transmitted through the brain (Neal Miller in America, W. R. Hess in Switzerland, Konorski in Poland, Anand in India, *et alii*). It has taken half a century, since the development of the technique of stereotaxic needle implants, to reach even such tiny thresholds as this. It was not until 1962 that physiologists, using microelectrodes, discovered how the eye transmits shapes to the brain. To move from this level to the postulate that TV is altering the neural functions of entire peoples or even one person — this could only strike a clinician as romanticism.

McLuhan, however, was ready for the criticism. He insisted he was not presenting a self-contained theory but making "probes." He sees himself as trying to open up the dark continent for systematic exploration by others. He says he is not drawing conclusions but using what facts are available as "means of getting into new territories." He even says that if he could persuade enough investigators to study the effects of the new technologies systematically, he would gladly return whence he came, viz., to "literary studies." At the same time, he has sought to give his theory some scientific underpinning by setting up psychological studies of sample groups in Canada and Greece, studying their "sensory balance" before and after the coming of TV to their locales. The Canadian study has been completed, and I understand that the results, unpublished as of this writing (January, 1968), were inconclusive.

What, then, has been the nature of McLuhan's extraordinary splash? It certainly has not been scientific, despite the fact that he now characterizes himself as a scientist, speaks of the "clinical spirit," and compares his methods to those of modern psychiatry, metallurgy, and structural analysis.

A clue, I think, may be found in the parallels between McLuhan's history and Freud's. In any historical perspective the two men are contemporaries (Freud died in 1939). Both have come forth with dazzling insights in a period (1850 to the present) of tremendous intellectual confusion and even convulsion following what Nietzsche called "the death of God"; and Max Weber, "the demystification of the world." Both men explain *all* in terms of — *Santa Barranza! something common as pig tracks! under our very noses all the time! so obvious we never stepped back to see it for what it was!* Freud: sex. McLuhan: TV. Both men electrified — outraged! — the intellectuals of their time by explaining the most vital, complex, cosmic phases of human experience in terms of such lowlife stuff: e.g., the anus; the damnable TV set. The biggest howl Freud ever caused was with a two-page paper that maintained that anal sensations in infancy were capable of imprinting a man's mature personality in a quite specific way. Freud was the subject of as much derision in his day as McLuhan in his; and, like McLuhan, benefited from it. Freud said to Jung: "Many enemies, much honor"; McLuhan might well say the same. After all, where there's smoke, there's . . . *what if he is right?* McLuhan said to his disciple and amanuensis, Gerald Stearn: "No one believes these factors have any effect whatever on our human reactions. It's like the old days when people played around with radium. They painted watch dials and licked the brushes. They didn't believe radium could affect people."

Freud, of course, was a doctor of medicine and a trained clinician and a more certifiably scientific thinker than McLuhan. But Freud, like McLuhan, strove after the cosmic insight. The more rigorous psychologists today, as well as most research physicians, regard Freud as a romanticist, almost a metaphysician. They cast the old boy as a sort of Viennese Bishop Berkeley. There is a suspicion that Freud poked around — *aha! very significant!* — amid the plump velvet and florid warps and woofs of a few upper-bourgeois Viennese households, including his own — *Dad, that bugger, seduced my sis* — and then rerouted his insights through the front door of the clinic as findings explaining the behavior of all mankind. One cannot help but wonder something of the sort about McLuhan. Here sits the master out back at the ping-pong table. And there, inside the house, sit the kids, gazing at their homework — amid a raging, encapsulating sensory typhoon of TV sets, transistor radios, phonographs, and telephones — and yet they make it through school all the same — *Very significant!* Amazing, even. A neo-tribal unity of the senses. "The family circle has widened. The worldpool of information fathered by electric media — movies, Telstar, flight — far surpasses any possible influence Mom and Dad can now bring to bear."

Ping-Pong

I walked into the living room.
They rocked me with a stereo boom.
No haven here downstairs at all.
Nymphets frug on my wall-to-wall
And boogaloo in my private den
And won't let poor work-a-daddy in.

How glorious!
Übermenschen! *golden gulls!*
With transistor radios plugged in their skulls.

Radiant! with an Elysian hue
From the tubercular blue of the television.
Such a pure Zulu euphoria
Suffuses their hi-fi sensoria!

How glorious.
I shall stand it long as I can,
This neo-tribal festival.
Their multi-media cut-up,
The audio-pervasion of their voices,
Leaves me with two choices:
Shall I simply make them shut up—
Or . . . extrapolate herefrom the destiny
Of Western Man?

Freud and McLuhan both became celebrities at the same period of life, their early fifties, and under similar circumstances. Both began with rather obscure cliques of academic followers. Freud had a little group of adherents who held discussions every Wednesday night in his waiting room and were known as the "Psychological Wednesday Society." McLuhan had his adherents in several Canadian universities, and they, plus Americans interested in his work, often met in his home. If one were to choose a precise date for Freud's emergence as a public figure, it would probably be April 26, 1908, when a *Zusammenkunft für Freud'sche Psychologie* (Meeting for Freudian Psychology) was held in the Hotel Bristol in Salzburg, with Jung, Adler, Stekel, and others in attendance. In McLuhan's case it would be January 30, 1964, when faculty members of the University of British Columbia staged what was known to his followers as a "McLuhan Festival" in the university armory. They suspended sheets of plastic from the ceiling, forming a maze. Operators aimed light projections at the plastic sheets and at the people walking through them. A movie projector showed a long, meaningless movie of the interior of the empty armory. Goofy noises poured out of the loudspeakers, a bell rang, somebody banged blocks of wood together up on a podium. Somebody else spewed perfume around. Dancers flipped around through the crowds, and behind a stretch fabric wall — a frame with a stretch fabric across it — there was a girl, pressed against the stretch fabric wall, like a whole wall made of stretch pants, and *undulating* and humping around back there. Everybody was supposed to come up and *feel it* — the girl up against the stretch fabric — to understand the "tactile communication" McLuhan was talking about.

Neither event, the Meeting for Freudian Psychology or the McLuhan Festival, received any very great publicity, but both were important if esoteric announcements that *this* is the new name to be reckoned with. As Freud says . . . As McLuhan says . . . McLuhan's friend, Carpenter, had already put it into words: "McLuhan is one of the epic innovators of the electronic age. His *Gutenberg Galaxy* is the most important book in the social sciences of this generation, overshadowing in scope and depth any other contribution."

Both Freud and McLuhan attracted another obscure but important source of support: young artists and young literary intellectuals who saw them as visionaries, as men "who divined the famed riddle" (Sophocles, *Oedipus Rex*), to quote from a medallion that Freud's Wednesday Society friends gave him on his fiftieth birthday in 1906. Both McLuhan and Freud present scientific theories, but in an ancient priestly-aristocratic idiom that literary and artistic souls find alluring. Both buttress their work with traditional literary erudition. Freud, of course, presents his most famous insight in the form of a literary conceit, i.e., "the Oedipus complex." To sense Freud's strong literary bias, one has only to read ten pages of Freud and then ten pages of Pavlov. The difference in mental atmospheres, the literary vs. the clinical, stands out at once. Freud had the typical literary respect for artistic genius. He depicted the artist as one who has the power to express openly and faithfully the world of fantasy — the link between the conscious and the unconscious — that ordinary mortals grasp only fitfully in daydreams. Freud became the patron saint of the Surrealists, who saw themselves as doing just that (Dali visited Freud shortly before Freud's death, sketched him, and told him that surrealistically his cranium was reminiscent of a snail).

McLuhan, of course, was trained as a literary scholar. He begins *The Gutenberg Galaxy* with three chapters carrying out a somewhat abstruse analysis of *King Lear.* A la Freud's Oedipus, he begins his discussion of "sensory ratios" with a Greek legend (the myth of Cadmus: the Phoenician who sowed dragon's teeth — and up sprang armed men; and introduced the alphabet to Greece — and up sprang specialism and fragmentation of the senses). It is all quite literary, this neurology. Joyce, Matthew Arnold, Dr. Johnson, Blake, Ruskin, Rimbaud, Pope, Cicero, Dean Swift, Montaigne, Pascal, Tocqueville, Cervantes, Nashe, Marlowe, Shakespeare, Ben Jonson, St. Augustine — they twitter and gleam like celebrities arriving by limousine.

Artists, meanwhile, have precisely the same role in McLuhan's galaxy as in Freud's. They are geniuses who detect the invisible truths intuitively and express them symbolically. They are divine *naturals,* gifted but largely unconscious of the meaning of their own powers. McLuhan sees artists as mankind's "early warning system." They possess greater unity and openness of the senses and therefore respond earlier to the alteration of the "sensory ratios" brought about by changes in technology. McLuhan today is the patron saint of most "mixed-media" artists and of many young "underground" moviemakers (for such dicta as "The day of the story line, the plot, is over"). He was very much the patron saint of the huge "Art and Technology" mixed-media show staged by Robert Rauschenberg and others at the 27th Street Armory in New York in 1967. The artists, incidentally, are apparently willing to overlook McLuhan's theory of how they register their "early warning." It is a rather retrograde performance, as McLuhan sees it. The "avant garde" of each period, he says, is actually always one technology behind. Painters did not discover The Landscape until the early nineteenth century, when the intrusion of machine-age industrialism caused them to see the technology of agriculture — i.e., The Land — as an art form for the first time. They did not discover machine forms (cubism) until the electric age had begun. They did not discover mass-produced forms (Pop Art: Roy Lichtenstein's comic strips, Andy Warhol's Campbell Soup cans) until the age of the conveyor belt had given way to the age of electronic circuitry. McLuhan says that this is the early warning, nevertheless — and the idea has made artists happy.

Older literary intellectuals, however, have reacted to McLuhan with the sort of *ressentiment,* to use Nietzsche's word, that indicates he has hit a very bad nerve. The old guard's first salvo came as far back as July, 1964, with a long piece by Dwight Macdonald. It contained most of the objections that have become so familiar since then: the flat conclusion that McLuhan writes nonsense (a typical reaction to Freud), that his style is repetitious and "boring," that he is anti-book and for the new barbarism (TV, electronic brains), or obversely, that he is amoral, has no values. Once again the example of Freud comes to mind. After Freud's Clark University lectures were published, the Dean of the University of Toronto said: "An ordinary reader would gather that Freud advocates free love, removal of all restraints, and a relapse into savagery." In fact, of course, Freud savaged and very nearly exterminated traditional Philosophy, the queen of the sciences throughout the nineteenth century. What was left of the lofty metaphysics of God, Freedom and Immortality, if they were products of the anus and the glans penis?

McLuhan, in turn, has been the savager of the literary intellectuals. He has made the most infuriating announcement of all: You are irrelevant.

He has hit a superannuated target. The literary-intellectual mode that still survives in the United States and England today was fashioned more than 150 years ago in Regency England with the founding of Magazines such as the *Edinburgh Review,* the *Quarterly, Blackwood's,* the *London Magazine,* the *Examiner* and the *Westminster Review.* They became platforms for educated gentlemen-amateurs to pass judgment in a learned way on two subjects: books and politics. This seemed a natural combination at the time, because so many literati were excited by the French Revolution and its aftermath (e.g., Byron, Wordsworth, Shelley, Hazlitt, Francis Jeffrey). The *Edinburgh Review* had covers of blue and buff, the Whig colors. Remarkably, the literary-intellectual mode has remained locked for more than a century and a half in precisely that format: of books and moral protest, by gentlemen-amateurs, in the British polite-essay form.

McLuhan has come forth as a man with impeccable literary credentials of his own to tell them that the game is all over. He has accused them of "primitivisim" and ignorance of the nature of the very medium they profess to value: the book; they "have never thought for one minute about the book as a medium or a structure and how it related itself to other media as a structure, politically, verbally, and so on. . . . They have never studied any medium." He has challenged them to come to grips, as he has, with the objective, empirical techniques of exploration developed in the physical and social sciences in the past fifty years; if the literary intellectual continues to retreat from all this into the realm of values, says McLuhan, "he's had it."

This has been the sorest point for the literary fraternities, as he calls them. During the past five years their response to the overwhelming sweep of scientific empiricism has been *the literary retrenchment* — an ever more determined retrenchment into the moralist stance of the Regency literati ("intellectual" protest against the tyrants and evils of the times). Literary intellectuals even sound the cry in so many words today, asserting that the task of the intellectual in a brutal age is the preservation of sacred values (e.g., Noam Chomsky's manifesto, "The Responsibility of the Intellectuals," in *The New York Review of Books*). Intellectuals thus become a kind of clergy without ordination. Macdonald, for example, has devoted the past two decades of his career to the *retrenchment.* He has been busily digging in against all forms of twentieth-century empiricism, from sociology to linguistics. He even sallied forth against so conservative and benign an intrusion of empiricism into the literary world as the third edition of Webster's Dictionary — on the quaint grounds that it had abdicated its moral responsibility to referee Good vs. Evil in grammar and diction. All the while, from inside the trench, he has been running up the flag of "values."

McLuhan's Nietzschean (*Beyond Good and Evil*) "aphorisms and entr'actes" on this subject have been particularly galling: "For many years I have observed that the moralist typically substitutes anger for perception. He hopes that many people will mistake his irritation for insight. . . . The mere moralistic expression of approval or disapproval, preference or detestation, is currently being used in our world as a substitute for observation and a substitute for study. People hope that if they scream loudly enough about 'values' then others will mistake them for serious, sensitive souls who have higher and nobler perceptions than ordinary people. Otherwise, why would they be screaming? . . . Moral bitterness is a basic technique for endowing the idiot with dignity."

Even more galling to the literati, I suspect, is that there is no medium they can turn to, books or otherwise, esoteric or popular, without hearing the McLuhan dicta thundering at them, amid the most amazing fanfare.

Ecce Celebrity.

McLuhan's ascension to the status of international celebrity has been faster than Freud's, due in no small part to the hyped-up tempo of *the media* today — and the fact that the phenomenon of Freud himself had already conditioned the press to exploit the esoteric guru as a star. Freud's ascension was more gradual but quite steady. His emergence, at the Meeting for Freudian Psychology, was in 1908. By 1910 his writings prompted barrages of heated reviews in both American and European intellectual journals, sometimes running to more than a hundred pages apiece. In 1915 his two essays, "Thoughts for the Times on War and Death," were a popular hit and were widely reprinted. By 1924 he was very definitely *Freud;* both the Chicago *Tribune* and the Hearst newspapers offered him huge sums, private ocean liners, etc., to come to the United States and make a psychoanalysis of the sensational thrill-killers, Leopold and Loeb (he declined).

Both Freud and McLuhan experienced their great publicity booms after trips to the United States, however. Freud's followed a series of lectures at Clark University in Worcester, Massachusetts, in 1909 on the twentieth anniversary of its founding. When his boat landed in New York on August 27, he was mentioned, and merely mentioned, in only one newspaper, and as "Professor Freu*n*d of Vienna," at that. By the time he sailed for Europe on September 21, he had his first honorary doctorate (from Clark) and was well on the way to becoming a proper sensation and outrage.

McLuhan's pivotal trip to the U.S. came in May, 1965. As I say, American corporations had already begun to import him for private lectures. The publication of *Understanding Media* in 1964 had prompted that. There was first of all the sheer intriguing possibility — *what if he is right?* There was also the strange wrong-side-of-the-tracks sense of inferiority such firms seem to feel toward the academic and intellectual worlds. Any scholar with good credentials who will take a serious, vaguely optimistic, or even neutral interest in the matters of the business world, e.g., technology, will be warmly received. McLuhan's May, 1965, trip to New York, however, was at the behest of two rather extraordinary men from San Francisco, Howard Gossage and Dr. Gerald Feignen.

Gossage is a tall, pale advertising man

with one of the great heads of gray hair in the U.S.A., flowing back like John Barrymore's. Feigen is a psychiatrist who became a surgeon; he is dark and has big eyes and a gong-kicker mustache like Jerry Colonna. He is also a ventriloquist and carries around a morbid-looking dummy named Becky. Gossage and Feigen started a firm called Generalists, Inc., acting as consultants to people who can't get what they need from specialists because what they need is the big picture. Their first client was a man who was stuck with an expensive ski lift in Squaw Valley that was idle half the year. They advised him to start a posh and rather formal restaurant-nightclub up the slope that could be reached only by ski lift. So he did. It was named High Camp and immediately became all the rage. One thing that drew Gossage and Feigen to McLuhan was his belief that the age of specialists (fragmentation of intellect) was over.

Gossage and Feigen invested about $6,000 into taking McLuhan around to talk to influential people outside the academic world, chiefly in the communications and advertising industries, on both coasts. Gossage says they had no specific goal (no fragmentation; open field). They just wanted to play it "fat, dumb and happy" and see what would happen.

So in May 1965 they had a series of meetings and lunches set up for McLuhan, at Laurent, Lutece, and other great expense-account feasteries of the East Fifties in Manhattan, with men of the caliber of Gibson McCabe. The first meetings and a cocktail party in Gossage's suite at the Lombardy were set for a Monday. McLuhan never showed up. Gossage finally got him on the telephone in Toronto that evening. Marshall, what the hell are you doing—

"I'm grading papers."

"Grading papers?"

"And waiting for the excursion rate."

"The excursion rate! What excursion rate?"

— the midweek excursion rate on the airlines. He could save about $12 round-trip if he didn't come to New York until Tuesday morning.

"But Marshall, you're not even *pay*ing for it!"

— but that was the English prof with the Pree-Tide tie. He had a wife and six children and thirty years behind him of shaving by on an English teacher's pay. So there he was in the bin, grading papers, scratching away —

"Listen," says Gossage, "there are so many people willing to invest money in your work now, you'll never have to grade papers again."

"You mean it's going to be fun from now on?" says McLuhan.

"Everything's coming up roses," says Gossage.

By January, 1966, the McLuhan boom was on, and with a force, as I say, that McLuhan himself never dreamed of. I remember seeing McLuhan in August, 1965, in Gossage's firehouse offices in San Francisco. Gossage and Feigen were putting on their own "McLuhan Festival," as they called it. They invited small groups of influential West Coast people in for Socratic dialogues with McLuhan every morning and every afternoon for a week. One afternoon McLuhan was sitting at the round table in Gossage's own big, handsome office with half a dozen people, Gossage, Feigen, Mike Robbins of Young & Rubicam, Herbert Gold the novelist, Edward Keating, then editor and publisher of *Ramparts* magazine, and myself.

Someone asked McLuhan what he thought of a large-scale communications conference that happened to be going on in San Francisco at that moment, at the Hilton Hotel, with a thousand scholars in attendance, headed by the renowned semanticist, S. I. Hayakawa.

"Well . . ." said McLuhan, pulling his chin in and turning his eyes up, "they're working from very obsolete premises, of course. Almost by definition."

By definition?

"Certainly. By the time you can get a thousand people to agree on enough principles to hold such a meeting, conditions will already have changed. The principles will be useless."

The Hayakawa conference . . . evaporated.

I thought of this remark four months later. McLuhan had a long-standing invitation to speak before the regular monthly luncheon meeting of a New York advertising group. This group always met in a banquet room off the mezzanine of the Plaza Hotel. Attendance was seldom more than a hundred. Suddenly McLuhan's appearance took on the proportions of a theater opening by a blazing new star. The luncheon had to be transferred to the Plaza's grand ballroom — and was attended by . . . a thousand.

McLuhan, as I look back on it, was magnificent that day. Rather than gratify the sudden popular clamor, he stood up at the podium and became his most cryptic, Delphic, esoteric, Oriental self. He was like a serious-faced Lewis Carroll. Nobody knew what the hell he was saying. I was seated at a table with a number of people from Time-Life, Inc. Several of them were utterly outraged by the performance. They sighed, rolled their eyeballs, then actually turned their chairs around and began conversing among themselves as he spoke. It could not have been more reminiscent of the Freud phenomenon fifty years before. *Many enemies, much honor!*

I have heard friends of McLuhan say that his publicity boom has become so intense, he is in danger of overexposure and trivialization. Perhaps; certainly some of his recent gestures, such as an article in *Look* on "The Future of Sex" (co-authored by a *Look* editor), have sounded trivial enough. But I think that all in all he has handled the whole thing like a champion. Like Freud, he never stops to debate a point ("I want observations, not agreement"). Mainly, he has just continued o pour it on, in every medium he can get hold of, books, magazines, TV, radio, lectures, seminars, symposia. He has even broken through the meaning barrier. As late as the winter of 1965–66 people from the Canadian Broadcasting Company told me they would like to put McLuhan on Canadian TV, but they felt he would be unintelligible to their audience. Today that objection would be a laugh, even at the CBC. It would be like saying, We can't show Richard Burton — he doesn't finish his sentences.

McLuhan's monomania for his theory — and his consecrated pursuit of it amid the whole spume of his celebrity — has lent him a weird peace. It is the peace of the eye of the hurricane or of what Professor Silenus, the architect, describes in Evelyn Waugh's *Decline and Fall.* Professor Silenus describes life as being like one of those whirling discs at the old amusement parks. They are like a gigantic phonograph record, 50 feet across. You get on the disc and it starts spinning, and the faster it goes, the more centrifugal force builds up to throw you off it. The speed on the outer edge of the disc is so great you have to hold on for dear life just to stay on. The closer you can get to the center of the disc, the slower the speed is and the easier it is to stand up. In fact, theoretically, at the very center there is a point that is completely motionless. In life, most people won't get on the disc at all. They shouldn't get on. They don't have the nerve or the *élan.* They just sit in the stands and watch. Some people like to get on the outer edge and hang on and ride like hell — that would be people like McLuhan's madman impresarios, Gossage and Feigen. Others are standing up and falling down, staggering, lurching toward the center. And a few, a very few, reach the middle, that perfect motionless point, and stand up in the dead center of the roaring whirlygig as if nothing could be clearer and less confused — that would be McLuhan.

Yes. I once took McLuhan to a Topless Lunch in San Francisco. This was at a place on North Beach called the Off Broadway, where the waitresses served lunch bare-breasted. Gossage, Feigen, and Herb Caen, the famous San Francisco columnist, joined us. All of us had heard about the Topless Lunch, but none of us had ever seen it. I found out that a curious thing happens when men walk for the first time into a room full of nude girls. Namely, they are speechless. I saw it happen many times that afternoon. The whole vocabulary of masculine humor about female nudity is actually based on the premise that they are partly clothed, that much is being revealed, but by no means all. When men walk into a restaurant and find a dozen girls walking around in nothing but flesh-colored cache-sexes and high heels, they just don't know what to say — not even a sophisticated boulevardier like Caen. Everyone was struck dumb; everyone, that is to say, except McLuhan.

Inside of thirty seconds McLuhan had simply absorbed the whole scene into . . . the theory. He tucked his chin down.

"Well!" he said. "Very interesting!"

"What's interesting, Marshall?"

"They're wearing *us.*" He said it with a slight shrug, as if nothing could be more obvious.

"I don't get it, Marshall."

"We are their clothes," he said. "We become their environment. We become extensions of their skin. They're wearing *us.*"

We sat down. The place was packed with businessmen. It was kept in a black-light gloom, apparently to spare embarrassment, just like in the old burlesque houses. Except that huge heavy expense-account lunches were being served by bare-breasted waitresses. Their breasts dangled and jiggled and sweated over your plate as they stretched in the meat crush to hand out the soups, the salads, the bread, the cocktails. You could barely see the plate in front of you, only glistening breasts in a nighttown gloom. It was a pure nutball farce, that was all one could seem to get out of it. Unless you were McLuhan.

"When you dim the visual sense," he said, "you step up the sense of taste. That's why these so-called 'dim-lit restaurants' work. That's why they are literally 'intimate.' You are brought together sensually and sensorially, forced out of the isolation of the visual man."

Later on we fell to discussing the relative charms of our sweating seraglio houris, and Caen happened to single out one girl as "good-looking" —

"Do you know what you said?" said McLuhan. "Good-*looking.* That's a visual orientation. You're separating yourself from the girls. You are sitting back and *looking*. Actually, the light is dim in here. This is meant as a *tactile* experience, but visual man doesn't react that way."

Everyone looks to McLuhan to see if he is joking, but it is impossible to tell in the tactile night. All that is clear is that . . . yes, McLuhan has already absorbed the whole roaring whirlygig into the motionless center.

Just after the meal, the Off Broadway presented its Style Show. This consisted of several girls with enormous tits — "breasts" just doesn't say it — blown up by silicone injections and sticking clear out of the various gowns and lingerie they were "modeling." All the while a mistress of ceremonies was at a microphone giving a parody version of that feathery female commentary you hear at fashion shows. "And here is Denise," she would say, "in her lace chemise" — and a young thing comes forward with a pair of prodigious dugs swollen out in front of her, heavily rouged about the nipples, and a wispy little stretch of lace dripped over her shoulder and tied with a bow at her neck. "This latest creation," says the M.C., "is made of *heavy-duty* Belgian lace . . . for that so, so *nec*essary *ex*tra support . . ."

After the show, McLuhan calls to the M.C., the woman at the microphone — she was clothed, by the way — he calls her over to our table and says to her, "I have something you can use in your *spiel*."

"What's that?" she says. Her face starts to take on that bullet-proof smile that waitresses and barmaids put on to cope with middle-aged wiseguys.

"Well, it's this," says McLuhan — and I have to mention that Topless performers had recently been brought into court in San Francisco in a test case and had won the trial — "It's this," says McLuhan. "You can say, you can tell them" — and here his voice slows down as if to emphasize the utmost significance — *"The topless waitress is the opening wedge of the trial balloon!"*

Then he looks at her with an unfathomable smile.

Her smile, however, freezes. The light goes out in her eyes. She suddenly looks like an aging pole-axed ewe. She stares at McLuhan without a word or an expression —

But of course!

— what if he is right?

The New Mutants

Leslie Fiedler

A realization that the legitimate functions of literature are bewilderingly, almost inexhaustibly various has always exhilarated poets and dismayed critics. And critics, therefore, have sought age after age to legislate limits to literature — legitimizing certain of its functions and disavowing others — in hope of insuring to themselves the exhilaration of which they have felt unjustly deprived, and providing for poets the dismay which the critics at least have thought good for them.

Such shifting and exclusive emphasis is not, however, purely the product of critical malice, or even of critical principle. Somehow every period is, to begin with, especially aware of certain functions of literature and especially oblivious to others: endowed with a special sensitivity and a complementary obtuseness, which, indeed, give to that period its characteristic flavor and feel. So, for instance, the Augustan Era is marked by sensitivity in regard to the uses of diction, obtuseness in regard to those of imagery.

What the peculiar obtuseness of the present age may be I find it difficult to say (being its victim as well as its recorder), perhaps toward the didactic or certain modes of the sentimental. I am reasonably sure, however, that our period is acutely aware of the sense in which literature if not invents, at least collaborates in the invention of time. The beginnings of that awareness go back certainly to the beginnings of the Renaissance, to Humanism as a self-conscious movement; though a critical development occurred toward the end of the eighteenth century with the dawning of the Age of Revolution. And we may have reached a second critical point right now.

At any rate, we have long been aware (in the last decades uncomfortably aware) that a chief function of literature is to express and in part to create not only theories of time but also attitudes toward time. Such attitudes constitute, however, a politics as well as an esthetics; or, more properly perhaps, a necessary mythological substratum of politics — as, in fact, the conventional terms reactionary, conservative, revolutionary indicate: all involving stances toward the past.

It is with the past, then, that we must start, since the invention of the past seems to have preceded that of the present and the future; and since we are gathered in a university at whose heart stands a library — the latter, like the former, a visible monument to the theory that a chief responsibility of literature is to preserve and perpetuate the past. Few universities are explicitly (and none with any real degree of confidence) dedicated to this venerable goal any longer. The Great Books idea (which once transformed the University of Chicago and lives now in provincial study groups) was perhaps its last desperate expression. Yet the shaky continuing existence of the universities and the building of new college libraries (with matching Federal funds) remind us not only of that tradition but of the literature created in its name: the neo-epic, for instance, all the way from Dante to Milton; and even the frantically nostalgic Historical Romance, out of the counting house by Sir Walter Scott.

Obviously, however, literature has a contemporary as well as a traditional function. That is to say, it may be dedicated to illuminating the present and the meaning of the present, which is, after all, no more given than the past. Certainly the modern or bourgeois novel was thus contemporary in the hands of its great inventors, Richardson, Fielding, Smollett and Sterne; and it became contemporary again — with, as it were, a sigh of relief — when Flaubert, having plunged deep into the Historical Romance, emerged once more into the present of Emma Bovary. But the second function of the novel tends to transform itself into a third: a revolutionary or prophetic or futurist function; and it is with the latter that I am here concerned.

Especially important for our own time is the sense in which literature first conceived the possibility of the future (rather than an End of Time or an Eternal Return, an Apocalypse or Second Coming); and then furnished that future in joyous or terrified anticipation, thus preparing all of us to inhabit it. Men have dreamed and even written down utopias from ancient times; but such utopias were at first typically allegories rather than projections: nonexistent models against which to measure the real world, exploitations of the impossible (as the traditional name declares) rather than explorations or anticipations or programs of the possible. And, in any event, only recently have such works occupied a position anywhere near the center of literature.

Indeed, the movement of futurist literature from the periphery to the center of culture provides a clue to certain essential meanings of our times and of the art which best reflects it. If we make a brief excursion from the lofty reaches of High Art to the humbler levels of Pop Culture — where radical transformations in literature are reflected in simplified form — the extent and nature of the futurist revolution will become immediately evident. Certainly, we have seen in recent years the purveyors of Pop Culture transfer their energies from the Western and the Dracula-type thriller (last heirs of the Romantic and Gothic concern with the past) to the Detective Story especially in its hard-boiled form (final vulgarization of the realists' dedication to the present) to Science Fiction (a new genre based on hints in E. A. Poe and committed to "extrapolating" the future). This development is based in part on the tendency to rapid exhaustion inherent in popular forms; but in part reflects a growing sense of the irrelevance of the past and even of the present to 1965. Surely, there has never been a moment in which the most naïve as well as the most sophisticated have been so acutely aware of how the past threatens momentarily to disappear from the present, which itself seems on the verge of disappearing into the future.

And this awareness functions, therefore, on the level of art as well as entertainment, persuading quite serious writers to emulate the modes of Science Fiction. The novel is most amenable to this sort of adaptation, whose traces we can find in writers as various as William Golding and Anthony Burgess, William Burroughs and Kurt Vonnegut, Jr., Harry Matthews and John Barth — to all of whom young readers tend to respond with a sympathy they do not feel even toward such forerunners of the mode (still more allegorical than prophetic) as Aldous Huxley, H. G. Wells and George Orwell. But the influence of Science Fiction can be discerned in poetry as well, and even in the polemical essays of such polymath prophets as Wilhelm Reich, Buckminster Fuller, Marshall McLuhan, perhaps also Norman O. Brown. Indeed, in Fuller the prophetic — Science-Fiction view of man is always at the point of fragmenting into verse:

men are known as being six feet tall
because that is their tactile limit;
they are not known by how far we can hear them,
e.g., as a one-half mile man
and only to dogs are men known
by their gigantic olfactoral dimensions. . . .

I am not now interested in analyzing, however, the diction and imagery which have passed from Science Fiction into post-Modernist literature, but rather in coming to terms with the prophetic content common to both: with the myth rather than the modes of Science Fiction. But that myth is quite simply the myth of the end of man, of the transcendence or transformation of the human — a vision quite different from that of the extinction of our species by the Bomb, which seems stereotype rather than archetype and consequently the source of editorials rather than poems. More fruitful artistically is the prospect of the radical transformation (under the impact of advanced technology and the transfer of traditional human functions to machines) of *homo sapiens* into something else: the emergence — to use the language of Science Fiction itself — of "mutants" among us.

A simpleminded prevision of this event is to be found in Arthur C. Clarke's *Childhood's End,* at the conclusion of which the mutated offspring of parents much like us are about to take off under their own power into outer space. Mr. Clarke believes that he is talking about a time still to come because he takes metaphor for fact; though simply translating "outer space" into "inner space" reveals to us that what he is up to is less prediction than description; since the post-human future is now, and if not we, at least our children, are what it would be comfortable to pretend we still only foresee. But what, in fact, are they: these mutants who are likely to sit before us in class, or across from us at the dinner table, or who stare at us with hostility from street corners as we pass?

Beatniks or hipsters, layabouts and drop-outs we are likely to call them with corresponding hostility — or more elegantly, but still without sympathy, passive onlookers, abstentionists, spiritual catatonics. There resides in all of these terms an element of truth, at least about the relationship of the young to what we have defined as the tradition, the world we have made for them; and if we turn to the books in which they see their own destiny best represented (*The Clockwork Orange,* say, or *On the Road* or *Temple of Gold*), we will find nothing to contradict that truth. Nor will we find anything to expand it, since the young and their laureates avoid on principle the kind of definition (even of themselves) for which we necessarily seek.

Let us begin then with the negative definition our own hostility suggests, since this is all that is available to us, and say that the "mutants" in our midst are non-participants in the past (though our wisdom assures us this is impossible), drop-outs from history. The withdrawal from school, so typical of their generation and so inscrutable to ours, is best understood as a lived symbol of their rejection of the notion of cultural continuity and progress, which our graded educational system represents in institutional form. It is not merely a matter of their rejecting what happens to have happened just before them, as the young do, after all, in every age; but of their attempting to disavow the very idea of the past, of their seeking to avoid recapitulating it step by step — up to the point of graduation into the present.

Specifically, the tradition from which they strive to disengage is the tradition of the human, as the West (understanding the West to extend from the United States to Russia) has defined it, Humanism itself, both in its bourgeois and Marxist forms; and more especially, the cult of reason — that dream of Socrates, redreamed by the Renaissance and surviving all travesties down to only yesterday. To be sure, there have long been anti-rational forces at work in the West, including primitive Christianity itself; but the very notion of literary culture is a product of Humanism, as the early Christians knew (setting fire to libraries), so that the Church in order to sponsor poets had first to come to terms with reason itself by way of Aquinas and Aristotle.

Only with Dada was the notion of an anti-rational anti-literature born; and Dada became Surrealism, i.e., submitted to the influence of those last neo-Humanists, those desperate Socratic Cabalists, Freud and Marx — dedicated respectively to contriving a rationale of violence and a rationale of impulse. The new irrationalists, however, deny all the apostles of reason, Freud as well as Socrates; and if they seem to exempt Marx, this is because they know less about him, have heard him evoked less often by the teachers they are driven to deny. Not only do they reject the Socratic adage that the unexamined life is not worth living, since for them precisely the unexamined life is the only one worth enduring at all. But they also abjure the Freudian one: "Where id was, ego shall be," since for them the true rallying cry is, "Let id prevail over ego, impulse over order," or — in negative terms — "Freud is a fink!"

The first time I heard this irreverent charge from the mouth of a student some five or six years ago (I who had grown up thinking of Freud as a revolutionary, a pioneer), I knew that I was already in the future; though I did not yet suspect that there would be no room in that future for the university system to which I had devoted my life. Kerouac might have told me so, or Ginsberg, or even so polite and genteel a spokesman for youth as J. D. Salinger, but I was too aware of what was wrong with such writers (their faults more readily apparent to my taste than their virtues) to be sensitive to the truths they told. It took, therefore, certain public events to illuminate (for me) the literature which might have illuminated them.

I am thinking, of course, of the recent demonstrations at Berkeley and elsewhere, whose ostensible causes were civil rights or freedom of speech or Vietnam, but whose not so secret slogan was all the time: *The Professor Is a Fink!* And what an array of bad anti-academic novels, I cannot help reminding myself, written by disgruntled professors, created the mythology out of which that slogan grew. Each generation of students is invented by the generation of teachers just before them; but how different they are in dream and fact — as different as self-hatred and its reflection in another. How different the professors in Jeremy Larner's *Drive, He Said* from those even in Randall Jarrell's *Pictures from an Institution* or Mary McCarthy's *Groves of Academe.*

To be sure, many motives operated to set the students in action, some of them imagined in no book, however good or bad. Many of the thousands who resisted or shouted on campuses did so in the name of naïve or disingenuous or even nostalgic politics (be careful what you wish for in your middle age, or your children will parody it forthwith!); and sheer ennui doubtless played a role along with a justified rage against the hypocrisies of academic life. Universities have long rivaled the churches in their devotion to institutionalizing hypocrisy; and more recently they have outstripped television itself (which most professors affect to despise even more than they despise organized religion) in the institutionalization of boredom.

But what the students were protesting in large part, I have come to believe, was the very notion of man which the universities sought to impose upon them: that bourgeois-Protestant version of Humanism, with its view of man as justified by rationality, work, duty, vocation, maturity, success; and its concomitant understanding of childhood and adolescence as a temporarily privileged time of preparation for assuming those burdens. The new irrationalists, however, are prepared to advocate prolonging adolescence to the grave, and are ready to dispense with school as an outlived excuse for leisure. To them work is as obsolete as reason, a vestige (already dispensible for large numbers) of an economically marginal, pre-automated world; and the obsolescence of the two adds up to the obsolescence of everything our society understands by maturity.

Nor is it in the name of an older more valid Humanistic view of man that the new irrationalists would reject the WASP version; Rabelais is as alien to them as Benjamin Franklin. Disinterested scholarship, reflection, the life of reason, a respect for tradition stir (however dimly and confusedly) chiefly their contempt; and the Abbey of Theleme would seem as sterile to them as Robinson Crusoe's Island. To the classroom, the library, the laboratory, the office conference and the meeting of scholars, they prefer the demonstration, the sit-in, the riot: the mindless unity of an impassioned crowd (with guitars beating out the rhythm in the background), whose immediate cause is felt rather than thought out, whose ultimate cause is itself. In light of this, the Teach-in, often ill understood because of an emphasis on its declared political ends, can be seen as implicitly a parody and mockery of the real classroom: related to the actual business of the university, to real teaching only as the Demonstration Trial (of Dimitrov, of the Soviet Doctors, of Eichmann) to real justice or Demonstration Voting (for one party or a token two) to real suffrage.

At least, since Berkeley (or perhaps since Martin Luther King provided students with new paradigms for action) the choice has been extended beyond what the earlier laureates of the new youth could imagine in the novel: the nervous breakdown at home rather than the return to "sanity" and school, which was the best Salinger could invent for Franny and Holden; or Kerouac's way out for his "saintly" vagrants, that "road" from nowhere to noplace with homemade gurus at the way stations. The structure of those fictional vaudevilles between hard covers that currently please the young (*Catch 22, V., A Mother's Kisses*), suggest in their brutality and discontinuity, their politics of mockery something of the spirit of the student demonstrations; but only Jeremy Larner, as far as I know, has dealt explicitly with the abandonment of the classroom in favor of the dionysiac pack, the turning from *polis* to *thiasos,* from forms of social organization traditionally thought off as male to the sort of passionate community attributed by the ancients to females out of control.

Conventional slogans in favor of "Good Works" (pious emendations of existing social structures, or extensions of accepted "rights" to excluded groups) though they provide the motive power of such protests are irrelevant to their form and their final significance. They become their essential selves, i.e., genuine new forms of rebellion, when the demonstrators hoist (as they did in the final stages of the Berkeley protests) the sort of slogan which embarrasses not only fellow-travelers but even the bureaucrats who direct the initial stages of the revolt: at the University of California, the single four-letter word no family newspaper would reprint, though no member of a family who could read was likely not to know it.

It is possible to argue on the basis of the political facts themselves that the word "fuck" entered the whole scene accidentally (there were only four students behind the "Dirty Speech Movement," only fifteen hundred kids could be persuaded to demonstrate for it, etc., etc.). But the prophetic literature which anticipates the movement indicates otherwise, suggesting that the logic of their illogical course eventually sets the young against language itself, against the very counters of logical discourse. They seek an anti-language of protest as inevitably as they seek anti-poems and anti-novels, end with the ultimate anti-word, which the demonstrators at Berkeley disingenuously claimed stood for FREEDOM UNDER CLARK KERR.

Esthetics, however, had already anticipated politics in this regard; porno-poetry preceding and preparing the way for what Lewis Feuer has aptly called porno-politics. Already in 1963, in an essay entitled *"Phi Upsilon Kappa,"* the young poet Michael McClure was writing: "Gregory Corso has asked me to join with him in a project to free the word FUCK from its chains and strictures. I leap to make some new freedom. . . ." And McClure's own "Fuck Ode" is a product of this collaboration, as the very name of Ed Saunders' journal, *Fuck You,* is the creation of an analogous impulse. The aging critics of the young who have dealt with the Berkeley demonstrations in such journals as *Commentary* and the *New Leader* do not, however, read either Saunders' porno-pacifist magazine or *Kulchur,* in which McClure's manifesto was first printed — the age barrier separating readership in the United States more effectively than class, political affiliation or anything else.

Their sense of porno-esthetics is likely to come from deserters from their own camp, chiefly Norman Mailer, and especially his recent *An American Dream,* which represents the entry of anti-language (extending the tentative explorations of "The Time of Her Time") into the world of the middle-aged, both on the level of mass culture and that of yesterday's ex-Marxist, post-Freudian avant-garde. Characteristically enough, Mailer's book has occasioned in the latter quarters reviews as irrelevant, incoherent, misleading and fundamentally scared as the most philistine responses to the Berkeley demonstrations, Philip Rahv and Stanley Edgar Hyman providing two egregious examples. Yet elsewhere (in sectors held by those more at ease with their own conservatism, i.e., without defunct radicalism to uphold) the most obscene forays of the young are being met with a disheartening kind of tolerance and even an attempt to adapt them to the conditions of commodity art.

But precisely here, of course, a disconcerting irony is involved; for after a while, there will be no Rahvs and Hymans left to shock — anti-language becoming mere language with repeated use and in the face of acceptance; so that all sense of exhilaration will be lost along with the possibility of offense. What to do then except to choose silence, since raising the ante of violence is ultimately self-defeating; and the way of obscenity in any case leads as naturally to silence as to further excess? Moreover, to the talkative heirs of Socrates, silence is the one offense that never wears out, the radicalism that can never become fashionable; which is why, after the obscene slogan has been hauled down, a blank placard is raised in its place.

There are difficulties, to be sure, when one attempts to move from the politics of silence to an analogous sort of poetry. The opposite number to the silent picketer would be the silent poet, which is a contradiction in terms; yet there are these days non-singers of (perhaps) great talent who shrug off the temptation to song with the muttered comment, "Creativity is out." Some, however, make literature of a kind precisely at the point of maximum tension between the tug toward silence and the pull toward publication. Music is a better language really for saying what one would prefer not to say at all — and all the way from certain sorts of sufficiently cool jazz to Rock'n'Roll (with its minimal lyrics that defy understanding on a first hearing), music is the preferred art of the irrationalists.

But some varieties of skinny poetry seem apt, too (as practised, say, by Robert Creeley after the example of W. C. Williams), since their lines are three parts silence to one part speech:

My lady
fair with
soft
arms, what
can I say to
you—words, words . . .

And, of course, fiction aspiring to become Pop Art, say, *An American Dream* (with the experiments of Hemingway and Nathanael West behind it), works approximately as well, since clichés are almost as inaudible as silence itself. The point is not to shout, not to insist, but to hang cool, to baffle all mothers, cultural and spiritual as well as actual.

When the Town Council in Venice, California, was about to close down a particularly notorious beatnik café, a lady asked to testify before them, presumably to clinch the case against the offenders. What she reported, however, was that each day as she walked by the café and looked in its windows, she saw the unsavory types who inhabited it "just standing there, looking — nonchalant." And, in a way, her improbable adjective does describe a crime against her world; for nonchaleur ("cool," the futurists themselves would prefer to call it) is the essence of their life-style as well as of the literary styles to which they respond: the offensive style of those who are not so much *for* anything in particular, as "with it" in general.

But such an attitude is as remote from traditional "alienation," with its profound longing to end disconnection, as it is from ordinary forms of allegiance, with their desperate resolve not to admit disconnection. The new young celebrate disconnection — accept it as one of the necessary consequences of the industrial system which has delivered them from work and duty, of that welfare state which makes disengagement the last possible virtue, whether it call itself Capitalist, Socialist or Communist. "Detachment" is the traditional name for the stance the futurists assume; but "detachment" carries with it irrelevant religious, even specifically Christian overtones. The post-modernists are surely in some sense "mystics," religious at least in a way they do not ordinarily know how to confess, but they are not Christians.

Indeed, they regard Christianity, quite as the Black Muslim (with whom they have certain affinities) do, as a white ideology: merely one more method — along with Humanism, technology, Marxism — of imposing "White" or Western values on the colored rest of the world. To the new barbarian, however, that would-be post-Humanist (who is in most cases the white offspring of Christian forebears) his whiteness is likely to seem if not a stigma and symbol of shame, at least the outward sign of his exclusion from all that his Christian Humanist ancestors rejected in themselves and projected mythologically upon the colored man. For such reasons, his religion, when it becomes explicit, claims to be derived from Tibet or Japan or the ceremonies of the Plains Indians, or is composed out of the non-Christian submythology that has grown up among Negro jazz musicians and in the civil rights movement. When the new barbarian speaks of "soul," for instance, he means not "soul" as in Heaven, but as in "soul music" or even "soul food."

It is all part of the attempt of the generation under twenty-five, not exclusively in its most sensitive members but especially in them, to become Negro, even as they attempt to become poor or pre-rational. About this particular form of psychic assimilation I have written sufficiently in the past (summing up what I had been long saying in chapters seven and eight of *Waiting for the End*), neglecting only the sense in which what starts as a specifically American movement becomes an international one, spreading to the *yé-yé* girls of France or the working-class entertainers of Liverpool with astonishing swiftness and ease.

What interests me more particularly right now is a parallel assimilationist attempt, which may, indeed, be more parochial and is certainly most marked at the moment in the Anglo-Saxon world, i.e., in those cultural communities most totally committed to bourgeois-Protestant values and surest that they are unequivocally "white." I am thinking of the effort of young men in England and the United States to assimilate into themselves (or even to assimilate themselves into) that otherness, that sum total of rejected psychic elements which the middle-class heirs of the Renaissance have identified with "woman." To become new men, these children of the future seem to feel, they must not only become more Black than White but more female than male. And it is natural that the need to make such an adjustment be felt with especial acuteness in post-Protestant highly industrialized societies, where the functions regarded as specifically male for some three hundred years tend most rapidly to become obsolete.

Surely, in America, machines already perform better than humans a large number of those aggressive-productive activities which our ancestors considered man's special province, even his *raison d'être.* Not only has the male's prerogative of making things and money (which is to say, of working) been preempted, but also his time-honored privilege of dealing out death by hand, which until quite recently was regarded as a supreme mark of masculine valor. While it seems theoretically possible, even in the heart of Anglo-Saxondom, to imagine a leisurely, pacific male, in fact the losses in secondary functions sustained by men appear to have shaken their faith in their primary masculine function as well, in their ability to achieve the conquest (as the traditional metaphor has it) of women. Earlier, advances in technology had detached the wooing and winning of women from the begetting of children; and though the invention of the condom had at least left the decision to inhibit fatherhood in the power of males, its replacement by the "loop" and the "pill" has placed paternity at the mercy of the whims of women.

Writers of fiction and verse registered the technological obsolescence of masculinity long before it was felt even by the representative minority who give to the present younger generation its character and significance. And literary critics have talked a good deal during the past couple of decades about the conversion of the literary hero into the non-hero or the anti-hero; but they have in general failed to notice his simultaneous conversion into the non- or anti-male. Yet ever since Hemingway at least, certain male protagonists of American literature have not only fled rather than sought out combat but have also fled rather than sought out women. From Jake Barnes to Holden Caulfield they have continued to run from the threat of female sexuality; and, indeed, there are models for such evasion in our classic books, where heroes still eager for the fight (Natty Bumppo comes to mind) are already shy of wives and sweethearts and mothers.

It is not absolutely required that the anti-male anti-hero be impotent or homosexual or both (though this helps, as we remember remembering Walt Whitman), merely that he be more seduced than seducing, more passive than active. Consider, for instance, the oddly "womanish" Herzog of Bellow's best seller, that Jewish Emma Bovary with a Ph.D., whose chief flaw is physical vanity and a taste for fancy clothes. Bellow, however, is more interested in summing up the past than in evoking the future; and *Herzog* therefore seems an end rather than a beginning, the product of nostalgia (remember when there were real Jews once, and the "Jewish Novel" had not yet been discovered!) rather than prophecy. No, the post-humanist, post-male, post-white, post-heroic world is a post-Jewish world by the same token, anti-Semitism as inextricably woven into it as into the movement for Negro rights; and its scriptural books are necessarily *goyish,* not least of all William Burroughs' *The Naked Lunch.*

Burroughs is the chief prophet of the post-male post-heroic world; and it is his emulators who move into the center of the relevant literary scene, for *The Naked Lunch* (the later novels are less successful, less exciting but relevant still) is more than it seems: no mere essay in heroin-hallucinated homosexual pornography — but a nightmare anticipation (in Science Fiction form) of post-Humanist sexuality. Here, as in Alexander Trocchi, John Rechy, Harry Matthews (even an occasional Jew like Allen Ginsberg, who has begun by inscribing properly anti-Jewish obscenities on the walls of the world), are clues to the new attitudes toward sex that will continue to inform our improbable novels of passion and our even more improbable love songs.

The young to whom I have been referring, the mythologically representative minority (who, by a process that infuriates the mythologically inert majority out of which they come, "stand for" their times), live in a community in which what used to be called the "Sexual Revolution," the Freudian-Laurentian revolt of their grandparents and parents, has triumphed as imperfectly and unsatisfactorily as all revolutions always triumph. They confront, therefore, the necessity of determining not only what meanings "love" can have in their new world, but — even more disturbingly — what significance, if any, "male" and "female" now possess. For a while, they (or at least their literary spokesmen recruited from the generation just before them) seemed content to celebrate a kind of *reductio* or *exaltatio ad absurdum* of their parents' once revolutionary sexual goals: The Reichian-inspired Cult of the Orgasm.

Young men and women eager to be delivered of traditional ideologies of love find especially congenial the belief that not union or relationship (much less offspring) but physical release is the end of the sexual act; and that, therefore, it is a matter of indifference with whom or by what method one pursues the therapeutic climax, so long as that climax is total and repeated frequently. And Wilhelm Reich happily detaches this belief from the vestiges of Freudian rationalism, setting it instead in a context of Science Fiction and witchcraft; but his emphasis upon "full genitality," upon growing up and away from infantile pleasures, strikes the young as a disguised plea for the "maturity" they have learned to despise. In a time when the duties associated with adulthood promise to become irrelevant, there seems little reason for denying oneself the joys of babyhood — even if these are associated with such regressive fantasies as escaping it all in the arms of little sister (in the Gospel according to J. D. Salinger) or flirting with the possibility of getting into bed with papa (in the Gospel according to Norman Mailer).

Only Norman O. Brown in *Life Against Death* has come to terms on the level of theory with the aspiration to take the final evolutionary leap and cast off adulthood completely, at least in the area of sex. His post-Freudian program for pan-sexual, non-orgasmic love rejects "full genitality" in favor of a species of indiscriminate bundling, a dream of unlimited sub-coital intimacy which Brown calls (in his vocabulary the term is an honorific) "polymorphous perverse." And here finally is an essential clue to the nature of the second sexual revolution, the post-sexual revolution, first evoked in literature by Brother Antoninus more than a decade ago, in a verse prayer addressed somewhat improbably to the Christian God:

Annul in me my manhood, Lord, and make

Me woman sexed and weak . . .
Make me then
Girl-hearted, virgin-souled, woman-docile,
maiden-meek . . .

Despite the accents of this invocation, however, what is at work is not essentially a homosexual revolt or even a rebellion against women, though its advocates seek to wrest from women their ancient privileges of receiving the Holy Ghost and pleasuring men; and though the attitudes of the movement can be adapted to the anti-female bias of, say, Edward Albee. If in *Who's Afraid of Virginia Woolf?* Albee can portray the relationship of two homosexuals (one in drag) as the model of contemporary marriage, this must be because contemporary marriage has in fact turned into something much like that parody. And it is true that what survives of bourgeois marriage and the bourgeois family is a target which the new barbarians join the old homosexuals in reviling, seeking to replace Mom, Pop and the kids with a neo-Whitmanian gaggle of giggling *camerados.* Such groups are, in fact, whether gathered in coffee houses, university cafeterias or around the literature tables on campuses, the peace-time equivalents, as it were, to the demonstrating crowd. But even their program of displacing Dick-Jane-Spot-Baby, etc., the WASP family of grade school primers, is not the fundamental motive of the post-sexual revolution.

What is at stake from Burroughs to Bellow, Ginsberg to Albee, Salinger to Gregory Corso is a more personal transformation: a radical metamorphosis of the Western male — utterly unforeseen in the decades before us, but visible now in every high school and college classroom, as well as on the paperback racks in airports and supermarkets. All around us, young males are beginning to retrieve for themselves the cavalier role once piously and class-consciously surrendered to women: *that of being beautiful and being loved.* Here once more the example to the Negro — the feckless and adorned Negro male with the blood of Cavaliers in his veins — has served as a model. And what else is left to young men, in any case, after the devaluation of the grim duties they had arrogated to themselves in place of the pursuit of loveliness?

All of us who are middle-aged and were Marxists, which is to say, who once numbered ourselves among the last assured Puritans, have surely noticed in ourselves a vestigial roundhead rage at the new hair styles of the advanced or — if you please — delinquent young. Watching young men titivate their locks (the comb, the pocket mirror and the bobby pin having replaced the jackknife, catcher's mitt and brass knuckles), we feel the same baffled resentment that stirs in us when we realize that they have rejected work. A job and unequivocal maleness — these are two sides of the same Calvinist coin, which in the future buys nothing.

Few of us, however, have really understood how the Beatle hair-do is part of a syndrome, of which high heels, jeans tight over the buttocks, etc., are other aspects, symptomatic of a larger retreat from masculine aggressiveness to female allure — in literature and the arts to the style called "camp." And fewer still have realized how that style, though the invention of homosexuals, is now the possession of basically heterosexual males as well, a strategy in their campaign to establish a new relationship not only with women but with their own masculinity. In the course of that campaign, they have embraced certain kinds of gesture and garb, certain accents and tones traditionally associated with females or female impersonators; which is why we have been observing recently (in life as well as fiction and verse) young boys, quite unequivocally male, playing all the traditional roles of women: the vamp, the coquette, the whore, the icy tease, the pure young virgin.

Not only oldsters, who had envisioned and despaired of quite another future, are bewildered by this turn of events, but young girls, too, seem scarcely to know what is happening — looking on with that new, schizoid stare which itself has become a hallmark of our times. And the crop-headed jocks, those crew-cut athletes who represent an obsolescent masculine style based on quite other values, have tended to strike back blindly; beating the hell out of some poor kid whose hair is too long or whose pants are too tight — quite as they once beat up young Communists for revealing that their politics had become obsolete. Even heterosexual writers, however, have been slow to catch up, the revolution in sensibility running ahead of that in expression; and they have perforce permitted homosexuals to speak for them (Burroughs and Genet and Baldwin and Ginsberg and Albee and a score of others), even to invent the forms in which the future will have to speak.

The revolt against masculinity is not limited, however, to simple matters of coiffure and costume, visible even to athletes; or to the adaptation of certain campy styles and modes to new uses. There is also a sense in which two large social movements that have set the young in motion and furnished images of action for their books — movements as important in their own right as porno-politics and the pursuit of the polymorphous perverse — are connected analogically to the abdication from traditional maleness. The first of these is nonviolent or passive resistance, so oddly come back to the land of its inventor, that icy Thoreau who dreamed a love which ". . . has not much human blood in it, but consists with a certain disregard for men and their erections. . . ."

The civil rights movement, however, in which nonviolence has found a home, has been hospitable not only to the sort of post-humanist I have been describing; so that at a demonstration (Selma, Alabama will do as an example) the true hippie will be found side by side with backwoods Baptists, nuns on a spiritual spree, boy bureaucrats practicing to take power, resurrected socialists, Unitarians in search of a God, and just plain tourists, gathered, as once at the Battle of Bull Run, to see the fun. For each of these, nonviolence will have a different sort of fundamental meaning — as a tactic, a camouflage, a passing fad, a pious gesture — but for each in part, and for the post-humanist especially, it will signify the possibility of heroism without aggression, effective action without guilt.

There have always been two contradictory American ideals: to be the occasion of maximum violence, and to remain absolutely innocent. Once, however, these were thought hopelessly incompatible for males (except, perhaps, as embodied in works of art), reserved strictly for women: the spouse of the wife-beater, for instance, or the victim of rape. But males have now assumed these classic roles; and just as a particularly beleaguered wife occasionally slipped over the dividing line into violence, so do the new passive protestors — leaving us to confront (or resign to the courts) such homey female questions as: *Did Mario Savio really bite that cop in the leg as he sagged limply toward the ground?*

The second social movement is the drug cult, more widespread among youth, from its squarest limits to its most beat, than anyone seems prepared to admit in public; and at its beat limit at least inextricably involved with the civil rights movement, as the recent arrests of Peter DeLissovoy and Susan Ryerson revealed even to the ordinary newspaper reader. "Police said that most of the recipients [of marijuana] were college students," the U.P. story runs. "They quoted Miss Ryerson and DeLissovoy as saying that many of the letter packets were sent to civil rights workers." Only fiction and verse, however, has dealt with the conjunction of homosexuality, drugs and civil rights, eschewing the general piety of the press which has been unwilling to compromise "good works" on behalf of the Negro by associating it with the deep radicalism of a way of life based on the ritual consumption of "pot."

The widespread use of such hallucinogens as peyote, marijuana, the "mexican mushroom," LSD, etc., as well as pep pills, goof balls, airplane glue, certain kinds of cough syrups and even, though in many fewer cases, heroin, is not merely a matter of a changing taste in stimulants but of the programmatic espousal of an anti-puritanical mode of existence — hedonistic and detached — one more strategy in the war on time and work. But it is also (to pursue my analogy once more) an attempt to arrogate to the male certain traditional privileges of the female. What could be more womanly, as Elémire Zolla was already pointing out some years ago, than permitting the penetration of the body by a foreign object which not only stirs delight but even (possibly) creates new life?

In any case, with drugs we have come to the crux of the futurist revolt, the hinge of everything else, as the young tell us over and over in their writing. When the movement was first finding a voice, Allen Ginsberg set this aspect of it in proper context in an immensely comic, utterly serious poem called "America," in which "pot" is associated with earlier forms of rebellion, a commitment to catatonia, and a rejection of conventional male potency:

America I used to be a communist
when I was a kid I'm not sorry.
I smoke marijuana every chance I get.
I sit in my house for days on end and
stare at the roses in the closet.
When I go to Chinatown I
. . . never get laid . . .

Similarly, Michael McClure reveals in his essay, *"Phi Upsilon Kappa,"* that before penetrating the "cavern of Anglo-Saxon," whence he emerged with the slogan of the ultimate Berkeley demonstrators, he had been on mescalin. "I have emerged from a dark night of the soul; I entered it by Peyote." And by now, drug-taking has become as standard a feature of the literature of the young as oral-genital love-making. I flip open the first issue of yet another ephemeral San Francisco little magazine quite at random and read: "I tie up and the main pipe [the ante-cobital vein, for the clinically inclined] swells like a prideful beggar beneath the skin. Just before I get on it is always the worst." Worse than the experience, however, is its literary rendering; and the badness of such confessional fiction, flawed by the sentimentality of those who desire to live "like a cunning vegetable," is a badness we older readers find it only too easy to perceive, as our sons and daughters find it only too easy to overlook. Yet precisely here the age and the mode define themselves; for not in the master but in the hacks new forms are established, new lines drawn.

Here, at any rate, is where the young lose us in literature as well as life, since here they pass over into real revolt, i.e., what we really cannot abide, hard as we try. The mother who has sent her son to private schools and on to Harvard to keep him out of classrooms overcrowded with poor Negroes, rejoices when he sets out for Mississippi with his comrades in SNCC, but shudders when he turns on with LSD; just as the ex-Marxist father, who has earlier proved radicalism impossible, rejoices to see his son stand up, piously and pompously, for CORE or SDS, but trembles to hear him quote Alpert and Leary or praise Burroughs. Just as certainly as liberalism is the LSD of the aging, LSD is the radicalism of the young.

If whiskey long served as an appropriate symbolic excess for those who chafed against Puritan restraint without finally challenging it — temporarily releasing them to socially harmful aggression and (hopefully) sexual self-indulgence, the new popular drugs provide an excess quite as satisfactorily symbolic to the post-Puritans — releasing them from sanity to madness by destroying in them the inner restrictive order which has somehow survived the dissolution of the outer. It is finally insanity, then, that the futurists learn to admire and emulate, quite as they learn to pursue vision instead of learning, hallucination rather than logic. The schizophrenic replaces the sage as their ideal, their new culture hero, figured forth as a giant schizoid Indian (his madness modeled in part on the author's own experiences with LSD) in Ken Kesey's *One Flew Over the Cuckoo's Nest.*

The hippier young are not alone, however, in their taste for the insane; we live in a time when readers in general respond sympathetically to madness in literature wherever it is found, in established writers as well as in those trying to establish new modes. Surely it is not the lucidity and logic of Robert Lowell or Theodore Roethke or John Berryman which we admire, but their flirtation with incoherence and disorder. And certainly it is Mailer at his most nearly psychotic, Mailer the creature rather than the master of his fantasies who moves us to admiration; while in the case of Saul Bellow, we endure the theoretical optimism and acceptance for the sake of the delightful melancholia, the fertile paranoia which he cannot disavow any more than the talent at whose root they lie. Even essayists and analysts recommend themselves to us these days by a certain redemptive nuttiness; at any rate, we do not love, say, Marshall McLuhan less because he continually risks sounding like the body-fluids man in *Dr. Strangelove.*

We have, moreover, recently been witnessing the development of a new form of social psychiatry[1] (a psychiatry of the future already anticipated by the literature of the future) which considers some varieties of "schizophrenia" not diseases to be cured but forays into an unknown psychic world: random penetrations by bewildered internal cosmonauts of a realm that it will be the task of the next generations to explore. And if the accounts which the returning schizophrenics give

[1] Described in an article in the *New Left Review* of November–December, 1964, by R. D. Laing, who advocates "ex-patients helping future patients go mad."

(the argument of the apologists runs) of the "places" they have been are fantastic and garbled, surely they are no more so than, for example, Columbus' reports of the world he had claimed for Spain, a world bounded — according to his newly drawn maps — by Cathay on the north and Paradise on the south.

In any case, poets and junkies have been suggesting to us that the new world appropriate to the new men of the latter twentieth century is to be discovered only by the conquest of inner space: by an adventure of the spirit, an extension of psychic possibility, of which the flights into outer space — moonshots and expeditions to Mars — are precisely such unwitting metaphors and analogues as the voyages of exploration were of the earlier breakthrough into the Renaissance, from whose consequences the young seek now so desperately to escape. The laureate of that new conquest is William Burroughs; and it is fitting that the final word be his:

"This war will be won in the air. In the Silent Air with Image Rays. You were a pilot remember? Tracer bullets cutting the right wing you were free in space a few seconds before in blue space between eyes. Go back to Silence. Keep Silence. Keep Silence. K.S.K.S. . . . From Silence re-write the message that is you. You are the message I send to The Enemy. My Silent Message."
The Naked Astronauts were free in space. . . .

Trash, Art, and the Movies

Pauline Kael

Like those cynical heroes who were idealists before they discovered that the world was more rotten than they had been led to expect, we're just about all of us displaced persons, "a long way from home." When we feel defeated, when we imagine we could now perhaps settle for home and what it represents, that home no longer exists. But there are movie houses. In whatever city we find ourselves we can duck into a theater and see on the screen our familiars — our old "ideals" aging as we are and no longer looking so ideal. Where could we better stoke the fires of our masochism than at rotten movies in gaudy seedy picture palaces in cities that run together, movies and anonymity a common denominator. Movies — a tawdry corrupt art for a tawdry corrupt world — fit the way we feel. The world doesn't work the way the schoolbooks said it did and we are different from what our parents and teachers expected us to be. Movies are our cheap and easy expression, the sullen art of displaced persons. Because we feel low we sink in the boredom, relax in the irresponsibility, and maybe grin for a minute when the gunman lines up three men and kills them with a single bullet, which is no more "real" to us than the nursery-school story of the brave little tailor.

We don't have to be told those are photographs of actors impersonating characters. We know, and we often know much more about both the actors and the characters they're impersonating and about how and why the movie has been made than is consistent with theatrical illusion. Hitchcock teased us by killing off the one marquee-name star early in *Psycho,* a gambit which startled us not just because of the suddenness of the murder or how it was committed but because it broke a box-office convention and so it was a joke played on what audiences have learned to expect. He broke the rules of the movie game and our response demonstrated how aware we are of commercial considerations. When movies are bad (and in the bad parts of good movies) our awareness of the mechanics and our cynicism about the aims and values is peculiarly alienating. The audience talks right back to the phony "outspoken" condescending *The Detective;* there are groans of dejection at *The Legend of Lylah Clare,* with, now and then, a desperate little titter. How well we all know that cheap depression that settles on us when our hopes and expectations are disappointed *again.* Alienation is the most common state of the knowledgeable movie audience, and though it has the peculiar rewards of low connoisseurship, a miser's delight in small favors, we long to be surprised out of it — not to suspension of disbelief nor to a Brechtian kind of alienation, but to pleasure, something a man can call good without self-disgust.

A good movie can take you out of your dull funk and the hopelessness that so often goes with slipping into a theater; a good movie can make you feel alive again, in contact, not just lost in another city. Good movies make you care, make you believe in possibilities again. If somewhere in the Hollywood-entertainment world someone has managed to break through with something that speaks to you, then it isn't *all* corruption. The movie doesn't have to be great; it can be stupid and empty and you can still have the joy of a good performance, or the joy in just a good line. An actor's scowl, a small subversive gesture, a dirty remark that someone tosses off with a mock-innocent face, and the world makes a little bit of sense. Sitting there alone or painfully alone because those with you do not react as you do, you know there must be others perhaps in this very theater or in this city, surely in other theaters in other cities, now, in the past or future, who react as you do. And because movies are the most total and encompassing art form we have, these reactions can seem the most personal and, maybe the most important, imaginable. The romance of movies is not just in those stories and those people on the screen but in the adolescent dream of meeting others who feel as you do about what you've seen. You do meet them, of course, and you know each other at once because you talk less about good movies than about what you love in bad movies.

II

There is so much talk now about the art of the film that we may be in danger of forgetting that most of the movies we enjoy are not works of art. *The Scalphunters,* for example, was one of the few entertaining American movies this past year, but skillful though it was, one could hardly call it a work of art — if such terms are to have any useful meaning. Or, to take a really gross example, a movie that is as crudely made as *Wild in the Streets* — slammed together with spit and hysteria and opportunism — can nevertheless be enjoyable, though it is almost a classic example of an unartistic movie. What makes these movies — that are not works of art — enjoyable? *The Scalphunters* was more entertaining than most Westerns largely because Burt Lancaster and Ossie Davis were peculiarly funny together; part of the pleasure of the movie was trying to figure out what made them so funny. Burt Lancaster is an odd kind of comedian: what's distinctive about him is that his comedy seems to come out of his physicality. In serious roles an undistinguished and too obviously hard-working actor, he has an apparently effortless flair for comedy and nothing is more infectious than an actor who can relax in front of the camera as if he were having a good time. (George Segal sometimes seems to have this gift of a wonderful amiability, and Brigitte Bardot was radiant with it in *Viva Maria!*) Somehow the alchemy of personality in the pairing of Lancaster and Ossie Davis — another powerfully funny actor of tremendous physical presence — worked, and the director Sydney Pollack kept tight control so that it wasn't overdone.

And *Wild in the Streets*? It's a blatantly crummy-looking picture, but that somehow works for it instead of against it because it's smart in a lot of ways that better-made pictures aren't. It looks like other recent products from American International Pictures but it's as if one were reading a comic strip that looked just like the strip of the day before, and yet on this new one there are surprising expressions on the faces and some of the balloons are really witty. There's not a trace of sensitivity in the drawing or in the ideas, and there's something rather specially funny about wit without *any* grace at all; it can be enjoyed in a particularly crude way — as Pop wit. The basic idea is corny — *It Can't Happen Here* with the freaked-out young as a new breed of fascists — but it's treated in the paranoid style of editorials about youth (it even begins by blaming everything on the parents). And a cheap idea that is this current and widespread has an almost lunatic charm, a nightmare gaiety. There's a relish that people have for the idea of drug-taking kids as monsters threatening them — the daily papers merging into *Village of the Damned.* Tapping and exploiting this kind of hysteria for a satirical fantasy, the writer Robert Thom has used what is available and obvious but he's done it with just enough mockery and style to make it funny. He throws in touches of characterization and occasional lines that are not there just to further the plot, and these throwaways make odd connections so that the movie becomes almost frolicsome in its paranoia (and in its delight in its own cleverness).

If you went to *Wild in the Streets* expecting a good movie, you'd probably be appalled because the directing is unskilled and the music is banal and many of the ideas in the script are scarcely even carried out, and almost every detail is messed up (the casting director has used bit players and extras who are decades too old for their roles). It's a paste-up job of cheap moviemaking, but it has genuinely funny performers who seize their opportunities and throw their good lines like boomerangs — Diane Varsi (like an even more zonked-out Geraldine Page) doing a perfectly quietly convincing freak-out as if it were truly a put-on of the whole straight world; Hal Holbrook with his inexpressive actorish face that is opaque and uninteresting in long shot but in close-up reveals tiny little shifts of expression, slight tightenings of the features that are like the movement of thought; and Shelley Winters, of course, and Christopher Jones. It's not so terrible — it may even be a relief — for a movie to be without the look of art; there are much worse things aesthetically than the crude good-natured crumminess, the undisguised reach for a fast buck, of movies without art. From *I Was a Teen-Age Werewolf* through the beach parties to *Wild in the Streets* and *The Savage Seven,* American International Pictures has sold a cheap commodity, which in its lack of artistry and in its blatant and sometimes funny way of delivering action serves to remind us that one of the great appeals of movies is that we don't have to take them too seriously.

Wild in the Streets is a fluke — a borderline, special case of a movie that is entertaining because some talented people got a chance to do something at American International that the more respectable companies were too nervous to try. But though I don't enjoy a movie so obvious and badly done as the big American International Hit, *The Wild Angels,* it's easy to see why kids do and why many people in other countries do. Their reasons are basically why we all started going to the movies. After a time, we may want more, but audiences who have been forced to wade through the thick middle-class padding of more expensively made movies to get to the action enjoy the nose-thumbing at "good taste" of cheap movies that stick to the raw materials. At some basic level they *like* the pictures to be cheaply done, they enjoy the crudeness; it's a breather, a vacation from proper behavior and good taste and required responses. Patrons of burlesque applaud politely for the graceful erotic dancer but go wild for the lewd lummox who bangs her big hips around. That's what they go to burlesque for. Personally, I hope for a reasonable minimum of finesse, and movies like *Planet of the Apes* or *The Scalphunters* or *The Thomas Crown Affair* seem to me minimal entertainment for a relaxed evening's pleasure. These are, to use traditional common-sense language, "good movies" or "good bad movies" — slick, reasonably inventive, well-crafted. They are not art. But they are almost the maximum of what we're now getting from American movies, and not only these but much worse movies are talked about as "art" — and are beginning to be taken seriously in our schools.

It's preposterously egocentric to call anything we enjoy art — as if we could not be entertained by it if it were not; it's just as preposterous to let prestigious, expensive advertising snow us into thinking we're getting art for our money when we haven't even had a good time. I did have a good time at *Wild in the Streets,* which is more than I can say for *Petulia* or *2001* or a lot of other highly praised pictures. *Wild in the Streets* is not a work of art, but then I don't think *Petulia* or *2001* is either, though *Petulia* has that kaleidoscopic hip look and *2001* that new-techniques look which combined with "swinging" or "serious" ideas often pass for motion picture art.

III

Let's clear away a few misconceptions. Movies make hash of the schoolmarm's approach of how well the artist fulfilled his intentions. Whatever the original intention of the writers and director, it is usually supplanted, as the production gets under way, by the intention to make money — and the industry judges the film by how well it fulfills that intention. But if you could see the "artist's intentions" you'd probably wish you couldn't anyway. Nothing is so deathly to enjoyment as the relentless march of a movie to fulfill its obvious purpose. This is, indeed, almost a defining characteristic of the hack director, as distinguished from an artist.

The intention to make money is generally all too obvious. One of the excruciating comedies of our time is attending the new classes in cinema at the high schools where the students may quite shrewdly and accurately interpret the plot developments in a mediocre movie in terms of manipulation for a desired response while the teacher tries to explain everything in terms of the creative artist working out his theme — as if the conditions under which a movie is made and the market for which it is designed were irrelevant, as if the latest product from Warners or Universal should be analyzed like a lyric poem.

People who are just getting "seriously interested" in film always ask a critic, "Why don't you talk about technique and 'the visuals' more?" The answer is that American movie technique is generally more like technology and it usually isn't very interesting. Hollywood movies often have the look of the studio that produced them — they have a studio style. Many current Warner films are noisy and have a bright look of cheerful ugliness, Universal films the cheap blur of money-saving processes, and so forth. Sometimes there is even a *spirit* that seems to belong to the studio. We can speak of the Paramount comedies of the Thirties or the Twentieth-Century Fox family entertainment of the Forties and CinemaScope comedies of the Fifties or the old MGM gloss, pretty much as we speak of Chevvies or Studebakers. These movies look alike, they move the same way, they have just about the same engines because of the studio policies and the *kind* of material the studio heads bought, the ideas they imposed, the way they had the films written, directed, photographed, and the labs where the prints were processed, and, of course, because of the presence of the studio stable of stars for whom the material was often purchased and shaped and who dominated the output of the studio. In some cases, as at Paramount in the Thirties, studio style was plain and rather tacky and the output — those comedies with Mary Boland and Mae West and Alison Skipworth and W. C. Fields — looks the better for it now. Those economical comedies weren't slowed down by a lot of fancy lighting or the adornments of "production values." Simply to be enjoyable, movies don't need a very high level of craftsmanship: wit, imagination, fresh subject matter, skillful performers, a good idea — either alone or in any combination — can more than compensate for lack of technical knowledge or a big budget.

The craftsmanship that Hollywood has always used as a selling point not only doesn't have much to do with art — the expressive use of techniques — it probably doesn't have very much to do with actual box-office appeal, either. A dull movie like Sidney Furie's *The Naked Runner* is technically competent. The appalling *Half a Sixpence* is technically astonishing. Though the large popular audience has generally been respectful of expenditure (so much so that a critic who wasn't impressed by the money and effort that went into a *Dr. Zhivago* might be sharply reprimanded by readers), people who like *The President's Analyst* or *The Producers* or *The Odd Couple* don't seem to be bothered by their technical ineptitude and visual ugliness. And on the other hand, the expensive slick techniques of ornately empty movies like *A Dandy in Aspic* can actually work against one's enjoyment, because such extravagance and waste are morally ugly. If one compares movies one likes to movies one doesn't like, craftsmanship of the big-studio variety is hardly a decisive factor. And if one compares a movie one likes by a competent director such as John Sturges or Franklin Schaffner or John Frankenheimer to a movie one doesn't much like by the same director, his technique is probably not the decisive factor. After directing *The Manchurian Candidate* Frankenheimer directed another political thriller, *Seven Days in May,* which, considered just as a piece of direction, was considerably more confident. While seeing it, one could take pleasure in Frankenheimer's smooth showmanship. But the material (Rod Serling out of Fletcher Knebel and Charles W. Bailey II) was like a straight (*i.e.,* square) version of *The Manchurian Candidate.* I have to chase around the corridors of memory to summon up images from *Seven Days in May;* despite the brilliant technique, all that is clear to mind is the touchingly, desperately anxious face of Ava Gardner — how when she smiled you couldn't be sure if you were seeing dimples or tics. But *The Manchurian Candidate,* despite Frankenheimer's uneven, often barely adequate, staging, is still vivid because of the script. It took off from a political double entendre that everybody had been thinking of ("Why, if Joe McCarthy were working for the Communists, he couldn't be doing them more good!") and carried it to startling absurdity, and the extravagances and conceits and conversational non sequiturs (by George Axelrod out of Richard Condon) were ambivalent and funny in a way that was trashy yet liberating.

Technique is hardly worth talking about unless it's used for something worth doing: that's why most of the theorizing about the new art of television commercials is such nonsense. The effects are impersonal — dexterous, sometimes clever, but empty of art. It's because of their emptiness that commercials call so much attention to their camera angles and quick cutting — which is why people get impressed by "the art" of it. Movies are now often made in terms of what television viewers have learned to settle for. Despite a great deal that is spoken and written about young people responding visually, the influence of TV is to make movies visually less imaginative and complex. Television is a very noisy medium and viewers listen, while getting used to a poor quality of visual reproduction, to the absence of visual detail, to visual obviousness and overemphasis on simple compositions, and to atrociously simplified and distorted color systems. The shifting camera styles, the movement, and the fast cutting of a film like *Finian's Rainbow* — one of the better big productions — are like the "visuals" of TV commercials, a disguise for static material, expressive of nothing so much as the need to keep you from getting bored and leaving. Men are now beginning their careers as directors by working on commercials — which, if one cares to speculate on it, may be almost a one-sentence résumé of the future of American motion pictures.

I don't mean to suggest that there is not such a thing as movie technique or that craftsmanship doesn't contribute to the pleasures of movies, but simply that most audiences, if they enjoy the acting and the "story" or the theme or the funny lines, don't notice or care about how well or how badly the movie is made, and because they don't care, a hit makes a director a "genius" and everybody talks about his brilliant technique (*i.e.,* the technique of grabbing an audience). In the brief history of movies there has probably never been so astonishingly gifted a large group of directors as the current Italians, and not just the famous ones or Pontecorvo (*The Battle of Algiers*) or Francesco Rosi (*The Moment of Truth*) or the young prodigies, Bertolucci and Bellocchio, but dozens of others, men like Elio Petri (*We Still Kill the Old Way*) and Carlo Lizzani (*The Violent Four*). *The Violent Four* shows more understanding of visual movement and more talent for moviemaking than anything that's been made in America this year. But could one tell people who are not crazy, dedicated moviegoers to go see it? I'm not sure, although I enjoyed the film enormously, because *The Violent Four* is a gangster genre picture. And it may be a form of aestheticism — losing sight of what people go to movies for, and particularly what they go to foreign movies for — for a critic to say, "His handling of crowds and street scenes is superb," or, "It has a great semi-documentary chase sequence." It does, but the movie is basically derived from our old gangster movies, and beautifully made as it is, one would have a hard time convincing educated people to go see a movie that features a stunning performance by Gian Maria Volonte which is based on Paul Muni and James Cagney. Presumably they want something different from movies than a genre picture that offers images of modern urban decay and is smashingly directed. If a movie is interesting primarily in terms of technique then it isn't worth talking about except to students who can learn from seeing how a good director works. And to talk about a movie like *The Graduate* in terms of movie technique is really a bad joke. Technique at this level is not of any aesthetic importance; it's not the ability to achieve what you're after but the skill to find something acceptable. One must talk about a film like this in terms of what audiences enjoy it for or one is talking gibberish — and might as well be analyzing the "art" of commercials. And for the greatest movie artists where there is a unity of technique and subject, one doesn't need to talk about technique much because it has been subsumed in the art. One doesn't want to talk about how Tolstoi got his effects but about the work itself. One doesn't want to talk about how Jean Renoir does it; one wants to talk about what he has done. One can try to separate it all out, of course, distinguish form and content for purposes of analysis. But that is a secondary, analytic function, a scholarly function, and hardly needs to be done explicitly in criticism. Taking it apart is far less important than trying to see it whole. The critic shouldn't need to tear a work apart to demonstrate that he knows how it was put together. The important thing is to convey what is new and beautiful in the work, not how it was made — which is more or less implicit.

Just as there are good actors — possibly potentially great actors — who have never become big stars because they've just never been lucky enough to get the roles they needed (Brian Keith is a striking example) there are good directors who never got the scripts and the casts that could make their reputations. The question people ask when they consider going to a movie is not "How's it made?" but "What's it about?" and that's a perfectly legitimate question. (The next question — sometimes the first — is generally, "Who's in it?" and that's a good, honest question, too.) When you're at a movie, you don't have to believe in it to enjoy it but you do have to be interested. (Just as you have to be interested in the human material, too. Why should you go see *another* picture with James Stewart?) I don't want to see another samurai epic in exactly the same way I never want to read *Kristin Lavransdatter.* Though it's conceivable that a truly great movie director could make any subject interesting, there are few such artists working in movies and if they did work on unpromising subjects I'm not sure we'd really enjoy the results even if we did *admire* their artistry. (I recognize the greatness of sequences in several films by Eisenstein but it's a rather cold admiration.) The many brilliant Italian directors who are working within a commercial framework on crime and action movies are obviously not going to be of any great interest unless they get a chance to work on a subject we care about.

Ironically the Czech successes here (*The Shop on Main Street, Loves of a Blonde, Closely Watched Trains*) are acclaimed for their techniques, which are fairly simple and rather limited, when it's obviously their human concerns and the basic modesty and decency of their attitudes plus a little barnyard humor which audiences respond to. They may even respond partly because of the *simplicity* of the techniques.

IV

When we are children, though there are categories of films we don't like — documentaries generally (they're too much like education) and, of course, movies especially designed for children — by the time we can go on our own we have learned to avoid them. Children are often put down by adults when the children say they enjoyed a particular movie; adults who are short on empathy are quick to point out aspects of the plot or theme that the child didn't understand, and it's easy to humiliate a child in this way. But it is one of the glories of eclectic arts like opera and movies that they include so many possible kinds and combinations of pleasure. One may be enthralled by Leontyne Price in *La Forza del Destino* even if one hasn't boned up on the libretto, or entranced by *The Magic Flute* even if one has boned up on the libretto, and a movie may be enjoyed for many reasons that have little to do with the story or the subtleties (if any) of theme or character. Unlike "pure" arts which are often defined in terms of what only they can do, movies are open and unlimited. Probably everything that can be done in movies can be done some other way, but — and this is what's so miraculous and so expedient about them — they can do almost anything any other art can do (alone or in combination) and they can take on some of the functions of exploration, of journalism, of anthropology, of almost any branch of knowledge as well. We go to the movies for the variety of what they can provide, and for their marvelous ability to give us easily and inexpensively (and usually painlessly) what we can get from other arts also. They are a wonderfully *convenient* art.

Movies are used by cultures where they are foreign films in a much more primitive way than in their own; they may be enjoyed as travelogues or as initiations into how others live or in ways we might not even guess. The sophisticated and knowledgeable moviegoer is likely to forget how new and how amazing the different worlds up there once seemed to him, and to forget how much a child reacts to, how many elements he is taking in, often for the first time. And even adults who have seen many movies may think a movie is "great" if it introduces them to unfamiliar subject matter; thus many moviegoers react as naïvely as children to *Portrait of Jason* or *The Queen.* They think they're wonderful. The oldest plots and corniest comedy bits can be full of wonder for a child, just as the freeway traffic in a grade Z melodrama can be magical to a villager who has never seen a car. A child may enjoy even a movie like *Jules and Jim* for its sense of fun, without comprehending it as his parents do, just as we may enjoy an Italian movie as a sex comedy although in Italy it is considered social criticism or political satire. Jean-Luc Godard liked the movie of *Pal Joey,* and I suppose that a miserable American movie musical like *Pal Joey* might look good in France because I can't think of a single good dance number performed by French dancers in a French movie. The French enjoy what they're unable to do and we enjoy the French studies of the pangs of adolescent love that would be corny if made in Hollywood. A movie like *The Young Girls of Rochefort* demonstrates how even a gifted Frenchman who adores American musicals misunderstands their conventions. Yet it would be as stupid to say that the director Jacques Demy couldn't love American musicals because he doesn't understand their conventions as to tell a child he couldn't have liked *Planet of the Apes* because he didn't get the jokey references to the Scopes trial.

Every once in a while I see an anthropologist's report on how some pre-literate tribe reacts to movies; they may, for example, be disturbed about where the actor has gone when he leaves the movie frame, or they may respond with enthusiasm to the noise and congestion of big-city life which in the film story are meant to show the depths of depersonalization to which we are sinking, but which they find funny or very jolly indeed. Different people and different cultures enjoy movies in very different ways. A few years ago the new "tribalists" here responded to the gaudy fantasies of *Juliet of the Spirits* by using the movie to turn on. A few had already made a trip of 8½, but *Juliet,* which was, conveniently and perhaps not entirely accidentally, in electric, psychedelic color, caught on because of it. (The color was awful, like in bad MGM musicals — so one may wonder about the quality of the trips.)

The new tribalism in the age of the media is not necessarily the enemy of commercialism; it is a direct outgrowth of commercialism and its ally, perhaps even its instrument. If a movie has enough clout, reviewers and columnists who were bored are likely to give it another chance, until on the second or third viewing, they discover that it affects them "viscerally" — and a big expensive movie is likely to do just that. *2001* is said to have caught on with youth (which can make it happen); and it's said that the movie will stone you — which is meant to be a recommendation. Despite a few dissident voices — I've heard it said, for example, that *2001* "gives you a bad trip because the visuals don't go with the music" — the promotion has been remarkably effective with students. "The tribes" tune in so fast that college students thousands of miles apart "have heard" what a great trip *2001* is before it has even reached their city.

Using movies to go on a trip has about as much connection with the art of the film as using one of those Doris Day–Rock Hudson jobs for ideas on how to redecorate your home — an earlier way of stoning yourself. But it is relevant to an understanding of movies to try to separate out, for purposes of discussion at least, how we may personally *use* a film — to learn how to dress or how to speak more elegantly or how to make a grand entrance or even what kind of coffee maker we wish to purchase, or to take off from the movie into a romantic fantasy or a trip — from what makes it a good movie or a poor one, because, of course, we can *use* poor films as easily as good ones, perhaps *more* easily for such non-aesthetic purposes as shopping guides or aids to tripping.

V

We generally become interested in movies because we *enjoy* them and what we enjoy them for has little to do with what we think of as art. The movies we respond to, even in childhood, don't have the same values as the official culture supported at school and in the middle-class home. At the movies we get low life and high life, while David Susskind and the moralistic reviewers chastise us for not patronizing what they think we should, "realistic" movies that would be good for us — like *A Raisin in the Sun,* where we could learn the lesson that a Negro family can be as dreary as a white family. Movie audiences will take a lot of garbage, but it's pretty hard to make us queue up for pedagogy. At the movies we want a different kind of truth, something that surprises us and registers with us as funny or accurate or maybe amazing, maybe even amazingly beautiful. We get little things even in mediocre and terrible movies — José Ferrer sipping his booze through a straw in *Enter Laughing,* Scott Wilson's hard scary all-American-boy-you-can't-reach face cutting through the pretensions of *In Cold Blood* with all its fancy bleak cinematography. We got, and still have embedded in memory, Tony Randall's surprising depth of feeling in *The Seven Faces of Dr. Lao,* Keenan Wynn and Moyna Macgill in the lunch-counter sequence of *The Clock,* John W. Bubbles on the dance floor in *Cabin in the Sky,* the inflection Gene Kelly gave to the line, "I'm a rising young man" in *DuBarry Was a Lady,* Tony Curtis saying "avidly" in *Sweet Smell of Success.* Though the director may have been responsible for releasing it, it's the human material we react to most and remember longest. The art of the performers stays fresh for us, their beauty as beautiful as ever. There are so many kinds of things we get — the hangover sequence wittily designed for the CinemaScope screen in *The Tender Trap,* the atmosphere of the newspaper offices in *The Luck of Ginger Coffey,* the automat gone mad in *Easy Living.* Do we need to lie and shift things to false terms — like those who have to say Sophia Loren is a great actress as if her *acting* had made her a star? Wouldn't we rather watch her than better actresses because she's so incredibly charming and because she's probably the greatest model the world has ever known? There are great moments — Angela Lansbury singing "Little Yellow Bird" in *Dorian Gray.* (I don't think I've ever had a friend who didn't also treasure that girl and that song.) And there are absurdly right little moments — in *Saratoga Trunk* when Curt Bois says to Ingrid Bergman, "You're very beautiful," and she says, "Yes, isn't it lucky?" And those things have closer relationships to art than what the schoolteachers told us was true and beautiful. Not that the works we studied in school weren't often great (as we discovered *later*) but that what the teachers told us to admire them for (and if current texts are any indication, are still telling students to admire them for) was generally so false and prettified and moralistic that what might have been moments of pleasure in them, and what might have been cleansing in them, and subversive, too, had been coated over.

Because of the photographic nature of the medium and the cheap admission prices, movies took their impetus not from the desiccated imitation European high culture, but from the peep show, the Wild West show, the music hall, the comic strip — from what was coarse and common. The early Chaplin two-reelers still look surprisingly lewd, with bathroom jokes and drunkenness and hatred of work and proprieties. And the Western shoot-'em-ups certainly weren't the schoolteachers' notions of art — which in my school days, ran more to didactic poetry and "perfectly proportioned" statues and which over the years have progressed through nice stories to "good taste" and "excellence" — which may be more poisonous than homilies and dainty figurines because then you had a clearer idea of what you were up against and it was easier to fight. And this, of course, is what we were running away from when we went to the movies. All week we longed for Saturday afternoon and sanctuary — the anonymity and impersonality of sitting in a theater, just enjoying ourselves, not having to be responsible, not having to be "good." Maybe you just want to look at people on the screen and know they're not looking back at you, that they're not going to turn on you and criticize you.

Perhaps the single most intense pleasure of moviegoing is this nonaesthetic one of escaping from the responsibilities of having the proper responses required of us in our official (school) culture. And yet this is probably the best and most common basis for developing an aesthetic sense because responsibility to pay attention and to appreciate is anti-art, it makes us too anxious for pleasure, too bored for response. Far from supervision and official culture, in the darkness at the movies where nothing is asked of us and we are left alone, the liberation from duty and constraint allows us to develop our own aesthetic responses. Unsupervised enjoyment is probably not the only kind there is but it may feel like the only kind. Irresponsibility is part of the pleasure of all art; it is the part the schools cannot recognize. I don't like to buy "hard tickets" for a "road show" movie because I hate treating a movie as an occasion. I don't want to be pinned down days in advance; I enjoy the casualness of moviegoing — of going in when I feel like it, when I'm in the mood for a movie. It's the feeling of freedom from respectability we have always enjoyed at the movies that is carried to an extreme by American International Pictures and the Clint Eastwood Italian Westerns; they are stripped of cultural values. We may want more from movies than this negative virtue but we know the feeling from childhood moviegoing when we loved the gamblers and pimps and the cons' suggestions of muttered obscenities as the guards walked by. The appeal of movies was in the details of crime and high living and wicked cities and in the language of toughs and urchins; it was in the dirty smile of the city girl who lured the hero away from Janet Gaynor. What draws us to movies in the first place, the opening into other, forbidden or surprising, kinds of experience, and the vitality and corruption and irreverence of that experience are so direct and immediate and have so little connection with what we have been taught is art that many people feel more secure, feel that their tastes are becoming more cultivated when they begin to *appreciate* foreign films. One foundation executive told me that he was quite upset that his teen-agers had chosen to go to *Bonnie and Clyde* rather than with him to *Closely Watched Trains.* He took it as a sign of lack of maturity. I think his kids made an honest choice, and not only because *Bonnie and Clyde* is the better movie, but because it is closer to us, it has some of the qualities of direct involvement that make us care about movies. But it's understandable that it's easier for us, as Americans, to see *art* in foreign films than in our own, because of how we, as Americans, think of art. Art is still what teachers and ladies and foundations believe in, it's civilized and refined, cultivated and serious, cultural, beautiful, European, Oriental: it's what America isn't, and it's especially what American movies are not. Still, if those kids had chosen *Wild in the Streets* over *Closely Watched Trains* I would think that was a sound and honest choice, too, even though *Wild in the Streets* is in most ways a terrible picture. It connects with their lives in an immediate even if a grossly frivolous way, and if we don't go to movies for excitement, if, even as children, we accept the cultural standards of refined adults, if we have so little drive that we accept "good taste," then we will probably never really begin to care about movies at all. We will become like those people who "may go to American movies sometimes to relax" but when they want "A little more" from a movie, are delighted by how colorful and artistic Franco Zeffirelli's *The Taming of the Shrew* is, just as a couple of decades ago they were impressed by *The Red Shoes,* made by Powell and Pressburger, the Zeffirellis of their day. Or, if they like the cozy feeling of uplift to be had from mildly whimsical movies about timid people, there's generally a *Hot Millions* or something musty and faintly boring from Eastern Europe — one of those movies set in World War II but so remote from our ways of thinking that it seems to be set in World War I. Afterward, the moviegoer can feel as decent and virtuous as if he'd spent an evening visiting a deaf old friend of the family. It's a way of taking movies back into the approved culture of the schoolroom — into gentility — and the voices of schoolteachers and reviewers rise up to ask why America can't make such movies.

The New Rock

Frank Zappa

Rock music is a necessary element of contemporary society. It is functional. It is healthy and valid artistically. It is also educational (how to ask a girl for a date, what love is like). It has all the answers to what your mother and father won't tell you. It is also a big business. This is a brief history of rock and its relationship to our society.

LO: PFF PFF. A nifty questionnaire to get you interested so you'll read the rest of the article:

Part One: The 50s

1. Who remembers beer? White port and lemon juice? For 10 points, what was the name of the guy in your school who used to buy your juice for parties . . .

2. Who remembers making out and getting hot? For 10 points, how old were you when it happened . . .

3. Who remembers duck tails, peggers, leather jackets, bunny shoes, brogans, tight sweaters, teardrops, full skirts with a million starchy petticoats, Sir Guy shirts and khakis? For 10 points, how much did you pay for your St. Christopher medallion . . .

4. Who remembers gang fights, tire chains, boys with razor blades in the toes of their wedgies, girls with razor blades in their hair, blood and sickening crunch? For 10 points, tell why the cops were afraid of your gang . . .

Part Two: The 60s

5. Who remembers speed? Smoke? Acid? Transcendental meditation? For 10 points, name your connection or guru . . .

6. Who remembers getting stoned and having an orgy? For 10 points, how old were you when you learned you were incapable of relating to others in a tender, personal way and finally discovered you had become asexual . . .

7. Who remembers electric hair, bell bottoms, plastic jackets, sandals, high boots, bulky knit sweaters, Guccis, miniskirts, De Voss shirts and velvet pants? For 10 points, look around the house, find your beads and bells, and recite Hare Krishna without laughing . . .

8. Who remembers demonstrations, truncheons, Mace, police dogs, the Pentagon, Century City, blood and sickening crunch? For 10 points, tell why you were afraid to cut your hair, infiltrate the establishment, and do it the easy way . . .

Our present state of sociosexual enlightenment is, to a certain extent, attributable to the evolution of rock and vice versa. Our story begins back in . . . the good old days, at the recreation centers, no Levis or capris please. "School functions" and "teen hops" were real swell and keen and acceptable to Mom and Dad. They were also dull unless you liked to dance a fox-trot as the high school swing band fumbled through an evening of Combo Orks and reprocessed Glenn Miller. The kids would be holding on to each other desperately and sweating. The chaperon would come along and say, "seven inches apart please," and hold a sawed-off ruler between you and the girl.

Society was very repressed, sexually, and dancing was a desperate attempt to get a little physical contact with the opposite sex. Free love, groupies, the Plaster Casters of Chicago and such bizarre variants as the G.T.O.s of Laurel Canyon in L.A. didn't exist then. Preoccupation with sexual matters accounted for a disproportionate amount of the daily conscious thought process and diverted a lot of energy from school work.

This, and the low quality of teaching in many schools, caused kids to seek education in the streets. Youth gangs with marvelous names and frightening reputations cruised the streets at night, searching for ways to compensate for the lack of sexually approachable girls. Vandalism and assorted manglings became acceptable substitutes for "teen sex." Young men would compete, like cowboy gunfighters, to be "the baddest cat." This dubious honor would generally entitle its bearer to boss the gang and, in some instances, preferential treatment from those few daring girls who would go "all the way."

Parents, unfortunately, have a tendency to misunderstand, misinterpret, and, worst of all, ridicule patterns of behavior which seem foreign to them. When they noticed a growing interest among teen-agers in matters pertaining to the pleasure-giving functions of the body, they felt threatened. Mom and Dad were sexually uninformed and inhibited (a lot of things wrong with society today are directly attributable to the fact that the people who make the laws are sexually maladjusted) and they saw no reason why their kids should be raised differently. (Why should those dirty teen-agers have all the fun?) Sex is for making babies and it makes your body misshapen and ugly afterward and let's not talk about it shall we?

The Big Note: Digression I

In the Abnuceals Emuukha Electric Symphony Orchestra Album *Lumpy Gravy* there is a section on side two where several unidentified characters discuss the origins of the universe. One of the characters explains the concept of the Big Note: everything in the universe is composed basically of vibrations — light is a vibration, sound is a vibration, atoms are composed of vibrations — and all these vibrations just might be harmonics of some incomprehensible fundamental cosmic tone.

How important is sound? I participated in a conversation recently with Herbie Cohen (our manager) about rumors of a government research project. The project, it seems, has been going on for several years. What does sound do to plants? According to Herbie, a field of corn increased its yield — the individual ears even got bigger — because the research team set up loudspeakers in the field and pumped in some music. According to Herbie, the next step is to find out what kind of music the vegetables like the best.

The ways in which sound affects the human organism are myriad and subtle. Why does the sound of Eric Clapton's guitar give one girl a sensation which she describes as "Bone Conduction"? Would she still experience Bone Conduction if Eric, using the same extremely loud thick tone, played nothing but Hawaiian music? Which is more important: the timbre (color-texture) of a sound, the succession of intervals which make up the melody, the harmonic support (chords) which tells your ear "what the melody means" (Is it major or minor or neutral or what), the volume at which the sound is heard, the volume at which the sound is produced, the distance from source to ear, the density of the sound, the number of sounds per second or fraction thereof . . . and so on? Which of these would be the most important element in an audial experience which gave you a pleasurable sensation? An erotic sensation? Look at kids in school, tapping their feet, beating with their fingers. People try, unconsciously, to be in tune with their environment. In a variety of ways, even the most "unconcerned" people make attempts to "tune up" with their God. Hal Zeiger (one of the first big promoters of rock entertainment during the 50s) says, "I knew that there was a big thing here that was basic, that was big, that had to get bigger. I realized that this music got through to the youngsters because the bit beat matched the great rhythms of the human body. I understood that. I knew it and I knew there was nothing that anyone could do to knock that out of them. And I further knew that they would carry this with them the rest of their lives."

Rock-around-the-Clock

In my days of flaming youth I was extremely suspect of any rock music played by white people. The sincerity and emotional intensity of their performances, when they sang about boyfriends and girlfriends and breaking up, etc., was nowhere when I compared it to my high school Negro R&B heroes like Johnny Otis, Howlin' Wolf and Willie Mae Thornton.

But then I remember going to see *Blackboard Jungle.* When the titles flashed up there on the screen Bill Haley and his Comets started blurching "One Two Three O'Clock, Four O'Clock Rock. . . ." It was the loudest rock sound kids had ever heard at that time. I remember being inspired with awe. In cruddy little teen-age rooms across America, kids had been huddling around old radios and cheap record players listening to the "dirty music" of their life style. ("Go in your room if you wanna listen to that crap . . . and turn the volume all the way down.") But in the theater, watching *Blackboard Jungle,* they couldn't tell you to turn it down. I didn't care if Bill Haley was white or sincere . . . he was playing the Teen-Age National Anthem and it was so LOUD I was jumping up and down. *Blackboard Jungle,* not even considering the story line (which had the old people winning in the end) represented a strange sort of "endorsement" of the teen-age cause: "They have made a movie about us, therefore, we exist. . . ."

Responding like dogs, some of the kids began to go for the throat. Open rebellion. The early public dances and shows which featured rock were frowned upon by the respectable parents of the community. They did everything they could do to make it impossible for these events to take place. They did everything they could to shield their impressionable young ones from the ravages of this vulgar new craze. (Hal Zeiger: "They did everything they could to make sure their children were not moved erotically by Negroes.")

From the very beginning, the real reason Mr. & Mrs. Clean White America objected to this music was the fact that it was performed by black people. There was always the danger that one night — maybe in the middle of the summer, in a little pink party dress — Janey or Suzy might be overwhelmed by the lewd, pulsating jungle rhythms and do something to make their parents ashamed.

Parents, in trying to protect their offspring from whatever danger they imagined to be lurking within the secret compartments of this new musical vehicle, actually helped to shove them in front of it whereupon they were immediately run over. The attitude of parents helped to create a climate wherein the usage of rock music (as a pacifier or perhaps anesthetic experience) became very necessary. Parents offered nothing to their children that could match the appeal of rock. It was obvious to the kids that anyone who did not like (or at least attempt to understand) rock music, had a warped sense of values. To deny rock music its place in the society was to deny sexuality. Any parent who tried to keep his child from listening to or participating in this musical ritual was, in the eyes of the child, trying to castrate him.

There was much resistance on the part of the music industry itself. (Hal Zeiger: "I remember a conversation with M — D —, a very famous song-writer, who has written many of our all-time favorites, wherein he chided me for being involved with this kind of music and entertainment and I said to him, 'M —, you are just upset because it has been discovered and revealed that a song written by some young colored child in a slum area can capture the fancy of the American public more effectively than a song written by you, who lives in a Beverly Hills mansion.' ")

Every year you could hear people saying, "I know it's only a phase . . . it'll poop out pretty soon. The big bands will come back." Year after year, the death of rock was predicted . . . a few times, as I recall, it was even *officially* announced: "Rock 'n' roll is dead, calypso is all the rage. . . ."

Oh, Those Great Rhythms: Digression II

The function of the drums in a rock music ensemble is to keep the beat. ("It has a good beat . . . I give it 10 points, Dick.") On early R&B records, the drum part was usually executed with brushes. All the arrangements required, generally, was a dull thud on the second and fourth pulse of the bar. There were very few "breaks" or "fills." When the drum fill (a short percussion outburst, usually at a cadence or resting point of a musical phrase) became popular in rock arrangements, it most often took the form of groups of triplets (three-note rhythmic figures, squeezed into the space of two beats . . . sounding like: ya-da-da ya-da-da ya-da-da ya-da-da-whomp). For a while, during the mid-50s, it seemed like every record produced had one or more fills of this nature in it. Eventually, with the improvements in studios and recording techniques, the drummers began to use sticks on the sessions and the cadence fills became more elaborate but, before and after the fill, the drummer's job was still to keep the beat . . . that same old crappy beat . . . the beat that made the kids hop around and scream and yell and buy records. A long process of rhythmic evolution has taken place since the early 50s. It is laughable now to think of that dull thud on the second and fourth as lewd and pulsating.

Green Visors

Hal Zeiger: "The problem at the time was basically this: trying to make the music acceptable, or, to try to get the right to expose it, and that took some doing. I knew the kids were listening to the radio stations . . . it was just a matter of how to merchandise this to get their dollars, too. I told Bill Graham (founder of the Fillmore and former manager of the Jefferson Airplane), 'You've got to understand when these things are underground, that's one thing. But the minute it goes over ground, the minute, you see, it looks like money, everyone wants in.' "

So to make R&B acceptable, the big shots of the record industry hired a bunch of little men with cigars and green visors, to synthesize and imitate the work of the Negroes. The visor men cranked out phony white rock. Highly skilled couriers then delivered the goods to American Bandstand along with a lot of presents (tokens of their esteem) to Dick Clark for all his marvelous assistance in the crusade to jam these products down the kids' throats. Pat Boone was notable, too, for his humanistic activities (bleaching Little Richard and making him safe for teen-age consumption).

One of my favorite Negro R&B groups during the 50s was Hank Ballard and the Midnighters. Their work was some of the most important sociosexual true-to-life commentary of that era, for instance: *Stingy Little Thing* (a song in protest about girls who wouldn't "put out"), *Work with Me Annie,* and *Annie Had a Baby.* Songs like these got played on the air every once in a while — the kids would hear *Annie Had a Baby* and say, "Hey, here's a song about a girl getting pregnant," and rush to tune it in — but an official of the station (with teen-age children of his own to protect) would "lay a pink memo on it," and the song would sort of "disappear."

The visor men, meanwhile, were magically purifying all this stuff. *Work with Me Annie* ("Please don't cheat/Give me all my meat") through the wisdom of their craft became *Dance with Me, Henry* ("If you want romancin'/You better learn some dancin' ").

Vaseline

White rock overproduced and shiny, nearly slickened itself to death. (Remember *Fats Domino with Strings?*) The music industry was slumping a bit. Was this to be the end of rock? Were we doomed to a new era of country Vaseline? Then, just in the nick of time, Beatlemania. New hope. There they were: cute, safe, white. The kids took to them immediately. Their music had real energy; it was sympathetic to their life style. It was music made for young people by other young people. No green visors. It seemed to radiate a secret message: "You can be free. You can get away with it. Look, we're doing it!"

I'm sure the kids never really believed all the Beatles wanted to do was *hold your hand.* And the girls were provided with "kissable closeups" (enlarged views of their idols' lips, teeth and gums) which they could kiss, touch, rub and/or hang on the bedroom wall. Girls forgot Elvis Presley. He was too greasy, too *heavy business:* sullen pouting and all that stuff.

The Beatles were huggable & cute & moptops & happy & positive. Beatlemania was fun to be involved in.

The record companies were at a loss to compete with the British threat. Zeiger relates another droll incident: "I remember Mike Maitland who was then vice president and sales manager of Capitol Records. He was decrying the fact that they couldn't get any hit singles, and I said to him, 'Well, Mike, the reason is because you have the wrong people working for you.' 'Well, what do you want me to do? Get some of these fellows with the tight pants to produce these records?' I said, 'Exactly. Two button records can't be produced by guys with three button suits. It's all a matter of buttons.' Look at Mike Maitland now. He's president of Warner Brothers Records and look at the kind of thing they're putting out . . . fellows with tight pants . . . or no pants . . . are producing the records.' "

72 Tracks and Itchykoo Park: Digression III

It might be interesting at this point to discuss the evolution of recording-studio techniques. In the very oldenest of days, the recording engineer's main function was to stand behind the singer holding him by the shoulders, and either push him forward or pull him away from a large funnel-shaped object attached to a bent pin or something that used to function as a primitive microphone to gather sounds to be transcribed on a wax cylinder.

During the early stages of R&B, most recording was done on very large acetate discs. Then came tape. Monaural recordings gave way to stereo . . . then to three-track . . . then four-track. Four-track recording was the "standard of the industry" for a while until some of those tight pants, no pants producers Zeiger mentioned put pressure on companies and manufacturers to obtain eight-track machines which would allow more creative freedom to the young musicians who were playing this wonderful new money-making form of music. Today, eight-track recording is common and the adventurous new breed of "pop experimenters" are hustling to get 12-track machines, 16-track machines, 24-track machines (the Beatles, I hear, are setting up a nifty studio with 72 tracks).

Audience Education

There seems to be a trend in today's music toward eclecticism. The people who make this music are examining a wide range of possible musical and nonmusical elements to incorporate into their bags. Through rock music, the audience is being exposed to an assortment of advanced musical and electronic techniques that five years ago might have sent them screaming into the street. Amazing breakthroughs have been made in the field of "audience education."

These improvements have been made almost against the will of the mass media. Suppression for racial and sexual reasons doesn't go on as much but radio stations still do not program progressive rock in proportion to the market which exists for it. Specific songs which seem most threatening to the established order don't get on radio and TV. Example: *Society's Child* by Janis Ian about interracial dating. (Mass media does more to keep Americans stupid than even the whole U.S. school system, that vast industry which cranks out trained consumers and technician-pawns for the benefit of other vast industries.) It is something of a paradox that companies which manufacture and distribute this art form (strictly for profit) might one day be changed or controlled by young people who were motivated to action by the products these companies sell.

The level of involvement with today's music is quite amazing. One example: Groupies. These girls, who devote their lives to pop music, feel they owe something personal to it, so they make the ultimate gesture of worship, human sacrifice. They offer their bodies to the music or its nearest personal representative, the pop musician. These girls are everywhere. It is one of the most amazingly beautiful products of the sexual revolution.

The Jimi Hendrix Phenomenon

Hendrix is one of the most revolutionary figures in today's pop culture, musically and sociologically. His success is a curious paradox in view of the historical prejudices outlined earlier.

Hendrix is 24 years old. He dropped out of a Seattle high school in the 11th grade. He was raised strictly by his parents: "They taught me to have manners." He is reasonably sincere and humble: "We are lucky to be listened to." He is apparently very happy with his commercial success. Partly because it allows him to act out some of his childhood fantasies (in his clothing, for instance): "I always wanted to be a cowboy or a *hadji baba* or the Prisoner of Zenda. . . ."

His strongest appeal is to the white female audience ranging in age from about 13 to 30, with the highest concentration of victims between 19 and 22. "I just carry advantages with me in my back pocket when I go off at a gig." His charisma also extends to a white male audience, 15 to 25.

He is realistic about his market appeal: "The black people probably talk about us like dogs . . . until we play." "When I see some of them in the street, they say, 'I see you got those two white boys with you.' . . . I try to explain to them about all this new music. I play them some records. First I play Cream . . . and when they say, 'Hey, that's great, who is that playing the guitar?', I tell them it's Eric Clapton and he's an Englishman. Then I might play them some of what we do. Sometimes they still think we're crazy."

Hendrix's music is very interesting. The sound of his music is extremely symbolic: orgasmic grunts, tortured squeals, lascivious moans, electric disasters and innumerable other audial curiosities are delivered to the sense mechanisms of the audience at an extremely high decibel level. In a live performance environment, it is impossible to merely listen to what the Hendrix group does . . . it eats you alive. (He is concerned about his live performance image: "I don't want everybody to solely think of us in a big flash of weaving and bobbing and groping and maiming and attacking and . . .")

In spite of his maiming and groping, etc., the female audience thinks of Hendrix as being beautiful (maybe just a little scary), but mainly very sexy. The male audience thinks of him as a phenomenal guitarist and singer. Boys will bring girls backstage for autographs. When signing their scraps of paper, shoulder blades, handbags and pants, Hendrix will frequently be asked: "Do you think of any particular girl while you're playing, or do you just think of sex itself?" Meanwhile, the boys will ask, "What kind of equipment do you use? Do you get high before you go on stage?"

The boys seem to enjoy the fact that their girl friends are turned on to Hendrix sexually; very few resent his appeal and show envy. They seem to give up and say: "He's got it, I ain't got it, I don't know if I'll ever get it . . . but if I do, I wanna be just like him, because he's really got it." They settle for vicarious participation and/or buy a Fender Stratocaster, an Arbiter Fuzz Face, a Vox Wah-Wah Pedal, and four Marshall amplifiers.

The Gas Co., The Electric Co. & The Music Co.: Digression IV

The loud sounds and bright lights of today are tremendous indoctrination tools. Is it possible to modify the human chemical structure with the right combination of frequencies? (Frequencies you can't hear are manifested as frequencies you can see in a light show.) Can prolonged exposure to mixed media produce mutations? If the right kind of beat makes you tap your foot, what kind of beat makes you curl your fist and strike? Do you cry if the violin is playing the melody *molto vibrato?*

Manifestations of response to music will vary according to the character of the music and the audience. Swooning to Kay Kyser is roughly equivalent to squealing for the Monkees or drooling over Jimi Hendrix. In each case the *swoonee, squealee,* or *droolee* is responding to the music in a manner which he feels is reasonably acceptable by current social standards in his peer group.

If you were drunk, and it was the middle of summer, Saturday night about 11:30, and you had your comfortable clothes on, and you were in a small beer joint dancing, and it's crowded (temperature about 82°), and the local Rock & Roll combo (Ruben and The Jets) is playing *Green Onions* (or something that sounds just like it . . . all full of parallel fifths moving monotonously through a root progression I, IIb, IV, IIIb . . . or something like that, over & over again), and the guitar player goes to take a solo and stomps his *fuzz-tone* into action and turns his amplifier all the way up so his guitar squeals and screams and sounds absolutely vicious, and he bends and mangles the strings & starts to really get it on, gyrating and going totally berserk and playing his ass off and everythin' . . . if you were drunk, and all this was going on, and you were out there dancing and sweating and really *feeling* the music (every muscle & fiber of your being, etc., etc.) and the music suddenly got louder and more vicious . . . louder and viciouser than you could ever imagine (and you danced harder and got sweaty & feverish) and got your unsuspecting self worked up into a total frenzy, bordering on electric Buddha nirvana total acid freak cosmic integration (one with the universe), and you were drunk & hot & not really in control of your body or your senses (you are possessed by the music), and all of a sudden the music gets EVEN LOUDER . . . and not only that: IT GETS FASTER & YOU CAN'T BREATHE (But you can't stop either; it's impossible to stop) and you know you can't black out because it feels too good . . . I ask you now, if you were drunk and all this stuff is happening all over the place and somebody (with all the best intentions in the world) MADE YOU STOP so he could ask you this question: *"Is a force this powerful to be overlooked by a society that needs all the friends it can get?"* Would you listen?

Shaman Songs

Gene Fowler

Hunting Song *a preface*

When the moon
stays into morning
when the river
calls loudest the dawn
it is our time to hunt
And we hunt
the first bear

Speak Shaman   How do we find
the bear

With the coming of night
build a fire
that you may see my words
With the coming of night
dance by the fire
that you may feel my words

We see Shaman   We see
your words
by the fire
We dance Shaman   We feel
your words
by the fire

Your bodies grow large
My words are flesh
on your limbs

We dance the flesh

Your skins grow shaggy
My words are fur
against the cold

We dance the fur

Your scent grows keen
My words are winds
with their secrets

We dance the scent

I

You run on fours
Run true on fours
My words are bears
with their secrets
We dance the bear
We dance the bear

Now you know the bear
We dance the bear

You know his ancestors
We dance the bear

You know his trails
We dance the bear

When the moon
stays into morning
you will catch the bear

My ancestors were shamans.
But i am not my ancestors.
I am shaman
to a tribe recently come.
A tribe with gas turbines.
A tribe with horror of Being
homosexual.
A tribe with a bomb.
A tribe with fear of the Other.
Foreign man.
Black man.
Sexed man.
High man.
Other.
A tribe with fear of the Other.
I wear animal skins
and cast huge shadows on the wall
And the old men sit in council,
sit at their fire.
They wonder
if i am their shaman.
Or if i am the Other.

2

on taking a coal from the fire
in naked fingers

The word
is in the hand.
Under the moon
in the hand.
At the head of the valley
in the hand.
It glows in the hand.
Here!
Look here
in the hand.
Look at the word
in the hand.
It glows.
A great translucence
in the hand.
Go thru the translucence
in the hand.
Into the world
in the hand.
The coals glow
in my fire.
Are words
for the hand.

3

You calld me, always, to heal you
when sickness came to you.

You calld me, always, to read you
the best path for the hunt.

Now you build
your fires big

but your skins
are not warm.

Now your pots
are empty

but you seek
no new game.

You calld me, always, to help you
and my magic was strong.

You calld me, always, to help you
when trouble came to you.

Then you said
my gods ate

what you could
not yet spare.

Then my songs
made you stand

where the storm
might come out.

You calld me, no more, to heal you
when sickness came to you.

You calld me, no more, to read you
the best path for the hunt.

Near my tent, you drop your head.
At my fire, your smile is stiff.
Still, you do not call.

4

I will journey
to a place where i may see
what each day we see.
These old friends will be
shaped and colord fires.
Heat and light will burn
within my eye.

I will journey
to a place where i may see
what we do not ever see.
I will write names in my blood.
When heard, the names will burn
within your eye.

I will journey
to a place where i may see
that which there is to see.
There, your eye and mine
will become a single eye.
That which i see will burn
as our eye.

5

I have journeyd.
I return with scarrd flesh.
I return with tattoos burnd
in my meat.

I have journeyd.
Now i sit at my tribal fire.
I sit and watch tattoos dance
on my skin.

I have journeyd.
Now i let you watch my flesh.
I let you watch stories unfold
on my surface.

I have journeyd.
Now i try to relate my stories.
You are lost in dancing images
on my corpse.

I have journeyd.
Let me return.

6

I have shown you
coals in the fire.

Words in the soul.

Look at one coal,
a single coal taken

up into my fingers,
safely in the flesh.

Look
deeply into the coal
til the eyes sting
til the eyes cry out.

Move close to the coal.
The flame does not flare
but it has not coold.
It has grown in heat.

See
the deep rooted fires.
See
the dark private places.

Move down into the coal.
Feel the flesh as flame.

Where is this place?
What are the names?

Who are the shapes
moving about you?

Who the live dark spots,
the living white flame?

Whose flesh is flame?
Where is your eye?

7

It is the woman who grows things.
He who would make the rain fall
must be as the woman.

The body must be cut and turnd.
The dark and moist soil of night
brought to the sun.

He who would make the rain fall
must walk unclothd in the night
must be as the woman.

Hold the seed in careful fingers.
Seed that comes from every field
with its songs told.

Seed that comes from every field
must be planted in the bright sun
and left in the night.

The seeded and moist soil of night
will call and join the sun and rain.
The moon will feed you.

8

The eye is clear with the dawn.
The nostrils are wide in the wind.
The legs are strong from their sleep.
The arms that reach for the sun
reach far over mountains.

Run fast as the deer.
Taste the wind as the rabbit.
Be strong as the bear.
See with the eagle's glint.
Hear as the lynx hears.

The known trails are dry and fast.
The new trails are wet for tracks.
The game is unrested, out and moving.
The legs that reach for the sun
reach far over mountains.

Trail as the jackal.
Change rivers as the beaver.
Strike slyly as the weasel.
Strike fast as the rattler.
Steal as the crow steals.

Bring our tribe the needed meat
sighting the cooking fires from far
the night growing behind you.

9

four invocations to fish

i

Night's wing hides the sun.

O, dark fish run fast
thru cold streams and rivers
that prowl in raven's house.

Dance in white waters.
Become many in black waters.

Become many and dance.

I will carry stones and earth
to mouths of rivers and streams
make deltas, make shallow places.

If the waters are made shallow
the fish must run near my hand.

O, dark fish run hard
into my quick hand.

ii

Night's wing falls
opens a thunder of sunlight.

O, bright fish run fast
thru spotted streams and rivers
that walk in long grasses.

Dance in light waters.
Become many in dark waters.

Become many and dance.

I will wade into the waters
til the two parts of my body
walk side by side.
I will catch the fish
if he does not know where i am.

O, bright fish run hard
into my quick hand.

iii

The raven and the golden hawk
have swallowed one another.

The birds of the sky are gone.
They took the sky with them.

I walk where day and night
do not embrace as lovers.

Many shades of day follow
and there is no beginning
and there is no end.

I wake and it is not light.
I sleep and it is not dark.

My only hope to find the day
my only hope to find the night
is to fish ghost waters, to fish
ghost waters for the coal fish.

I must fish with a dance.
I must fish with a song.
I fish for the night.
I fish for the day.

O, coal fish come burn
with light and dark places.

O, coal fish hurry now
into my quick hand.

I will reach into your
fiery heart, pull out
the sky

iv

I hide the day in one hand.
I hide the night in one hand.

I fish in eight directions.
I fish among the many suns.

The fish i hunt will run
the spotted sky

dance away in light waters
we call stars

become many in dark waters
we call distances.

All forms are his form.

O, terrible fish run hard
into my quick hand.

And your fire and dark
will be my flesh.

10

each man's lust is a cult

The rains are warm.
Our valleys and plains are almost green
—under blades of grass so slight
a blade is seen only by a keen eye
from the height of a walking man.

The strong women who have born sons are restless.
The ripe girls who have come thru the winter
watch the sun walk across the day.
Their eyes gentle as the wind, tender as the new grass.

The shaman's tent is prepared for fire and dances.
The ripe girls who have come thru the winter
watch the sun go away across the day.
The men look at the girls' throats and breasts in wonder.

Night lands, breathes
its strange winds around our closed tents, and fires
breathe their forms onto the circling hides.

Women must be torn from girls in a cruel stench
of dance filld flesh and full thighs.

On stretcht hides of the shaman's tent
woman Gods mimic the first wild dances
—thundercloud dancers in a sacrament.

Stolen tusk of a grandfather buffalo.
Unfalling carvd phallus of our tribe.
My corded arm is painted to the elbow
in the red rains of our Spring.

The sudden woman shine at the river, trickt
from winter with a dance's thundercloud rise.

The rains are warm, our valley and plains green.

11

O, thunder cloud
buffalo robe
of the sun—
how can you warm the sun?

The woman's belly
swells, summer melon
ready to split.
It warms my fingers

Dreamer's eye
a magic star, grows
in one night
to twice its old size.

Thru the grey cloud
lies a hidden sun
roasting potato—
no one to eat its warmth.

O, thunder cloud
roasting robe
of the sun—
i will rip you open.

12

We have made hawks
that fly
where no hawks have flown.

We have made hard sky
and look out at the rain.

We have made warm hides
from no animal yet slain.

We have made horses
that stride
as no horses ever known.

But, we are weak.
On our wounded plains, we are alone.

We have forgotten
the shape and cry of our bellies.

We have forgotten
the dances of our own faces,
the songs of our own voices.

We have forgotten
the chants of the souls
in our running feet.

Now, we remember.
In our weeping tents, we are alone.

13

shaman stands on the pre-dawn mountain, a dark mane on a thundercloud

i

One by one, all the old men of the tribe die, one by one, all the old women, all the young men,
all the young women,
even our children—
They all die.
The crows steal our eyes and fly beyond mountains.

The people of our tribe curl in trees, take on the color of the desert, and the desert begins
to swallow our plains, to pull down our mountains,
to burn our winds into blackend breaths.
Our skin and bones grow old as the desert, become rock of the desert.
Where our eyes lookt out, there are now dark caves in twisted desert trees.

Ha he ye ya he ha-a-aa
I walk among the trees.

Ha he ye ya he ha-a-aa
Faces are gone with ghosts.

Ha he ye ya he ha-a-aa
I bury them in trees.

Ha he ye ya he ha-a-aa
Sorrow shakes my knees.
I, too, find my tree.

Ha he ye ya ha-a-aa
Ha he ye ya he ha-a-aa

When the dawn fire rises, where will we be?

ii

You few, who have listend, must rise
and leave the tree.

You few, who have heard, must gather
your magic and go.

I cannot tell you
what you take with you

but, it burns, a coal
planted in your center.

I cannot tell you
the magic names you know

but, they wait, alive
planted in your center.

You few, who have listend, have known
my magic was strong.

You few, who have heard, will know
your magic is strong.

You have seen my gods
and given them more

than you had to spare.
You must grow your gods.

Skin and bones must become
rock, the ghost must rise

and fill you and burn.
You must grow your gods.

You few, who have listend, have calld
my magic and eaten.

You few, who have heard, must call
your magic and grow.

Near my tent, you lift your throat.
At my fire, your smile beckons.
Still, you must not call.

iii

When those who left the trees
have no more magic

when the ghosts who left
are in ghost trees

stronger shamans than i, shamans whose
eyes burn as suns
in the sky
shamans whose
eyes burn as stars
in the night
will come.

Their magic will stand on the shoulders
of my magic, my
strong magic.

Their magic will ride on my magic
as a tall warrior
rides, standing
on the shoulders of
a great stallion.

And brushing the ghost trees with
fingers warm as suns
those ghost shamans
will make the ghosts to walk
again in great tribes.

Bibliographical Index

John N. Bleibtreu spent twelve years as a stock broker, before his concern with the relationship between the sciences and the humanities led him to become a writer. He writes both fiction and non-fiction. Bleibtreu's most recent book is *Parable of the Beast* (1967).

William S. Burroughs (1914–), the grandson of the inventor of the Burroughs adding machine, was educated at Harvard and the University of Vienna. From his thirtieth to his forty-fifth year — until he was cured by apomorphine treatment in England — Burroughs was addicted to "junk" (opium and its derivatives). At various times in his life he has worked as a newspaper reporter, a private detective, an exterminator, and a bartender. He is best known as the author of two "novels," *The Naked Lunch* (1959) and *The Soft Machine* (1961), which portray an apocalypse of death, drugs, and sexual perversion. As a novelist, Burroughs has no use for plot or story. He sees himself as a machine, a recording instrument, that registers sensory impressions at the moment of writing and later scrambles these at random, or combines them randomly with the texts of other writers, using a "cut-out" or "fold-in" technique. Burroughs has been widely praised and imitated; he has also been called "a dirty-minded neurotic" with "a third-rate sensibility" who writes "bogus-highbrow filth."

Eldridge Cleaver (1935–) was born in Little Rock, Arkansas, and grew up in Los Angeles. Sentenced to prison (San Quentin and Folsom) in 1959 for assault with a deadly weapon and attempted murder, Cleaver was paroled after serving seven years, much of it spent in solitary confinement. In prison he used his time to study and to write many of the essays that later were included in *Soul on Ice* (1968). After his release from prison, he joined the Black Panther Party and became one of its most articulate voices as well as its Minister of Information. In 1968 Cleaver was a Peace and Freedom Party candidate for President, and in November of that same year he became a fugitive from justice when U.S. Supreme Court Justice Thurgood Marshall turned down an appeal to prevent the revoking of Cleaver's parole, and Cleaver, free on bond, failed to report to San Quentin as ordered.

Harvey G. Cox (1929–) a clergyman and theologian, is on the faculty of Harvard University. He was graduated from the University of Pennsylvania in 1951, received his B.D. *cum laude* from Yale in 1955 and his Ph.D. from Harvard in 1963. From 1955–1958 he was the director of religious activities at Oberlin College; from 1958–1962 he was a program associate for the American Baptist Home Mission Society; from 1962–1965 he was on the faculty at the Andover Newton Theological School. His books include *The Secular City* (1965) and *God's Revolution and Man's Responsibility* (1965).

Midge Decter, a member of *Harper's* staff since 1967, is from Minnesota. Articles by her include "The Peace Ladies," "The Young Divorcee," and "Sex, My Daughter and Me." She has contributed to other magazines, including *Commentary* and *Partisan Review.*

Martin Duberman (1930–), an historian, is currently on the faculty at Princeton University. He received his B.A. from Yale in 1952, his M.A. from Harvard in 1953, and his Ph.D., also from Harvard, in 1957. He received the 1962 Bancroft prize for his book *Charles Francis Adams, 1807–1866,* and the 1963–1964 Vernon Rice Award for *In White America.* His latest book is *James Russell Lowell* (1966).

Ralph Ellison (1914–), a distinguished American Negro writer, attended Tuskegee Institute from 1933–1936. He has taught Russian and American literature at Bard College, and creative writing and American studies at the University of Chicago, Rutgers, and Yale. Ellison set out early in life to be an artist; he studied jazz, classical music, and sculpture before he began his writing career in 1937, under the tutelage of Richard Wright. The novel *Invisible Man* (1952), for which Ellison received the National Book Award, is widely recognized as one of the best works of fiction published since World War II. The novel gives an ironic, surreal account of a black man who struggles to succeed in white America, remaining invisible, but finally accepting his social responsibility and his Negro identity. *Shadow and Act* (1964), a collection of essays is Ellison's "intellectual and spiritual autobiography."

James A. Emanuel (1921–) is Assistant Professor of English at City College of the City University of New York. Mr. Emanuel has published poetry and literary criticism, and has edited, with Theodore L. Gross, an anthology entitled *Dark Symphony: Negro Literature in America* (1968).

Lawrence Ferlinghetti (1919–), one of America's most popular poets, was educated at the University of North Carolina, Columbia University, and the Sorbonne. *Pictures of the Gone World* (1955) established his reputation as a Beat poet who writes of American life with trenchant and sardonic insight; *A Coney Island of the Mind* (1958) and *Starting from San Francisco* (1961) have confirmed that reputation. Ferlinghetti believes that the poet must be engaged and committed, that he must not abdicate his responsibility to society by concentrating merely on technique. In pursuit of that philosophy, Ferlinghetti has attempted to bring poetry to the public through his experiments with poetry and jazz and his frequent public readings. He is also well known as the owner of San Francisco's City Lights Books, a bookstore and publishing house prominent in the Beat movement of the 1950's. Through City Lights, Ferlinghetti has published a number of America's literary rebels, including William Burroughs, Allen Ginsberg, Gregory Corso, Michael McClure, and the late Jack Kerouac.

Leslie Fiedler (1917–) received his B.A. in 1938 from the University of New York and Ph.D. in 1941 from the University of Wisconsin. He has taught English at Columbia, Princeton, Indiana, and Montana State Universities, and now teaches at the University of Buffalo. Mr. Fiedler views American literature, customs, and institutions with an iconoclastic disdain for genteel, scholarly niceties, as he has abundantly demonstrated in his criticism: *An End to Innocence* (1955), *Love and Death in the American Novel* (1960), and *Waiting for the End* (1964). He has also published several works of fiction, including *Pull Down Vanity* (1962), *The Second Stone* (1963), *Back to China* (1965), and *The Last Jew in America* (1966).

Gene Fowler (1931–) has been a nightclub comic, a soldier, an armed robber, a prison inmate, a door-to-door salesman, a file clerk, a computer programmer, a college student, a skid-row derelict, and a research assistant at the University of California's School of Criminology at Berkeley. He is now an established poet and critic, an inventive painter. Since 1965 he has published three books of poetry — *Field Studies* (1965), *Shaman Songs* (1967), and *Her Majesty's Ship* (1969) — and hundreds of poems, essays, and short stories. In 1967 Buckminster Fuller wrote: "In all my life, I have found no more brilliant, no more naturally articulate thinker than Gene Fowler" ("Gene Fowler as Thinker," *Eikon,* Winter, 1967). Mr. Fowler now lives in Berkeley, California, with his wife, the poet Hilary Ayer Fowler.

Hilary Ayer Fowler (1944–), the youngest writer in this book, is the daughter of the late Richard G. Ayer — a prominent Bay Area painter and sculptor — and the wife of the poet Gene Fowler. Like her husband, whom she met during her one year at the University of California at Berkeley, Mrs. Fowler never finished college. Her poems are characterized by wit, gentle humor, intelligence, musical language, and fine perception. She has published two books of poetry, *Mind Dances* (1966) and *Colors* (1968); and her poems have appeared in many little magazines.

Herbert Gold (1924–), a resident of the San Francisco Bay Area, is a writer of novels, short stories, and essays. Gold received his B.A. from Columbia in 1948 and his M.A. in 1949. His novels include *Birth of a Hero* (1951), *The Prospect Before Us* (1954), *The Man Who Was Not With It* (1956), *The Optimist* (1958), *Therefore Be Bold* (1961), *Salt* (1963), *Fathers* (1967). A collection of his short stories, *Love and Like,* was published in 1960, and a collection of essays, *The Age of Happy Problems,* in 1962.

Alan Harrington (1918–) received his B.A. from Harvard in 1939. He has been a wire-service correspondent, a public relations man in an advertising agency, and an editor at the Republic of Indonesia Information Office in New York; has also served on the public relations staff at the Crystal Palace, a pseudonym for one of the twenty-five largest corporations in the country. Harrington's works include *The Revelations of Dr. Modesto* (1955), *Life in the Crystal Palace* (1959), and *The Secret Swinger* (1966).

Ernest Havemann (1912–), educated at Washington University, has been a magazine reporter and an associate editor of *Time* and *Life.* Since 1956 he has worked as a free-lance writer. His publications include *They Went to College* (1953), *I Never Thought We'd Make It* (1953), *Age of Psychology* (1958), and *Men, Women, and Marriage* (1962). Mr. Havermann has won several national awards for his writings on scientific and economic subjects.

Nat Hentoff (1925–) was educated at Northeastern University, Harvard, and the Sorbonne. Mr. Hentoff has served as the New York editor of *Downbeat* and as a staff writer for *The New Yorker;* he has published widely in such magazines as *Commonweal, The Reporter,* and *Playboy.* His special subjects are jazz, civil rights, and poverty. His books include *The Jazz Makers* (1957), *The Jazz Life* (1961), *The New Equality* (1966), *Jazz Country* (a novel, 1965), *Call the Keeper* (a mystery novel, 1966), and *Our Children Are Dying* (1966).

John Clellon Holmes (1926–) was educated at Columbia University and the New School for Social Research. He has written articles on the Beat generation and the Hip generation for *Holiday, Playboy,* and *Esquire.* his novels include *Go* (1952), *The Horn* (1958), and *Get Home Free* (1964).

Ernest Hemingway (1898–1961) was born in Oak Park, Illinois, on July 21, 1898, the second of six children of Dr. Clarence Edmunds Hemingway and Grace Hall Hemingway. Violence shaped Hemingway's life and his work. He came to view life as a battle that all men lost to fate, so that only one thing truly mattered: the way a man faced his dying. As a boy, Hemingway liked violent sports — boxing, football, hunting and fishing up in Michigan with his father; as a man, he liked big-game hunting, deep-sea fishing, and bullfights. He sought out violence: he was badly wounded during World War I, in which he served as a volunteer with an Italian infantry unit; he was in Spain during the Spanish Civil War; and he worked as a war correspondent during the Sino-Japanese War and World War II. And violence came to him: in 1928 his father committed suicide by shooting himself; in 1961 Ernest Hemingway too committed suicide, when he put his favorite double-barrelled shotgun into his mouth and pulled both triggers at once.

Hemingway's stories and novels present man's struggle with fate in a spare, lean, tough prose, marked by short repetitive sentences and parallel structure — a formal style, influenced, according to Hemingway, by the style of the Old Testament. His books include *In Our Time* (short stories, 1924), *The Sun Also Rises* (1926), *A Farewell to Arms* (1929), *Death in the Afternoon* (1932), *For Whom the Bell Tolls* (1940), *The Old Man and the Sea* (1952), and *A Moveable Feast* (a memoir of his days in Paris as a member of the "lost generation" of the 1920's, published posthumously in 1964). In 1953 he won the Pulitzer Prize for *The Old Man and the Sea.* In 1954 he received the Nobel Prize for his total contribution to literature.

Langston Hughes (1902–1967), educated at Columbia and Lincoln universities, was probably America's greatest and most prolific Negro writer: he was a distinguished poet, humorist, essayist, editor, playwright, translator, song lyricist, lecturer, reader, short-story writer, and novelist. Hughes' life had as much variety as his work. He traveled widely, not only in the United States but in Mexico, Africa, Western Europe, Cuba, Haiti, Russia, Korea, Japan, and China. And he worked, as a young man, at many jobs: he taught English in Mexico, he farmed in New York, he served as a messboy on a steamship bound for Africa, he washed dishes in a nightclub in Paris.

Hughes took the black man's experience of America as his dominant subject, and explored it with intelligence, style, humor, and profound understanding of black and white alike. As a poet — in such volumes as *The Weary Blues* (1926), *Fine Clothes to the Jew* (1927), *Dear Lovely Death* (1931), and *Lament for Dark People and Other Poems* (1944) — he rejected traditional form and experimented with jazz, blues, and gospel rhythms. As a humorist, he made a lasting contribution to American literature in creating Jesse B. Semple, often known as Simple, that "Negro Everyman" who cuts through the soft intellectual flab of black and white alike with the edge of his shrewd, unlettered, sweetly cynical mind. Besides the volumes of poetry noted above, Hughes' published work includes his novels *Not Without Laughter* (1930) and *Simple Speaks His Mind* (1950); his nonfiction for young people, *The First Book of Negroes* (1952), *The First Book of Rhythms* (1954), and *Famous Negro Heroes of America* (1958); two anthologies which he edited, *The Poetry of the Negro, 1746–1949* (with Arna Bontemps, 1949) and *Poems from Black Africa* (1963); his autobiographies, *The Big Sea* (1940) and *I Wonder as I Wander* (1956); and collections of his short stories, *The Ways of White Folks* (1940), *Laughing to Keep from Crying* (1951), and *The Best of Simple* (1961).

Kristin Hunter (1931–) graduated from the University of Pennsylvania in 1951. She has worked as a columnist, feature-writer, and advertising copywriter. Now a full-time free-lance writer, she is the author of two novels, *God Bless the Child* (1964) and *The Landlord* (1965), and a TV documentary, *Minority of One,* produced by CBS in 1956.

Donald Justice (1925–) was educated at the University of Miami, Florida, the University of North Carolina, and the State University of Iowa. He has published two volumes of poetry, *The Summer Anniversaries* (1960) and *A Local Storm* (1963), and has edited *The Collected Poems of Weldon Kees* (1960). He has taught at the University of Missouri, Hamlin University, and the State University of Iowa, where he is now an Associate Professor of English.

Pauline Kael (1920–), a native Californian and a graduate of the University of California, Berkeley, now makes her home in New York City where she currently reviews films regularly for the *New Yorker* magazine. In her role of film critic and lecturer, she has appeared at universities across the country and on numerous radio and TV programs as well. She has written about movies for *The Atlantic, Holiday, Life, Mademoiselle, New Republic, Vogue,* and other periodicals. She has made documentary and experimental short films, and written hundreds of highly literate program notes. Her books include *I Lost It at the Movies* (1965), *Kiss Kiss Bang Bang* (1968), and *Pauline Kael . . . Take Three* (1970).

Alfred R. Lindesmith (1905–) is a professor of sociology at the University of Indiana. In 1962 he was a delegate to the White House Conference on Drug Abuse; in 1965 he was a member of the Indiana Citizens Council on Crime and Delinquency. He has served as advisor to and on the editorial boards of the National Association for the Prevention of Addiction to Narcotics. He has authored or co-authored *Opiate Addiction* (1947), *Social Psychology* (1949), *Drug Addiction: Crime or Disease* (1961), *Anomie and Deviant Behavior* (1964), and *The Addict and the Law* (1965).

Leo E. Litwak (1924–), author of *To the Hanging Gardens* (1964) and *Waiting for the News* (1969), is currently on the English faculty of San Francisco State College. He has contributed short stories to *Esquire, Midstream,* and *Partisan Review.* He is the recipient of the 1952 O Henry Award and the 1959 Longview Foundation Award. He attended the University of Michigan and Wayne State University from which he received his B.A. degree in 1948. In addition, he did graduate study at Columbia from 1948–1951.

Robert Lowell (1917–), who can trace his ancestry to two important nineteenth century American poets, James Russell Lowell and Amy Lowell, was born in Boston, Massachusetts. He attended Harvard from 1935–1937, then transferred to Kenyon College, where he majored in classics and studied under the poet-critic John Crowe Ransom. In 1940 he graduated from Kenyon *summa cum laude,* married the novelist Jean Stafford, and became a Roman Catholic. During World War II, Lowell twice tried to enlist in the Navy but was rejected. In 1943, however, he was drafted; when Lowell refused induction into the Army on conscientious grounds, he was tried, sentenced to one year and one day, and served five months of this term. In 1948 he divorced Jean Stafford; and in 1949 he married Elizabeth Hardwick, a novelist and critic. He and his wife and daughter now live in New York City. Lowell has taught at Kenyon, Boston University, and Harvard.

As a poet, Robert Lowell most often uses a powerful, complex, compressed language to explore religious and psychological themes, frequently in the form of dramatic monologues. His publications include *Lord of Unlikeness* (1944), *Lord Weary's Castle* (1946), *The Mills of the Cavanaughs and Other Poems* (1951), *Life Studies* (1959), *Imitations* (1961), and *For the Union Dead* (1964). He has won many national awards and prizes, most notably the Pulitzer Prize in 1947 for *Lord Weary's Castle* and the National Book Award in 1960 for *Life Studies.*

Robie Macauley (1919–) is currently an editor at *Playboy.* He received his B.A. from Kenyon College in 1941 and his M.F.A. from the State University of Iowa in 1950. Macauley has been on the English faculty at Bard College, at the State University of Iowa, and at the University of North Carolina. He has written *The Disguises of Love* (1951) and *Techniques in Fiction* (1964).

Robert Mezey (1935–), educated at the University of Iowa, has at various times worked in mental hospitals and factories. He has taught at the University of Iowa, Western Reserve University, Fresno State College, and Memphis State College. His book *The Lovemaker* (1961) won the Lamont Poetry Award.

Warren Miller (1921–1966), educated at the University of Iowa, was a creative-writing teacher, magazine editor, and novelist. He is perhaps best known for his novel *The Cool World* (1959), which so effectively captured the language, ideas, and moods of contemporary Harlem adolescents that James Baldwin, in his review of the book for the *New York Times,* pointed out that he could not tell whether the author was black or white. Baldwin added that the book was "one of the finest novels about Harlem" that had ever come his way. Warren Miller also wrote *The Sleep of Reason* (1956) an early criticism of Senator Joseph McCarthy, *The Way We Live Now* (1958), *Flush Times* (1962), *Looking for the General* (1964), and *The Siege of Harlem* (1964). He died of lung cancer in 1966.

Theodore Roethke (1908–1963), perhaps the greatest lyric poet of our time, was born and raised in Saginaw, Michigan, where his father and uncle owned a greenhouse that was to influence his work profoundly. Roethke grew up close to the natural struggle of plants to survive and reproduce; and many of his best poems celebrate the unity of man with every growing thing. Educated at the University of Michigan, Roethke taught English at Lafayette Collete, Pennsylvania State College, Bennington College, and — for the last sixteen years of his life — the University of Washington, where he was recognized as a truly great teacher as well as a fine poet. In 1953 he married Beatrice Heath O'Connell, a former Bennington student.

Roethke's poems were published in the following volumes: *Open House* (1941), *The Lost Son and Other Poems* (1949), *Praise to the End!* (1951), *The Waking: Poems 1933–1953* (1953), *The Collected Verse of Theodore Roethke: Words for the Wind* (1961). *I Am! Says the Lamb* (1961), and *The Far Field* (1964). Roethke won many national prizes and awards for his poetry, including the Pulitzer Prize in 1954 for *The Waking,* the Bollingen Prize in 1958, and the National Book Award in 1965 for *The Far Field.*

Arthur Schlesinger Jr. (1917–), currently the Schweitzer professor of Humanities at City University of New York, has been a leading spokesman for liberal political thought during the 1950's and 1960's. He was a member of the campaign staff of Adlai Stevenson in 1952, of John F. Kennedy in 1960, and of Robert F. Kennedy in 1968. From 1961–1964 he was special assistant to the President of the United States. Schlesinger received his A.B. degree *summa cum laude* from Harvard in 1938 and taught on the history faculty there from 1946–1961. His books include *Orestes A. Brownson: A Pilgrim's Progress* (1939), *The Age of Jackson* (1945), *The Vital Center* (1949), *The General and the President* (with R. H. Rovere, 1951), *The Crisis of the Old Order* (1957), *The Coming of the New Deal* (1958), *A Thousand Days: John F. Kennedy in the White House* (1965).

Anne Sexton (1928–) was a fashion model and then a mother before she became a poet. She wrote her first poems at the age of 29, during a period when she was recovering from a nervous breakdown. Like Robert Lowell and W. D. Snodgrass, with whom she is often compared, she writes a personal, confessional poetry with a heavy emphasis on her own psychological traits. Her published volumes include *To Bedlam and Part Way Back* (1960), *All My Pretty Ones* (1962), *Selected Poems* (1964), and *Live or Die* (1966).

Jerry L. Simmons (1953–) is currently on the sociology faculty at the University of California at Santa Barbara. He received his B.A. degree from the University of Iowa in 1959 and his Ph.D. in 1963. He has conducted research and published widely on deviance and alienation. He is the co-author of *Identities and Interaction* (1966), *It's Happening* (1966), and the author of *Marihuana: Myths and Realities* (1967).

Paul Simon (1941–), whose lyrics and music have been called "inventive and poetic" by Leonard Bernstein, has a wide audience: according to critics, his music bridges the generation gap. His music has a message of literate protest that deals with the pangs of youth and the pathos of old age, with the hypocrisies of the middle class and the middle-aged. Paul Simon, guitarist, singer, composer, Brooklyn Law School graduate, is half of one of the two top attractions in the pop music concert field today: Simon and Garfunkel command up to $50,000 a performance and as a team earn over two million dollars per year. A teen-age act (Tom and Jerry) a decade ago, nothing much happened until 1964 when Simon interested Columbia Records in some of his original songs, with the result that he and Garfunkel, then a student at Columbia, recorded their first album, "Wednesday Morning, 3 A.M." The album was a flop except for one song, "The Sounds of Silence," which, as one critic noted, seems to have become the "anthem of a generation." Simon and Garfunkel have recorded four additional albums since 1967: "The Sounds of Silence," "Parsley, Sage, Rosemary, and Thyme," "Bookends," and the original sound track from "The Graduate."

William Jay Smith (1918–) received his B.A. and M.A. degrees from the University of Washington and did advanced work at Columbia, Oxford, the University of Florence, and the University of Poitiers. He has taught English at Williams College, and English and French at Columbia. His publications include three volumes of poetry — *Poems* (1947), *Celebration at Dark* (1950), and *Poems: 1947–1957* (1958) — and two volumes of criticism — *The Spectra Hoax* (1961) and *Herrick* (1962). His poems and articles have appeared in such magazines as *Harper's, Poetry* (Chicago), *The Nation, Evergreen,* and *Yale Review.*

Kenneth Tynan (1927–), the only non-American in this collection, is a British drama critic, author, the literary manager of the National Theatre since 1963. He was educated at Magdalen College, Oxford. A film critic for *The Observer,* he has also criticized drama for English newspapers and periodicals and the *New Yorker* magazine. He is the author of *He That Plays the King* (1950), *Persona Grata* (with Cecil Beaton, 1953), *Alex Guinness* (1953), *Bull Fever* (1955), a play for the BBC, *"The Quest for Corbett"* (with Harold Lang, 1956), and *Curtains* (1961). He conceived of and wrote part of "Oh! Calcutta!" (1969).

John Updike (1932–), educated at Harvard and at The Ruskin School of Drawing and Fine Arts, writes both poetry and fiction. He is best known for his novels *Rabbitt, Run* (1960), *The Centaur* (1962) for which he won the National Book Award, and *Couples* (1968), a story of the involved and unhappy sex lives of Eastern suburbanites.

George Wald (1906–) is a professor of biology at Harvard and a corecipient of the Nobel Prize for medicine in 1967. He received his B.S. degree from New York University in 1927, his M.A. from Columbia in 1928, and his Ph.D., also from Columbia, in 1932. His publications include *Twenty-Six Afternoons of Biology* (1962), as well as numbers of science papers on vision. He has been awarded honorary degrees by the University of Berne, Yale, Wesleyan University, N.Y.U., and McGill University.

Barry Winograd, co-author of *It's Happening* (1966, with J. L. Simmons), when last heard from was a teaching fellow at the University of California at Santa Barbara. He has been both observer of and participant in student movements and student life. He also has been a working journalist on the West Coast.

Tom Wolfe (1921–), once a semi-pro baseball player, has been swinging at the fences of the outrageous and pretentious ever since. Thomas Kennerly Wolfe Jr. received his B.A. degree from Washington and Lee in 1951 and his Ph.D. in American studies from Yale in 1957. He has written for the *Springfield (Mass.) Union,* the *Washington Post,* the *New York Herald Tribune,* and the *New Yorker* magazine. He has contribued essays to *Esquire, Harper's Bazaar,* and other periodicals. Wolfe's essays specialize in shrewd, comic analyses of American culture. His prose has a sharply visual and aural appeal; it sparkles with a psychedelic pattern of wild sounds, colors, and images. Every Tom Wolfe essay is a happening. His essays have been collected in *The Kandy-Kolored Tangerine-Flake Streamline Baby* (1965), *The Electric Kool-Aid Acid Test* (1968), and *The Pump House Gang* (1968).

Richard Wright (1902–1967) was born near Natchez, Mississippi, and received what formal education he had from a Seventh Day Adventist School. At the age of 15 Wright was already on his own. In 1935 he joined the Federal Writers' Project in Chicago and in 1937 he went on to the Federal Writers' Project in New York. At about the same time, he began writing for smaller magazines. His writings include *Uncle Tom's Children* (1938), *Native Son* (1940), *Black Boy* (1945), *Black Power* (1954), *White Man, Listen* (1957), and *The Long Dream* (1959).

Frank Zappa (1931–), lyricist-composer, is the "chief mother" of the Mothers of Invention, a rock group. Voted 1968 Pop Musician of the year in *Jazz and Pop* magazine's annual poll, Zappa, according to critics, is second only to John Lennon as the leading creative talent in pop music. In addition to being the moving force behind the Mothers of Invention, Zappa is the composer and orchestrator of a ballet, "Lumpy Gravy," to be marketed (as are all Mothers' albums) by the Nifty Advertising Agency, whose president is Frank Zappa. Zappa's headquarters near Los Angeles are in a huge log cabin built by Tom Mix, who buried his horse, Tony, under it.

2 3 4 5 6 7 8 9 0